Policing Protest

Social Movements, Protest, and Contention

Series Editor: Bert Klandermans, Free University, Amsterdam

Associate Editors: Sidney G. Tarrow, Cornell University
Verta A. Taylor, The Ohio State University

Policing Protest

The Control of Mass Demonstrations in Western Democracies

Donatella della Porta and Herbert Reiter, editors

Afterword by Gary T. Marx

Social Movements, Protest, and Contention
Volume 6

 University of Minnesota Press
Minneapolis • London

A version of chapter 2 was published as "L'institutionalisation de la contestation aux États-Unis" in *Les Cahiers de la Sécurité Intérieure* 27 (1997): 16–35; reprinted by permission.

Published by the University of Minnesota Press
111 Third Avenue South, Suite 290
Minneapolis, MN 55401-2520
http://www.upress.umn.edu

Library of Congress Cataloging-in-Publication Data

Policing protest : the control of mass demonstrations in Western democracies / Donatella della Porta and Herbert Reiter, editors ; afterword by Gary T. Marx.
    p. cm. — (Social movements, protest, and contention ; v. 6)
    Includes bibliographical references and index.
    ISBN 0-8166-3063-1 (hardcover : alk. paper). — ISBN 0-8166-3064-X (pbk. : alk. paper)
    1. Riot control—Europe, Western.   2. Riot control—United States.
  3. Demonstrations—Europe, Western.   4. Demonstrations—United States.
  5. Protest movements—Europe, Western.   6. Protest movements—United States.
  I. Della Porta, Donatella, 1956–   II. Reiter, Herbert.   III. Series.
  HV6485.E85P65 1998
  363.3′2—dc21   97-48500

10 09 08 07 06 05 04 03 02 01 00 99 98   10 9 8 7 6 5 4 3 2 1

Contents

Afterword
Some Reflections on the Democratic Policing of Demonstrations
Gary T. Marx

Introduction

The Policing of Protest in Western Democracies

Donatella della Porta and Herbert Reiter

One specific aspect of state response to political dissent is the policing of protest, which we define as the police handling of protest events—a more neutral description for what protesters usually refer to as "repression" and the state as "law and order." Although the repression variable has been included in several models on the preconditions for collective action (among others, Tilly, 1978, in particular 101–6; Skocpol, 1979; McAdam, 1982), empirical research on the relationship between police and protesters in Western democracies is still rare. There is, therefore, a significant gap to be filled in the literature with comparative studies on protest and policing. Moreover, protest policing is a particularly relevant issue for a thorough understanding of the relationship between social movements and the state: "Police may be conceived as 'street-level bureaucrats' who 'represent' government to people" (Lipsky, 1970, 1).

Police intervention has, indeed, a strong impact on protesters' perceptions of the state reaction to them (della Porta, 1995). Waves of protest, in turn, have important effects on the police, as Jane Morgan (1987) observed in her historical research on the police in Great Britain. Protest policing would appear to be, in fact, a key issue for the professional self-definition of the police. For the process of modernization and professionalization of European police forces in the nineteenth century, it was of decisive importance that the police should become the principal agency responsible for safeguarding internal security and public order, thus marginalizing the military in this role. As the example of postwar Germany illustrates, the way in which the police deal with protest in contemporary democratic societies seems to be a significant, if not dominant, aspect of their self-image (Winter, in this volume). The importance of these reciprocal repercussions highlights the need for an in-depth study of protest policing in a comparative perspective.

This need is addressed by the chapters in this volume, which are revised versions of contributions to an international conference on the theme "The Policing of Mass Demonstrations in Contemporary Democracies" organized by the Robert Schuman Center of the European University Institute in Florence in October 1995.[1] In the following, we shall attempt to locate the contributions to this volume within the framework of the social science literature related to the topic; at the same time, we shall propose some hypotheses on the origins, development, and consequences of different models of police protest control. Part I presents a description of the long-term national styles and recent developments in protest policing before discussing in a comparative perspective the hypotheses emerging from the studies collected in this volume on the significant historical cross-national differences in protest policing and on the recent trend toward a "softer" and more tolerant attitude in Europe. In Part II, we propose a model for explaining protest policing styles. Drawing on the research presented and on the literature on state responses to protest, we illustrate our hypothesis that protest policing is determined on a first level by (*a*) the organizational features of the police, (*b*) the configuration of political power, (*c*) public opinion, (*d*) the police occupational culture, and (*e*) the interaction with protesters. All of these influences are filtered, on a second level, by (*f*) police knowledge, defined as the police's perception of external reality, which shapes the concrete policing of protest on the ground. We also discuss the effects of the most recent trends in protest policing, as they emerged from the research of our contributors on the fate of social movements.

Trends and Cycles in the Evolution of Protest Policing

In order to reflect on the consequences of protest policing, we need to understand how the policing of protest varies: How can different ways of policing protest be characterized? Which cross-national differences can be identified? How did they evolve over time? Pertinent to a characterization of different ways of policing protests are the suggestions in social movement literature on the classification of the forms and nature of state control. Gary T. Marx (1979) distinguished repressive actions according to their specific aims: for instance, the creation of an unfavorable public image; information gathering; restriction of a movement's resources and limitation of its facilities; de-recruitment of activists; destruction of leaders; fueling of internal conflicts;

encouragement of conflicts between groups; sabotage of particular actions. Charles Tilly's typology (1978, 106–15) classified political regimes on the basis of the degree of repression and "facilitation" they manifest toward various collective actors and actions.

Police studies formulated a series of typologies about police styles in order to characterize the intention and impact of different ways of policing. For instance, police interventions have been distinguished as oriented toward mediation, separation, coercion, or counseling (Bayley, 1986); styles of social control such as the penal style, the conciliatory style, the therapeutic style, and the compensatory style (Black, 1980, 130–32); police officers as professionals, reciprocators, enforcers, and avoiders (Muir, 1977); police tactics such as fire-brigade policing, local intelligence policing, and community policing (Baldwin and Kinsey, 1982).

Research on state building and democracy indicates the existence of different national styles for dealing with challengers. States with an equilibrium of power among the different social classes (particularly among the monarchy, the aristocracy, and the bourgeoisie), first-comer nation-states, and small states facing strong competition in the international markets developed integrative styles, while the other states tended to be exclusive (see, for instance, Marks, 1989; Kriesi et al., 1995). Moreover, experiences with authoritarian regimes tend to have long-lasting consequences on police style (see Jaime-Jiménez and Reinares, and Reiter, in this volume).

Drawing on these various approaches, it is possible to develop more specific and detailed categories for the study of protest policing. Some relevant dimensions are presented in figure 1 (see also della Porta, 1995). A combination of these dimensions describes the protest policing style (understood as a subcategory of police style) employed by the police forces at protest events. For instance, police who repress a large number of protest groups, prohibit a wide range of protest activities, and intervene with a high degree of force are employing a diffused, repressive, and "brutal" protest policing style.[2]

With regard to traditional police styles, the "civilized" British "bobby"— unarmed, integrated in the community, and more or less autonomous from political power—has been contrasted with the militarized continental police, who live in barracks and are dependent on political power. Already in the nineteenth century, the London Metropolitan Police were viewed by the liberal press on the continent as an example of what a police force should be. For instance, an article published in the German illustrated journal *Die Gartenlaube* in 1878 on "the blue men of London" started, as any article on the London police in a German illustrated journal might have a hundred years

- "brutal" versus "soft"
  referring to the degree of force used
- repressive versus tolerant
  referring to the number of prohibited behaviors
- diffused versus selective
  referring to the number of repressed groups
- illegal versus legal
  referring to police respect of the law
- reactive versus preventive
  referring to the "timing" of police intervention
- confrontational versus consensual
  referring to the degree of communication with the demonstrators
- rigid versus flexible
  referring to the degree of "adaptability"
- formal versus informal
  referring to the degree of formalization of the rules of the game
- professional versus artisanal
  referring to the degree of "preparation"

Fig. 1. Variables relevant in order to define styles of "protest policing"

later, with the cliché of the friendly bobby giving directions to a foreign tourist (Katscher, 1878). It also noted the traditional "low-profile response" of the London police and their positive relationship with the public. Particular emphasis was placed on the accountability of every policeman, which assured that neither the single bobby nor the London police force as a whole was a threat to individual or collective liberty. Two lines of argument were generally used to explain these characteristics of the English police, as in the case of this article in *Die Gartenlaube*: on the one hand, the common-law tradition in England in contrast with the Roman law tradition on the continent and, on the other hand, the origins of the English police in the tradition of community policing. As Robert Reiner shows in his contribution to this volume, however, "the ideal British police model was not a reflection of some natural, in-built harmony or order in British society and culture." On the contrary, pioneers of the British police tradition "encouraged a low-profile, legalistic, minimal force strategy *because of,* not despite, the bitter political protests and acute social divisions of early nineteenth-century Britain."

On the European continent the countermodel to this strategy was formed by the French tradition of a "king's police," that is, a state police dependent on and under strict control of the central government, charged with a very wide range of tasks, and originally standing as a synonym for the interior state administration. At the same time, the French example served as a model for the police forces in other European countries and was drawn upon during debates on the institution of the London Metropolitan Police as a scarecrow to warn against the liberticidal aspects of this type of law enforcement (Bunyan, 1977, 63).

Myths aside, there do in fact appear to be visible differences between the record of the English police and the continental police forces in the field of protest policing in relation to the "old" challengers, that is, the democratic and labor movements. On the continent, police action against challengers seemed to aim at defending not only a general system of power, but a concrete government. If combined, as was often the case, with a weak respect for civil rights, the consequences of this modality for the policing of protest are easily imaginable. The protest policing styles traditionally dominant on the continent were more "brutal," more repressive, more confrontational, and more rigid than in England.

It should be noted, however, that significant differences also existed within the overall framework of the continental police systems, both over time and between countries, stretching from the French police of the Third Republic to the police system of National Socialist Germany.[3] After World War II, differences continued to exist on the continent. Latin police styles, based on the unconstrained use of force, were distinguished from the Central European style, characterized by respect for the *Rechtsstaat* (constitutional state). A comparison of Italy and Germany from the 1960s to the 1990s (della Porta, 1995, chap. 3) described the Italian protest policing style during this thirty-year period as more "brutal," more diffused, more illegal, more informal, and more artisanal than the German style.

For the decades since the 1960s, the studies collected in this volume point to a progressive assimilation of the different models of European policing, including protest policing. In Great Britain, a "militarization" thesis developed, based on the premise that the British police were moving toward the militarized, continental model in the control of public order. The riots in several British cities at the beginning of the 1980s, as well as the policing of the miners' strike later on, have been met with a "tougher" policing (Jefferson, 1990)—

although the availability of legal and technological resources for paramilitary intervention does not automatically mean that these resources are actually implemented (Waddington, 1994b).

On the "continent," a contrary trend was singled out. Connecting police professional culture with the main frames about protest policing in Germany, Martin Winter's (1991) analysis of specialized police journals during the 1960–90 period shows a shift toward a growing acceptance of forms of direct action. Winter argues that the debate on the military- versus the civil-oriented character of the police overlapped in Germany with the debate on protest strategy, with the traditionalists claiming the need for a hard line against the "anarchists" in order to "state an example" and the reformists— among whom the reform-oriented police trade union—defending a "soft approach." Although prior to 1968 demonstrations were largely identified with "Störung der öffentlichen Ordnung" (disturbing public order) and the potentially dangerous "crowds" had to be controlled in a paramilitary way, in the 1970s the reformist *Neue Linie* inside the police instead recognized demonstration as a basic right. After some rollbacks during the period of terrorism and the antinuclear campaign, the debate was dominated from 1985 on by the implications of the Brokdorf decision of the German Federal Constitutional Court. This judgment stated that "the right to demonstrate must be protected," thus a *Bürgerpolizei* conception now tends to prevail.

Interpreted as parallel movements, the convergent trends in England and Germany seem to confirm the progressive assimilation of the different styles of European protest policing observed earlier. Over time, cross-national differences between the European countries seem to have diminished. The research of the contributors to this volume on protest policing in England, France, Germany, Italy, and Spain (but also the United States) brought forth similar conclusions.[4] A general trend emerges regarding protest policing styles, which, on the basis of the variables presented in figure 1, can be defined as "soft," tolerant, selective, legal, preventive, consensual, flexible, and professional.

On the basis of the research presented in this volume, in fact, the three most significant tactical tendencies characterizing protest policing in the 1990s appear to be (*a*) underenforcement of the law; (*b*) the search to negotiate; (*c*) large-scale collection of information. First, the strategy used during the 1980s and up to the present appears to be dominated by the attempt to avoid coercive intervention as much as possible. Lawbreaking, which is implicit in several forms of protest, tends to be tolerated by the police. Law enforcement is usually considered as less important than peacekeeping. This implies a considerable departure from protest policing in the 1960s and

1970s, when attempts to stop unauthorized demonstrations and a law-and-order attitude in the face of the "limited rule-breaking" tactic used by the new movements maneuvered the police repeatedly into "no-win" situations.

Second, in order to avoid disorder, complicated procedures of negotiation emerged. This tendency is not new. For the Germany of the 1960s, Martin Winter notes that, following public criticism of the "hard line" adopted by the police, public relations efforts were increased and the support of police psychologists was institutionalized. Other research indicates an increasing formalization of bargaining techniques. For the United States, McPhail, Schweingruber, and McCarthy document in this volume the sharp contrast between the general practices of protest policing in the 1960s, characterized by escalated force, and those of the 1980s and 1990s, characterized by negotiated management, which found significant expression in the development of a protest permit system. In his study of the London police, P. A. J. Waddington observed: "The principal method of securing compliance was through negotiation with the organizer of the protest" (1994b, 69). In the course of his research, Waddington noted a considerable bureaucratization and formalization of the entire procedure, with the effect of reinforcing obedience to the law. Without matching the level of bureaucratization of the British case, other countries, including France, Germany, and Switzerland, have witnessed the growing role of police officers responsible for "public relations," acting as mediators between demonstrators and the forces of order.

Third, the collection of information has received substantial attention by the police. The use of intelligence in the control of protesters is not a new trend. In his book on the "Red Squads," the specialized units employed against subversion that proliferated in American cities, Frank Donner (1990) suggests that there was a shift during the 1930s from traditional interventionist practices to "intelligence," that is, information gathering and surveillance, including the compilation of files and their aggressive use to damage the protesters. The role of the Red Squads was strengthened in the 1960s, when the FBI was thwarted by its own old conception of the left as "communists" and by millions of dossiers of old—or dead—radicals. Technological advances allowed for an increasing level of control.[5] In more recent times too, the availability of new techniques, together with growing professionalization, has been reflected in an ever-increasing attention to the collection of information—as may be seen, for instance, in the control of soccer crowds (see della Porta and De Biasi, in this volume).

If this seems to be the common general trend, both in Great Britain and in continental Europe, protest policing within any given country is *selective*, with a different treatment for different social groups, and in some cases "antagonistic" protest policing styles remain manifest. Our research, in fact, indicates the contemporary presence of diverse protest policing styles, implemented in different situations and directed toward different actors. For France, Fillieule and Jobard in this volume describe a paternalistic model of intervention (based on a "soft" management of violent demonstrations). In the case of the farmers' demonstrations, in particular, both tactical and political necessities have often seemed to push the police toward tolerating certain episodes of violence. In other instances, however, the French police have shown an antagonistic attitude, resorting to a repressive policing style. Within the general trend toward a more tolerant style, della Porta singles out four different models of protest policing for Italy: a model of cooperation, based on collaboration between the police force and demonstrators, and an inconspicuous police presence; a model of negotiation, based on a more active police presence with the objective of mediating between the demonstrators and "nondemonstrators" who are said to suffer the disruptive effects of protests; a model of ritualistic standoff, based on a more "aggressive" police presence, but often at a distance; and a model of total control, based on a massive presence and close involvement of the police forces.

Although the general trends described can be observed in all countries under review, some differences remain visible in a cross-national comparison. The very terms of the British debate on "militarization" suggest that the civilian character of the "bobby" is more deeply rooted than critics tend to-concede. With respect to underenforcement of the law, the degree of toleration of lawbreaking appears to be higher in countries such as Italy and France, where the discretionary power of the police is greater, than in a country such as Germany, where legal constraints are more restrictive. The internal differences between French-speaking and German-speaking cantons in Switzerland, analyzed by Dominique Wisler and Hanspeter Kriesi in this volume, appear to confirm this trend. So too, the degree of formalization of negotiation practices shows considerable variance: rather informal in Italy, more formalized in Germany, fairly formalized in Great Britain. Constraints on the use of information-gathering techniques also vary. The Italian case, for instance, seems to be characterized by a lack of limits and controls on information-gathering activities by the *Digos* (the political police), which functions as an "epistemological" organ of the state, with the role of collecting information on all the political actors and interest groups and having a special direct relationship with the government (in this volume, see della Porta; for historical tradition, Reiter). These remaining differences highlight the need for further comparative and focused research.

A Model for the Explanation of Protest Policing Styles

How to explain the cross-national and intranational differences in protest policing styles, as well as their evolution in time? Figure 2 provides an outline of the different analytical levels that appear to be relevant in answering these questions.

First of all, protest policing styles are influenced by the political system—in particular, by what researchers of social movements have defined as the Political Opportunity Structure (POS) (McAdam, 1982; Tarrow, 1983, 1994; della Porta and Diani, 1997). A first analytical level refers to the stable opportunities in which a certain style of policing develops. Institutional features—such as police organization, the nature of the judiciary, law codes, and constitutional rights—may play an important role in defining the opportunities for and constraints on protest policing, as they set the conditions for the actual protest policing strategies. Moreover, aspects of the political culture, particularly those referring to conceptions of the state and citizens' rights, have similarly important effects (Brand, 1985; Kitschelt, 1986; Kriesi, 1991). Police studies have suggested that the very conditions of policing bring about the development of a particular police culture, including a series of stereotypes about disorders.

In addition to the relatively stable context, policing styles depend on a second, more "volatile" set of political opportunities. Various collective actors, in fact, put forward their interests or opinions, forming what Kriesi (1989) refers to as a "configuration of power." First of all, the government defines some general lines on how protest should be handled. In addition, social movements intervene on issues relating to citizens' rights and police tasks—they organize protest actions to denounce police brutality, they demand more democracy. Political parties, interest groups, trade unions, and voluntary associations conflict or cooperate with one another on the issue of how to police protest. Like-minded actors take sides on the issue, forming law-and-order coalitions on the one hand, and, on the other, civil rights coalitions (della Porta, 1997). The media are part of this picture, partially as a "spokesperson" of one or the other coalition, and partially following an "autonomous" logic.

The impact of the stable opportunities and the more volatile ones on protest policing styles is filtered by police knowledge—that is, the police's construction of external reality, collectively and individually—which we consider to be the main intervening variable between structure and action. The influence of institutional characteristics of the police, police culture, governments, and public opinion on protest policing finds a concrete expression

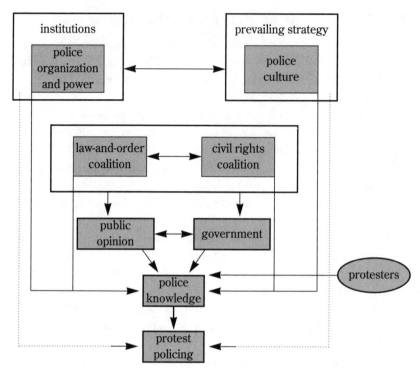

Fig. 2. A model to explain styles of "protest policing"

only insofar as it becomes part of the knowledge of the police. This level of analysis is all the more important when institutional actors enjoy—as is the case with the police—a high degree of discretionary power.

Institutional Characteristics of the Police and Protest Policing Styles

One of the institutional variables relevant to police behavior is constituted by the legal framework, including legislation on constitutional rights (right of movement, right of expression), defendants' rights (preventive detention, presence of one's attorney at interrogations, right of the police to interrogate a defendant), and prisoners' rights (privacy, contact with the external world). The Brokdorf decision of the German Federal Constitutional Court shows the extent to which legal decisions can open new spaces for protesters and restrict the range for police intervention (Winter, in this volume). A contrary dynamic was created by the failure of the Italian parliament to revise the fascist police laws, which remained on the books until the mid-1950s, effectively

obstructing legal popular protest and facilitating a wide range of police interventions (Reiter, in this volume). The final turning point for a democratic
policing of protest in post-Franco Spain came about in 1983 with the new law
on meeting and demonstration rights (Jaime-Jiménez and Reinares, in this
volume).

A second institutional variable relevant to police behavior is the organizational structure of the police. Particularly pertinent questions on the characteristics of police organizations refer to (a) centralization (How much
power do decentralized units have? How powerful is the central government?), (b) accountability to the public (Do policemen wear identifying numbers or name tags? Are their actions subject to independent review? How
easily can citizens bring formal complaints?), and (c) militarization (How dependent are the police on the defense ministry? Do they live in barracks? Are
they part of the army? How great is the emphasis on "discipline"? What type
of armaments do they use? Are the police unionized?).[6]

The effects of these features of police organization on police styles are un-
clear, however. According to Geary (1985, 123), centralization undermined
the use of police forces as an employer's private army in Great Britain at the
beginning of this century and led to a more impartial style of law enforcement. The fact, however, that the centralization process was initiated at the
same time as the Labor Party won the majority in some local councils also
indicates that centralization can have different aims.

Opinions also differ on the effects of centralization on police accountability. In a study of the police and labor disputes in England and Wales in the
first four decades of this century, Jane Morgan (1987) suggested that one
effect of centralization is a reduction of the accountability of the police to the
democratic bodies. P. A. J. Waddington, however, studying the British police
in the 1980s, observed: "Local control would not guarantee that the police
would be employed in ways that liberal and radical critics would like"
(Waddington, 1991, 134).[7]

Analyses of the effects of militarization on the police have drawn similarly
contradictory conclusions.[8] In general, a militarily organized police force is
considered to be more prone to brutality since it implies a hierarchical organization with "blind" obedience to order. Looking at the evolution of the
British police, however, several scholars noted that militarization, with its implication of stricter control on rank-and-file officers, could actually help prevent brutality. As Reiner (1991, 54–55; see also Waddington, 1991, 136) remarked: "In violent confrontations, a 'non-militaristic' response by police (i.e.,
without adequate training, manpower, coordination, and defensive or even of-

fensive equipment) could mean that injuries will be multiplied. This doesn't just mean injuries to the police, but also to others who will suffer from undisciplined and excessive violence from constables who lose their cool or their courage."

Our own research indicates that the problems of centralization and militarization take on different dimensions in old and new democracies. It can be stated that an authoritarian or totalitarian regime is inconceivable without a militarized and centralized police. In the Italian and Spanish transition to democracy (respectively, Reiter and Jaime-Jiménez and Reinares, in this volume), reformist pressure was especially directed against these organizational features. This was not only because the dominant police model of the victors of World War II as well as of the Cold War was the Anglo-Saxon one, but also because police decentralization and demilitarization were considered necessary in order to ensure democratic accountability. As the example of Italy shows, failure to modify the centralized and militarized structures of the police forces emerging from an authoritarian or totalitarian regime can result in a circle of continuities, only broken by a complete generational turnover. The Spanish experience offers a more successful, if cautious, attempt to transform the Francoist security forces into a democratic police. The Italian police reform, which finally took place at the beginning of the 1980s, provides a further example of the contribution that organizational changes (such as demilitarization, unionization, recruitment of female police officers) can make toward an "opening up" of a police force (della Porta, in this volume).

The argument in old democracies seems to be conducted on a different level. The general trend toward a "softer" protest policing style developed in all the countries dealt with in this book, regardless of the different levels of centralization and militarization of the respective police forces (although a high level might have had a retarding effect). The practical impact of different degrees of centralization and militarization on police deployment and intervention in concrete public order cases has not yet been the subject of comparative research. However, the contributions of Fillieule and Jobard on France and of Waddington on England suggest that militarization and centralization are important elements in influencing protest policing styles when the police, to use Waddington's expression, have decided "to die in a ditch." In this case, a centralized police force with paramilitary capacities will be a far more formidable instrument than a decentralized civilian one. As a body it may tend to intervene more aggressively, even though a centralized, military organization will allow the leadership to exercise greater restraining control over the officers on the ground until the moment of intervention. Comparative research is needed to ascertain whether the same mechanisms can be found in special militarized riot units within generally decentralized civilian forces.

Police Culture and Protest Policing Styles

Although less formalized, the political culture of the different countries under review and the occupational culture of their police forces also constitute stable opportunities. Together with the organizational features, they provide the long-term underlying influences on protest policing styles. Kriesi applied to social movements the concept of national strategies of conflict resolution, elaborated in the analysis of industrial conflicts: "National strategies set the informal and formal rules of the game for the conflict" (1989, 295). Traditions are, in fact, embedded not only in laws but also in the political culture. Protest policing seems to be particularly sensitive to the cultural understanding of civil rights and police power. In particular, the "rootedness" of a democratic culture seems to have important consequences on the reactions of elites to emergent challengers, and vice versa. In both Italy and Germany, the institutional and emotional legacy of prewar fascist mass movements and their "legal revolutions" was reflected—well into the 1970s—in a "weak" acceptance of certain democratic rights. Thus, protest was perceived as a threat to democracy by the institutions, and state reactions were perceived as a sign of fascism by movement activists (della Porta, 1995, chap. 3). Generally speaking, however, the postwar years in Europe saw a continuous development and strengthening of a democratic political culture, which influenced the police and contributed to the emergence of the new protest policing styles.

In the analysis of police behavior, sociological research developed the concept of police culture. In seeking an explanation of policing styles, past research on the police—based mainly on ethnographic approaches to urban subdivisions of police at work—emphasized certain characteristics of the professional culture and, especially, of the operational culture widespread among officers. In his seminal work, Skolnick (1966, 231) suggested that the policeman understands his role as "craftsman rather than legal actor . . . skilled worker rather than civil servant obliged to subscribe to the rule of the law." Maureen Cain (1973) observed, in her research on the English police, that constables were oriented mainly toward crime fighting, although only a minor portion of their time was devoted to this task. Various studies have converged in indicating that, because of the very characteristics of their job, policemen develop such attitudes as a tendency to secretive behavior and a lack of confidence in the external world (Rubinstein, 1973; Manning, 1979; Holdaway, 1984).

Some characteristics of the police culture have been noted as facilitating repressive attitudes. Referring to the Brixton riots, Benyot (1984) observes that the commonly held macho attitudes among rank-and-file policemen lead them to privilege crime fighting over peacekeeping. Analyzing the policing of the British miners' strike in the 1980s, Sarah McCabe and Peter Wallington suggested that since police activity tends to be tedious (waiting for something that almost never happens), the protests of the 1960s and 1970s may have produced some excitement among police officers (McCabe and Wallington, 1988, 43). According to Lipset (1971, 29), the general job experiences of policemen "enhance the possibility that whatever authoritarian traits they bring from their social background will increase rather than decrease. . . . In general, the policeman's job requires him to be suspicious of people, to prefer conventional behavior, to value toughness." Policemen tend to see themselves surrounded by a hostile world, which, especially in combination with certain organizational features such as militarization, can lead to isolation from society and aggressive feelings against those who are perceived as "diverse."

Two aspects in particular of the police culture generated by the work experience of policemen have important repercussions on protest policing. As already mentioned, the police, although bound by the law, form an institution with great discretionary power. This fact is worth underlining not only for the institution as a whole, but also for the individual policeman on the beat. Historical changes—even the obligation to follow the legality principle and to report any violation of the law—in practice did little to alter the situation. Most police interventions and sanctions continued to be triggered by situational moments, prejudice, stereotypes, and other imponderables and depended only to a lesser extent on the bureaucratic transposition of well-defined rules (Jessen, 1995, 32f.). The need to take on-the-spot decisions about whether to intervene or not makes policemen develop stereotypes about people and situations perceived as creating trouble or representing a danger. What is relevant about these stereotypes is that they become a kind of guideline for police intervention—for instance, the police images of Liverpool's Toxteth district pushed toward the tough policing style that eventually led to riots in 1981 (Brogden and Brogden, 1982, 245).

The long-term continuities in the conduct of policemen and the practice of policing resulting from these characteristics of police culture have been repeatedly stressed (Lüdtke, 1992, 20). Recent research, however, tends to view with increasing skepticism the notion of an immutable police culture. Styles of conflict management, although surely resilient to a certain extent, change with time. As was observed, for instance, in a comparison of state responses to the antinuclear movements, traditionally exclusionary states may adopt very flexible tactics in order to avoid escalation, while traditionally inclusive states may use repression (Flam, 1994, 345). Historically relevant events can become turning points: in learning from past mistakes, collective actors develop new strategies (della Porta, 1995, chap. 3). Together with the transformation in the police environment, some features of the police's professional culture may also be changing. Such trends as a demilitarization of the police and their professionalization may be reflected in a higher class background, as well as in an increasing integration into society. Although the police still tend to consider themselves "craftsmen," an increasing emphasis on training, and a shift in its content, may also have effected changes in the police culture. Cross-national differences in the development of these phenomena may be one reason for the existing cross-national differences in protest policing in the countries under review.

Governments and Protest Policing Styles

The evolution of protest policing may be influenced in the long run by stable institutional and cultural opportunities and constraints. The relevant changes over time suggest, however, that, in addition to this stable context, protest policing is also dependent on the "volatile" configuration of power. As Roger Geary observed, "Of course, constitutionally the police are supposed to be a neutral law enforcement agency independent of political influence. However, there seems little doubt that the Government does influence the policing of industrial disputes both in terms of the overall approach and in terms of particular operational decisions" (1985, 125–26). In fact, the degree of political control on protest policing, which varies cross-nationally and over time, influences police styles. Political control on the police can, however, play in different directions. Shifts in the policing of protest—or techniques of repression—have often been traced to changes in the government's makeup. In his model of the determinants of repression in the United States, Goldstein (1978) considered the ideological position of the president as the most important variable. Several historical examples indicate that the policing of protest was an issue on which parties did in fact polarize along the traditional left-right cleavage. In his study on the policing of industrial disputes in Great Britain, Geary attributed the shift from a "hard style" to a "soft style" of protest policing—a shift that he situated in about 1910—to political considerations that constrained the behavior of the authorities, in particular to the fact that "the Liberals, in order to maintain a majority over the conservatives, frequently had to rely on the support of Labor and Irish nationalist Members of Parliament" (1985, 117). Left-wing parties, with vivid memories of state repression of the labor and socialist movements, tended to rally in favor of civil liberties; conservative parties, fearful of losing votes to parties further to their right, often advocated law and order. A comparative study of Italy and Germany (della Porta, 1995) shows that, in general, protest policing was "softer" and more tolerant when the left was in government, whereas conservative governments were inclined to use "harder" tactics. In Italy, the center-left governments of the 1960s broke with the tradition of allowing the police to shoot at demonstrators. In Germany, the first Social Democratic-Free Democratic (SPD-FDP) government of Willi Brandt (1969–72) developed a more tolerant style of protest policing and liberalized laws concerning public marches and citizens' rights. In Great Britain in the 1980s, a partial rollback to a "harder" protest policing was instead connected with the political choices of the conservative government led by Margaret Thatcher.

It would be inaccurate, however, to claim that left-wing governments are always more tolerant of protest than conservative governments. Indeed, there seem to be periods in which the main parties do not greatly differ in their position on internal security policy (on Germany, see Funk, 1990). One possible reason for this is that protest policing is, in fact, a tricky issue for left-wing governments. The comparative study on Italy and Germany (della Porta, 1995) indicated, for instance, that left-wing governments often have to face difficult law-and-order campaigns launched by the conservative opposition (as happened in Germany under Chancellor Brandt). It is especially when the left feels the need to legitimate itself as "fit to govern" that it has to make concessions to the hard-line proponents of law and order. Such compromises not only inevitably disappoint social movement activists (usually to the advantage of the most radical wings), they also elicit internal criticism. Just as left-wing governments are not automatically lenient toward protest, so too conservatives in power do not always implement repressive policies. For instance, the swing from left to right in the state government amid the turmoil of the Berlin squatters' movement in 1981 did not interrupt the negotiations for a political solution, although some incidents did escalate into violence simply because the squatters anticipated a harder reaction by the conservative government (CILIP, 1981).

As the case studies presented in this volume indicate, government obviously retains a great potential influence on protest policing. The example of Italy in the immediate postwar period analyzed by Reiter shows the extent to which orders from the central government can affect protest policing at the local level. In this case, the government not only named "the enemy," but also outlined the types of police intervention to be exercised and evaluated the results achieved. For both France and England, our contributors emphasize the strong influence maintained by political powers, albeit with perceivable differences, on the question of when to intervene. Reporting on the criticism voiced by police officers on this interference, Fillieule and Jobard propose that it is more appropriate to speak of political antagonism than of police antagonism in those cases where the government, basing its decisions on political considerations, orders an antagonistic police intervention. The influence of government on protest policing styles also makes itself felt in a more general way, as is shown by the existence of two protest policing "lines" (one of Social Democratic-governed North Rhine-Westphalia and the other of conservative-governed Bavaria) in the Federal Republic of Germany (see Winter, in this volume). On the other hand, P. A. J. Waddington (in this volume), while underlining the influence of political power, also stresses the considerable degree of autonomy of the police, who, in the case of an anarchist demonstration in Trafalgar Square, would not be compelled to "die in the ditch" by the minister whose actions were perceived as arbitrary and partisan.

The recent developments toward a "softer" protest policing style seem to have gone hand in hand with a retreat of government from direct intervention. Our research indicates two connected developments: in general, governments increasingly tend to leave the technical side of policing protest to the police, who, in turn increasingly perceive their role in policing social and political conflicts as problematic, criticizing politicians for handing responsibility over to the police for situations that can be resolved only politically. Historically, the absence of instructions on protest policing from the political power has led to disorientation among the police, with contrasting consequences—in most cases tending more toward apathy than toward aggressive activism. In serious public order events, the lack of such political guidance might lead to a dominance of on-the-ground emotions and to an escalation of the confrontation between protesters and police into a win-or-lose battle.

Public Opinion, the Media, and Protest Policing Styles

Government choices on protest policing are sensitive to the pressures of various actors. Political parties, interest groups, and movement organizations express their preferences on protest policing, addressing either their constituency, the public, or the policymakers directly. Their discourses are then filtered through the media, thereby influencing public opinion.

Protest policing is an issue on which the more radical actors often find alliances, leading to the formation of civil rights coalitions. For instance, in his research on the policing of industrial disputes in Great Britain, Geary stated: "In the past the use of lethal force against defenseless working people had been counterproductive in several ways. Opposition from a broad section of political opinion could be expected and this often proved extremely embarrassing for the Government" (1985, 117). When the police are perceived as "overreacting," a process of "solidarization" is set in motion between those who are the direct target of repression and larger—often more moderate—forces. The reaction in England to the Peterloo Massacre in 1819 offers a historical illustration of this point: "For a time ultra-radicals and moderates buried their differences in a protest movement with which many Whigs were willing to associate" (Thompson, 1968, 756).

Moments can occur, however, when the public (or a part of the public) asks for a "tougher" intervention, and law-and-order coalitions arise. The "majoritarian"—or more vociferous—public opinion of the day is, in fact, not always a "liberal" one. Historical examples can readily be located in which hard-line policies were implemented in response to pressure exerted by law-and-order coalitions. According to Zwerman (1987), the "harder" counterterrorist policies of the Reagan administration resulted from the pressure of right-wing groups (such as the Moral Majority) on the national government. Thus, "tough" police intervention may be criticized by some, while appreciated by others. A study on the impact on the public of the policing of the 1984–85 miners' strike in Great Britain showed that, while alienating the strikers, the police's hard line improved the image of the police among nonstrikers (Green, 1990, chap. 3). Phases of "moral panic" (Cohen, 1972) have often generated demands for "law and order."

The media enter this picture partly as a "spokesperson" of one or the other coalition and partly with their own "autonomous" logic. Media attention to social protest seems to have the effect of generating a shift toward more tolerant policing. In particular since the seventies, the daily press appeared to be more critical toward "tough" police interventions, and more pluralistic (della Porta, 1997). The mere presence of journalists, in fact, appears to have a de-escalating effect on the police, although the fact that this presence does not always discourage the police from a "hard" style of intervention is testified to by the very existence of media coverage of such interventions. First of all, appreciation of the influence maintained by the media and interested coalitions on protest policing styles in contemporary European democracies should not lead to an overestimation of their weight in general. Although studies on the police in transition phases to democracy show that the police are very sensitive and dependent on public support during such periods, the Italian case in particular also demonstrates the degree to which, even in a democracy, the police may use repressive policies, despite the opposition of a large and well-organized minority (Reiter, in this volume). This is especially true when the police enjoy unlimited government support and receive clear directives, that is, if they know that the difficulties of the job, considerable if they have to suppress a large minority, are outweighed by the possible trouble that could result if they fail to follow the government's orders. Second, there are also cases where the media become the promoters of law-and-order campaigns. One example is the coverage by the Springer press, especially the tabloid *Bild*, of the student movement in Germany, most notably in Berlin. Third, there are indications that media coverage by its very nature can work as an agent of escalation. Certain characteristics of news production seem to generate a media "bias" in favor of the police. As Murdock (1984, 78) observed, "Contrary to the 'high' and 'low' conspiracy theories favored by some critics of the news media, the answer does not lie in interventions from on high or in the personal prejudices of journalists and editors, but in the routine business of news production and the practical and commercial pressures which shape it." First among these characteristics is the fact that in news gathering journalists rely on official sources—and among them the police are usually a preferred one.[9] Not only are police spokespeople given ample space in accounts of disorders, even the pictures reflect the police "point of view" since, for security reasons, they are usually taken from behind the police. A second characteristic of the "business of news production" that can produce a biased image of protesters is the rule that a "good story" should focus on dramatic and violent actions, involving large numbers of participants, and not on the incidents that originally triggered off such mass events (D. Waddington, 1992, 177). Third, like other actors, the press uses stereotypes that oppose rampaging crowds to sober citizens, that identify troublemakers with hooligan youth.

Although they do not deal directly with public opinion and the media, the chapters in this volume indicate a growing public stigmatization of coercive police management of political demonstrations and social protest. This is at least the perception by the police, as we shall see in more detail. However, as suggested by Wisler and Kriesi in this volume, public opinion seems to be less tolerant of disruptive protest behavior when other protest channels are available. Moreover, coercive policing is better accepted, or even advocated, if directed against violent protesters.

The Interaction between the Police and Protesters and Protest Policing Styles

Another variable that undoubtedly influences protest policing styles is the interaction between protesters and the police, a dynamic that is not restricted to single protest events. The police, in fact, seem to be equipped with an elephant's memory: the history of previous interactions with protesters is an important element shaping today's protest policing.

The prohibition of a demonstration can set up violent dynamics. Research on disorderly demonstrations in London over a period of one hundred years has shown that "violence has tended to occur whenever protesters have been castigated as 'subversive,' 'unpatriotic,' or 'communistic'; when their activities were likely to prove embarrassing to the government, monarchy or 'national reputation,' or when the demonstration was technically illegal, occurring in a defiance of legal prohibition" (D. Waddington, 1992, 29). As the police leaders recognize, the implementation of a ban on demonstrating is a source of violent escalation (for instance, Wisler, Barranco, and Tackenberg, 1996, 7; see also Fillieule, 1995a).

Moreover, certain police techniques can lead to escalation during interaction with demonstrators. As Gary T. Marx (1972, 79) explains, "Contrary to riot control manuals (and usually the wishes of higher authorities) as police encounter a crowd they may break ranks, raise their nightsticks above their shoulders and hit people on the head rather than the body." The dispersal of crowds, in fact, is a delicate task, and the main instrument of coercive police intervention—the baton charge—easily leads to escalation:[10]

> The reason why baton charges are difficult to control is known colloquially in the Metropolitan Police as "the red mist". This refers to a potential cocktail of psychological conditions which diminishes any person's self-control, and from which the police are not exempt. Baton charges require officers to act aggressively in conditions of relative anonymity . . . they may be wearing protective clothing with visors to obscure their facial features; and they will almost certainly be acting, not as individuals, but as a group. The target of their actions will not be other individuals, but an equally anonymous collective—"the crowd", "Them"—who will have insulted and physically attacked "Us"—the police. Officers' anger and frustration will thus have been aroused, and a baton charge will allow retaliation in conditions which minimize individual responsibility. (Waddington, 1991, 177–78)

Particularly in crowd dispersal, an additional risk of escalation derives from organizational dynamics. As Monjardet observed (1990, 217ff.), there are at least three main mechanisms in police intervention that favor escalation: the dialectic of centralization and autonomy in police units, the difficulties of co-ordinating the different groups, and uncertainty about the aims of the inter-vention. Although a police force may have well-developed techniques for controlling large masses, it may be ill prepared to isolate and control small groups operating within larger crowds (ibid., 233). In Italy and Germany (della Porta, 1995), certain much-criticized "hard" police interventions—that eventually led to escalation—occurred during peaceful mass demonstrations "infiltrated" by small radical groups. In such situations, the handling of law and order indeed called for a difficult equilibrium between control of the rad-icals and respect for the rights of the moderates. Moreover, especially in Ger-many in the 1980s, claims of police brutality often followed the authorities' decision to deploy units from different states to police protest events. In these cases, lack of coordination and a poor knowledge of the territory may have led to the escalation of conflicts, even when a strategy of de-escalation had been planned by the police leadership.[11] Moreover, as Gary T. Marx (1972, 89) noticed, police riots may occur:

> The above, superior officers may lose the power to control their men. The chain of command and communication between and within enforcement agencies, often unclear to begin with, may completely break down. . . . Some police be-havior seems as much, or more, inspired by the desire for vengeance, retalia-tion and "to teach the bastards a lesson" as by the desire to restore law and order.

However, the effects of police-protester interactions are not restricted to the dynamics of a single encounter. Individual incidents may have long-term repercussions on police attitudes toward protest. If the image of a "weak" police—especially when "promoted" by political entrepreneurs—can produce fear in the public and calls for more "effective" repression, the impression of having been "defeated" will also have important consequences within the police. These consequences go beyond immediate reactions such as promises to take revenge, and extend to tactical and structural changes. In Great Britain, a perceived police "defeat" during a picketing action in Saltley in the 1970s led to the organization of a system of mutual aid between the var-ious local police forces, as well as to the establishment of a National Record-ing Center. Later on, the visible weakness of the police during the riots of the early 1980s allowed for an increasing specialization and armament of the "an-tirioting" branches (in this volume, see Waddington, Reiner). As Geary

(1985, 127) has observed, "It's only after you have been seen by the public to lose at one tactical level that you can escalate to the next level."

The history of interactions between protesters and police is of great importance in explaining protest policing dynamics. Such interactions are the concrete expression of the national strategies developed to deal with challengers, as mentioned earlier. For the police, the history of their relations with specific protest groups constitutes an important element in decisions on tactics to be applied. For this reason, the impact of the virtuous circle of less and less violence on public demonstrations has to be stressed. These mechanisms are already taking us into the category of police knowledge, to which we now turn.

Police Knowledge and Protest Policing Styles

As police research has often revealed, the police are a bureaucracy with a very high degree of discretion. Several studies have addressed the question of police behavior, explaining the different strategies adopted by police officers and/or police units. In particular, a "situational" approach relates police choices to environmental characteristics, while an "attitudinal" approach concentrates on the individual preferences of police officers (for a review, see Worden, 1989). Both approaches share the persuasion that (*a*) a large degree of discretion exists in police behavior, and (*b*) there are systematic variations. As Manning observed, "Policing tends to be shaped by adaptations made by actors to structural patterns, to the reality they perceive, construct and maintain" (1979, 48–49). For a full understanding of protest policing styles it is not enough to look at the variables discussed so far. We also have to examine police knowledge; that is, the police's perception of their role and of the external reality. For organizational features, police culture, governments, public opinion, and interaction with protesters to have an influence on protest policing styles, their input has to be taken up by the police and transformed into knowledge.

Why do we refer to the police's perception of their role and of external reality as "knowledge" and not just as "images"? A first reason is connected with the *great discretion* that the police enjoy as an organization and as individual officers. In an apparent reversal of the mechanism typical of bureaucracies, which sees increased discretionary latitude at the top of the hierarchy, the rank-and-file policemen on the spot hold a very extensive power of definition over the situation. Police officers seem to intervene first of all on the basis of their appreciation of the situation, and only secondarily on the basis of rules and regulations (Jessen, 1995, 32f.). In this sense, the police's perception of external reality serves as the equivalent of the specialized knowledge of other parts of the bureaucracy.[12] It is not subordinate to rules and regulations contained in written manuals, but is equally important for the carrying out of police duty, and is not restricted to certain shortcuts and tricks of the trade taught by experience.

A second reason for the use of the term "knowledge" can be found in the range and depth of police knowledge, which is not limited to fleeting images, stereotypes, and prejudices, but extends to the *core problems* of protest policing. To give an example, Waddington in this volume calls the policing of protest in democracies "intrinsically morally ambiguous: protesters are not criminals, but citizens participating in the political process; . . . any conflict between protesters and the police tends to be a battle of moral equals in which both sides are seeking the approval of bystanders." Interviews with police officers, which served as the main tool for the study of police knowledge in our research, show that they are aware, precisely for this reason, that protest policing is a particularly delicate task. As a British superintendent observed, "In our society if we arrest a man for stealing everybody else says, 'serves him right,' but where you get into an area where you are arresting a man in relation to his work [i.e., during a strike] then there are emotions involved here that are not as clear-cut to the average guy" (in Geary, 1985, 127).

A third reason for the use of the term "police knowledge" lies in the *interconnection* of perceptions of external reality. These perceptions do not remain isolated images, but form a body of knowledge. To take the example of a feature of the police occupational culture, namely, police images about protesters and demonstrations: the distinction made by the police between "ordinary decent protesters" and "professional protesters," which will be discussed in detail later, reflects the institutional pressure, that is, the political impact (Waddington, in this volume). It is furthermore based on instruction and on past work experiences. It represents an adaptation of general stereotypes developed by the police about disorders and disordered behavior, and takes into account the dynamics of police interaction with some specific groups—because "Demonstrators' and policemen's images reflect each other. The image the demonstrators have of the police will have an impact upon the images the police have of the demonstrators" (McClintock et al., 1974, 102). In the final score, it is influenced by the media and public opinion in general, but also by a reflection on the media coverage of demonstrations. With police knowledge, we refer, then, to the police's "construction of the external reality" (Berger and Luckman, 1966).

The way in which police knowledge translates into a protest policing style will be discussed in what follows by means of the examples of police stereotypes of "protesters." The process works for protest policing in the same way as for police work in general: "The action of the police, as a force of social control, depends of course on the received order (authorized demonstration or non authorized demonstration), but also on the images that the policemen have of those very groups they have to police. . . . Control or dispersion of the demonstrators will be more or less brutal according to this image" (McClintock et al., 1974, 102). In his explanation of the brutal police repression of protests during the 1968 Democratic Convention in Chicago, Donner (1990, 116) observed that the police believed that an army of demonstrators had planned to invade the city (some movement literature had boasted an invasion of the city of between one hundred and two hundred thousand demonstrators, although no more than five thousand came). They also believed the "threats" disseminated by Yippies as a sort of theater provocation to "burn the city down" or flood the city sewers with gasoline or dump LSD in the water supply (ibid., 116–17).

Stereotypes about protesters may overlap with those of other groups usually included in the (socially constructed) definition of public disorders. In their analysis of certain examples of public behavior understood as constituting public disorder and in response to which public order law was or could have been used (with particular regard to youth gangs, soccer hooligans, vagrants and traveling people, industrial conflict, and inner-city riots), Nicola Lacey, Celia Wells, and Dirk Meure noted the presence of recurring themes, such as the ideas of the young, outsiders (such as immigrants, ethnic minority members, or "agents provocateurs"), deviants, and disadvantaged socioeconomic groups as being especially implicated in public disorder (1990, 71). In addition to "old" stereotypes, some of which, like the "conspiracy theory," enjoy a surprising life span and vitality, "new" ones can emerge during waves of protest.[13] Stereotypes about one form of public disorder can spread to others. Taking the example of Great Britain again, it was observed that the experiences of the 1970s in Northern Ireland surfaced in the "framing" of the riots of the early 1980s, and then spread to the policing of the miners' strike. Commenting on the Tactical Options Manual distributed in 1982 to senior police officers in Great Britain—a manual that introduced maneuvers of an essentially military character and redirected police methods from the individual-oriented tradition to that of the team, and from the reactive tradition to a proactive one—McCabe and Wallington affirm:

> The style of policing reflected in the Tactical Options Manual was consciously copied from the crowd control methods developed in colonial police forces (such as Hong Kong) and in Northern Ireland. . . . While the 1981 riots may

have been the principal catalyst to the drawing up of the manual, and perhaps future urban riots the main intended occasion for its practical implementation, in the event the first full-scale use of the type of maneuvers envisaged was during the miners' strike, most spectacularly during the confrontations at Orgreave. (McCabe and Wallington, 1988, 48–49)

Research has indicated that the police have quite complex images of demonstrators. Helmut Willems and his collaborators (1988) discovered that policemen have surprisingly little knowledge of protesters' motives. Nevertheless, the image of demonstrators was found to be a complex one, in which "peaceful demonstrators" are set in opposition to "hooligans." According to the police, "Peaceful demonstrators have a pragmatic interest, and a clear aim, for which they engage themselves with a lot of involvement and credibility. They make use of their basic right to demonstrate. Normally, they are peaceful demonstrators . . . with a direct interest in the conflict. . . . They are willing to discuss, they are well informed" (Willems et al., 1988, 153). Violent hooligans, on the other hand,

> are not interested in the topic of the conflict, but only in rioting, in reducing their aggression in the struggle with the police. They are described as destructive and misinformed. They travel from demonstration to demonstration, are probably supported and financed by wire-pullers. . . . In comparison with the peaceful demonstrators, they are a relatively small group, many of them are very young, and for this reason are easy to influence. Normally, they are not interested in discussions. (Ibid., 153–54)

The police distinction between "good" and "bad" demonstrators is based on their conception of "legitimate" protest, as well as on their expectations of the demonstrators' behavior. As P. A. J. Waddington noticed, legitimate protest, linked to social problems and organized by people aiming to make themselves heard in order to solve the problems, is sharply contrasted to protests by "professional demonstrators," who upset public order because they enjoy provocation and revolt (Waddington, 1994b, 112–13). In the Italian case (see della Porta and De Biasi in this volume), a widespread perception among the police is that the principal actors producing disorder in the 1990s were motivated not by political beliefs—considered to be "noble" ends—but by an impulse toward "hooliganism," which reflects the existence of social problems. In fact, a distinction is made between "good" demonstrators, who protest to achieve comprehensible ends and are well organized in their actions, and "bad" demonstrators, whose objectives appear to be more confused and whose actions are disorganized. Among the former category are "workers" or "family men"—according to the definitions of interviewees—who demonstrate in defense of their jobs or in favor of union demands, and who have both a long experience of demonstrations and a noteworthy capacity to manage them. Among the second category are the hooligans and young people from social centers, whose demands are considered at best to be "confused," and whose behavior often appears "unpredictable." Similar observations emerge from the French case study (Fillieule and Jobard, in this volume). As Gary T. Marx (1972, 79) had already noticed studying the American police reaction to urban riots and as our research confirms, police images of protesters define their strategic choices and behavior: "When the disturbance seems apolitical, unfocused and primarily expressive, and when there is no minimal organization among rioters . . . authorities may have no alternative—from their viewpoint—but the graduated use of force."

Police knowledge intervenes as a filter on all the levels of figure 2, and not only for the occupational culture of the police, from which the examples of stereotypes discussed earlier are taken. The presumed impact of organizational features such as centralization and militarization on police officers' perception of their role fueled police reform efforts in various countries. As far as the legal framework is concerned, the underenforcement of the law, singled out as one of the most significant tendencies characterizing protest policing in the 1990s, provides a clear example of the way in which police knowledge acts as a filter. For instance, in his discussion of the Brokdorf decision of the German Federal Constitutional Court, Martin Winter emphasizes that it was the reception of this legal decision by the police that gave it its impact on protest policing.

Police knowledge works in the same way in terms of the impact that the political powers have on protest policing styles practiced in specific cases. Waddington (in this volume) emphasizes that "institutional power is refracted through the lens of how the police define their task." The London police do not need a specific order to protect the memorial to Britain's war dead from desecration; their knowledge of the consequences for their image should it be profaned is sufficient. In Germany, there are cases of *vorauseilender Gehorsam* (obedience in advance) (Winter, in this volume). In countries like Italy, where the police have a tradition of political dependence, the efforts of the police are oriented toward perceiving "which way the wind is blowing," so that, for instance, the governmental change in Italy in 1994 led to a period of extreme caution for the police as they waited for political directives on the management of public order (della Porta, in this volume).

Police knowledge also "filters" the demands coming from the public and "published" opinion. As Nigel Fielding observed, "Few mothers and children have been prosecuted for disrupting traffic while demanding pedestrian crossings. . . . Obstruction and even conspiracy charges could have been applied, if the group were not one to whom the police judged most people to be sympathetic" (1991, 77). The police are not only conscious of the presence of the mass media at demonstrations, but are also knowledgeable about the mechanisms of media coverage. According to a British superintendent:

> We are very much aware of the media which controls to some extent police action. So that action, when it's seen on the film, has got to be seen to be reasonable. If we act unreasonably, then yes, we could alienate the public, not in the issue, but in the way that we deal with them [demonstrations]. . . . We have got to protect our image. (Ibid., 130)

To conclude this discussion of police knowledge, it is worth underlining that a study of this subject must confront certain difficulties, beside the fact that it is not only written knowledge which is being analyzed. An analysis of interviews with police officers will show that "the" police and consequently "the" police knowledge do not exist.[14] The control exercised over the police by political authorities, for instance, is perceived differently on different levels of the police hierarchy. In the British case, the more attentive awareness of senior officers seems to have had a restraining effect on rank-and-file members. As one inspector observed:

> These senior officers, they are into this low profile, softly, softly, community relations approach, and let these strikers get away with just about every offense short of murder. . . . We ought to just once move in hard—that's all it would take and we'd have no more problems. These senior officers, well, they are too scared to do that. They are worried about questions being asked in Parliament, about their chances of promotion, about being criticized . . . about whether the Home Secretary would call for a report, etc., etc. (In Geary, 1985, 125)

Furthermore, the police themselves do not appear to reflect critically on their construction of external reality as knowledge, interpreting it as "experience" and "on-the-job learning." Police knowledge is therefore probably shifting and possibly contradictory, different for different levels of police hierarchy and for different police branches.

Escalation and De-escalation: The Consequences of Protest Policing

We can turn now to the effects of protest policing on social movements, and particularly on protest tactics. The social science literature provides us with several hypotheses on this point. Some scholars have stated that a reduction in repression facilitates the development of revolutions and social movements (Skocpol, 1979; McAdam, 1982; della Porta, 1995). A high degree of repression and an illiberal political culture have often been associated with radical behavior on the part of challengers (Goldstein, 1983, 340; Kitschelt, 1985, 302-3). As a reaction to police repression, the protest focus tends to shift from the single issue to the meta-issue of protest rights (Escobar, 1993, 1485). As mentioned, the general trend since the 1970s and 1980s has been toward a more tolerant, selective, and "soft" policing style, which tends to institutionalize many forms of protest. This de-escalation seems to be based on a "virtuous circle." The "institutionalization" of protest and social movements provides an additional reason to foresee the prevalence of more tolerant behavior—also on the side of the police—as we can in fact expect that the more instrumental movement would have a greater interest in maintaining the support of public opinion. In particular, this would be true of those movements that are more strictly affiliated with a political party. The labor movement in Great Britain offers a good example. Geary observed, in fact, that the trade unionists he interviewed were "highly sensitive to the political implications of industrial disorder" and attributed their sensitivity to their "close identification with the Labor Party" (Geary, 1985, 120). As one trade unionist stated, "Miners are not fools. They almost all vote Labor and they are aware of the effect trouble at the picket line would have on the election" (ibid., 123).

The fact that violent behavior tends to be more and more stigmatized can, however, produce new cycles of more repressive attitudes. In the late 1960s, Allan Silver (1967), commenting on a general trend toward increasing stigmatization of violence, observed the risk of no longer seeing the possibility of a political solution for violent behavior. Looking at the reactions to violent forms of protest in the 1980s, it seems that Silver was right. To provide just one example, writing about the 1980 Bristol riot, Joshua and Wallace stress the refusal of the Home Office and the national government to acknowledge the political and social reasons behind the events. The main reaction was instead the "armament" of the police with "aggressive" riot equipment (the shock had been the fact that the police had had to withdraw from the Saint Paul's district during the riots): "Then in the space of a few weeks riot equipment and tactics once considered unacceptable, i.e. crash helmets, new riot shields, new protective uniforms, and the use of police Land Rovers to break up crowds became the norm. CS gas was used and officially sanctioned, as were water cannons, plastic bullets, and armored police vehicles as 'a last resort'" (Joshua and Wallace, 1983, 127).

This mechanism may be reinforced by some of the police tactics characterizing protest policing in Europe today: the de-escalating efforts of modern protest policing—with underenforcement of the law, the search to negotiate, and large-scale collection of information—may backfire. Waddington's research in particular has illustrated the potential of control that can be achieved with this tactic, a form of control that may result in making protest invisible. Should the police yield to the temptation to "overcontrol" protest, protesters might get the impression that their demonstration is useless because invisible, and change to more spectacular tactics in order to make themselves seen and heard. Similar reactions may be provoked by the emphasis on large-scale collection of information, which is also characteristic of the general trend toward increasing control. In fact, agencies that deal with intelligence gathering and the prevention of crime or subversion have shown an inherent tendency to expand (Marx, 1979, 112; Garret, 1981, 224–25). A parallel trend was singled out by police historians who suggested that the retreat of the police force from its welfare functions was compensated for by a progressive expansion of the security concept to include ever greater risks, so that the new concept of police in practice also included the order of the whole society (Jessen, 1995, 31).

These last observations lead to the question: In which direction will protest policing in contemporary democracies move? Will the adoption of a "soft," tolerant, selective, legal, preventive, consensual, flexible, and professional protest policing style be definitive? It is not our intention to foretell the future, but the results of the research presented in this volume give certain indications. Not only the character of these changes, but also the nature of the continuities in protest policing can give us an idea about the reversibility of the trend toward a "softer" and more tolerant protest policing style.

One theoretical possibility for a reversal of the trend lies in a change of the environment. Our research has shown that, in their dealings with protest, the police will react to shifts in the demands from outside. If these demands come from the government, the police are likely to fulfill them, even if they remain unconvinced about their usefulness or effectiveness, although they might voice protest. As historical examples show, police forces will fulfill demands by the government, even without regard for their correspondence with democratic rights. With this we do not wish to imply in any way that there are indications that such orders might be given, nor do we want to question the fact that democratic principles are more deeply rooted in today's police forces than in earlier periods. In most European countries, in fact, the visible government input in the wake of the 1960s has been predominantly in the direction of greater respect for democratic rights, and consequently "softer" protest policing—and there are no indications of a development in the contrary direction. However, the nature of the relationship between the police and government is such that if a government were to order a change in public order policies, the police would feel bound to comply.

At least of equal importance to government input for the development of more tolerant protest policing styles is the pressure of public opinion, which over the last decades has veered in the direction of a growing acceptance of a wide range of previously condemned protest activities. This shift was perceived by the police and translated into a different policing of protest. Underlying this attitude is the fact that a failure to perceive the preferences in the public would have to be paid for by a loss of legitimation, a fact about which the police are very conscious. Any such loss could be compensated for only by the government's willingness to shield the police from criticism and to back the stepping up of coercive and repressive measures, a choice possible only to a certain degree.[15] In the absence of such support the police would not "die in the ditch" for any abstract notions about order, but would try to accommodate the demands of the public. In the same way, however, the police will try to accommodate eventual demands by the public for "harder" protest policing.

By following popular shifts, the police show a capacity to learn. Changes and learning processes of the police are initiated by an analysis of problematic public order interventions, that is, the police learn by analyzing their failures.[16] Over the last decades, the police forces in Europe have proved to be capable of incorporating new experiences into their body of police knowledge, making the continuation of a "soft" and tolerant protest policing style more likely. The importance of the body of past experience, however, seems such that it prevents the police from anticipating change. Tactical and strategic errors in confrontations with new movements and protest forms may trigger off a relapse into an antagonistic protest policing style.

Notwithstanding the changes in protest policing over the past three decades, there are also significant elements of continuity. The police remain the state agency for the protection of order and security, which they establish, if need be, by means of force. The range of options for intervention theoretically open to the police has remained basically unchanged. As underlined several times, the dominant protest policing style in Europe is selective, that is, different police styles are used for different actors. In this way, "brutal" and repressive styles have survived. These styles are connected with the same kind of stereotypes about professional disturbers of the peace, conspirators, and so on, as before. The difference today is that these stereotypes and protest policing styles are now applied only to a small minority among the protesters, whereas historically they were used against large sections of the population, such as the members and associations of the working-class movement. It is this kind of continuity in the role of the police, in the range of options theoretically open to them, and in the mechanisms with which they individuate and label "dangerous" enemies that makes arrest or reversal of the trend toward "softer" and more tolerant protest policing styles a possibility of which we have to be aware.

Notes

We are grateful to the Robert Schuman Centre of the European University Institute, and in particular to its director Yver Mény, for interest in our research. We also wish to thank Michel Dobry, Alessandro Pizzorno, and Arpad Szakolczai, who acted as discussants at the conference, for their valuable comments.

1. At the conference, two additional contributions were presented on the Hungarian case (Szabo, 1995; Szikinger, 1995) that are not included in this collection.

2. According to Wisler, Barranco, and Tackenberg (1996), the different dimensions tend to define two coherent protest policing styles, one more opportunist, tolerant, soft, selective, and flexible, the other legalistic, repressive, hard, diffuse, and dissuasive.

3. Lüdtke (1992, 17) sees the long-term changes in Germany since the nineteenth century in a process of professionalization and *Verrechtlichung*, as well as a growing pressure for public justification.

4. A similar trend also appeared in the Hungarian case (see Szabo, 1995; Szikinger, 1995).

5. Since the prime emphasis of the urban units was identification, photography became an operational focus. Technological sophistication in this field allowed for expansion in the area covered (from half a mile away) and for an extended time (twenty-four hours a day, thanks to infrared circuits). Other techniques of control included wiretapping, electronic bugging, and the planting of informers.

6. Some characteristics of the secret services and the judiciary can also be of relevance to protest policing. For instance, the specialization of the secret services in internal versus external security and their relative dependence on the military are also important factors in any attempt to define the context for protest and protest policing.

7. Waddington added: "Police in countries like the USA, who were under local political control and where citizens were protected by a Bill of Rights, saw *more, not less*, violence" (1991, 134–35).

8. Jessen (1995, 30) recalls that a partial militarization of the police was the price to be paid for the retreat of the military from the arena of social conflicts.

9. "The police are news," writes Nigel Fielding (1991, 17).

10. For an analysis of the escalation of confrontations during the student movement of the sixties in West Germany, see Sack, 1984.

11. This point is also made by Marx (1972, 85). On escalation and unforeseen consequences of police intervention, see also Monet (1990).

12. Max Weber defined "specialized knowledge" as the knowledge acquired via a specific education, and "service knowledge" as the knowledge—available only to the functionaries—of the concrete events necessary to control the administration ([1922] 1974, 735).

13. Other widespread stereotypes are those of the "rotten apple" and "communist agitators" (among others, see McClintock et al., 1974, 127–30; McCabe and Wallington, 1988, 43–44).

14. On this point, see also Winter in this volume.

15. Even in totalitarian states, the police depended on the acquiescence and collaboration of the population. The sheer numerical relationship between the police, especially the political branch, and the population would have made any kind of policing based on pure coercion impossible. The Gestapo, for instance, was not ever-present, and if it seemed to be all-knowing, this resulted from the propagation of a myth and was based on large-scale cooperation or collaboration. On this subject, see the contributions in Paul and Mallmann (1995).

16. For instance, recalling the negative political consequences of the police killing of demonstrators in February 1934, Monjardet (1990, 214–15) suggested that the French police are still trained to consider demonstrators not as an enemy, but as a temporary adversary, and to avoid injuring or killing people.

Part I

Policing Protest in Established Democracies

Chapter 1

Policing, Protest, and Disorder in Britain

Robert Reiner

Protest and Policing in British History

The origins of modern British policing are intimately related to changing perceptions and patterns of disorder and protest. There is a long-running debate in historical analyses of the early development of the police in Britain between those who stress the centrality of riot and disorder to it (e.g., Silver, 1967, 1971), those who emphasize the role of everyday crime (e.g., Reith, 1956), and those who see police expansion as fundamentally a reflex of the bureaucratization of government in general (e.g., Monkkonen, 1981).

The debate is partly a function of the ideological perspective of the author: more orthodox, conservative interpretations seek to depoliticize the significance of the creation of the police and attribute such disorder as cannot be ignored in their accounts to ordinary criminality (e.g., Reith, 1956, 122); more critical analyses see an implicit political dimension to everyday crimes, especially against property, and see the police role as primarily protection of a dominant, oppressive social order. As one Marxist account puts it, "The existence of the modern police force owes little to the exigencies of combating professional crime and was developed primarily as an instrument of political control and labour discipline" (Hirst, 1975, 225).

The debate is also partly a question of which phase of police development is concentrated on. The first parliamentary attempt to establish a modern police force, Pitt's abortive Police Bill of 1785, was immediately inspired by the Gordon riots (anti-Catholic riots in 1780 when for several days London seemed at the mercy of mobs). But it was informed by nearly a century of campaigning by advocates of a professional police as the answer to a perceived scourge of everyday crime, led by such prominent figures as the Fieldings. When Sir

Robert Peel was finally successful in piloting the Metropolitan Police Act through Parliament in 1829, after a further half century of futile attempts by himself and others, this was in part by defusing opposition to what many regarded as a potentially politically oppressive force by stressing its role in preventing routine crime. His speech made much of statistics purporting to demonstrate a growth in theft, and he made reference to riot only briefly in the ensuing debate. But the subsequent 1839 County Police Act was almost entirely motivated by fears engendered by the growth of political disorders associated with Chartism. The parliamentary debates were dominated by impassioned arguments about whether new police forces in the provinces would exacerbate or dampen disorder (Watts-Miller, 1987, 47–48). The 1856 County and Borough Police Act, which spread the new police throughout the country, cannot be readily explained as a response to either crime or disorder, and is probably more an illustration of the proposition culled from a study of the spread of American policing: "growth of uniformed urban police forces should be seen simply as a part of the growth of urban service bureaucrats" (Monkkonen, 1981, 55).

Thus the centrality of public order to the development of policing in Britain can be disputed according to ideological standpoint, and it varies between specific periods. But there cannot be much doubt that concerns about the policing of political disorder have been crucial in affecting the style and standing of the police in different periods. In turn, the mode of policing conflict and disorder has had important consequences for the stability of British society.

This essay will trace the shifting patterns of policing protest and disorder since the creation of the modern British police in the early nineteenth century. It will be suggested that between 1829 and the mid-1980s the style of policing political conflict and disorder went through a long-term U-turn (Geary, 1985). Starting from a context of considerable political conflict and criticism, the mode of policing protest in the 1950s and 1960s had become one of tolerance, compromise, and accommodation, which (incorrectly) has been seen as the quintessence of British policing (Reiner, 1992b, chaps. 1 and 2). In the 1970s and early 1980s this shifted back to conflict and controversy, as a transformation in what is often described as a "paramilitary" mode occurred (Waddington, 1987, 1991, 1993a, 1994b; Jefferson, 1987, 1990, 1993; Northam, 1988; Hills, 1995). Since the mid-1980s, both the practice and the perception of public order policing have moved to a pragmatic yet brittle acceptance of a style with greater coercive potential. These changes correspond to broader moves in the politics of policing, and beyond that in the structure and culture of British society.

Public Order Policing 1829–1985: A Historical U-Turn

The Demand for Order and the Creation of the Police

Particular stages in the creation of the modern British police were more marked by concern about the policing of protest and disorder than others. But there can be little doubt that the process as a whole was a consequence of what has been described as a growing "demand for order in civil society" (Silver, 1967). Historians have debated the extent to which the perception of contemporary commentators that there was a rapid rise of criminality in the growing cities of industrializing Britain in the eighteenth and early nineteenth centuries was accurate, or an example of the "respectable fears" about declining morality that can be found in all periods, especially periods of rapid change (Gatrell and Hadden, 1972; Pearson, 1983).

But regardless of the objective truth, the upper-class perception of crime and disorder was changing. Routine crime came to be seen as symptomatic of a deeper threat to the social order as such, stemming from the "dangerous classes," the burgeoning mass of the urban poor (Silver, 1967, 3). The moral economy of feudalism, which saw prices and economic relationships as embedded in traditional (albeit rigidly hierarchical) conceptions of justice, was replaced by a pure market economy, governed only by impersonal laws of supply and demand (Thompson, 1975, 1992). Traditional practices of workers retaining some of the product they handled was supplanted by the pure cash nexus of the money wage, and such payment in kind was redefined as theft (Bunyan, 1977, 61; Brogden, 1982, 55).

The meaning of collective disorder changed in a parallel way. Historians like Rude and Hobsbawm have shown how, up to the early nineteenth century, riotous protest was an accepted and mutually understood means by which the politically unrepresented masses communicated grievances to the ruling elite: "collective bargaining by riot." But with the spread of industrial capitalism, riot came to be regarded not as a form of protodemocracy but as a fundamental threat to the social and political order (Hobsbawm, 1959, 116; Storch, 1980, 34). Whether or not it was increasing in frequency or scale, riotous protest came to be seen as a fundamental threat to the stability and integrity of society. "The market system was more allergic to rioting than any other economic system we know" (Polanyi, 1944, 186).

The increased demand for order was not only a question of concern about collective protest. Industrial capitalism required a higher level of routine, everyday order. The new mechanized conditions of factory production necessitated that the formally free labor force be subject to tighter discipline in both work and "leisure" time to fit the rhythms and regimentation of industrial organization. This produced a "criminalisation of traditional street pastimes which were solely recreational" (Cohen, 1979, 120–21). The new police officer became a "domestic missionary" (Storch, 1976), "the moral entrepreneur of public propriety" (Cohen, 1979, 128), charged with converting savage street dwellers to respectability and decency.

Overall, emerging industrial capitalism required a tighter disciplining of hitherto loosely regulated aspects of social relations (Foucault, 1977). Not only overt demonstrations or rioting which were regarded as threatening the social order, but routine crime and everyday disorderliness were themselves seen as having crypto-political significance, eroding the viability of social organization. "A stable public order was a precondition of rational calculation on the part of industrial capitalists" (Spitzer and Scull, 1977, 277).

The creation of a modern, professional, bureaucratized police came increasingly in the course of the early nineteenth century to be seen as the best means of supplying the higher level of order demanded. Traditional means of responding to collective protest or disorder were either the army or a variety of forms of citizen force: the militia (raised by compulsory ballot of all inhabitants by the Lord Lieutenant of a county), the yeomanry, and the special constabulary. The use of the army to suppress protest was often a counterproductive sledgehammer. It could only alternate "between no intervention and the most drastic procedures—the latter representing a declaration of internal war with lingering consequences of hate and resentment" (Silver, 1967, 12). Moreover, as soldiers were also recruited from the poor, they were on occasion politically unreliable in dealing with collective protest (Stevenson, 1977, 33–34). This problem applied also to the militia, as those selected often employed deputies, who would be drawn from the same social strata as rioters.

Although volunteer forces, especially the yeomanry, might be politically reliable, they were problematic in other ways. Urban bourgeois manufacturers were less ready to answer a call to arms—"the classic confrontation of an agrarian military tradition and a pacific commercial and industrial one" (Silver, 1967, 10). This was not only a matter of urban elites being more timorous than their hunting and shooting rural counterparts. They also saw personal involvement in suppressing protest as politically provocative. "The use of social and economic superiors as police exacerbated rather than mollified class violence" (ibid.). This was explicitly argued by the 1839 Royal Commission on the Rural Constabulary, which preceded the County Police Act of that year: "The animosities created or increased, and rendered permanent by arming master against servant, neighbour against neighbour, by triumph on the one side and failure on the other, were even more deplorable than the outrages actually committed."

The attraction of a professional police organization that purported to represent impersonal and impartial legal authority was that it could depoliticize the control of protest and riot. Deployed on regular patrol, it could defuse spontaneous disorders before they reached a stage requiring military intervention. Discipline could become a routinized aspect of everyday life, not an occasional thunderbolt from on high. Above all, the control of protest could be represented as a professional enforcement of impartial law, not the exercise of political power. A "bureaucratic police system that . . . drew attack and animosity upon itself . . . seemed to separate the assertion of 'constitutional' authority from that of social and economic dominance" (Silver, 1967, 11–12).

"Softly, Softly": The Institutionalization of Protest and the British Police Tradition

There were heated debates among contemporaries about the form the new police should take. Some argued—especially in the 1830s and 1840s, the heyday of Chartist protest seeking the extension of the franchise—that the police should have an overtly military structure and capability. After the passage of the Reform Bill of 1832, for example, the Duke of Wellington claimed that "From henceforth we shall never be able to carry on a government without the assistance and support of a military body. If we cannot have a regular army in such a state of discipline and efficiency as that the King can rely on them, we must and we shall have a National Guard in some shape or other" (cited in Silver, 1971, 185). Many of the rural constabularies set up following the County Police Act of 1839 *did* assume a military model (Steedman, 1984, 21–25) and were prompted directly by fears of political agitation and disorder.

However, the conception of policing that held sway eventually was more subtle. Precisely because of their recognition of the precarious state of political stability in the face of widespread conflict and protest, the main architects of the predominant direction of British policing (such as the home secretary, Sir Robert Peel, and Rowan and Mayne—the first two Metropolitan Police Commissioners) argued that the police must strive to achieve the support or at least the acquiescence of the mass of the population. "The preservation of public tranquillity"—Mayne's famous 1829 definition of the prime police function, notably resuscitated by Lord Scarman in his 1981 Report on the Brixton disorders (Scarman, 1981, paras. 4.55–4.60)—was to be given the highest priority, even if this occasionally meant that immediate and full law enforcement or order maintenance was sacrificed. Discretion became the better part of policing valor.

A particular, celebrated model of British policing emerged gradually as a result. It has been encapsulated as follows by one American historian: "What people in our own age think of when we hear the words 'English police' is an unarmed police force of constables who are ordinarily courteous to tourists, patient, and restrained in confronting crowds" (Thurmond Smith, 1985, 5). This benign image of the British bobby still resonates around the world as a potent myth, even if the apparent militarization of the policing of public disorder and scandals about abuse of powers have begun to challenge it.

What is often lost sight of is that the ideal British police model was not a reflection of some natural, built-in harmony or order in British society and culture, a sort of collective stiff upper lip, as some celebratory accounts in the heyday of the myth may have implied, such as the adulatory histories by police buffs like Charles Reith (e.g., Reith, 1938, 1943, 1956). One problem with this story that recent historical critiques have emphasized is that British policing in colonial situations—including John Bull's Other Island—has always been militaristic, and often brutal and oppressive in suppressing protest (Brogden, 1987; Palmer, 1988). The benign model was exclusively for domestic consumption and not for export.

In mainland Britain itself, the development of a restrained and dignified style of policing was not an automatic reflex of social homogeneity or tranquillity. On the contrary, Peel and the other pioneers of the British police tradition formulated their approach precisely in the light of the tense and conflict-ridden domestic political context, in which the very idea of police was strongly contested (Miller, 1977). They encouraged a low-profile, legalistic, minimal force strategy *because of*, not despite, the bitter political protests and acute social divisions of early nineteenth-century Britain. This policing policy of compromise and co-optation between classes was a part of a wider pattern in British statecraft. As Moore has summed it up: "Governing in the context of rapidly growing industrial capitalism, the landed upper classes . . . avoided serious defeat by well-timed concessions. This policy was necessary in the absence of any strong apparatus of repression" (Moore, 1967, 39). What needs to be stressed in the policing context is that "the absence of a strong apparatus of repression" was itself a tactical choice, which rejected the advice of those (like the Duke of Wellington) who advocated it.

The strength of opposition to the very creation of the modern police as a tool of political oppression has been stressed in most historical accounts. It was symbolized four years after the birth of the Metropolitan Police by the dramatic Coldbath Fields episode. On May 13, 1833, during a meeting of the National Political Union, fighting broke out between protesters and police. A constable, P. C. Culley, was fatally stabbed. The inquest jury returned a verdict of "justifiable homicide." Although this was quashed on appeal by the Court of King's Bench, it symbolized the deep and widespread popular suspicion that faced the new police. Conservative histories have seen this as the high point of antipolice protest. For example, the authorized history published on the Met's 150th birthday claimed: "The police, though they did not then know it, had won their final and conclusive victory over the Ultras. More importantly, they had won an even greater victory in the long-term—the seal of public approval" (Ascoli, 1979, 105). In fact, as more critical historians had already demonstrated, antipolice protest and riot continued into the latter part of the nineteenth century as new police forces spread to the industrial towns of the north (Storch, 1975).

This widespread opposition was defused in part by a set of deliberate strategies adopted by Peel and his associates (Reiner, 1992b, chap. 2). They encouraged the development of a highly disciplined force, insulated from direct political control, strictly accountable to the rule of law, operating primarily by preventive uniform patrol, and performing a variety of services to people in need—not least in managing the problems of criminal victimization. One of the key ingredients in this was the cultivation of a nonmilitaristic image. In the phrase much used by official discourse, the police were merely "citizens in uniform," paid to do tasks that other people could and should carry out as civic duties. An essential ingredient of this was the restriction of the arms and coercive powers and equipment of the police, especially in the policing of collective disorder and protest that had a political dimension.

The most famous encapsulation of the traditional British police crowd control strategy was coined by Sir Robert Mark, Metropolitan Police Commissioner in the early 1970s: "The real art of policing a free society or a democracy is to win by appearing to lose." Public sympathy was a more powerful weapon than water cannon, tear gas, or plastic bullets. He illustrated this by the probably apocryphal story that the Met had trained an especially attractive horse—the "Brigitte Bardot" of police horses—to collapse and feign death on command from its rider.

Although the British police have never acted with kid gloves, there has been the deliberate cultivation of a low-key, minimal force image. The strategy encouraged by the Home Office after the 1856 County and Borough Police Act spread modern forces around the country was prevention of crime and disorder by "a police force essentially civil, unarmed and acting without any assistance from a military force" (Steedman, 1984, 33). Police officers were unarmed apart from truncheons on routine patrol, and other weapons (pistols, cutlasses) were resticted to especially selected and trained officers, who were issued with them only on especially dangerous assignments. During the course of the nineteenth century, the use of the army in controlling disorder was gradually supplanted by the nonlethally armed police, although the army remained (and remains) available as a last resort. However, the army has not been used to deal with protest or disorder on the mainland since the 1919 Liverpool police strike.

Minimum force is a relative term. Probably all forces would claim to use the minimal force possible in their circumstances. Until recently, however, there can be little doubt that the British police had developed an image of relying on less coercive force in containing protest and disorder than the police in most other countries. Apart from anything else, they simply lacked the riot control hardware and equipment common elsewhere. This does not mean that they used no or even little force, and there are many occasions when the policing of protest produced plausible complaints of excessive police violence and violations of civil liberties. This is especially true during periods of intensified industrial conflict or political protest: the clashes between police and the organized unemployed of "Outcast London" in the 1880s (Bailey, 1981); the rise of the suffragette movement before World War I; the bitter industrial disputes around the turn of the century and World War I, and in the mid-1920s; conflicts between police and the unemployed movement, and with antifascist demonstrators in the 1930s (Morgan, 1987; Weinberger, 1991).

In the unprecedented economic and political crisis of the 1930s, the policing of protest and public order did become an issue in a way it had not been since the mid-nineteenth century. Violence surrounding fascist meetings was the stimulus for the 1936 Public Order Act. Concern about violence used to suppress marches of the National Unemployed Workers' Movement (NUWM) led to the 1934 foundation of the National Council for Civil Liberties.

Even during times of crisis, however, the Home Office generally attempted to encourage the appearance of low-key policing. During the 1887 protests in Trafalgar Square it tried to ensure that police tactics stayed within the bounds of legality (Bailey, 1981). Despite much evidence of bias and brutality by police against the NUWM and antifascists during the 1930s, on the whole "the police do seem to have reacted less in political terms than in response to the challenge to public order and to their own position as the custodians of law and order" (Stevenson and Cook, 1977, 243). In the crucial area of industrial disputes, there was a long-term trend to declining levels of violence between police and pickets after the 1890s that was sustained up to the late 1970s. Although, during the bitter South Wales coal strike, the home secretary, Winston Churchill, was continuously involved in the policing of the dispute, despite the fiction of locally controlled policing, and organized the deployment of troops for the contingency of serious disorder, the Home Office's main concern remained long-run stability rather than short-term suppression (Morgan, 1987). In the post–World War II period, industrial conflict changed from a quasi war to something resembling a sporting contest, especially in the 1950s (Geary, 1985). It became rare for any picket-line violence to go beyond ritualized pushing and shoving.

What made this transformation possible was not just the farsighted statesmanship of the police elite. The increasing aversion to violent tactics came earlier and more completely from the citizenry and organized labor than from the police. During the interwar years in particular, the authorities remained ready to see protorevolutionary potential in many industrial conflicts and political protests organized by leaders with impeccable commitment to reformism and constitutionality (Jeffery and Hennessy, 1983, 6–9). They responded at elite level with contingency plans for emergency powers, and at street level the use of rough tactics, including baton charges against primarily peaceful protesters, remained all too common. But the realization was growing in the government and the police elite that overharsh policing could destabilize the security of the state by stiffening the resolve of protesters and by forfeiting public support for the establishment. Despite frequent atavistic reversions to repression in the 1920s and 1930s, the trend was toward a more pacific mode of policing protest and conflict.

Ultimately the declining level of violence by both protesters and police is a reflection of broader processes of increasing social integration, civility, and "institutionalisation of class conflict" (Marshall, 1950; Dahrendorf, 1959; Giddens, 1973, 56, 201–2). Violent protest—"collective bargaining by riot"—gave way to more formalized modes of collective bargaining. Strikes became one weapon in negotiations, not all-out class war. Demonstrations and industrial conflict came to be seen as accepted processes within the confines of particular rules, not inherently subversive threats to the social order. The working class, the main structurally rooted source of opposition to the police in the nineteenth century, gradually, unevenly, and incompletely came to be incorporated into the institutions of British society, most obviously in the post–World War II period. This process of incorporation always had very clear limits. It enabled the bulk of the population to share in the fruits of economic growth, at any rate until the late 1970s. But class inequality remained almost unaltered in relative terms (Westergaard and Resler, 1975; Goldthorpe, Llewellyn, and Payne, 1980; Miliband, 1982). Nevertheless, the gulf between the "two nations" that yawned so wide in the mid-nineteenth century as the police came into being had become blurred and attenuated by the mid-1950s.

The Militarization of Minimal Force

During the late 1970s and the 1980s, the British police apparently underwent a transformation in their style of dealing with public order. This has often been referred to, by critics and supporters, as a process of "militarization," though there is disagreement about the connotations of this term, as well as the source and significance of the changes (Bowden, 1978; Bunyan and Kettle, 1980; Ackroyd, Rosenhead, and Shallice, 1980; Reiner, 1980; Manwaring-White, 1983; Gregory, 1985; Brewer et al., 1988; Northam, 1988; McCabe and Wallington, 1988; Waddington, 1987, 1991, 1993a, 1994b; Jefferson, 1987, 1990, 1993; Waddington, Jones, and Critcher, 1989; Vogler, 1991; Fielding, 1991; D. Waddington, 1993). The essence of the shift is the availability and occasional use of riot control hardware and protective uniforms and equipment, together with changes in training, organization, intelligence, and routines of mobilization aimed at the rapid deployment of squads intended to maintain or restore order with force if necessary. Although the case for an overt specialist riot control force has been rejected, it has often been argued that the current arrangements amount to de facto "third forces" within the guise of traditional British policing (Morris, 1985). I have summed up the changes as the replacement of the image of the British police represented by Dixon (the eponymous hero of a seminal BBC TV police series running from 1956 to 1974) by Darth Vader (Reiner, 1992a, 89). This has certainly been a major factor in the gradual loss of legitimacy and public support and affection which the police have suffered over the last thirty years (Reiner, 1992a, 1992b). To many it seems that the celebrated "winning by appearing to lose" strategy has been replaced by a determination to win each battle, leading to a loss of the war for public sympathy.

The police themselves would argue plausibly that each ratchet upward in the militarization process has been preceded by an earlier escalation in the violence of protest and disorder, necessitating the toughening of police responses. As one distinguished chief officer put it:

> I would like to take issue with some of the things you have written on this. In some of . . . your writing you develop a sort of scenario where the police have

been tooling up. . . . I just can't see it that way. I describe it like this. You can identify various milestones along the way. Probably the first significant milestone was 1976, the time of the first Notting Hill riot, following the Carnival. We saw the terrifying spectacle of policemen having to pick up dustbin lids to defend themselves against really quite a furious barrage of bottles and stones. Really as a reaction to that, the police thought, well, we'd better have shields. And I can remember the training which was given at the time, which was very, very definite in indoctrinating constables in the notion these were for defence only, they were not to be regarded as offensive tools but just to protect them. . . . And then there was the first time they were actually deployed, in 1977 in Lewisham (a clash between National Front and Anti-Nazi League protestors), in I think a good cause. Then we go to 1980 and again we have this in Bristol, the unedifying spectacle of constables virtually leaving the centre of the place undefended. Much to the discontent of traders and so on. And there was a lot of agonised thinking. This great preoccupation to retain the traditional image, the introduction of reinforced ordinary policemen's helmets, and a little more beefing-up in training. And then, of course, 1981 was the trauma of petrol bombs. As a defensive reaction to that, the introduction of flame-proof overalls and all the rest of it . . . the impression has been given by you that the police had a conscious policy of tooling up. Whereas in fact it has always been a reluctant, incremental reaction to a developing situation. (Interview cited in Reiner, 1991, 171)

The development of the police reaction to disorder has been largely reactive. During a decade and a half of escalating frequency of protest, starting with antinuclear demonstrations in the 1950s and culminating in the anti-Vietnam War and student protests of the late 1960s and early 1970s, the police continued to adhere to a low-key response, despite increasing internal anxiety. The generally restrained policing of the 1968 Grosvenor Square protests outside the U.S. Embassy in particular was celebrated by many as the finest hour of a pacific style of controlling protests, which one leading police historian analyzed as *The Conquest of Violence* (Critchley, 1970). This was, however, already fraying at the edges. Rank-and-file police were expressing increasing concern and resentment at being required to act in a relatively passive and restrained way in the face of what they saw as escalating provocation, lawbreaking, and violence by demonstrators.

The turning point was the establishment panic engendered by the 1972 miners' strike, notably the apparent defeat suffered by police at the hands of flying pickets who succeeded in forcing the closure of Saltley coke depot despite police attempts to keep it open. In a sense, official anxiety about this was warranted: the industrial disputes of the 1972–74 period did ultimately bring about the fall of the Heath government. These years precipitated the beginnings of government and police plans to bolster their capacity to prevent such success for trade-union picketing or other mass protest activity against government policy in the future. The strategy initiated secretly in the early 1970s for enhancing the training and coordination of the police in dealing with disorder bore fruit ultimately in the defeat of the 1984–85 miners' strike, largely through a nationally coordinated policing operation on an unprecedented scale (McCabe and Wallington, 1988). Each stage of the process may well have been justified situationally in the way indicated by the previously quoted police chief. But there is no doubt that the end result was a transformation in the image of the British policing style that caused considerable public controversy and concern.

The change in public image may have exaggerated the change in underlying policy. Not only did commitment to minimal force remain in principle, although the level of force felt to be needed to cope with greater disorder was of course higher, but the basic British policing style of underenforcement of the law, using discretion to preserve tranquillity rather than the strict letter of the law, has remained intact even in the highly charged field of policing political protest. This is shown by P. A. J. Waddington's seminal empirical study of the policing of protest in London since the 1986 Public Order Act (bitterly attacked as a draconian assault on civil liberties by many critics), *Liberty and Order*—one of the most significant books on policing in the last decade and the last word on public order policing for the time being. On the whole, police use persuasion and some Machiavellian manipulation to gain protesters' compliance with their way of doing things. Usually they manage the balance between words and force well enough to avert outbreaks of violence. When they fail it is mainly because of errors of judgment rather than the underlying paramilitary capacity, which is normally kept in the background as a last resort.

In a long-running debate with Waddington, sustained over three books and two rounds of exchanges in the *British Journal of Criminology* (Jefferson, 1987, 1990, 1993; Waddington, 1987, 1991, 1993a, 1994b), Tony Jefferson has argued that this account fails to deal with the profane reality of conflict on the ground. He argues for a "bottom-up" view, in which paramilitary capacity is provocative and intimidating to protesters, frequently producing self-fulfilling prophecies of violence, and inherently likely to spin out of control in the tense heat of actual confrontations. Perhaps his most telling point is that what Waddington regards as a vindication of paramilitarism—that on many occasions he observed that successful tactics prevented large-scale disorder from erupting—Jefferson turns around from his "bottom-up" perspective: what has happened from the point of view of making the protesters' case is that their demonstration has been ineffective. It has been orderly, restrained, peaceful—but made correspondingly little impact.

This suggests that at bottom the disagreement is not in the analysis but in political position. Waddington would concede that paramilitary tactics will not work according to blueprint every time. Humans err, and wheels can come off. Whilst Jefferson contends that in practice militaristic tactics can often be counterproductive and escalate violence, his main point seems to be that when they succeed in their own terms—that is, order is maintained—this is at the expense of the protesters being able effectively to make their case. Ultimately, this seems to point to some of the thorniest issues of democratic theory. How is a just balance between liberty and order to be arrived at? Waddington implicitly adopts the priority of peace and tranquillity enshrined in traditional British police rhetoric—albeit he, and the police, would wish to allow adequate liberty for orderly protest. From Jefferson's "bottom-up" perspective, this appears to be saying that protest is permitted so long as it is not effective. It seems to me that this issue is an essentially contested one. There cannot be an overarching Olympian position from which the positions of both sides in a conflict can be really satisfied, though acceptable pragmatic compromises may be accepted as second-best solutions, but the best practicable, for both sides.

Public Order Policing 1986–Present: A Postmodern Turn

This essay has tried to chart how between 1829 and the mid-1980s British policing of protest and public order transcribed a historical U. Beginning with a position of militaristic policing of deep political conflicts, police tactics and the institutionalization of class conflict succeeded in achieving relative orderliness and domestic peace by the mid-twentieth century. In the early 1970s, however, this trajectory was reversed. Conflict intensified and police public order tactics became more militarized again. Justified or not, effective or counterproductive, this paramilitary turn was certainly controversial and contributed to a more widespread politicization of policing (Reiner, 1992b). This in turn was a reflection of a deeper politicization of social and industrial conflict. It reached its high point in the mid-1980s strikes in the mining and printing industries, and the urban riots of the early 1980s.

Since then a paradoxical development has occurred. There has been no diminution in serious public order incidents. A litany of the most serious would include the protests over the poll tax in the late 1980s, worsening conflicts over the policing of leisure activities such as hippie convoys, pop festi-

vals, raves, acid house parties, and "joyriding," which have on occasion resulted in very serious violent disorders. Most recently, clashes between police and protesters against live animal exports have often been bitter and provoked many complaints of heavy-handed police tactics. These are remarkable
for involving respectable middle-class people with backgrounds of complete
support for the police.

The potential is there in terms of both the seriousness of clashes and the
social credibility of many contemporary protesters, for the policing of public
order to become a major political issue. Certainly there has been no diminution in police maintenance of paramilitary capability, although arguably they
have become much more expert in exercising it with appropriate finesse.
Nonetheless, there has been sufficient concern about specific incidents of
strong policing of protest to suspect that the explanation of why this has not
continued to be a major issue lies deeper.

Social and cultural changes in the last two decades or so have arguably
transformed the political meaning and significance of both policing and protest. These are often summed up as the advent of "postmodernity" and their
impact on policing has been and will be profound (Reiner, 1992a, 1994). In
brief, two intertwined processes have made both policing and protest more
fragmented, piecemeal, and diffused in their political significance. As implied
by the earlier arguments about their historical legitimation, the police stood
as the symbolic acme of modernization: the historical movement toward
more homogeneous, integrated mass societies. As modern industrial society
became increasingly interdependent and disciplined ("organically solidary,"
in Durkheim's language), it became increasingly "allergic" to disorder. Protest
represented not specific demands but a potential threat to the overall social
order. Policing played its domestic missionary role, disciplining the masses
and representing a dominant morality.

Contemporary "postmodern" societies have experienced simultaneous
processes of greater cultural heterogeneity and economic fragmentation and
global diffusion. This renders it far less likely that particular protests or disorders will be seen as other than single issues, local troubles, however serious they may be in themselves. Conversely, the police are seen not as sacred
totems of a disappearing national consensus, but as more or less effective
deliverers of practical, specific services, measured by the same calculus as
any other businesslike enterprises. Paramilitary capacity may be regarded as
abused on specific occasions without undermining the legitimacy of policing
as such, in much the same way as objects of protest have become a series of
single issues, not emblems of whole ways of life.

Chapter 2

Policing Protest in the United States: 1960–1995

Clark McPhail, David Schweingruber, and John McCarthy

Students of collective action have given great attention to the sources, processes, and consequences of changing repertoires of collective action across space and time. One important focus of this scholarship has been the integral role of interaction between protesters and the police (e.g., Kritzer, 1977; McAdam, 1983; Tilly, 1978, 1995). The actions of each modify the environments of the other, creating intermittent opportunities and obstacles that result in ongoing reciprocal adjustments of each party's purposive efforts. As the agents of the state devise ways of blunting, blocking, or finessing the actions of the protesters, the latter devise variations and innovations in their collective actions to circumvent the control efforts of the former. Della Porta (1995) has advised that we cannot understand protest repertoires and their evolution without understanding the interaction between protesters and the police. Only recently, however, has focused attention been given to the actions of the police.

Our interest in this topic began during an investigation of selection and description bias in media accounts of demonstrations in Washington, D.C. (McCarthy, McPhail, and Smith, 1996). During this research, which used police permit records, we became familiar with the highly elaborate permitting system used by the three major Washington, D.C., police agencies (the National Park Service police, the U.S. Capitol Police, and the Metropolitan Police of the District of Columbia). This permitting system is one aspect of a public order management system (POMS), a term we use to describe the organizations charged with managing public disorder problems, their policies and programs, their individual and collective policing actions, and their enabling technologies. The POMS that was developed in Washington, D.C., has since been replicated, with some modifications, in many state capitals, large cities, and university campuses across the United States. Significant components of this system recently have been adopted in South Africa and in Belarus and facsimiles are present within the protest policing systems of England, Germany, France, Switzerland, and Spain.

This essay presents an investigation of the development of the U.S. POMS between 1960 and 1995. First, we contrast U.S. policing practices in the 1960s, which were marked by "escalated force," to those in the 1980s and 1990s, which have been characterized by "negotiated management." Second, we offer a historical account of the development of the negotiated management style during the 1960s and 1970s, including the contributions of several federal agencies in diffusing elements of the current U.S. POMS. Finally, we suggest the theoretical implications of our empirical findings for investigating other public order management systems.

Two Styles of Protest Policing

This section describes the phenomenon to be explained in this essay the striking differences between U.S. protest policing practices in the 1960s and those in the 1980s and 1990s. Although we have observed the policing of many U.S. demonstrations in each of the decades from the 1960s to the 1990s, we do not claim that those observations alone are representative. We have constructed a broader picture from an examination of social science scholarship on demonstrations and an extensive review of police literature that reports perspectives, policies, training programs, and problem-solving procedures developed by municipal, state, and federal policing agencies.[1] We do not know the extent to which what is reported in this literature describes what was actually done or how widely or consistently the policies and procedures described were practiced. However, we do believe there are some very general practices that characterize the policing of protest in the 1960s and that these practices contrast sharply with those used to police protest in the 1980s and 1990s. The policies and practices of the 1960s are characterized by *escalated force*, while those of the 1980s and 1990s are characterized by *negotiated management*.

Well-known demonstrations in which police used the escalated force approach include those in the Birmingham civil rights campaign (May 1963), the 1968 Chicago Democratic Convention, and the confrontation between student protesters and National Guard soldiers at Kent State University (May 1970).[2] During each of these demonstrations, police or soldiers used force in an attempt to disperse demonstrators, even demonstrators who were peacefully attempting to exercise their First Amendment rights—as the vast majority of them were.

Demonstrations in which police used negotiated management tactics are generally not as memorable as those previously mentioned because they are relatively uneventful. Under the negotiated management system, police negotiate with demonstrators before the demonstration so that demonstrators can exercise their First Amendment rights with minimal conflict with police. These demonstrations include thousands each year in Washington, D.C., such as the annual March for Life, the 1993 Lesbian, Gay, and Bisexual March, and the 1995 Million Man March. Even in demonstrations in which protesters break the law as a form of civil disobedience, such as the 1983 anti-MX missile demonstrations in Washington, nationwide antiapartheid demonstrations in 1985, and abortion clinic blockades, police following the negotiated management style use minimal force and may even make prearrest arrangements with demonstrators.[3]

Five Dimensions of Protest Policing

We have identified five key characteristics of policing practices. We refer to these as dimensions of protest policing since each is a continuum along which can be placed the policing practices of any particular policy agency regarding any particular demonstration. These dimensions are (1) the extent of police concerns with the *First Amendment rights* of protesters, and police obligations to respect and protect those rights; (2) the extent of police *tolerance for community disruption*; (3) the nature of *communication* between police and demonstrators; (4) the *extent and manner of arrests* as a method of managing demonstrators; and (5) the *extent and manner of using force* in lieu of or in conjunction with arrests in order to control demonstrators. For each of the five dimensions, we will describe police practices under both styles of protest policing.

1. First Amendment Rights   In the escalated force style of policing, First Amendment rights were either ignored or disregarded as mere "cover" for demonstrators. The right to protest was denied and permits were not issued.

Under the negotiated management style of policing, the protection of First Amendment rights is a primary goal of the police, equal in importance to protecting property or lives (Burden, 1992; Sardino, 1985). Even the most provocative speakers are permitted and protected as the courts have ruled that the threat of counterdemonstrator violence is not a legal reason for withholding a permit (*King Movement Coalition v. Chicago*, 1976).

2. Tolerance for Community Disruption   Under the escalated force style of policing, only familiar and "comfortable" forms of political protest were tolerated, those police described as "peaceful rallies" and "polite picketing." They showed no willingness to tolerate the disruption caused by civil rights (and subsequently antiwar) demonstrations, which involved unfamiliar forms of protest, disruptive tactics, violation of social norms, and often illegal (although usually peaceful) activities. Even disruption of normal traffic patterns was often seen as unacceptable and civil disobedience was equated with anarchy (Whitaker, 1964, 1966; LeGrande, 1967).

Under the negotiated management style, an "acceptable level of disruption" is seen by police as an inevitable by-product of demonstrator efforts to produce social change. Police do not try to prevent demonstrations, but attempt to limit the amount of disruption they cause. They recognize that large demonstrations almost invariably involve disruptions of traffic patterns and other normal routines in the community. Police attempt to steer demonstrations to times and places where disruption will be minimized, a restriction allowed by public forum law. Even civil disobedience, by definition illegal, is not usually problematic for police; they often cooperate with protesters when their civil disobedience is intentionally symbolic. The new police goals of protecting First Amendment rights while keeping disruption to acceptable levels required changes in protest policing tactics, which we take up in our examination of the final three dimensions.

3. Communication   Communication between police and demonstrators was minimal under the escalated force style of policing. The principal exception was undercover police infiltration of demonstrator groups to secure information with which to thwart the demonstration efforts or to act as agents provocateurs in order to entrap demonstration members (Marx, 1974). Police did not confer, let alone negotiate, with demonstration organizers before or during the demonstration. This lack of communication often caused misunderstandings, which inconvenienced both demonstrators and police, and which could result in the use of force as police attempted to enforce their interpretation of demonstration requirements (Stark, 1972). Police did not cede any control of the demonstration to the demonstrators themselves.

Police using the negotiated management style believe that communication with demonstrators is necessary if the former are to successfully protect the First Amendment rights of the latter and keep disruption to an acceptable level (Kleinknecht and Mizell, 1982; Sandora and Petersen, 1980). Extensive interaction between demonstrators and police is part of the permit application, negotiation, granting, and protection process. Applicants are informed of time, place, and manner restrictions and any conflicts over these restrictions are negotiated. Even civil disobedience arrests may be planned by police and demonstrators (Brothers, 1985; Sandora and Petersen, 1980). Police also help organizers prepare for demonstrations by consulting with them regarding transportation, restroom facilities, and first aid. Finally, demonstrators are required to have trained marshals who understand demonstrator goals and police responsibilities as well as the negotiated plans and procedures, and who can therefore knowledgeably "police" other demonstrators. Thus, the increased communication facilitates internal control of demonstrations by demonstration leaders instead of external control by police.

4. Extent and Manner of Arrests   Under the escalated force style of policing, arrests quickly followed any violation of the law and sometimes occurred where no law had been broken. Arrests were forceful and were used strategically by police to target and remove "agitators." The main exception to the rule of immediate arrest was when police used physical punishment in lieu of arrests (Stark, 1972).

Under negotiated management policing (Chandler, 1986; Sardino, 1985), arrests are used only as a last resort and then are used selectively, only against those who violate the law. Participants in nonviolent civil disobedience are not arrested immediately, but are informed repeatedly that they are breaking the law (often by trespassing) and given every opportunity to desist (Brothers, 1985). Arrests deemed necessary are carried out in an orderly manner designed to avoid injuring the demonstrators and with proper documentation. In order to promote orderly arrests, efficient booking processes, and quick releases from jail, police attempt to negotiate arrests with demonstrators before the demonstration. Police provide prearrest forms and request estimates of how many arrestees there will be and whether they will actively or passively resist arrest.

5. Extent and Manner of Using Force   As its name indicates, the escalated force style of protest policing was characterized by the use of force as a standard way of dealing with demonstrations. Police confronted demonstrators with a dramatic show of force and followed with a progressively escalated use of force if demonstrators failed to abide by police instructions to limit or stop their activities (e.g., Applegate, 1969; Momboisse, 1967).[4] Police used riot control techniques such as tear gas, batons, fire hoses, electric cattle prods, riot formations, and dogs. Police frequently used force in lieu of arrests.

Under the negotiated management style of protest policing, only the minimum necessary force is used to carry out duties such as protecting persons or property and arresting lawbreakers (Chandler, 1986; International Association of Chiefs of Police, 1992). Police attempt to avoid the need to use force by cordoning off the demonstration area, especially if counterdemonstrators are present, and through prior negotiations with demonstrators (Burden, 1992; Gruber, 1990).

The Development of One Public Order Management System

The initial changes from the escalated force style of policing toward the negotiated management style were introduced during the wave of U.S. protests and riots in the 1960s and 1970s. During this period national and local agents of social control searched for solutions to these problems. Although there is no national police force in the United States, the federal government was instrumental in developing and disseminating new strategies to decentralized state and municipal police agencies. Several federal agencies, reacting to different aspects of the same problem, were involved in this process. First, three national commissions investigated aspects of the current cycle of protests and riots and issued findings and recommendations. Second, the Supreme Court and various federal district courts issued a series of opinions in legal cases arising from earlier municipal, state, and federal government efforts to restrict protest. Third, the National Park Service developed an elaborate permit system to accommodate protest in Washington, D.C. Fourth, the U.S. Army Military Police School created a national civil disorder training program for local police officials. After a brief review of the riots and demonstrations during the period, we describe each of the contributions made by the federal government.

Riots and Demonstrations

Beginning with the Bedford-Stuyvesant and Harlem riots in New York City in 1963 and then the Los Angeles (Watts) riot in 1964, the United States was confronted with urban riots more or less every summer through 1968. These riots varied in intensity and duration as well as geographical location (e.g., Chicago, Illinois, in 1965; Omaha, Nebraska, in 1966, and Newark, New Jersey, Detroit, Michigan, and Milwaukee, Wisconsin, in 1967). In April 1968, Martin Luther King was assassinated. Immediately in the wake of the assassination there were 125 urban riots, the largest simultaneous period of urban rioting in the nation's history. One of the most severe riots occurred in Washington,

D.C. Massive vandalism, looting, and arson occurred less than one mile from the White House (Gilbert, 1968).

These urban riots were preceded by several years of repeated protest campaigns in the civil rights movement, including the 1963 March on Washington. The last large and sustained civil rights demonstrations in Washington—the Poor People's Campaign in May and June of 1968—followed the Martin Luther King riots. During the mid-1960s, the Vietnam War gradually supplanted civil rights as the focal issue around which the majority of demonstrations were mobilized nationwide. Early demonstrations, such as a November 1967 demonstration (100,000 people) sponsored by Mobilization Against the War in Vietnam (hereafter, MOBE), were marked by confrontations with authorities and arrests. But during later demonstrations, relations between demonstrators and authorities were less contentious. These demonstrations include the January 1969 counterinaugural demonstrations, the November 1969 MOBE rally (500,000 people), the May 9, 1970, MOBE rally (100,000), and the April 1971 U.S. Capitol rally (500,000) sponsored by the People's Coalition for Peace and Justice (PCPJ). The peak of antiwar demonstrations across the nation was in May of 1970 when, following the shooting deaths of four Kent (Ohio) State University students by National Guardsmen during an antiwar demonstration, protests against that tragedy and U.S. foreign policy erupted on more than 1,250 campuses.

Commissions of Inquiry and Their Recommendations

Between 1967 and 1970, U.S. presidents appointed three national commissions to investigate riots and demonstrations. The National (Kerner) Commission on Civil Disorder was established in July 1967, in the wake of major riots in Newark, New Jersey, and Detroit, Michigan, and issued its report in March 1968. The National (Eisenhower) Commission on the Causes and Prevention of Violence was established in June 1968, following the post–King assassination riots, and issued an initial report in January 1969; a final report in November 1969 summarized several commission task force studies of protest (e.g., Graham and Gurr, 1969; Sahid, 1969; Skolnick, 1969b; Walker, 1968). The National (Scranton) Commission on Campus Unrest was established in May and reported in September 1970. As their titles indicate, these commissions focused on slightly different phenomena, which, nonetheless, share some common features bearing on the policing of demonstrations.

The Kerner Commission was primarily concerned with urban rioting and found that in half of the twenty-four riots investigated in detail, police actions were pivotal in the initiation of the riots. The commission recognized that few communities had adequate numbers of police officers to deal with "major crowd control problems," thus necessitating that those existing officers be better trained and equipped. The Kerner Commission recommended that training for civil disorder prevention and control include all levels of personnel and be ongoing from the initial training of recruits to the regular review, repetition, and practice required for junior and senior police officers to function collectively and in collaboration with state and federal control agencies. The Kerner Commission further recommended that public officials establish fair and effective mechanisms for "the redress of grievances against police" and that they review and eliminate "abrasive policing practices." Finally, it criticized the use of deadly force, which too frequently incites further violence, and recommended instead the principle of using only the "minimum force necessary to effectively control the situation" (Kerner, 1968, 330).[5]

The Eisenhower Commission had a much broader charge than the Kerner Commission but devoted a great deal of attention to questions of policing demonstrations in democracies. First, the commission recognized that "group protest is as American as cherry pie," but that protest violence is the rare exception, not the rule. Second, protest is protected by the First Amendment; thus, the president, the attorney general, and the federal court systems must take whatever actions are necessary to protect against threatened or actual interference with First Amendment guarantees. Third, the "excessive use of force is an unwise tactic for handling disorder . . . [and] often has the effect of magnifying turmoil not diminishing it" (Eisenhower, 1969). Fourth, the respect for protest, the willingness to negotiate its time, place, and manner, and the granting of permits for protest are the best means of avoiding the necessity of policing, not to mention the use of unnecessary levels of force. The commission recommended that the policing of protest at the 1968 Chicago Democratic Convention should be taken as an example of how officials should not proceed; rather, it recommended the exemplary policies and practices that resulted in comparatively orderly and relatively nonviolent protest in Washington's January 1969 counterinaugural demonstrations, in Chicago's October 1969 Weatherbureau Days of Rage,[6] and in Washington's November 1969 massive antiwar rally. Fifth, the Eisenhower Commission's recommendations were much more mixed for dealing with civil disobedience as a form of protest. Seven members criticized this form as the first step toward social and political disaster in a democracy, citing contemporary India as a case in point; six other members defended civil disobedience with a variety of justifications.

The Scranton Commission was the last of the three major inquiries to make its report, but its conclusions and recommendations complemented those already noted. In the cover letter to the president, chairperson William Scranton wrote: "Campus unrest is a fact of life. It is not peculiar to America. It is not new and it will go on" (Scranton, 1970). Scranton further noted that campuses are places of intellectual restlessness, which can lead to protest, much (if not most) of which is neither disruptive nor violent; and, although violent protest should be met with firm and just responses, the use of deadly force is rarely required.

The Development of Public Forum and Protest Law[7]

The use of escalated force to control and disperse demonstrations, the arrest of of protesters, and the denial of demonstration permits produced a series of legal challenges. Many of the affected citizens believed that these actions were infringements of their constitutional rights to assemble, speak, and seek redress of their grievances and they sought relief through the courts. The amount of litigation around this issue escalated along with the wave of protests, importantly as a result of an aggressive campaign waged by the American Civil Liberties Union (ACLU), much of it in Washington. The Supreme Court decisions resulting from these cases created a substantial body of First Amendment decisions that came to be known as "public forum law."[8] Although these were certainly not the first significant court decisions on First Amendment guarantees, the 1960s, 1970s, and 1980s were the most concentrated period of such legal decisions in U.S. history.[9]

The public forum doctrine relies on a series of distinctions between categories of physical setting: the "traditional public forum," the "limited" or "designated public forum," the "nonpublic forum," and private property (Post, 1987). Traditional public forums include commons, public streets, parks, sidewalks, and other spaces that, "by long tradition or by government fiat," have come to be used for expressive activity in every community (An, 1991). First Amendment activity in these areas can only be limited by reasonable time, place, and manner restrictions, which cannot be based on the content of protesters' messages. When imposed, time, place, and manner restrictions must be narrowly drawn and unavoidable in the service of "compelling state interests" (Smolla, 1992, 208). Content-based restrictions are forbidden in public forums because they target the communicative impact of speech activity, restricting expression because of its subject matter, speaker identity, or viewpoint. Content-neutral restrictions are acceptable only if they aim at the noncommunicative impact of speech and even if they incidentally limit speech. Such restrictions are justified only under the strictest scrutiny in the case of traditional public forums, but are more readily accepted in other categories of forums (Tribe, 1988, 789–90).

Limited public forums are those government properties previously closed to "expressive activity" but which, upon review of the evidence, were found not to threaten "compelling state interests." These were then reclassified as "limited public forums" and include places such as airports, university meeting spaces, and municipal theaters. Speech restrictions in these places must be justified by the same standards that are required in traditional public forums.

A third category, the nonpublic forum, "includes governmental property that is not a public forum 'by tradition or designation'—such as a post office or jail. Restriction on speech in nonpublic forums need only be reasonable and not an effort to suppress expression merely because public officials oppose the speaker's view" (An, 1991, 63–66).

In addition to this central body of public forum law, between 1960 and 1995 the federal courts handed down a large number of decisions bearing on the content, time, place, and manner of protest in the public forum. First and foremost among these were decisions bearing on the sanctity of protest content, including *Brandenburg v. Ohio* (1969) and *Watts v. United States* (1969), which protect even the right to advocate violence if there is no call for immediate violent action. Furthermore, *Chicago v. Mosely* (1972) was but the first of several decisions to reiterate that the "First Amendment means that government has no right to restrict expression because of its message, its ideas, its subject matter, or its content," regardless of how provocative and offensive those may be. These ranged from the protection of civil rights marchers from hostile onlookers (*King Movement Coalition v. Chicago*, 1976) to the protection of Nazis from counterdemonstrators (*Skokie v. National Socialist Party*, 1978) to the protection of the right to burn the U.S. flag (*United States v. Eichman*, 1990). Across this same time period, there were a number of very important court decisions limiting restrictions on the *time* (*Collins v. Chicago Park District*, 1972), the *place* (*Heffron v. International Society for Krishna Consciousness*, 1981; *Quaker Action Group v. Hickel*, 1969; *Quaker Action Group v. Morton*, 1975), and the *manner* of protest (*Blasecki v. Durham*, 1972; *Skokie v. National Socialist Party*, 1978).[10]

Tracing the extent and scope of court decisions affecting the rights of protesters between 1960 and 1995, it is obvious that the courts were important in shaping the dimensions of the shift between the two forms of protest policing, setting the stage for, if not mandating, negotiated management. But these evolving constitutional principles had to be implemented in practical situations, and that is where the evolving protest permit system assumed central importance in turning those lofty principles into practical bureaucratic guidelines for managing protest.

The Development of a Protest Permit System

Permits are essential components of a protest management system because they specify the time, place, and manner in which protest may take place under police protection of First Amendment guarantees. Permits typically, though not invariably, depend on protesters' prior notification of public officials of their intentions to demonstrate. This is ordinarily conveyed by means of a permit application form on which the applicant minimally is asked to (1) identify himself/herself and the group or organization seeking the permit, (2) the time and date proposed for the demonstration and the place (or places in the event of a march), (3) the manner or activities planned to constitute the demonstration, (4) the purpose of the demonstration, and (5) the number of people expected to participate. Officials may also ask applicants to provide more details about the schedule of activities, perhaps to list the speakers, as well as props or equipment required to carry out the demonstration, and in all likelihood the number (and perhaps training and experience) of marshals to coordinate and control the demonstration. Finally, officials may wish to know if the applicants expect or anticipate the possibility of counterdemonstrations and if so, the names of the organizations or individuals who might mount such opposition.

This information is important because it provides the basis on which preliminary discussions can take place between prospective protesters and the officials responsible for the jurisdictions in which the protest is proposed. This may provide the first opportunity for officials to discuss with applicants the full range of responsibilities that the police are sworn to uphold, including the protection of protesters' First Amendment rights as well as the persons and property of protest targets and bystanders. This creates a context for discussing the goals of both protesters and police and how each can make plans and preparations to realize their respective purposes within the framework of existing laws. Sometimes these discussions are few in number and brief in duration. In other instances, they may be repeated and extensive as protesters and police negotiate their differences.

At the beginning of the time period under consideration there was but a mere semblance of the permit system now in place. The Federal Code in December 1959 required a mere one page in the Federal Register to detail the legal code covering parades and public meetings in the National Park Service (NPS) jurisdiction. Those regulations and guidelines were to undergo considerable revision over the next five years but no doubt were employed in negotiating permission to hold the 1963 March on Washington (Gentile, 1983).

Shortly after the first large antiwar demonstration in April 1965, a memorandum was issued by the Department of the Interior (June 1965) stating some demonstration guidelines. These guaranteed the protection of demonstrators' First Amendment rights in National Park Service jurisdictions while reserving restrictions over time, place, and manner. The guidelines further emphasized NPS representatives' contact, negotiation, and cooperation with applicants for demonstration permits and guaranteed their protection by the National Park Police. Permits were issued on a first-come, first-served basis. And although there was explicit emphasis on cooperation with leaders of groups seeking to demonstrate, these individuals were urged to apply sufficiently in advance of the proposed time of the demonstration to permit negotiation of mutually acceptable ground rules. Even so, neither failure to apply for a permit nor the absence of a permit were grounds for prosecution. In the same (1965) guidelines, NPS representatives were urged to develop cooperative relationships with other nearby local, state, and federal officials.[11]

Although this primitive permit system was in place, the outcome of negotiations involving the civil rights and antiwar demonstrations was more a function of who was negotiating between police agencies and demonstration organizers than it was of the permit system itself.[12] In the 1960s, the representative for the government agency or agencies was appointed (or at least endorsed) by the White House and therefore bargained in terms of the political preferences of the incumbent administration. The dramatic differences in the negotiations for the permits for Martin Luther King's 1963 March on Washington, with the support of the Kennedy administration, stand in marked contrast to the negotiations for the 1967 March on the Pentagon, with opposition from the Johnson administration, or the negotiations for the majority of antiwar demonstrations, with opposition from the Nixon administration.

Two large demonstrations—the January 1969 counterinaugural protests and the May 9, 1970, antiwar rally—resulted in government reports that significantly influenced the future permit system. An Eisenhower Commission staff report (Sahid, 1969) titled *Rights in Concord* describes in some detail the police agencies of the Park Service and the Metropolitan District of

Columbia and the negotiations for the January 1969 demonstration permits, with one negotiator representing all government agencies.

In June 1970, the Department of Justice published *Demonstration and Dissent in the Nation's Capitol*, which claimed to describe the cooperation and negotiation procedures that led to the successful May 9, 1970, demonstration, and further claimed that the same procedures had been used in the November 1969 antiwar demonstration. These claims are arguable at best. Demonstration organizers believed the orderly outcome of the May 9 demonstration was a function of government delay, happenstance, and the organizers' own ineptitude. The MOBE had planned a sit-down in front of the White House—a symbolic house arrest—but its plans were designed at the last moment and were poorly scripted and implemented.[13] What is more, the government did not in fact follow the policies and procedures set forth in the 1970 document. Nonetheless, subsequent policing practices were more likely consistent with that document, as the massive and orderly April 1971 antiwar rally illustrates. Moreover, those policies and procedures served as benchmark and guidelines for demonstration management in Washington for the next decade and beyond. They placed emphasis on First Amendment guarantees and on the importance of contact and communication between demonstrators and government negotiators with the objective of cooperation and negotiation of mutually agreeable protections of the interests, rights, and responsibilities of all parties.

The next benchmark in the development of the current system was the 1982 document *Demonstrating in the District of Columbia*, created by the ACLU's Capitol Area Chapter. There is more than a ten-year gap between this document and the 1970 statement by the Department of Justice. The earlier document is replete with descriptions of how the system should work; the later one details how the system did work in 1982. In between those two dates, we have already noted, were at least nine court decisions protecting First Amendment guarantees. Between 1982 and 1991, there were many more, all of which are brought together in the American Civil Liberties Union publication *The Right to Protest* (Gora et al., 1991). While the guidelines for demonstrations on U.S. government properties at the beginning of the time period under consideration required but one page in the 1959 Federal Register, the current (1993) guidelines require seven pages.

Today, instead of negotiators handpicked or endorsed by the White House to represent status quo interests, the negotiator is a civil servant from the National Park Service, the Metropolitan Police Department, and/or the U.S. Capitol Police. And although it would be naive to think that the status quo interests of White House incumbents are never figured into the negotiations, we believe it is frequently the case today that the terms of the permit are more rigorously decided in terms of the corpus of public forum and First Amendment law that has accumulated since 1970.

The Development of New Policing Principles and Techniques: SEADOC

After the U.S. urban riots of the summer of 1967, the Department of Justice directed the United States Army Military Police School (hereafter, USAMPS) at Fort Gordon, Georgia, to develop a civil disturbance orientation course (CDOC, hereafter SEADOC) for civilian police officials in the tradition of its long-standing training of U.S. Army personnel for riot control duties. This weeklong course was introduced in February 1968 and was offered fifty-six times before it was abruptly terminated in April 1969. We will refer to this course as SEADOC I. In May 1970, SEADOC reopened and was taught regularly at Fort Gordon until 1975, when the Military Police School was moved to Fort McClelland, Alabama. The course was continued there at least through 1978. We will refer to this course as SEADOC II.

Both versions of SEADOC clearly played a major role in diffusing protest policing practices. In an earlier paper (McCarthy, McPhail, and Crist, 1995), we estimated that as many as ten thousand police administrators, police officers, and other public officials may have gone through the SEADOC courses. This is consistent with Cherry's (1975, 55) characterization of SEADOC as "the best and most complete course available in civil disturbance planning" and his estimate that "thousands of [civilian] police executives" attended and garnered a wealth of detailed advice and checklists enabling them to develop a program in their local communities.

The emphasis in the SEADOC I instruction (1968–69) was on planning by and coordination among municipal, county, state, and federal officials and agencies for civil disturbance control operations (USAMPS, 1972a, 1972b, 1972c, 1972d).[14] SEADOC I was organized around four general and related phases of civil disturbance control planning and operations: (1) prevention, (2) preparation, (3) control, and (4) after-action. The control phase in SEADOC I instruction placed emphasis primarily on "shows of force" and controlled escalation of force in dispersing gatherings, protecting properties, and apprehending law violators.[15] This emphasis must be considered in the context of the primary forms of civil disorder—urban riots—which preceded and gave rise to the initial SEADOC program. It should be no surprise that the focus of SEADOC I was almost exclusively on riot control.

SEADOC II was redesigned in its orientation and emphasis, reflecting the recommendations of both the Kerner Commission (1968) and the Eisenhower Commission (1969). Both commissions had emphasized that the escalated force strategy for "riot control" was perhaps better suited to quelling labor conflicts of the 1930s, the racial riots of the 1940s, and the urban riots of the mid-1960s than it was to controlling the wider variety of forms of civil disorder that marked the late 1960s and early 1970s: "Many of the confrontations occurring across the United States today cannot be simply classed as 'riots.' Such widely varying situations as mass demonstrations, nonviolent protests and acts of political terrorism have necessitated extensive reevaluation of the basic concepts for controlling civil disturbances" (USAMPS, 1972c, 1).

One of the concepts introduced in SEADOC II was "confrontation management." This reflected a sensitivity to the Kerner and Eisenhower (and the later Scranton) commission reports' claims that traditional policing actions risked provoking more disorder rather than its resolution. "Confrontation management is a strategy concept . . . which seeks to counter the attempts of dissident organizations" to radicalize their ranks by provoking police to overreact (USAMPS, 1972a, 1).[16]

The new course continued "to stress inter-agency planning and coordination, but places new emphasis on civil disorder management concepts and principles" (USAMPS, 1972b, 1). Like its predecessor, SEADOC II was designed to address contemporary types of civil disorder. By 1970, these were antiwar protests, which often incorporated civil disobedience tactics in a variety of innovative ways. Thus, it comes as no surprise that SEADOC II offered a reconceptualization of civil disorder and of the kind of policing required to deal with these "new" phenomena.

First, SEADOC II lectures emphasized that civil disorders could take a variety of forms, ranging from mass demonstrations through civil disobedience and other forms of idealistic protest to rioting and terrorism. Second, SEADOC II lectures emphasized variations in the extent of disruption to the social and political status quo likely to result from those various forms of civil disorder. Such an analysis, therefore, justified variations in the form of confrontation management employed by police. Instead of following the older rule of the escalation of force to quell disorder, the newer formulation emphasized "a high degree of flexibility and selectivity in the response to a civil disturbance situation" (USAMPS, 1972b, 3). The result is the strategic concept of "confrontation management" and the complementary "tactical shift in field operations in accordance with the rule of minimum necessary force" (ibid., 4). "The primary rule which governs the actions of federal forces in assisting state and local authorities to restore law and order is that you must at all times use only the minimum force required to accomplish your mission. This paramount principle permeates all civil disturbance operations."

In addition to the principles taught by SEADOC II faculty to civilian police officials, in December 1970 the U.S. Army issued to all federal military personnel (and all National Guard personnel) revised "Special Orders," which they were to carry on their person while on duty in any civil disturbance operation (USAMPS, 1972d, 1–2). Noteworthy here are three of the orders: (1) "Use only the minimum amount of force required to accomplish your mission and, if necessary, to defend yourself"; (2) "You are not authorized to use firearms to prevent offenses which are not likely to cause death or serious bodily harm, nor endanger public health or safety"; (3) "When firing is necessary, shoot to wound, not to kill."

Public Order Management Systems and Their Environments

The U.S. POMS was developed as police officials attempted to devise a set of practices for managing problems of public disorder within their political and legal environments. We suggest three sets of variables necessary for understanding the development of a POMS: (1) the POMS itself, that is, the organizations charged with managing public disorder problems, their policies and programs, their individual and collective policing actions, and their enabling technologies; (2) the public order environment, that is, the frequency, variety, and severity of public disorder that police organizations encounter; (3) the political and legal environment within which POMS are developed.

Components of Public Order Management Systems

Public order management systems consist of (1) civilian and/or military police organizations, (2) the public order policies of these organizations, (3) these organizations' programs for recruiting and training personnel (civilian or military) to enact these policies, (4) the actual practices of these policing personnel, and (5) the technology and equipment used while carrying out these practices.

Police organizations vary considerably in size, resources, the way they are organized, and the ways they are connected to other organizations. Some nation-states have nationalized and centralized police forces (e.g., France and Japan); in others, police agencies are decentralized and responsible to municipal civilian authorities (e.g., the United States). Within these organizations, designated units (e.g., the Special Operations Division, Metropolitan

Police of the District of Columbia) and divisions (e.g., permit procedures) may specialize in public order management.

Police organizations also vary in their links to one another within metropolitan or regional areas (e.g., through mutual assistance pacts), to county and state police and fire agencies (e.g., through centralized communication and dispatcher systems), to federal police agencies (e.g., fingerprint and record search services of the Federal Bureau of Investigation), and through memberships in national and global professional police organizations (e.g., the International Association of Chiefs of Police and Interpol). These connections are increasingly both more accessible, rapid, and extensive (e.g., through the Internet and the World Wide Web and a variety of other satellite and telecommunications systems, which supplement more traditional means of contact and interaction such as professional association meetings, periodicals, workshops, and seminars). Several other important distinctions among police organizations are related to the public order environment and the political and legal environment in which they operate. These variations are taken up in subsequent sections.

As indicated earlier, significant changes in public order policing policies and practices in the United States took place between 1960 and 1995. The five dimensions of protest policing discussed earlier are an attempt to conceptualize the possible variation in these policies and practices. An important question that we do not address here is how the policies a police organization adopts and trains its officers to carry out may differ from their actual implementation in the field.

Protest policing recruitment and training may be highly specialized or may involve all personnel in a police agency. Increasingly in the United States, prospective police officers must meet both educational and physical criteria for admission to basic police-training academies. Many, but not all, police academies offer some basic training dealing with large public gatherings and various forms of civil disorder. After graduation from the academy and two or three years of routine police work, some officers may be recruited to, or may apply for specialized training in, public order policing. Thereafter, they may be assigned to special operations units (e.g., Washington, D.C.) or may have general policing responsibilities from which they can be readily summoned and rapidly mobilized to participate in civil disorder policing operations. Some police agencies have periodic refresher training in civil disorder policing throughout the calendar year and concentrated briefings and refresher training in advance of special assignments (e.g., papal visits, cham-

pionship games, massive political demonstrations, or projected announce-
ment of court decisions in controversial legal proceedings).

Additionally, technologies of public order policing changed dramatically
between 1960 and 1995. These include sophisticated communication technologies, defensive technologies (helmets, Plexiglas face masks and body
shields, and protective clothing), and offensive technologies (batons, tear
gas, rubber bullets, and specialized firearms).

The Public Order Environment

Police organizations vary enormously in the frequency, variety, and severity of the public disorder they are called on to manage. This public order environment varies temporally and geographically. Major temporal variations
may be significant in the creation of POMS as well as in their decline or fad-
ing into disuse. In the U.S. case, the wave of protests and riots in the 1960s
and 1970s was critical in the development of the current POMS.

Geographic variation in the public order environment produces important
differences in police organization. Police agencies in large metropolitan
areas, particularly those with decision-making centers of international scope
(e.g., the United Nations in New York City) or of national and international
scope (e.g., legislative, judicial, and executive branches of the U.S. government in Washington), may develop special units and elaborate permit systems for managing public disorder. Other police agencies that face regular
protest activity include those in state capitals and university campuses.

We have been concerned here primarily with political demonstrations, but
there are also disturbances to public routines that stem from large and otherwise extraordinary religious gatherings (e.g., papal visits), sport gatherings
(e.g., celebrations following championship games), and even prosaic gatherings on beaches and in the streets of resort communities and other recreation
sites during collegiate spring holidays. Communities are likely to adopt and
adapt POMS that address their routine public order problems. For instance,
police in large metropolitan areas that host national and international sports
championship tournaments or games develop, adopt or adapt programs for
managing those events and subsequent celebrations that may become disorderly. Larger municipal police agencies (e.g., Washington, San Francisco) frequently develop their own manuals of procedures and tactics as part of their
continuing training of officers for public order policing. In smaller cities
where large protest demonstrations are rare, local police may consult with
other agencies and/or make use of mutual assistance pacts when faced with

such a demonstration. However, these police may have standard practices for dealing with more common types of public gatherings, such as patriotic parades and ceremonies.

Political and Legal Environment

Among the most important historical considerations for understanding the sources and processes of public order has been the autonomy of policing organizations and institutions from the political regime in which they function. There has been a steady decoupling of police from regime as a function of the post–World War II modernization of nation-states around the world (Bayley, 1985). In the United States, with the routinization of the permit system in Washington, the influence of incumbent presidential administrations in making demonstration management decisions has waned and the role has been taken over by police agencies. A related political consideration has been the relative mix of military and civilian policing of public order. In some nations, there is virtually no separation, or at best a minimal one, between military and paramilitary policing of public order. In the United States, there is a very sharp distinction enforced by the *posse comitatus* act, which prevents the military from policing civilian public order unless or until civilian authorities determine that they are no longer capable of maintaining order and formally request from the president of the United States the authorization of military assistance to their community. Civilian oversight and regulation of policing as well as military forces varies from nation to nation. These variations range from civilian review boards of police practices in the local community to civilian secretaries of defense in the national cabinet to whom military chiefs of staff are accountable. In the United States, three presidential commissions of inquiry, which included distinguished civilian and military police officials, were influential in the development of the current POMS.

It appears that some version of the basic right to public assembly is common to most democracies old and new, but the scope and details of these rights vary. In the United States, there is a constitutional guarantee—the First Amendment—to public assembly, speech, and petition for the redress of grievance; no equivalent guarantee exists in Great Britain. The details of public forum law are also unique to the United States. This right may or may not be counterbalanced by the legal obligation of prospective protesters to notify local authorities of their intention to demonstrate and the right of authorities to impose restrictions on the time, place, and manner of protest. In other nations, however, it may be illegal to protest publicly regarding some or all issues.

Summary

In this essay, we have used the concept of public order management systems (POMS) to refer to those organizations charged with policing public disorder, and to their policies, programs, practices, and technologies for doing so. We first contrasted U.S. policing practices in the 1960s, which were marked by "escalated force," to those in the 1980s and 1990s, which have been characterized by "negotiated management." We described both of these styles and presented five dimensions of protest policing, which can be used to conceptualize these and other protest policing styles. Second, we offered a detailed historical account of the development of the negotiated management style during the 1960s and 1970s. This account emphasized the wave of demonstrations and riots during this period, the development of legal, political, and other social institutions in response to this problem, and the contributions of several federal agencies in creating and diffusing elements of the current U.S. Public Order Management System. Finally, we suggested the theoretical implications of our empirical findings for investigation of other public order management systems. The diffusion and adoption of the new style of protest policing is far from uniform across the United States.[17] It has become the increasingly likely practice of police organizations in large cities, at state capitols, and on major university campuses where protest and other large public gatherings are frequent occurrences. The extent to which it has been adopted and implemented in those locales is an intriguing empirical question that remains to be investigated, and one we hope to pursue in the not too distant future.

Notes

1. Our review of the police literature included an examination of every issue of *The Police Chief* (1963–94) and the *FBI Law Enforcement Bulletin* (1964–94) during the entire period of our study for articles on the policing of crowds, demonstrations, and riots in the United States. We also were able to examine issues of *Law and Order* (1971–75, 1979–93), the *Police Journal* (1963–94), the *Police Yearbook* (1963–77, 1982–88), *Police Studies* (1978–93), and two unrelated journals called *Police* (1963–71 and 1987–92) for portions of the relevant time period. Articles from these and other periodicals were also obtained through searching indexes that cover these periodicals.

2. See Williams (1987), Branch (1988), and Morris (1993) for excellent detailed accounts of the Birmingham campaign; Walker (1968) for a comprehensive account of police-protester interaction at the 1968 Chicago Democratic Convention; and Michener (1971) and Adamek and Lewis (1973) for alternative accounts of the Kent State massacre.

3. See Brothers (1985), Ochs (1985), and Sardino (1985) for detailed accounts of police-protester interaction during the antiapartheid campaign on U.S. college campuses.

4. One of the possible consequences of these early training manuals and guidelines for policing demonstrations can be seen in the manner by which antiwar protests were handled at the 1968 Democratic National Convention in Chicago. These actions led a subsequent

commission of inquiry to coin the term "police riot" (Walker, 1968). Similar uses of police force in lieu of arrest and due process are described and analyzed in Stark's (1972) monograph *Police Riots*.

5. The Federal Bureau of Investigation states the same principle in its 1967 manual for the *Prevention and Control of Mobs and Riots*.

6. This campaign of demonstrations, observed and recorded by the first author, involved a number of planned, rehearsed, and effectively executed sequences of violence against property (and sometimes persons) by the Weatherbureau. Even though the police expected this, they nonetheless granted permits for the rallies and marches that preceded the violent actions and were remarkably restrained in their efforts to curtail the violence and arrest the perpetrators. By comparison with protest policing efforts the previous year during the Democratic National Convention, and the deliberately violent tactics of the Weatherbureau, police followed the principle of minimum necessary force in quelling the Days of Rage demonstrations in October 1969.

7. This section relies heavily on McCarthy, McPhail, and Smith (1994).

8. Snyder (1985) and Gora et al. (1991) each include different but useful summaries of the "public forum" doctrine.

9. Significant early court decisions on First Amendment guarantees include *Hague v. C.I.O.* (1939) and *Cox v. New Hampshire* (1941), both of which were landmark rulings on the public forum issues that were so frequently raised in the 1970s, 1980s, and 1990s.

10. Gora et al.'s (1991) excellent summary of First Amendment law provides details of further court decisions protecting the specific forms of protest by manner of assembly, parade, leafleting, picketing, signs, and posters.

11. Toward these goals, a weekend training seminar in "demonstration management" was offered in May 1965 for National Park Service administrators (Department of the Interior, 1965).

12. A very useful account of the planning, organization, mobilization, and permit negotiations for the 1963 March on Washington is presented in Gentile (1983). Local police agencies were not sympathetic, despite their own accounts to the contrary (see Covell, 1963). Absent the firm support of Attorney General Robert Kennedy for the demonstration, it is unlikely that negotiations would have gone as smoothly as they did.

13. Wells (1994, 445) notes that "The government contributed to the MOBE's failure. By granting the Ellipse, it moved the demonstration away from the front of the White House, where civil disobedience would have been easier. And by doing it at the last minute, it gave the MOBE scant time to devise a plan. And [principal MOBE organizer David] Dellinger called the government move 'a master stroke of public relations.'"

14. Our description of SEADOC is based on examination of the extensive course textbook used by students at Fort Gordon, Georgia, during the week of July 16–21, 1972. To date we have only been able to examine the text materials used in SEADOC II, but from discussions with USAMPS historians, we are confident that the structure of both courses was very similar, differing only in the orientation and emphasis discussed here.

15. We surmise this emphasis by our inspection of the Army Field Manual FM 90-15, which was in effect at the time of SEADOC I.

16. Provoked or not, police use of deadly force in quelling demonstrations appears to have had effects like those to which SEADOC II authorities referred. Adamek and Lewis (1973) surveyed Kent State University students shortly after the May 4, 1970, shooting by Ohio National Guardsmen. Kent students who witnessed the shootings had significantly more antigovernment attitudes than Kent students who were absent from campus the day those shootings occurred.

17. Elsewhere (McCarthy and McPhail, 1997), we examine the diffusion and adoption of innovations in a population of police organizations.

Chapter 3

The Policing of Protest in France: Toward a Model of Protest Policing

Olivier Fillieule and Fabien Jobard

In *Demonstration Democracy* (1970), Amitai Etzioni stated that the recourse to direct expression of opinion through protest was becoming an increasingly common practice in democratic countries. According to Etzioni, this was noticeable both in the rise in the number of demonstrations and in the spread of this practice to all levels of society. This analysis is in line with the French situation of the 1980s and the 1990s. In fact, the legitimacy of protest is now well recognized by French public opinion. Its use is widespread among all socioprofessional categories (Fillieule, 1997) and the legal framework has developed to the extent that the right to protest is now considered a constitutional right.[1] Furthermore, demonstrations rarely give way to the use of violence on the part of demonstrators or the forces of law and order. Studies conducted by Favre and Fillieule have in fact shown that only 5 percent of demonstrations become violent in the form of destruction of public/private property or attacks on other persons (Favre and Fillieule, 1994).[2]

These observations strongly suggest that demonstrating has become a usual and peaceful process in France, which therefore places it among the broad range of conventional political practices. Thus, the common image of the police battling with demonstrators has become rather misleading. Disorder is rare, even in the biggest and most problematic protest events. By and large, demonstrators cooperate with the police, assemble at a previously agreed-upon location, proceed along an agreed route, and disperse peacefully, regardless of the perceived results of their action.

Thus, the issue to address is how the police have extended such a high degree of control over protest action by cooperation with demonstrators rather than by repression. How is the policing of protests organized in France? On

POLICING OF PROTEST IN FRANCE 71

what principles and professional knowledge is it based? These are some of the questions that this essay will deal with.

The theoretical significance of these issues is not simply confined to sociological studies of the police. In its broader framework, studies of the maintenance of law and order should become one of the central elements of the analysis of social movements. Indeed, the development of social movements depends largely on the state's structures and its responses. In the majority of existing works, however, the extreme diversity of actors and agencies constituting the state is oversimplified by their being placed in general categories such as strong state and weak state. This would suggest a concerted action on the part of the state. In such an analysis, police forces and their actions are considered as pure instruments and are categorized under "police repression." The sole actor that the protesters confront is the government in power representing the state. This body, through the police, thus decides whether to increase repression or to give way to the demonstrators' demands. From a judicial point of view emanating from Max Weber, the police appear as an armed instrument of political power.

In this essay, we propose a model for ways in which protests are handled that presents street demonstrations as part of a triangular game in which the rules are prone to change during the course of the event. In effect, it can be argued that an understanding of the methods of protest management should include three major actors: the forces of law and order, the government, and the protesters themselves. The analysis constantly returns to the freedom of maneuver at the disposal of these actors in order to establish the rules of the game and then to act within them. This room for maneuver necessitates an examination of events as a result of a complex interactive and tactical process incorporating the social movement, police officers (senior officers and rank and file) on the ground, and political authorities. From this angle, our model differs slightly from that of della Porta, which emphasizes police knowledge and tactics. It is also different from the model proposed by McCarthy, McPhail, and Crist (1995), which, in addition to police tactics, analyzes the relationship between public order policy and the legal and political environment. In our view, the model is incomplete without giving equal importance to the role of the demonstrators themselves.

Taking this as a starting point, we explore three central questions: What are the established rules of the game (legal norms, structure of police organization and professional conduct, hierarchical relations between police authorities and political authorities)? How, in practice, do the different actors play the game (by a strict or relaxed application, depending on the individual circumstances and vested interests at the time? What impact does the development of the game have on any modifications of the rules? In other words, what determines modifications of the rules?[3]

Our work relies on three kinds of material: first, a series of formal interviews, conducted in Paris as well as throughout the country with the senior officers most frequently involved in the negotiating, planning, and command of order operations; second, observation of numerous protest events and participation in the planning process of demonstrations in Marseilles and Nantes; finally, a database of almost five thousand protest events that occurred between 1979 and 1989 in the cities of Marseilles, Nantes, and Paris. We have constructed this data from the national police archives (Fillieule, 1997). This database allows us to make a quantified corroboration of the police officers' assertions. By this multiplication of sources and methods, we hope that our conceptualization of protest policing will not be as impressionistic as ethnographic studies sometimes appear to be.

We begin by briefly pointing out what we consider to be the main organizational characteristics of the handling of protests in France: a highly centralized and unified framework, even if, in the purest French tradition, the case of Paris is quite unique. We then present the philosophy on which this maintenance of order is based. We will show the extent to which these effective rules of the game are based less on legal prescriptions than on actual informal practices. Third, we will see how these rules of the game are applied in different ways on the ground, depending on the orders given by the government and the police perception of the groups involved.

Forces of Law and Order in France: A Diverse but Highly Centralized Model

For historical reasons that cannot be elaborated on here, the forces responsible for the maintenance of public order in France are both varied and numerous. There are military forces (*gendarmes mobiles*) and the national police force (specialized divisions of these and more general sections).[4] However, behind this diversity is hidden a highly centralized and uniform organization in terms of leadership, policy implementation, and methods. This will be briefly illustrated in this section with reference to the organization of the specialized forces and the urban police in Paris as well as in the provinces.

The Specialized Forces

The specialized forces are first of all composed of the *gendarmes mobiles*, which come under the Ministry of Defense but are at the disposal of the

Ministry of the Interior, and second of the CRS (Compagnies Républicaines de Sécurité), drawn from the mainstream police forces.

The first characteristic feature of these forces is that they are composed of mobile units with a national jurisdiction. CRS and *gendarmes mobiles* squads rarely act in the area where they are actually based. Second, these specialized forces undertake specific training. They follow regular training sessions in the form of simulated operations. The professional code of practice on which the training of the two types of forces is based, judging by the manual used in these sessions, is virtually identical.

The essential training in the maintenance of order is concentrated on a small set of simple rules. Whatever situation they are applied to, these rules are based on the necessity of a strong collective discipline and absolute respect for orders given by the senior officers. In effect, the CRS and the *gendarmes mobiles* must always act as complete units under the authority of their own senior officers. It follows that the training of the rank and file is relatively neglected, with the emphasis remaining on that of the senior officers.

The civil authorities—that is, the prefect or the deputy prefect (*sous-préfet*), the mayor or one of his associates, and the police commissioner (*commissaire*)[5]—are responsible for the use of coercive measures when considered appropriate. On the ground, however, the execution of policy legally depends on the hierarchy of squads made available. Once the decision to use coercion is taken, with the orders given by the civil authorities, the heads of each squad can give orders and supervise the action of their men in the field.

This rational partition of labor, however, conceals a lack of clarity regarding the exact nature of the relationships between the orders given by the civil authorities from the command room or on the ground and the actual implementation of these orders by the chiefs of each squad. This lack of clarity can sometimes be magnified in important cases of maintaining order, given the wide range of forces that could intervene and the frequent interventions of political power in the technical decisions to be taken. In the light of these observations, it seems necessary not to reduce the interactions in demonstrations to a simple conflict between demonstrators and the police. Just as demonstrators can oppose each other, so the forces of order do not necessarily act in a unified way. There are no clearly defined structures governing the relationships on the ground—a state of affairs that could potentially result in disorder.

Urban Police in the Provinces and in Paris

For the majority of routine demonstrations, the urban police are the only force involved. In the provinces, they are characterized by two features: first, there is no specific training on the maintenance of order, either in the initial course or in subsequent ones; professional knowledge is only acquired by experience. Second, maintaining order is just one aspect among others of their general duties. In Paris, however, the young recruits are integrated into intervention squads (*compagnies d'intervention*), which receive training in maintenance of order but are not a constituent part of the specialized forces. They also assume numerous tasks related to anticrime initiatives.

Created in June 1959, the *compagnies d'intervention* benefited in the 1960s from a regular and very similar type of training program to that of the CRS and the gendarmes. Then, in 1978, their role was extended to include an anti-crime component. As a result, specific training for demonstrations diminished and finally disappeared. At the end of the 1970s, they were less and less frequently used as individual units. This development was reinforced in 1983 with the dispersal of these squads among the different police stations in Paris. There was thus a loss of technical expertise to the point of incompetence, with dangerous implications.

This brief description of the different forces dealing with protest policing shows well how important the unification of the national context is in France. Apart from distinguishing Paris from the rest of the country—which is really only due to a question of political requirements—we can say without doubt that protest policing is exerted in a unified manner all over the country. Every aspect converges toward this unification: from the procedures for recruiting within the different forces, to the nature and quality of the training offered to the specialized units, the lack of such training for protest policing within the urban police, and the doctrine on which the training and the organization of the command are based. We could add that all commissioners (*commissaires*) in charge of protest policing go through the school of Saint-Cyr-au-Mont-d'Or, where they receive an identical preparation for the maintenance of public order, and that information in Paris and out of Paris is collected by the same intelligence service (Renseignements Généraux). The result is that a specific "philosophy of protest handling" has been built up nationally in France, elements of which may be found within each police force and all over the country. We will now examine the essential characteristics of this "philosophy."

Fundamental Doctrine and Practice in Protest Policing in France

It would be misleading to base an explanation of the handling of protests solely on an analysis of the legal and material means at the disposal of political authorities. In France, the practice of protest policing is characterized pre-

cisely by the two following aspects: first, the continual search, through negotiation and compromise, for agreement even if such agreement is not necessarily based on the range of legal means; second, the underuse of available
coercive means. The "philosophy" of protest policing can be summed up in
the following three principles:

1. The first objective of policing is to prevent trouble so that the police
will not have to use force. Police intelligence is therefore essential in for-
mulating preventive measures.

2. When police intervention is necessary to reinforce order, such intervention must not exacerbate the situation.

3. Protest policing has as its primary objective the control of the situation
at all times, regardless of costs.

Predicting the events, constant negotiation with the other side, and control of
the situation, which is implemented by a wait-and-see approach in which a
strong coercive response is at one end of a range of possible reactions, are the
three basic rules of the doctrine of protest policing. We will now examine the
meaning of these three principles and the way in which they are implemented.

The Use of Intelligence and Planning

Before the event, intelligence and planning are an essential part of protest
handling. According to most senior officers interviewed, failed policing above
all occurs "when we are surprised. The worst thing that can happen is when
we are surprised."

The Law of 1935 circumscribes the right of protest with an obligation on
protesters to give the police three days' notice of a march. This prior notification must be sent to the town hall or to the police headquarters in Paris. Even
if the legal procedure is not strictly followed by the organizers of demonstrations (we will give more information on this point later), the police try to get
in touch with the organizers to find out their intentions and to discuss the
details of the march. At the same time, the intelligence service produces a
detailed report in which it provides its own information about the expected
number of demonstrators, the aims of the march, and the spirit of the protesters themselves. Based on these elements, the local police chief (or the
subdirector of public order in Paris) formulates a plan of action within the
framework of the prefect's orders. The organization of the operation depends
on two factors: the previous and/or the declared goals of the demonstrators,
and the will of the political authorities.

At this point, police headquarters determines the number of police officers required during the event. The prefect approves the requisitioning of
these men, from the local urban police (*compagnies d'intervention* in Paris)
and, in the case of large or risky marches, gendarmes and/or CRS. After the
national police headquarters has assigned all available forces, the local police
leadership forms a plan of action consisting in the disposition of forces, the
designation of senior officers (*commissaires*) who will lead these forces, and
the requisitioning of specific materials (water tanks, antibarricade trucks,
etc.). This plan is established during one or more preparative sessions. On
the day of the event, units gather one hour before the event is scheduled to
begin. In most cases, when the CRS or gendarmes are required, they are
briefed by a senior officer in command as to the general plan and the objectives set by the prefect at each point in the operation.

Negotiation and Compromise

The planning done before a demonstration is based in the main on contact
with protest groups. Most of the time the event takes place in a spirit of mutual recognition and respect, and cooperation is secured through negotiation
with the protest organizers, before as well as during the march. This negotiation process relies more on informal means than on legal norms.

By far the most illustrative example of this informal way of managing
protests is that of the notification requirement contained in the Law of 1935.
As already noted, this law requires notification to the police no less than three
days before the intended date of the action. A march for which notification is
not properly made and which refuses to disperse when asked by the police
would be treated as an unlawful assembly. In such cases, the police are legally
authorized to use force, and can arrest and prosecute the organizers as well
as the participants.

However, there is a gap between this legal framework and practice. It is extremely rare for organizers to comply with the law or even to know its prescriptions, except in Paris where the principle of preliminary notification is
generally respected. In other places, prior notification is the exception rather
than the rule, as illustrated by figure 3.1 for Marseilles. Only 8.5 percent of
the events recorded between 1987 and 1991 were notified to the police or the
town hall. If the police were to bring the law into operation, French demonstrations would for the most part be considered "unlawful assemblies" and
would be strictly forbidden. As one can see, this did not happen.

In the same way, it would be misleading to try to understand the way
French political authorities deal with demonstrations simply by observing

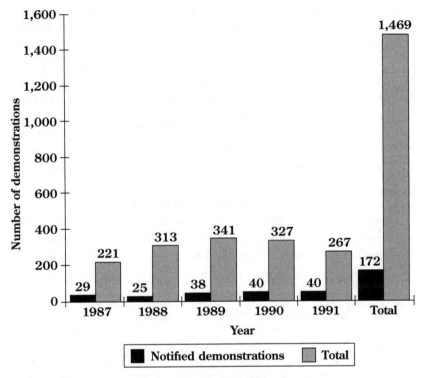

Fig. 3.1. Notified demonstrations in Marseilles, 1987–91

the changing legislative regime. The recent change in French law gives a
very clear example of this. Under pressure from the law-and-order lobby, the
legal framework was tightened during the course of the overall reform of the
penal code undertaken in 1994. This might logically lead one to conclude that
there has been a move toward greater repression in France. But that is not
the case at all: the political reasons that prompted the passing of this set of
laws are far removed from the reality of protest handling. This is confirmed
by the interviews we conducted in July 1995 with the officers in charge of the
Parisian police. First, and this is quite surprising, these police chiefs only had
limited knowledge of the new laws. Second, they all insisted on the theoretical aspect of these laws, which could only be applied in the case of a very serious crisis.

Protest policing cannot be adequately analyzed in terms of the legal norms.
As a rule, police do not use the whole set of legal means at hand to maintain
order and the basis of their actions is essentially informal negotiation.[6]

To give an illustration of that point, in Paris, where prior notification of demonstrations is much more frequent than in the provinces, we can see that directors of public order, rather than sticking to the strict provisions, seek to establish negotiations with the protesters. These negotiations must lead to a compromise so that unexpected risks are minimized. The police head-quarters considers this step to be a central element in the means at its disposal and the chief of police himself meets in his office with the people involved in organizing the demonstration. These organizers may have asked for the meeting or the police may have invited them.

According to the chief of police, negotiation with demonstrators must fulfill the following requirements:

1. Requirements of public order (for instance, the police may prefer a specific route and deny another) and political considerations (that is, the orders of the prefect) must never be presented to the demonstrators as flat requirements based on law; on the contrary, the goal of the negotiation is to make the demonstrators think that the restrictions are in their own interests, that it is simply friendly advice. As the chief of police told us:

> If there is some small problem, perhaps with the route, I try to make them aware of it before they arrive at the Prefecture. So they can think about changing their route. If, for example, they want to go down the Champs-Élysées, this is not possible.[7] But rather than say to them that it is not possible, I would explain to them that they have to park fifteen hundred coaches, which is an enormous number. A coach is twenty meters long. You need dozens of streets in which to park them. They haven't thought of that. So, I suggest to them Saint-Augustin, since they can park their coaches in the Boulevard Malesherbes, and so they agree and go away satisfied.

2. Organizers must always go away from the meeting with the feeling that negotiating helped them in organizing the march. That is why the chief of police presents his requirements in the form of helpful advice. For instance, in the case of inexperienced demonstrators, it is frequent for senior officers to give the organizers some instructions on how to organize marshals and how to direct them. In fact, the police have an important advantage: they usually hold a monopoly of expertise, which they use to a greater or lesser degree to advise and assist organizers who are unfamiliar with practices and procedures. In doing so, they guide organizers along a path acceptable to the political authorities.

3. Police always act so that the organizers feel that they hold the main responsibility for the demonstration. They ask about their marshaling and plans, pointing out (and even exaggerating) all the potential dangers found at

this kind of event. The goal here is to encourage the organizers to be as co-operative as possible and to ensure that they recognize the importance of the liaison officer who will be the link between the organizers and the police on the day of the event. But also, if the organizers fear dangerous or violent acts from their own participants or from other outside groups, this encourages a shared interest, between the police and the organizers with regard to those who might be considered troublemakers.

4. Finally, the purpose of negotiation is to establish a climate of mutual confidence, with the organizers being persuaded that the police will respect their undertakings. To fulfill this aim, the chief of police may reveal some part of the means at his disposal, in a spirit of openness, but also in order to exclude the possibility of ambiguous situations or surprises arising on the day the event takes place.

Clearly, these four informal principles on which negotiations are based are applied to a greater or lesser extent according to the nature of the groups in question. The degree of cooperation can vary greatly. For instance, when demonstrators show no readiness to cooperate, and even refuse to meet with the police, the chief of police may content himself with a simple telephone negotiation, with the route and conditions being sent by fax.

After the preliminary negotiations, it is worth stressing how much the search for compromise influences the forces of law and order as events are actually taking place. To further this spirit of compromise, a liaison officer is appointed for every protest, with the task of maintaining constant contact with the organizers. During very large protests, he is always a senior officer of the police force.[8] On the other hand, civilian police representatives are specifically charged with establishing contact between the organizers and the political authorities targeted by the demonstration. These representatives lead the negotiation, for example, for the receiving of a delegation at a public administration building and are in charge of the group while it is inside the building and as it leaves. These agents usually work in the different arrondissements (administrative districts of Paris), so they are perfectly familiar with the various heads (in each district) who can receive a delegation. Negotiation with demonstrators is thus facilitated.

This process of constant negotiation in the field very often produces a close cooperation between the police and the demonstrators' marshals, since they share common interests. As one police official explained:

> If there is a march of more than eight hundred meters, we must be able to isolate troublemakers from the crowd, and protect those that have a right to be there. This works very well with the CGT [General Confederation of Labor] and

other professional organizations. They have marshals in place who know that we will isolate those that shouldn't be there. They will put up barriers and if necessary will stop the demo, speed it up, or cut it short. Sometimes, they will come to us and tell us that they are going to lead the troublemakers up a certain street. And we can be waiting at the other end of the street to greet them! But for student demos, the marshals do not like to do that, because it is seen as collusion with the police. Some marshals at student protests even play a double game.

Once, I conducted a baton charge at the head of the CGT stewards. It was one of the 1987 demonstrations in memory of Malik Oussekine,[9] with many young people. The CGT was responsible for the marshaling. I was in charge of coordinating the forces in the field. When we arrived in Place de la Bastille, the organizers came to me and said: "OK, our deal is over, we called for dispersion, good-bye." I said good-bye to them and at that very moment, an unmarked police car was turned upside down and anarchists started in wrecking everything around them; a few dozen, not many more. So, I went back to the guy from the CGT and he told me: "Yes, but we called for dispersion." I said to him: "Listen, we have to do something." You know, even if there were some police units, the rest of the march was still arriving. There were lots of young people. The guy from the CGT understood perfectly well that we could not do anything. It was a very delicate task, it was worse than bad. The CGT guy consulted his men. He asked the one he had to ask, and then he came back to me and said: "OK, let's go." Then, with twenty big guys, we all together charged the hooligans. And I must tell you: they use methods we gave up a long time ago. Everything was then back in order.

Here may be seen one of the considerations that is most important for senior police officers: professionalism of the adversary. The more the organizers are used to the practice of a demonstration, the more senior police officers find it a "pleasure to work with them" (to use an expression often repeated in our interviews).

In this analysis, we have shown that one of the major weapons of the police lies not in a repressive or legalistic approach, but rather in the art of negotiating with the organizers, bringing them onto the police's home ground where they can keep the initiative and use their expertise to the fullest. This weapon would suffice if demonstrations only opposed senior officers and organizers. When the event is under way, however, the central problem becomes one of controlling troops—on the side of the demonstrators as well as on the side of the police.

Distance as a Means of Control

Two different obstacles stand against us in the field of protest policing. On the one hand, we find those who have organized and signed the preliminary notification. But the organizers have great difficulties when explaining this to their own constituency, and it is exactly the same thing when we try to make it clear for police officers. The average demonstrator does not know that people come here and sign an official paper, that routes are negotiated with us, that some maneuvers are decided before the event begins: "When you get here, we'll move this squad. Behind you, there will be this other unit. In front of you, a CRS squad will move ahead." The organizers know this. I tell them everything again when I get in touch with them. I tell them: "So, now, we want this, we let another squad stand behind you." But the rest of the march only sees cops wearing helmets who are ready to go. And our officers only see people moving and shouting. We always have some difficulty explaining to them that demonstrations are a kind of role playing. It is a part of the urban ethnology, and our two grass roots do not understand this very well.

This observation from the director of training at the Paris Police Prefecture clearly demonstrates our point: the central issue faced by those responsible for maintaining law and order at protest events is that of control among their rank and file as well as among the demonstrators. This distrust toward their own troops demonstrates how the doctrine of protest policing is largely based on the desire to avoid any confrontation between police officers and demonstrators. Protest policing in France is locked in a weighty contradiction expressed, on the one hand, by increasing pressure from the government and public opinion to control the demonstrations and, on the other hand, by what is still a main characteristic of police action, that is, whatever happens, "one is always hostage to the last legionnaire of the last century." In other words, protest policing is at the mercy of the weakest link.[10]

In the case of urban police, the question of control is even more important since the profession of "guardian of the peace" attracts into its ranks a population of undermotivated young people whose only wish is to move out of the ranks of the unemployed. Furthermore, senior officers claim that new recruits do not stand up well to the various daily constraints of the job because their missions are completely incompatible with the romantic idea they had about the job before they joined the police force:

> Now, most of the young recruits join because of the pressure of joblessness. They come from the provinces and their one aim is to go back there. But what is of utmost importance is that they have no idea of the job they will have to do, and what they imagine it will be is completely false. This image is in fact the one promoted by trash TV series like *Starsky and Hutch*. The young officer sees himself patrolling the streets all day long with no defined goal in a big car with a revolving flasher, in regular clothes, and doing a good job every day. . . . When they find themselves controlling traffic at intersections, they very quickly sing a different tune.

These comments help us to better understand why, in Paris in particular, but also among the specialized forces, those in command are wary of their rank and file. A veritable schism exists in effect between the goals of the senior officers and the way the rank and file think with regard to what constitutes good policing of protests. Nonintervention and a dispassionate approach are two criteria for excellence in the senior officers' view, but their men do not consider the operation a success without some kind of physical confrontation or without having evened the score with the demonstrators.

> You know, most of the time, when we are engaged in policing a protest, we do not confront demonstrators. If there is no violence, I think the officers resent it in a way that is—I will say it frankly—it's disappointing. Because they want to go into battle. Some of them, however, more philosophically, think it is not so bad. Policing of protests does not always mean baton charges, tear gas, beatings. That is what we try to explain to our young recruits. A lot of them think they are strong because they are numerous, and within a large force. Then, they would like . . . they would like . . . to be more violent. But we, on the other side, we watch over it. We just say, "Stop!"
>
> The men always want to give a personal touch to the debate. Before a baton charge, one can often hear within the ranks: "I'm gonna kick that one, because he threw ten Molotov cocktails." If one says, "We'll arrest him," it is OK; but if he says, "This one, we'll smash him on the corner of the bridge and then we won't take him back," that's another story. It is the duty of the commanders to listen to what is said and to draw aside those who start this kind of argument, which can lead to seriously injured people, even among themselves, among those who had their sprint alone to solve their little problem. Finally, they made their film on their own. And the opposite is true as well. The demonstrator who fixes an officer in his memory because the officer is a little bit bigger. He fixes the poor little copper and he'll receive his jab because he was on his own.

The concern to restrict the autonomy of policemen at the front line has increased in importance in recent years, notably after the student demonstrations of November and December 1986, during which one specialized motorcycle unit (Peloton Voltigeur Motocycliste [PVM]) behaved in a particularly violent manner, with one squad even going so far as to beat a demonstrator to death. This especially dramatic episode, in which the freedom of movement granted to the field resulted in the death of a man, reemerges time and time again in discussions among senior officers as a particularly tragic example of how a demonstration can go wrong when police officers are not well enough handled by their commanders.

To control the rank and file, a whole set of techniques, based on the idea of a necessary distance between demonstrators and officers, has been progressively developed. These various techniques are, in a certain sense, the action repertoire for different interventions.

The main elements of this repertoire are based on the use of specific types of action depending on the situation. Ideally, these responses aim to avoid physical harm to the demonstrators on each occasion and, at the same time, to allow the police officers to be protected and feel reassured. To achieve these two objectives, the method employed concentrates on maintaining a *necessary distance* and on utilizing the *ritualization of aggression*.

Ritualization of aggression and necessary distance are based on various methods. In Europe, different methods, such as smoke screens, have been tried to this end. In France, the standard response is based essentially on the use of tear gas, and in a less systematic way, water tanks. As Bruneteaux (1993) notes, tear gas was employed for the first time in 1947 and became commonplace at the end of the 1960s. Following on lacrimatory methods, gradation was introduced in the scaling of repression from 1955 on with the invention of the offensive grenade, a missile designed to cause traumatic shock.

The use of water undoubtedly represents one of the oldest tools, in the form of deployment by firemen. Nevertheless, it was not until May 1968 that the first water tank model was employed to create a brief moment of crisis among protesters and force a no-man's-land between them and the police forces so that all contact could be avoided.[11]

Ritualization of aggression is implemented in specific ways that present themselves to the demonstrators, move in the urban space, and make certain gestures that policemen who were questioned referred to as rituals:

> The purpose of the training is to be able to carry out very compact and uniform maneuvers in order to give the impression of a large force. Gendarmes have understood this very well for a long time: they hit their shields, a ritual, a gesture quite like the ones animals use. I often compare it to Konrad Lorenz's books. It is the same with the demonstrators. Shouting, colors. It is just like Sioux war paintings. And on our side, we answer with another kind of gesture: wearing helmets, putting our visors down, beating the shields, letting the men progress in a line or in a column. We all know this. But it is rather difficult for our men to understand it.

When all other means of intimidation fail and it is no longer possible to maintain a line, senior officers have recourse to the baton charge. In the thinking of the police commanders, this is the ultimate means at their disposal, in the sense that it is used only when confrontation with the demonstrators is absolutely unavoidable.[12] But it should also be noted that, in many cases, the baton charge is considered a means of intimidation whose function is to leave the demonstrators untouched but to forcibly create a no-man's-land that prevents person-to-person contact. The charge with baton drawn and the use of coercive methods against demonstrators, according to the doctrine, is considered to be a last resort.

Differentiation in the Management of Protesting Groups

Over and beyond a general doctrine of policing protests that would be theoretically applicable to all situations, both field observation and analysis of police archives clearly show that protest handling styles are determined by three interconnecting factors: police perceptions of protest groups, political considerations, and the strategy of protest groups themselves. In this final section, we will argue that to understand actual policing styles, each event must also be analyzed in terms of a three-way interaction involving government officials, security forces, and demonstrators themselves.

Although protest handling is a technique (oriented by a doctrine) materialized by a set of practices (the determinants of which are to be sought in police perceptions of the groups in conflict), it is also a *policy* in the sense that it involves choices made within the framework of a government strategy (Monjardet, 1990). For this reason, we will now examine how, in addition to the organizational and technical elements already analyzed, protest handling poses a number of problems that can be interpreted on a cultural and political level.

Police Perception of Conflict Groups

The doctrine of protest handling as it is taught does not confine its scope to delineating tactical and strategic methods inherent in police work. It inevitably develops an ideology as well. To the extent that policing protests implies resorting to force—in other words, striking citizens while going to great lengths to assert that they are not enemies—it is hard to avoid developing a normative philosophy to rationalize the practices adopted. This normative philosophy, employed to justify the use of force, is basically built on a declaration of *impartiality*.

Although the police claim that their intervention takes place within the law of the republic and admit the legitimacy of protest action, they analyze demonstrations through the very peculiar prism of crowd psychology handed down through the works of Tarde and Le Bon. The resulting conception of the demonstrator consequently appears, in our opinion, first to justify the patience the police are asked to exercise in the event of an assault or property damage, then to legitimize the use of strong-arm tactics when the civil authorities have decided to call for intervention or in situations of self-defense.

This is why anticipation, throwing projectiles, and hurling insults are at first tolerated by men who have been conditioned to believe that they are dealing with children, or at least "people who have taken leave of their senses." But at the same time—and this is not contradictory—this vision of things contains the principal justification for intervention, both because the irresponsible crowd has become dangerous and because in its midst are leaders that have to be neutralized. Commissioner Berlioz (1987, 13) aptly expresses this conception when he writes that an angry crowd

> is obviously dangerous, because the individual feels liberated. The slightest slogan, even the most unreasonable one, is instantly taken as a primal truth and acted on without reservation. The intransigence and intolerance of this mass preclude all discussion and negotiation; thus, the only solution open to someone in charge of public order is to check the eruption of this crowd before it is too late.

The predominance among police cadres, as well as men in the ranks, of a type of reasoning inspired by crowd psychology might lead one to conclude that their vision of protesting crowds is an undifferentiated one. In reality, this is not so.

Notwithstanding the official line of the law, which holds that every demonstrator has the right to equal treatment, it has become clear both through studying demonstration reports and through conducting interviews with police officers that they always pass an implicit judgment on the demonstrators' legitimacy, according to the perceived characteristics of the protest organization:

> In some cases, people are desperate. I've seen some who had come from little provincial towns like that. That's desperation, when the factory is closing down. It happens when the whole town depends on practically one single business. Or worse, when two spouses work in the same company. For people like that it's a disaster because they won't find another job. They haven't got much else to lose and you can understand why they resort to violence. You've got to understand.

These perceptions obviously play a role in the type of strategy implemented by the police force. Again, Monjardet's analyses of the professional ideology of the CRS are enlightening. In his view, the attitude of the CRS "depends on the demonstrators' behavior and very directly on the tension they themselves display. It also depends, in a different way for each CRS member, on the nature of the demonstrators: their social characteristics, the types of demands." This allegedly leads to "a certain sympathy for workers' demands and a certain aversion regarding young, privileged, student senseless looters" (1988, 101).

Protest Handling under High Political Surveillance

Police perceptions of demonstrators are not enough to explain differences in styles of protest handling. Political involvement also has to be taken into account. As we have already noted, calling in any sort of security force is always the result of a decision on the part of the administrative authorities (the prefect). This state of legal subordination suggests that we should examine both the instructions given by the civil authorities and how they are implemented in the field. We will first see that the intransigence displayed at times by the political authorities makes the outbreak of violence highly probable.[13] Conversely, government representatives sometimes handle conflicts in a paternalistic manner. The methods and justifications of this policing style remain to be explored.

The case in which security forces, on orders from the civil authorities, most clearly take a repressive attitude toward demonstrators is during illegal demonstrations not tolerated by the government. For example, on November 30, 1988, opponents of the Turkish government planned a demonstration to protest Prime Minister Turgut Özal's visit to Paris. Although it was banned by the prefect, a meeting was planned at Place de la Concorde in front of the Hôtel Crillon to boo Özal, an official guest of France. Security forces had strict orders from the government to prevent any gathering at the Concorde and to make arrests. As early as 10 A.M., small groups of demonstrators were coming out of the metro. Soon some thirty people were gathered near the obelisk. The CRS commandant then received orders to proceed with arrests, which he refused to do for lack of buses. A half hour later, the protesters numbered about two hundred: the security forces moved to scatter them and the first clashes began (the demonstrators were carrying batons). About fifty arrests were made. At 10:25 A.M., the remainder of the demonstrators, who were crouched down to avoid being carried off, were ordered to disperse. The security forces intervened by blocking the demonstrators against the fence surrounding the obelisk, which allowed the officers to make arrests in greater numbers. During this operation, tear gas was used to neutralize the most militant demonstrators. A withdrawal maneuver initiated by the CRS then allowed the crowd to disperse along the Quai des Tuileries. At 10:45 A.M., it was all over. The CRS counted fourteen wounded among their ranks; one demonstrator, "suffering from the effects of tear gas, fainted and was taken by civilian prefecture staff over to the obelisk fence and handcuffed to it until the first aid team arrived," states the CRS report. Numerous arrests must have taken place as several prefecture vehicles were sent out.

This example provides a perfect illustration of the difference in treatment that demonstrators receive depending on the instructions given by government authorities: given the orders to disperse immediately, police intervention preceded any demonstration of violence; in contrast with most protest policing operations, the aim of the maneuver was less to disperse the demonstrators than to make arrests. Therefore, opponents were blocked against the fence around the obelisk, a procedure about which the CRS itself expressed reservations given the violence it sparked; warnings were issued only after an initial effort to drive the crowd back and some fifty arrests were made; finally, plainclothes officers from the prefecture were there to filter the press so as to avoid too much publicity.

Another typical method of direct political involvement in the policing of demonstrations (unfortunately little research has been devoted to it) is antagonism. The existence of agents provocateurs has been the focus of many debates in France, either put forth as an argument for propaganda purposes or denounced as a cause of violence when trying to establish the facts of a given case. As Gary T. Marx (1974) points out, the sociology of mobilizations and police specialists have scarcely taken an interest in the phenomenon, despite the abundant historical examples of its use (in his article, Marx studies some twenty cases in the United States). In France, the practice resurfaces periodically, the most striking cases in recent years being the steelworkers' demonstration on March 23, 1979,[14] and the lycée student protest on November 12, 1990.

Deliberate antagonism on the part of political authorities is most often at the expense of the police themselves, who reiterate their hostility to the orders given. Rather than speak of "police antagonism," it would thus be more accurate to speak of "political antagonism." For the November 12, 1990, demonstration, for instance, the prefect authorized the young protesters to cross the Seine River and disperse along the Champs-Élysées. He also set up a large concentration of troops on the Right Bank, leaving the Left Bank relatively unattended. The general staff unanimously expressed its disapproval based on technical considerations. But no changes to the plans were allowed. The result concurred with police predictions: the first incident of pillaging prompted the prefect to prohibit the march from crossing the Seine, provoking a fury among the mass of demonstrators. Furthermore, the operation was set up in such a way that the police had immense trouble controlling access to the bridges. The demonstration ended in several hours of violent clashes, considerable property damage, and some one hundred wounded.

Though certain social groups or demands probably receive more severe treatment than is usually the case, in certain circumstances political authorities show greater tolerance toward illegal protest activity. Most cases involve demonstrations of farmers, and, to a lesser degree, those of students.

On the most transparent level, political authorities issue orders not to make arrests, even when individuals who have perpetrated violence can be identified. This is particularly to avoid refueling protest dynamics. Security forces, unconvinced of the efficacy of this method, often complain of government leniency, the effect of which, in their opinion, is more to assure the protest group of the usefulness, or even the necessity, of violent action.

Variations in the degree of tolerance shown by the civil authorities are manifest in other instances as well. It is not uncommon, as we have seen, for "zones of tolerance" during predemonstration negotiations between organizers and the authorities, to be defined, the purpose of which is to circumscribe beforehand the type and degree of violence that will not give rise to police intervention. These are the negotiation procedures with political authorities that we have shown to have crucial repercussions on police operations. Delimiting degrees of acceptable illegality fulfills a dual function: it allows the civil authorities to define acceptable targets for violence and to reject others deemed more sensitive or costly (for instance, public buildings, private property, and so on), and, at the same time, it does not cut off the organizers from their popular base, which is sometimes determined to see some action no matter what, and thus allows the leadership to maintain control.

Conclusion

To conclude, we wish to underscore the importance of the communication process in protest interaction. This communication can be analyzed as an insurance game, that is, an exchange in which the action depends on anticipating the adversary's next move: demonstrators adjust their actions in accordance with what they believe the police will tolerate, while the civil authorities implicitly or explicitly set tolerance thresholds depending on the nature of the protagonists. Figure 3.2 outlines this mechanism by identifying four ideal types of protest styles.

Type A refers to routine demonstrations that follow the procedures outlined earlier and that take place in a climate of mutual cooperation. Type B covers situations in which the police, on orders from the political authorities or their own chief, have a distinctly repressive and/or antagonistic attitude toward nonviolent demonstrators. Most banned and nontolerated demonstrations fall into this classification.[15] Type C considers situations in which the authorities handle illegal protests in a soft manner. The police take a wait-and-see stance with regard to public and private property damage. Type D

	Police style (possibly under political pressure)	
Action of the demonstrators	*peaceful/cooperation*	*violent*
peaceful/ cooperation	**A** peaceful demonstrations	**B** nontolerated demonstrations
violent	**C** paternalistic handling	**D** crisis demonstrations

Fig. 3.2. Ideal types of protest styles in France

characterizes demonstrations in which protesters and security force commanders alike adopt a position of open conflict. Our essay demonstrates that, apart from a few exemplary cases, differences in policing conflicts do not fall neatly into these four categories. We have shown that attitudes during a demonstration are in constant flux; for instance, a demonstration being handled according to the soft method as long as protest violence remains within certain bounds can turn into an open clash and the dispersion of the protesters as soon as security forces implement repressive methods. Figure 3.2 serves only to stress the ways the authorities—be they in the political arena or the police in the field—perceive protest groups, and thus the treatment the latter receive is obviously not uniform.

The main reason for this is that government authority as it is manifested in protest handling is brought into action through a multitude of actors, whose interests, subcultures, and attitudes vary greatly. Police handling of protests can therefore not be interpreted solely according to a logic of pure instrumentality of the security forces in the service of political choices, given the leeway agents at all levels are granted. We thus conclude that there is a need to analyze the police machinery as a full-fledged actor in the structure of political opportunities. Yet it would be misleading to concentrate attention on police work alone and not take into account the role of political authorities or the nature of protest groups. Only a combination of these three elements can enable us to identify a series of factors that can be said to play a role in the type of protest handling that is implemented.

Notes

1. Cf. Constitutional Court, no. 94–352 DC 01/18/1995 and Favre (1993).
2. For both practical and theoretical reasons we cannot go into in this essay, we define a protest event much more narrowly, as follows: an event in which a nongovernmental actor

occupies a public space (public buildings, streets) in order to make a political demand, to experience in-process benefits, or to celebrate something, which includes the manifest or latent expression of political opinion. For a further explanation of the reasoning behind this definition, see Fillieule (1995a).

3. Because the development of an answer to this last question would lead us too far from the framework of this essay, we will not deal with it here. Suffice it to say that, historically, the constitution of police knowledge, police practices, and legal tools to deal with demonstrations was mostly initiated as a reaction to the changing tactics of demonstrators (see 1893–98, 1934, 1968, 1990–93 as major examples). The fact that the demonstrators themselves led the way reinforces our argument that the analysis of protest handling must be undertaken on three levels (see also Fillieule, 1995a).

4. In addition to these forces of intervention are those of the intelligence service (the Renseignements Généraux) whose task it is to provide the ground forces with all necessary information to conduct their work. We will return to this later.

5. The term *commissaire* refers here to a person responsible for law and order, a civil representative of the prefect, not a post in the police hierarchy.

6. We should keep in mind, however, that the eventuality of a crisis situation can lead to a strict interpretation of the law, which would allow a very high level of repression.

7. It is a tradition in Paris, for symbolic and practical reasons, that there are no demonstrations on the Champs-Élysées.

8. This practice originates from the end of the 1970s, when the Police Prefecture in Paris generally opened large marches with police buses placed several hundred meters in front of the demonstration. It was during a demonstration of steelworkers on March 23, 1979, that for the first time a police officer was in charge of the link. Since the student demonstrations of December 1986 in Paris, this method has been systematically employed. It can sometimes be highly visible: during the annual demonstration of the National Front in honor of Joan of Arc on May 1, 1988, a car with a sign saying "liaison police/organizers" opened the march.

9. A student who died as a result of a police beating during a demonstration on December 4, 1986.

10. The assistant to the director of public security in Paris expresses it nicely in the following terms: "In the contemporary policing of protests, the chief of police, under pressure from cabinet ministers and Agence France-Presse, tends toward a push-button response to police actions in the same vein as electronic games. But Nintendo has not yet provided the solution."

11. Following a nurses' demonstration during which water tanks were used without any significant harm, a campaign of complaints led to a restriction on the use of this method, despite its effectiveness.

12. On the psychological effects of the baton charge on the officers, see Waddington (1991, 171–78).

13. This has already been suggested by Skolnick (1969, 47). See also D. Waddington (1992, 50–51), based on many case studies of suffragettes, antifascists, and student demonstrations in Great Britain.

14. For a complete analysis of this spectacular case, see Fillieule (1997).

15. We know that the banning of a demonstration is no longer a sufficient reason to provoke a systematic dispersion. There must be a political decision taken by the authorities. Banning a demonstration just reinforces differences in the treatment of authorized and nonauthorized demonstrations.

Chapter 4

Public Order, Protest Cycles, and Political Process: Two Swiss Cities Compared

Dominique Wisler and Hanspeter Kriesi

The Approach

The "political process" perspective in research on social movements (McAdam, 1982; Tilly, 1978; Kitschelt, 1986), which emphasizes the crucial role played by the state on trajectories of contention, has been less concerned with the constitutional mechanisms by which the state responds to protests than with the windows of opportunity that such occasions temporarily offer challengers. Phrasing it in another way, research has been focused on the input side of the "political opportunity structure" (POS), defined as open or closed, and has neglected its output side. To be fair, it should be acknowledged that proponents of the political process approach have never been entirely mute on the output side of the POS. In his seminal work, Doug McAdam (1982), to give just one example, underlined the weakening effect on social control resulting from a restructuring of power favorable to a movement. However, the study undertaken by Donatella della Porta on Germany and Italy (1996) has pioneered the field by importing the insights of the political process approach into police sociology. This work breaks new ground in its systematic discussion of the relationship between the POS and protest policing. According to della Porta, protest policing is a "barometer" of the POS, and police styles can be explained in terms of political institutions, political culture, and the distribution of power between the coalitions of law and order and those of civil rights.

Police style also results from the process of interaction with social movements during protest cycles, a phenomenon that has been illustrated by McCarthy, McPhail, and Christ (1995) for the American case. Protest cycles are particularly relevant to protest policing not only because there is an especially intense interaction between police and protest movements during such cycles, but more importantly because, according to Tarrow's analysis (1989b), it is precisely during protest cycles that the police confront changing repertoires of collective action. As pointed out by McAdam (1983), the police force responds to these innovations by adapting its tactics and, we will add, its organization. A specific organizational adaptation can pave the way for what Monjardet refers to as a "hierarchical inversion" with respect to decision making on the use of force. The notion of hierarchical inversion is particularly relevant to understanding the use of police force during public order operations. Thus, protest policing styles are shaped by the POS on the one hand, and police responses to protest cycles on the other.

The impact of these two influences—the POS and protest cycles—on policies relating to public order will be discussed in this chapter by means of a comparison of the use of force, and related decision making, during public demonstrations in two Swiss cities: Zurich and Geneva. Our analysis begins with an outline of the evolution of the use of force and related decision-making procedures in Zurich and Geneva since 1968. In this first part, the analysis of protest policing will focus mainly on the protest cycles and the alliance configurations. By moving one level higher in the POS analysis, the second part of this study aims to identify political mechanisms that help to constitute the specific configuration of force regarding mass protests and the police.

Two concepts—"politicization" and "routinization"—will be used extensively throughout this chapter. "Politicization" refers to a process whereby political authorities gain control through decision making over the use of force during public order operations. Decreasing political involvement in the recourse to force by the police is described as a process of "routinization." Further, increasing delegation of decisions to lower ranks of the police hierarchy indicates increased routinization. By the same token, politicization clearly begins with a claim by the police chief to retain entire control over decisions during a public demonstration. It should be clear from these definitions that routinization can ensue from political will, but, in this case, political authorities consciously delegate specific powers to the police chiefs or to lower-ranking officers in the police hierarchy.

The data for this study derive from three main sources: first, interviews with past and present police officers in charge of public order operations; second, a preliminary analysis of parliamentary debates on protest policing since 1965; third, a provisory analysis of police files and newspaper reports on public order interventions during mass demonstrations collected systematically for the period from 1965 to 1994 in four Swiss cities (Basel, Bern, Geneva, and Zurich).

Why Study Zurich and Geneva?

The focus on the "local" in Switzerland is justified first of all by the fact that, strictly speaking, there is no "Swiss" police in this country. Recent attempts to "nationalize" police units in charge of public order have all failed in the face of federalist resistance and a strong civil rights movement.[1] As a result, police organization, training, and philosophies are still fragmented today along the territorial lines of the cantons. Unlike centralized states like France and Italy, where the central government, through the prefect system, is responsible for protest policing, in Switzerland local-level authorities have retained sovereignty in this respect. Depending on the particular canton, responsibility for public order policies lies either with the cantonal authorities, as is the case in Geneva and Basel (usually small city cantons), or with the municipal authorities, as in cantons like Zurich or Bern that have delegated such powers to their biggest cities. In the case of these two last-mentioned cities, this delegation of powers, unaccompanied as it has been by a concomitant transmission of legislative power to the municipal parliaments, has meant that the city executives are entirely isolated from their local legislative bodies in terms of public order policies. Typically, decisions on matters of public order—for example, on the use of the public domain for political demonstrations—are taken by means of ordinances in Zurich and Bern, whereas they have to pass through the cantonal legislative bodies in Geneva or Basel. Moreover, as will become clear from our description of the local POSs, huge variations exist among Swiss cantons with regard to their political institutions, including direct democratic instruments, electoral laws, and practices. We will also see that political cultures in relation to public order vary along regional lines in Switzerland and that political parties are defined primarily at the local, and not the national, level. In other words, practically all the POS variables relevant to an explanation of protest policing are locally based in Switzerland.

The two cities under consideration in this study have been the theater of very different kinds of mobilization in terms of protest movements and cycles. In French-speaking Switzerland, new social movements have been generated to a much smaller degree than in the German-speaking region (Giugni, 1991, 91). On the other hand, the labor movement has been comparatively weaker in the latter region. Furthermore, while Zurich and many other Swiss cities experienced the strongest protest cycle of their postwar history in 1980–81, with the radicalization of the Autonomen movement, Geneva was almost completely insulated from this protest wave at that time (figure 4.1). Given our hypothesis that police style depends at least in part on

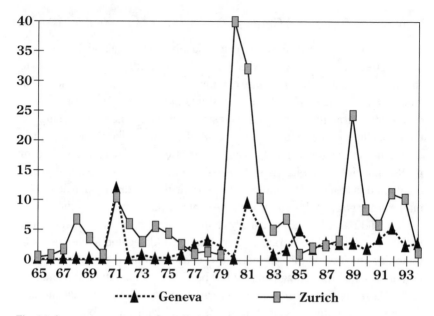

Fig. 4.1. Autonomen protest cycles in Zurich and Geneva

the specific interaction between police and social movements during a protest cycle, we should expect diverging protest policing trajectories in these
two cities.

Decision Making and the Use of Force in Zurich and Geneva:
The Story of Protest Cycles

Zurich

Tear gas has been available to the Swiss police since the late 1940s in the
form of a modified hand-thrown army grenade. To our knowledge, the only
canton to have resorted to this form of control prior to 1968 is that of Bern. In
Zurich, the use of tear gas in 1968 was tightly controlled by the political authority in charge of the Zurich police, the *Polizeidirektor*. Even during the
worst riot of that year, when a large number of police officers and firemen
were injured, no tear gas was used. The Zurich police doctrine was based on
what might be called the "classical model," which prescribes the use of the
baton charge to disperse turbulent assemblies. However, soon after the
Globus riot,[2] a new doctrine—the "distance model"—emerged, finding its first
formulation in a directive issued by the Zurich city executive in March 1969.

This directive, which did not require the approval of the city parliament but was simply adopted by the city government as part of its responsibilities for public order in Zurich, set down a five-step procedure for police interventions during demonstrations: canalization, followed by the use of body power (only for small assemblies), the water cannon, water mixed with tear gas, and, as a last resort, the baton. It thus inverted the classical hierarchy of control methods; until 1968 the baton had been the primary form of crowd control, while tear gas was considered the *ultima ratio*. This new hierarchy reflects a shift from crowd control by means of close presence to "crowd control by distance." Besides the water cannon, tear gas is believed to be the most effective means of keeping a distance between police officers and demonstrators, thereby providing the greatest protection to police from injuries. Three technical innovations, largely the result of intensive cooperation between Swiss army weapons experts and the police, made this reversal possible: a modified version of the army's flamethrower, which allows a tear gas-water solution to be sprayed to a distance of about thirty meters, was introduced in 1969; in the same year, modern water cannons able to spray the same solution on demonstrators were brought into use; then, in 1973, the so-called TW-73 (tear gas launcher, *Tränengas-Werfer*), a Swiss army rifle with a short-cut barrel adapted thus to launch tear gas grenades to a distance of eighty meters, was developed. All of these new forms of protest control expanded the spectrum of distance and resolved, to a certain extent, the tactical problem caused by hand-thrown tear gas grenades that could easily be thrown back at the police by demonstrators.

The new directive specified that orders for the use of the new control methods, namely, water and tear gas, had to come from the *Polizeidirektor*. At the same time, it mentioned the possibility of a delegation of powers to the commanding officer in charge of a particular police intervention for situations of self-defense or emergency ("In allen Fällen aber ist der Einsatz weitergehenden Mittel durch den *verantwortlichen Kommandierenden* zu befehlen"). This first slight routinization of the use of tear gas was slowly reinforced during the 1970s and it was not rare during this period for officers in charge of large units (companies or sections) to be granted responsibility for the use of tear gas. The Zurich police make a crucial distinction between "mission" and "command" tactics. With mission tactics, the commanding officer retains complete control over the police operation by being the only person with power to give orders regarding the use of force. As one interviewee stated:

> In principle, the commanding officer in Zurich is omnipotent, meaning that he can do anything that is thought to be necessary in the course of the action. We command according to the "mission" tactics, not "command" tactics; that is, we give the commanding officer the mission and also the competence over any decision that is necessary and he is also responsible for what happens. He can then delegate up front, to the section chief or even to the group chief, responsibility for the use of gas and other hard methods. The same is not true in Germany. There, competences are kept in the highest ranks of the police hierarchy and this produces delays that can have a negative impact on the situation on the ground when the "guys" (the rank-and-file police) think we are not allowed and, second, when they are in a difficult situation, and then . . . (Interview with Zurich cantonal police officer, April 1995)

During the 1970s, however, "mission" delegation of competences remained restricted to police officers, generally section chiefs, and did not yet extend to group chiefs (usually noncommissioned policemen). The number of police officers present at a demonstration depended largely on the potential level of trouble: demonstrations that were expected to be peaceful were not necessarily even commanded by an officer, while the number of police officers varied between four and ten for difficult protests in Zurich.

This shift in protest policing philosophy and the gradual routinization in decision making on the use of tear gas resulted, following its initial use in January 1971, in a moderate diffusion of this method of control during the 1970s. For practical reasons (too heavy, unable to circulate in the small streets of the center), the water cannon was increasingly marginalized and rarely appeared in the police operation structure. This quasi abandonment, however, was done quietly, with complete disregard for the official doctrine.

No major changes occurred during this decade, and indeed we have to wait until the next protest cycle—the Autonomen movement of 1980–81—to see a fundamental revision of the public order doctrine and an adaptation of tactical and organizational police methods in Zurich. The 1980 revision included an almost complete routinization of the use of tear gas (decisions were now made by noncommissioned officers), the introduction of "rubber bullets," and a new concept of intervention based on high police mobility and a far-reaching decentralization of police forces.

The protest cycle of the early 1980s in Zurich was articulated around the demand for an autonomous youth cultural center. The immediate trigger was a referendum for the renovation of the Opera House, which would cost sixty billion francs. The referendum was supported by a large coalition, which, however, did not include the city's strong Social Democratic Party. The Social Democrats claimed that "alternative" popular culture would be further marginalized by the unilateral allocation of such a huge sum to elite culture. More accurately, they were split on the issue, with the unionists supporting the referendum as a job-creating project. The Autonomen movement emerged with the referendum campaign and was immediately supported by the non-unionists—the progressives—of the Social Democratic Party. This new protest cycle turned out to be unusually violent as the law-and-order coalition gathered increasing strength. During the campaign, it appears that the dividing line between the law-and-order and the civil rights coalitions was exactly the same as the division between the proponents and opponents of the Opera bill; it crossed directly through the Social Democratic Party, with the party unionists joining the other conservative parties in demanding more repression. The position of this wing of the Social Democrats was crucial since all the Social Democrats of the city executive (four out of the nine members) were unionists. With the elections of March 1982, the divisions over public order policies ended in a split in the party, and the unionists once again won all the Social Democratic seats in the city executive.

An attempt in 1981 by the progressive Social Democrats of the city parliament to prohibit the use of tear gas by means of the so-called individual initiative led to a juridical battle over the right of the parliament to legislate on the issue.[3] The fight was eventually lost by the parliament through a 1985 Federal Constitutional Court decision, and thus did not result in a repoliticization process in decision making on the employment of this coercive method. Indeed, quite the opposite occurred. During the Autonomen protest cycle, we may observe a further routinization of decision making regarding tear gas. Delegation of responsibility for the use of tear gas was no longer limited to police officers, but, as we will see, was extended to small four-man riot police units. Moreover, the 1980–81 protest cycle witnessed the introduction of a new coercive control method in public order operations in Zurich: "rubber bullets." These bullets are made of small rubber pieces, manufactured in Switzerland, which can be fired with TW-73. They were first developed by the British for use in the conflict in Northern Ireland. Although they were purchased by the Zurich municipal and cantonal police forces in 1977, it was not until the Opera demonstration organized by the Autonomen movement on June 30, 1980, that they were used for the first time in Zurich.[4] Use of this coercive method of control during this protest cycle became routinized along the same lines as occurred with tear gas.

In addition to the strength of the law-and-order coalition, another independent phenomenon contributed to this routinization process, namely, the development of a new concept of police intervention in response to a radical change in protest tactics during the Autonomen protest cycle. In response to the "early" police dispersion of demonstrations, which aimed to increase the cost of participation in unauthorized marches, demonstrators innovated by introducing a set of tactics labeled by the media as "cat-and-mouse" tactics.[5] Following the police order to disperse, demonstrators split into small groups (*Splittergruppen*) and simultaneously created disorder (damage to property, looting, barricades, or surprise attacks on police) in different parts of the city. This new strategy completely changed the "image" of demonstrations. Whereas the typical image of a demonstration in the 1970s was one of a strong and compact form, which, in the case of trouble, would attack the heavily equipped (with batons and helmets) police forces frontally, Autonomen demonstrations of the 1980s produced the image of several groups acting independently of one another, moving very quickly and equipped with baskets or roller skates and small rucksacks.

Police adaptation to the cat-and-mouse tactics became visible in late August 1980. It should be recalled that a typical public order operation of the 1970s was structured on several (two to four) large units of sixty to eighty policemen, each of which was divided into three sections of twenty to thirty policemen. During this decade, the sections acted as "closed" (*geschlossen*), cohesive units, with each single unit in principle under the command of an officer. Although mobile, they were relatively slow-moving as each unit was assigned to one huge police vehicle (the *fourgon* or so-called MTW— *Manschaftstransportwagen*). In comparison, the new organizational structure of police operations that appeared in the mid-1980s protest cycle was extremely flexible and decentralized. The traditional four heavy units were now each divided into two sections; one of these continued to act as a larger cohesive unit (twenty to forty policemen) with one transport vehicle, while the other was subdivided into several groups of four men, each with their own vehicle.

This new structure, known first as *Jagdgruppen* and later as the "TW-taxi groups," was a real innovation, for which, it should be noted, the Zurich (cantonal) police claim paternity.[6] In the mid-1980s, it was not uncommon to see the heavy police sections completely replaced in public order operations with the smaller TW-taxis groups, whose number would vary for large-scale interventions from eighteen to thirty. Within this new concept, each TW-taxi group was mobile, with its own vehicle—a police patrol car or small van[7]— and was fully equipped with TW-73, the tear gas launcher that, as noted, had been adapted in the mid-1970s to be able to fire both tear gas grenades and rubber bullets. These small mobile units undertook the new mission of patrolling the city before, during, and after a demonstration, accompanying marches tightly on the flanks, and surveilling and following small and isolated groups of troublemakers.

The "personnel" problem had rapidly reached acute proportions in Switzerland because there is no federal police force that could be called on for help in the case of an enduring protest.[8] Although individual policemen receive basic public order training in Zurich, the large police operation structure soon proved to be unable to sustain a protest cycle. Thus, the TW-taxi group structure not only was a tactical response to the protests, but it also sought to answer the growing problem of inadequate police personnel. The 1980–81 protest cycle required the mobilization of uniformed policemen almost every day, or at least several days a week. Other police duties suffered, police were forced to do overtime, weekends were done away with, and so on. Thus, with time, the need was increasingly felt for a concept of police intervention that would be less demanding on human resources and still efficient enough for the police to adequately control protests. The TW-taxi group concept provided such a solution, as our interviews with Zurich police officers confirmed. TW-taxi groups proved to be less demanding on policemen since one or two mobile TW-taxi groups could control bigger areas, with the possibility of requesting reinforcements in case of trouble. While a large police operation of the 1970s in Zurich required about four hundred policemen, it became unusual, from August 1980 on, to see police operations involving more than two hundred policemen, despite the radicalization of protests. The TW-taxi concept was thus responsible for the smaller-sized police intervention structure and allowed the contingent of police personnel to be cut by about half. It was found to be so efficient that it became established as the dominant public order intervention structure in Zurich in the 1980s. Today, even small and peaceful demonstrations are controlled by a couple of TW-taxi groups.

In order to compensate for the reduced numbers of police and the lost dissuasive effect of large-scale units of riot police, the TW-taxi groups were granted wider latitude in the use of tear gas and rubber bullets. They received a "mission," meaning that they themselves could choose between the available methods to fulfill their mission. Most important, since each four-man unit could not include an officer, but was at best led by a noncommissioned officer, decisions on the use of tear gas and rubber bullets were now delegated to the lowest ranks of the police hierarchy. This authorization of responsibility to the TW-taxi groups, especially for turbulent demonstrations, is confirmed by interviews with Zurich cantonal and municipal police officers.[9] In other words, mobility and decentralization of police forces induced a truly "hierarchical inversion" in Zurich public order operations. With the concept of "hierarchical inversion," Monjardet (1984) grasped a widely acknowledged fact in police literature, namely, that the police rank and file were given wide latitude in decision making as part of the ever-present danger of their duties in patrol units. Although, taking the example of France, Monjardet believes that protest policing is not included in the above-mentioned description of police work, we can see that the latitude given to individual policemen varies greatly during public order operations depending on the organizational structure of police intervention (centralized versus decentralized). In the case of Zurich, the policing of protests is no different today than other traditional police duties with respect to the degree of decision-making discretion delegated to lower ranks, since the small TW-taxi groups are entirely comparable in this respect to their peer police units of patrol cars. The de facto routinization of decision making on coercive methods of protest control induced by the TW-taxi concept was codified only much later with an official shift of doctrine concerning competences for the use of force by the police. A directive issued by the city authorities in 1984 explicitly states that the 1969 doctrine has aged and that decisions regarding the use of tear gas and rubber bullets can now be made by the "responsible on-site chief."

It is worth noting that this routinization process, completed during the 1980–81 protest cycle, ended up with the reverse situation of 1968: where the use of tear gas had been controlled by a politician, decisions were now taken by the lowest ranks of the police hierarchy. This routinization was also accompanied by a further diffusion of the use of coercive means of protest control in Zurich. From 1980 on, rubber bullets and tear gas became a routine part of control methods for disorderly demonstrations.

Toward the end of the 1980s, however, there was a reversal in the routinization of police use of coercive methods and we may observe a repoliticization of decision making regarding the use of tear gas. The immediate trigger for this process was the drama surrounding the Chernobyl demonstration in Bern. But there was also another major change in the local political context of the Zurich police: for the first time in the postwar history of Zurich, the left, in alliance with the Ecologist Party, won with a majority in the 1990 elections.

With regard to the Chernobyl demonstration, a conflict over a prohibited route led to the massive use of tear gas by the Bern police to disperse the largely peaceful crowd of antinuclear protesters—fifteen thousand people, according to police estimates—that had gathered in the central area of the city on a Saturday afternoon to commemorate the first anniversary of the Chernobyl nuclear plant accident. Many bystanders, peaceful demonstrators, and children became the target of this heavy police operation, which, because the protest was considered an important event, was under the command of the Bern city police chief himself.

The police immediately became the focus of harsh criticism from politicians and public opinion through the media. The cantonal head of police, which had a contingent under city command in the operation, publicly criticized the operation as being disproportionate. In the Bern municipal parliament, more than twenty parliamentary interpellations and motions—an unusually high number—were lodged within a few days, a parliamentary inquiry commission was set up, and two legal experts on the police intervention (one from the municipal authorities and one from the parliament) were commissioned. During the parliamentary debates following the operation, many members of the conservative parties joined the civil rights coalition formed initially by the Greens and the leftist parties. Radical demands to prohibit tear gas and rubber bullets during mass demonstrations in the future were rejected, but more moderate calls to limit their use found strong support in the municipal legislative body. The legal experts did not agree on whether the police intervention was proportionate to the situation or not. The legal opinion commissioned by the authorities (a retired federal court judge, Dr. Harald Huber, and a university professor, Hans Schulz) concluded that it was, whereas the opinion ordered by the parliament (a professor of constitutional law in Fribourg, Thomas Fleiner) came to the opposite conclusion. The core debate, however, was not proportionality but rather the so-called troublemaker principle. In other words, the issue brought to the fore by the Bern police operation, as stated in the Bern daily *Der Bund*, was whether or not the police could have focused their coercive measures on the small number of troublemakers rather than indiscriminately dispersing the whole crowd. This debate, in fact, echoes the earlier German Brokdorf Federal Constitutional Court (*Bundesverfassungsgericht*) decision (1985), which granted demonstrators the fundamental right to demonstrate and, as a consequence, restricted the use of police force on troublemakers (Burfeind, 1993).

The Chernobyl demonstration debate did not remain confined within the cantonal borders, but rapidly became national in scope. National television was present during the escalation and dramatic images were broadcast on the evening news. A leading national newspaper, der *Tages-Anzeiger*, wrote of the "Bern catastrophe" (April 26, 1987) in its morning edition. Repercussions of this debate were felt on an administrative level eight months later in the formal demand by the president of the Conference of Cantonal Police Department [political] Heads (CCDCJP) to the Conference of Swiss Police Chiefs (CCPCS) to formulate a new set of tactics and techniques that explicitly take into account the troublemaker principle in the control of demonstrations. On December 31, 1989, the "working group" of the CCPCS issued a directive that asserted the need to isolate troublemakers and to refrain from using coercive means on peaceful demonstrators.[10] At the same time, it remained rather vague and inconclusive on the question of decision making concerning the use of force during a protest escalation. Nevertheless, the document does specify that "it seems at least tactically correct to give competences for a massive intervention involving heavy methods to the intervention chief, or at least to issue specific rules about the conditions of their use" (p. 10).

The second important event in the repoliticization of the use of tear gas in Zurich was the 1990 electoral victory of the civil rights coalition in the municipality of Zurich. A majority in both the city government and the city parliament was won by an alliance between the Social Democrats and the Ecologist Party. In addition, a Social Democrat, Robert Neukomm, became head of the police department. This electoral victory of course played a major role in the repoliticization of the use of tear gas. An attempt was also made to restrict the use of rubber bullets and, during the first year of Social Democratic control of the city, their use also appears to have been repoliticized. Following the very first case of a municipal police officer being sentenced (February 1991) by a district tribunal to a fine for having ordered the use of rubber bullets in inappropriate circumstances, Neukomm was quoted by a newspaper as saying that the time had come for a "fundamental revision of the use of rubber bullets" (*Volkssrecht*, February 8, 1992). On a few occasions, police cordons and "pushing" were even reintroduced. This early goodwill on the part of Neukomm was overshadowed, however, by his later refusal to follow a call of the civil rights coalition in the municipal parliament for a ban on rubber bullets in public order operations in Zurich.[11] Two reasons motivated this failure to comply: first, unlike tear gas, rubber bullets are believed to be well suited to the troublemaker principle since they can be directed against a small group of persons; second, the TW-taxi concept had not been modified, and this concept quite simply does not work without an efficient means of keeping a distance from protesters and a wide latitude in decision making for the TW-taxi groups.

Geneva

The history of fluctuations in the decision-making process regarding the use of tear gas and rubber bullets in Geneva is very different from—and much shorter than—that of Zurich. Decision making on the use of coercive methods of control, including the baton, was highly politicized in 1968, and, as a consequence, essentially strategic. In the early 1970s, the use of force was delegated to the police, but remained, over the next decades, relatively high in the police hierarchy and did not experience the degree of routinization of the Zurich police.

As in Zurich, some routinization occurred in the early 1970s after an earlier period during which the use of coercive means of force was more strictly controlled by the political head of the police. During the protest cycle of 1968, the political head of the cantonal police, Henri Schmitt, retained control over police operations and is known to have been present himself on the streets during interventions. As a result, he was referred to with the nickname "Schmitt the baton." In one interview with a police officer in Geneva, this process was described in the following terms:

> Before, the overall plan of action was centralized and, as a consequence, relatively slow. If the chief of the intervention wanted to use coercive methods, he had to ask permission from the police chief, who was in the command room at the main police station. . . . To complicate the whole thing, there was often a politician in the command room. Things changed in 1972–73. The delegation of competences increased and politicians became less involved in the decision-making process. The chief of an intervention in the street basically received the competences for the use of coercive methods and could delegate them further to the section chief. (Interview, Geneva, June 20, 1994)

The use of tear gas was routinized in the early 1970s, becoming a matter of tactical, rather than strategic, choice. Interestingly, the first use of tear gas seems to correspond to the years of changes as described in the interview regarding political involvement in decision making. We retrace it to January 13, 1973, during the course of a Vietnam War demonstration. As in Zurich, this routinization was restricted to the police-officer level in the 1970s.[12] This control was thus strict since there were seldom more than three police officers involved in demonstrations in Geneva.[13] Rank-and-file policemen could make decisions on the use of tear gas only in situations of *légitime défense* or if communication was cut with the commanding officer. In general, the head of the police intervention (usually the chief of the uniformed police) retained complete control over the use of tear gas and other officers in the streets were required to seek his permission to use it. Thus, while Zurich opted for the control of social protests by means of "mission tactics," Geneva used the more classical "command tactics." Furthermore, the Geneva police did not adopt the Zurich doctrine of crowd control by distance in the 1970s, but instead stuck with the classical doctrine of protest policing by means of the cordon and the baton charge as primary coercive tools. As a result, the use of tear gas remained exceptional in Geneva during this decade.

Basically, neither the decision-making procedure nor the intervention doctrine for social protests underwent profound changes in Geneva during the 1980s. Not only did decision making on the use of tear gas remain strictly controlled by the higher echelons of the police hierarchy, requiring that an order be given by an officer at the least, but more important, rubber bullets were not introduced in public order operations. Although rubber bullets were indeed purchased by the Geneva police in 1975, following the escalation of the Jura conflict (Interview, Geneva, June 20, 1994), decision making on this method of control was highly politicized. In order to use rubber bullets during a police intervention, a specific order by the chief of police was required. It was unlikely, however, that the chief of the Geneva police would ever give such an order without prior consultation with the political head of the police. Asked about this particular method, the police chief of Geneva observed:

> From a symbolic point of view, firing on the populace, even with rubber bullets, would not be accepted by the Geneva mentality. . . . The day I gave this order, I would not be police chief anymore. Personally, I can't allow firing in a stretched trajectory (rubber bullets) on people, because then they are no longer considered as adversaries but they become enemies. (Interview, Geneva, September 24, 1996)

Unlike Zurich, where we have seen that rubber bullets became the "favorite" form of coercive police control in the late 1980s, they have never been used in Geneva. We may add here that there is a surprising dividing line between the German-speaking part of Switzerland, where rubber bullets are routinely used, and the French-speaking part, where they have never been used.

Two major reasons explain the continuity of decision making in Geneva and the comparatively high degree of politicization in the use of tear gas, and especially rubber bullets. First, the civil rights coalition has always been much larger in Geneva than in Zurich. During the 1980–81 protest cycle, the most prominent advocate of civil rights and political dialogue with the Autonomen movement was a conservative, Guy-Olivier Segond, who was a member of the Geneva city government and was also president of the Federal Youth Commission. This commission, largely influenced by its president, issued a list of recommendations in November 1980 to Swiss political authorities promoting greater tolerance and dialogue with the Autonomen movement.[14] Far from being an isolated figure in Geneva, Segond represented the view of the progressive wings of the two major local conservative parties, the

Radicals and the Liberals, on issues relating to public order. There is a broad consensus in Geneva on the notion that the role of the political authorities is to maintain social peace rather than blindly implement legal order. Important contributions to social peace are believed to derive from negotiation with social movements and the promotion of nonescalating police tactics, rather than from repression and use of the hard-line forms of control favored by the Zurich authorities. The strength of the civil rights coalition in Geneva is well expressed by the consistently tight control maintained over the use of "hard" methods within the police hierarchy since 1968.

The second reason underlying the continuity in decision making in Geneva is that this city was largely spared from the Autonomen protest cycle of 1980–81. Although the movement did mobilize later, mostly in the second half of the decade, the pronegotiation orientation of the Geneva authorities helped to deradicalize the conflict. The absence of this early 1980s radical protest wave and its "cat-and-mouse" tactical innovation explains why the Geneva police felt no need to adopt the new mobility and decentralization of the Zurich intervention structure. Mobility in Geneva in the 1980s was only slightly enhanced as compared to the 1968 situation. Riot police no longer patrolled in heavy *fourgons*, but rather each group of ten men moved about in a small van. Geneva police mastered the problem of mobility in the 1980s (and the problem of "real" trouble) by using its "intervention group," trained for anti-terrorist policies, and its version of the French *peloton mobile*, a single unit of twelve men trained for special security problems. Both were used in hot spots of protest policing (see the June 20, 1994, interview at the beginning of this section). By the same token, some level of decentralization has become observable over time. Today, the biggest unit, the company, is divided into several sections, which are in turn subdivided into three to six groups, depending on the mission of the section (static or mobile, for example). Neither in terms of size nor methods used by these groups, however, can a comparison be made with Zurich's TW-taxi groups. Unlike the four-man TW-taxi groups, the Geneva groups consist of about ten men. Moreover, only one Geneva group—the so-called support group—in each section is equipped with two TW-73s or other tear gas material; the others have only batons. Thus, arithmetically, we find that in Geneva there are two TW-73s in a section of about thirty men, whereas an equivalent section in Zurich has eight TW-73s. In contrast to Zurich, an increase in the use of tear gas did not occur in Geneva in the 1980s and the "classical" model of crowd control, with police cordons and baton charges during violent demonstrations, remained the dominant mode of protest policing.

From this description of the diverging evolution in the use of coercive methods of protest control in Zurich and Geneva we can draw several conclusions. In both cities, decision making in relation to coercive means was delegated from the political level to high-ranking police officers in the early 1970s and, as a result, the use of tear gas increased during disorders. Contrary to the course of events in Zurich, however, there was no hierarchical inversion in Geneva during the following decade. This was due first of all to the fact that the Geneva police did not have to confront the "cat-and-mouse" tactics of the Autonomen movement during the 1980–81 protest cycle. Although there was a wave of Autonomen protest later in the decade in Geneva, the police did not use escalating tactics and politicians chose to integrate the movement. Therefore, because the Geneva police did not have to deal with cat-and-mouse tactics developing within a repression-violence dynamic, they were not forced to adapt their intervention structure and adopt the highly flexible and decentralized character of Zurich police interventions. The second—and obviously related—reason for the absence of a hierarchical inversion in Geneva was the fact that the civil rights coalition in Geneva remained strong in the city despite the protest wave, whereas in Zurich the Autonomen protest cycle ended up strengthening the law-and-order coalition. In the late 1980s, after the catastrophe of the Chernobyl demonstration in Bern, the use of tear gas on crowds was once again restricted and more tightly controlled by the police hierarchy in Zurich. The repoliticization of the use of tear gas in Zurich in the 1990s accompanies the victory of the civil rights coalition in the 1990 municipal election. Whereas the use of rubber bullets remains highly politicized in Geneva, they are still routinely employed during public order operations in Zurich. The civil rights coalition has not yet been able to limit their use—a battle it fought throughout the 1980s—partly because the police have not revised their TW-taxi doctrine and because of the autonomy of the executive regarding public order policies vis-à-vis the local parliament.

The POS Context and Response Mechanisms to Protest Policing

The differences between Zurich and Geneva are quite intriguing, given that the left has remained in the minority for most of the period studied in both cities. It is indeed surprising that the Geneva chapter of the conservative party—the Radicals—shared a roughly similar view on protest policing with the progressive wing of the Social Democrats in Zurich, whereas the Zurich chapter of the Radicals was the strongest advocate of repression within the law-and-order coalition. Furthermore, the leading conservative press in these two cities—the *Neue Zürcher Zeitung*, close to the Radical Party in Zurich, and the *Journal de Genève*, close to the Liberal Party in Geneva—also contrasted along the same lines in their "diagnostic" and "prognostic" frames in relation to protest policing.[15] From 1968 until 1995, the *Neue Zürcher Zeitung* was consistently a leading advocate of strong repression and no-negotiation policies with protest movements, framed emphatically as a self-defense of the *Rechtsstaat* (constitutional order) against anarchy. In contrast, the *Journal de Genève* has favored some degree of tolerance and consistently defended a pronegotiation policy with social movements as part of a broader view that society is changing faster than the constitutional order.

The distinctive character of the political culture and the degree of openness of political institutions in these two cities can help to explain the contrasting strengths of the civil rights coalitions (and public opinion) in Zurich and Geneva. Political institutions and political culture intervened in the process of shaping divergent political coalitions in relation to public order policies. Our focus in this final section will thus be on the specific attributes of these two political structures and identification of the mechanisms shaping political coalitions and protest policing in Switzerland.

Political Culture

The term "political culture" refers to a general and, over time, consistent consensus of political elites on the definition of public order. Clearly, these definitions differ radically along regional lines in Switzerland and are a product of cultural diffusion from Germany and France (Wisler, 1995). In German-speaking Switzerland, public order is defined legalistically with the notion of the *Rechtsstaat* or constitutional order. A breach of the constitutional order by protest movements is synonymous with disorder and requires an intervention by the state to restore public order. An anecdotal, but illustrative, note can be made about this point. Early in the protest cycle of the Autonomen movement, the mayor of Zurich, member of a center party, sought to justify initiating a dialogue with the movement with the comment "Human beings are not made for the *Rechtsstaat*, but the *Rechtsstaat* is made for them." Not only did this view not prevail during later interaction with the movement, but it became the focus of a polemical and virulent criticism by the *Neue Zürcher Zeitung* the next day. The *Neue Zürcher Zeitung* (June 28–29, 1980) claimed that the mayor had used this saying in the wrong way—without the protection of the *Rechtsstaat*, society would return to a state of anarchy equivalent to the Hobbesian description of the state of nature.[16] In fact, the mayor's remark did not resonate in a political culture that identifies legality with public order.

In French-speaking Switzerland, on the other hand, constitutional order is not the overarching principle and public order is better understood as "social peace." Society may change faster than legislation and protest may be an expression of social change. In the final analysis, as several leading articles in the conservative *Journal de Genève* have put it, protest, and even illegal actions, can be interpreted as a "revitalization of the political system" rather than the "return to anarchy" feared by the *Neue Zürcher Zeitung*.[17] The task of the state is to restore social peace rather than to implement outdated legislation. Protest policing is, then, primarily an act of finding a delicate balance between accommodating social change and implementing constitutional order. The Geneva political culture regarding public order might be defined as "opportunist" because the police repression option is considered inopportune as soon as an escalation of the conflict is expected. The remark by the Zurich city mayor mentioned earlier, that the law is for human beings rather than the other way round, would never have been a matter of dispute in Geneva: it is the traditional and official understanding of public order in that city.

While Zurich defines public order as being *immanent* to the constitutional order, Geneva sees it as being *transcendent* to it. Both of these definitions, of course, are reminiscent of the opposition between the legalistic political culture of Germany and the more state-oriented political culture of France. The state in Germany is itself limited by its "fundamental" law, whereas the *raison d'État* provides the French state with a rationale to transcend the limits imposed by the law.[18] More generally, the legalistic and the opportunistic definitions of public order seem to be constitutive of two distinct concepts of the police, called elsewhere the Latin and the German families (Wisler, 1995).

These two different traditions are expressed in the diverging strengths of the civil rights and pronegotiation coalitions in Zurich and Geneva. Radical protest is considered to threaten the spirit of democracy in Zurich, to echo a Hobbesian state of nature, and the state is required to restore constitutional order rather than accommodate demands. In Geneva, radical protest is seen as an expression of social change and there is an understanding that the state can, through opportunity, accommodate demands and try to find a new equilibrium between the constitutional order and society.

Political Institutions

Political institutions, defined restrictively as the formal rules of political participation, also play a role in protest policing through two mechanisms that we refer to as the "cognitive-cultural" and "structural" mechanisms. In order to remain within the scope of this chapter, we will develop the argument by focusing on one specific political institution, namely, direct democratic instruments, which arguably play a major role in both mechanisms. It should be recalled, however, that direct democratic instruments are not alone in structuring these mechanisms; electoral laws and the degree of centralization of the state are other indexes of the degree of openness of a given institutional context that a more complete analysis should take into account. Let us simply state that on both counts—that is, with regard to electoral laws and the centralization of the state—Zurich is much more open than Geneva (Wisler, Kriesi, and Barranco, 1995). Before discussing these mechanisms, it is necessary to document the differences between Zurich and Geneva in relation to the degree of openness of direct democratic instruments.

Two direct democratic channels, the initiative and the referendum, may be distinguished. The initiative begins a legislative process, whereas the referendum closes such a process. Swiss cantons all have these instruments, but important variations exist concerning (1) their availability at the municipal level, (2) the political level of their application (administrative, legislative, and constitutional) and their form (mandatory or facultative), and (3) their accessibility in terms of the number of signatures required.

Broadly speaking, direct democratic instruments in Geneva display a much more closed character than is the case in Zurich. First, Zurich has known the municipal initiative since the end of the last century, whereas it was introduced in Geneva only in 1981. Thus, prior to that year movements that challenged policies within the competences of the municipality of Geneva, such as the housing policy, had no direct democratic instruments to initiate a legislative process. Second, although the referendum is available in both Zurich and Geneva at the administrative, legislative, and constitutional levels, Zurich is unique in having a *mandatory* referendum for financial expenses. Third, the differences between the two cities in terms of the proportion of the voting population required to sign a direct democratic instrument is quite dramatic. Thus, if the canton of Zurich requires that 1 out of 147 voting citizens sign a referendum to give way to a popular vote, the Geneva ratio is 1 out of 20. If we add that the required number of signatures must be gathered within a much shorter period of time in Geneva than in Zurich, we can readily understand that access to direct democratic instruments in Geneva is much more restricted than it is in Zurich. Table 4.1 illustrates the variation in the degree of openness of direct democratic instruments in Swiss cantons and four cities.

These differences are translated in table 4.2 into the differential use of these instruments during the 1980s in several Swiss cantons and cities, including Zurich and Geneva.

Table 4.1. "Entry price" of direct democratic instruments in Swiss cantons and four cities

Canton/city	Number of signatures required as percentage of electorate			Maximum number of days for collecting the signatures		
	Constitutional Initiative	Legislative Initiative	Optional Referendum	Constitutional Initiative	Legislative Initiative	Optional Referendum
Glarus	0.00	0.00	–	–	–	–
Inner-Rhoden	0.01	0.01	2.03	–	–	30
Ausser-Rhoden	0.18	0.18	–	–	–	–
Aargau	0.83	0.83	0.83	360	360	90
Basel-Land	0.87	0.87	0.87	–	–	56
Uri	1.19	1.19	1.19	–	–	90
Zurich	1.31	1.31	0.66	180	180	45
Zurich (city)	1.74	1.74	1.74	180	180	20
Lucerne	1.78	1.78	1.33	360	360	60
Solothurn	1.85	1.85	0.93	540	540	90
Schaffhausen	2.08	2.08	2.08	–	–	90
Bern	2.24	2.24	1.50	180	180	90
Obwalden	2.40	0.01	0.48	–	–	30
Schwyz	2.56	2.56	2.56	–	–	30
Saint Gall	2.88	1.44	1.44	180	180	30
Thurgau	2.97	2.97	1.48	180	180	90
Basel-Stadt	3.07	3.07	1.54	–	–	42
Basel (city)	1.6	1.6	0.8	–	–	30
Vaud	3.38	3.38	3.38	90	90	40
Lausanne	x	x	7.69	x	x	40
Zug	3.40	3.40	2.55	–	–	60
Valais	3.45	2.30	1.72	360	360	90
Jura	3.95	3.95	3.95	360	360	90
Fribourg	4.04	4.04	4.04	90	90	90
Grisons	4.09	2.45	2.45	360	360	90
Geneva	4.96	4.96	3.47	120	120	40
Geneva (city)	4.66	4.66	4.66	120	120	40
Niedwalden	5.00	0.00	5.00	60	–	60
Ticino	5.25	3.68	3.68	60	60	30
Neuchâtel	5.85	5.85	5.85	180	180	40

Note: French-speaking cantons and cities are italicized. An "x" indicates that the instrument does not exist.

Sources: Documentation Center on Direct Democracy (University of Geneva), Kriesi and Wisler (1996)

The cognitive-cultural mechanism is more related to the "input" aspect of direct democratic instruments (the initiative), whereas the structural mechanism is more concerned with their "output" character (the referendum) regarding state action.

Table 4.2. Number and types of referenda and initiatives submitted to a vote in several Swiss cities and cantons between 1980 and 1990

	Lausanne city	Geneva canton	Geneva city	Winterthur city	Bern city	Zurich city	Basel city	Basel canton
Mandatory referendum								
Financial	–	–	–	52	62	70	–	–
Annual budget	–	–	–	–	10	–	–	–
Others	–	–	17	16	41	26	–	4
Optional referendum								
Exceptional	1	–	–	–	–	–	–	–
Counterproject	–	–	6	7	2	5	–	1
Parliamentary	–	–	–	–	–	11	–	–
Others	6	11	10	6	4	9	6	54
Total referendum	7	11	33	81	119	121	6	59
Initiatives								
Individual	–	–	–	–	–	17	–	–
Others	–	2	10	11	11	22	–	26
Overall total	7	13	43	92	130	160	6	85
Annual means	0.6	1.2	3.9	8.4	11.8	14.5	0.5	7.6

Sources: Stadtkanzlei Zürich, Basel, Winterthur, Bern, and Lausanne, Staatskanzlei Basel, Chancellerie d'État de Genève

The Cognitive-Cultural Mechanism

The cognitive-cultural mechanism links the degree of openness of political institutions to the cultural status of public protests within a democracy. The more open a political system is—that is, the more institutional channels are available for challengers to participate in the political process—the less legitimate demonstrations are. In other words, noninstitutional forms of collective action, such as public protests, appear to be redundant and even illegitimate since they are often linked to disorders, if other institutional channels are (easily) accessible for challengers. Arguably, direct democratic instruments play an important role in this mechanism.

Opinion polls in Switzerland confirm the low cultural status of public protests in a model of institutionally open political systems (38 percent of respondents in a national opinion poll in Switzerland, and 50 percent of the respondents in the five largest Swiss cities, found it legitimate to demonstrate in 1987), whereas public demonstrations enjoy a high status in the prototype of an institutionally closed democracy—namely, France. Favre (1990) refers to an opinion poll conducted in Grenoble in 1987 in which about 80 percent of responses were favorable to public demonstrations. The role of direct democratic instruments in this mechanism cannot be overstated. In its important

Brokdorf decision (1985), for example, the German Federal Constitutional Court noted the lack of direct democratic instruments in Germany's political system as the main rationale for the recognition of public demonstrations as a fundamental right.[19] Clearly, the right to demonstrate is asserted as a functional equivalent to direct democratic instruments. One leader of the 1968 student movement in Zurich, Thomas Held, held that the availability of direct democratic instruments in Switzerland could explain the repressive reaction of political elites toward street protests in this country. "In many comments on the events in Germany and France," Held wrote, "it was said that a non-parliamentary opposition has no justification whatsoever in Switzerland because the citizens, with the initiatives and the referenda, are themselves already some sort of a nonparliamentary opposition" (*Neue Zürcher Zeitung*, June 16, 1968).

The legitimation mechanism of public demonstrations through the closedness of formal political institutions facilitates the emergence of a consensus over the democratic aspect of street protests. In an essay on the case of France, Favre (1990) emphasizes the "democratic essence" of mass demonstrations as a challenge to a strong government. In an institutionally open system, the existence of direct democratic instruments heavily constrains the potential development of a coalition oriented toward the defense of civil rights. Although the French-speaking part of Switzerland shares with France a view of public demonstrations as essentially democratic, they are often discarded in Zurich or Bern as "intolerable pressures of the streets." As a result, public demonstrations in front of the Federal Assembly or the local Bern Assembly during parliamentary sessions are banned and the Swiss-German authorities resort relatively often to their right to prohibit potentially turbulent demonstrations. In contrast, Geneva, throughout the period under consideration, has practically never resorted to any such prohibitions and has a long tradition of tolerance for "illegal" (not formally authorized) public demonstrations.

The Structural Mechanism

The tendency of the authorities to negotiate with or repress movements not only stems from the cognitive-cultural mechanism and political culture, but is also structurally influenced by the degree of openness of the referendum system. Indeed, the "output" capacity of the authorities—that is, their capacity to negotiate with protesters—varies greatly as a function of accessibility to the referendum. Especially relevant to the interaction between the authorities and the Autonomen movement in Zurich, for example, is the mandatory referendum for financial bills, since the Autonomen demands involved substantial expenditures. This kind of referendum, unknown in Geneva, specifies that recurrent (yearly) expenses above half a million Swiss francs must be submitted to popular vote. Thus, the Zurich authorities were not empowered to negotiate in their own right a substantial agreement with the movement during the 1980–81 protest cycle, regardless of which political coalition was in power. Although it is certainly reasonable to acknowledge that concessions to the movement in 1980 did not fit the municipal cultural policy of the time, which was oriented toward an elitist cultural image (Rothmayr, 1994), it might also be said that political prudence advised the authorities that a referendum on an autonomous center would probably have been rejected by the electoral college through the referendum, as had been the case in a referendum in 1974 for a (too) ambitious youth center project costing thirty million dollars. Thus, the no-negotiating stance of the Zurich municipal authorities is not simply a matter of orientation or ideology of the political elite, but is also the consequence of the requirement for a financial referendum in that city.

By contrast, political institutions in Geneva give the authorities the room for maneuver needed to negotiate substantial agreements with protesters, allowing them to balance problems of public order and political concessions in order to preempt protest movements. Political decisions are rarely challenged through the referendum system and financial bills are not subject to a mandatory referendum. It is true that the financing of the alternative cultural center of the *Usine*, involving an initial cost of three hundred thousand dollars and an annual operating cost of $150,000, could have been challenged by opponents through referendum, but the high number of signatures required and the short period for collecting them constitute major obstacles for any challenging group. Table 4.2 shows that direct democratic instruments are not frequently used in French-speaking cantons and cities as compared to the German-speaking region.

The "state-oriented" decision style, which Ladner (1994) found to be characteristic of most French-speaking cities, is arguably induced by the strictures of the referendum system in this region, while the availability of direct democratic instruments seems to play a major role in the "societal style" that predominates in German-speaking Swiss cities.[20] Interactions between the political authorities and social movements in Geneva are structured by direct and informal negotiation channels, whereas in Zurich they are channeled through direct democratic instruments. This second case inevitably involves the participation of the media and pressure groups in the decision-making process to a much greater extent than in a state-oriented system and has usually proven to be detrimental to marginal and unpopular social groups like the Autonomen movement.

Conclusion

The conjunction in Geneva of a high legitimacy of public demonstrations, a broad latitude for maneuver on the part of the political authorities, and an opportunistic definition of public order makes a favorable terrain for the emergence of the strong civil rights (and pronegotiation) coalition that our analysis detected. It also at least partially explains the high degree of politicization of "hard" methods of protest policing in this city and the reticence expressed by the current Geneva police chief to use rubber bullets in public order operations. By contrast, in Zurich, given the low legitimacy of public demonstrations, the weakness of the political authorities, and the legalistic tradition of public order, it is not surprising that the civil rights coalition has been much narrower and that "hard" methods like rubber bullets are used routinely in public order operations.

At the same time, our analysis has stressed that another process contributed to the more routine recourse to coercive methods of protest control by the Zurich police. Geneva was completely spared from the Autonomen protest cycle, whereas Zurich found itself at its epicenter. During this cycle, the movement responded to the closure of the POS and a repressive police stance by innovatively developing highly disruptive "cat-and-mouse" tactics, a set of tactics that the Zurich police adapted to by adopting a mobile, flexible, and decentralized concept of intervention. This model proved to be so successful that it was eventually established as the dominant mode of crowd control throughout the 1980s. The crucial point in Zurich's public order policies is the hierarchical inversion it implies with respect to the use of force and its consequences on the use of "hard" methods. In contrast, Geneva, having been insulated from this protest wave, continued with the "classical" doctrine of crowd control by means of police cordons and the baton charge. Despite only minor adaptations, control over the use of "hard" methods in Geneva has been consistently retained by the police hierarchy.

Notes

1. The most recent attempts, motivated by the revitalization of protest in Switzerland (Kriesi, 1981), have been proposals to create an "intercantonal mobile police force" (IMP) and a "federal uniformed police" (BUSIPO). The IMP proposal failed in the early 1970s as a result of strong resistance from several crucial cantons, one of which was Zurich. Zurich op-

posed the project for two reasons, according to evidence from the parliamentary debates: first, for political reasons, the canton did not want to become involved in the repression of the French-speaking Jura separatist movement and, second, having the largest Swiss police force would have made Zurich the largest contributor to the IMP. The BUSIPO, promoted as a federal project, was rejected in a referendum by a large majority in 1978.

2. The June 1968 Globus riot, named after the building of the Globus stores where it started, was the first violent demonstration in postwar Zurich; forty-one people were injured and about a hundred arrested.

3. In Zurich, a single elector may propose a legislative bill ("individual initiative"), which, if supported (today) by half the members of the local parliament, leads to a referendum.

4. Rubber bullets are mostly associated with a "colonial model" of protest policing and became known in Switzerland through the Jurassian conflict in the mid-1970s. Rubber bullets were used for the first time in the Jura in 1975 by the Bern police.

5. See, for example, *Neue Zürcher Zeitung*, September 1, 1980.

6. One of the authors has been able to observe the use of a concept similar to that of the TW-taxi groups in the Netherlands today. "TW" = *Tränengaswerfer* (tear gas launcher).

7. Zurich municipal police use Ford Transits; Zurich cantonal police use Volvo Breaks.

8. During the eighteen months of the Autonomen protest cycle, Zurich never requested the support of other cantons, probably because other city and cantonal police units trained in public order intervention work were dealing with the same protest cycle in their own cities.

9. For cantonal police, see the earlier quotation from April 1995. In an interview in the *Neue Zürcher Zeitung* (September 19, 1992), the chief of the municipal uniformed police stated: "In the municipal directives on nonpeaceful police intervention it is written that each intervention is led by the 'commanding officer in the street,' who, depending on the situation, can be a *group leader* or a section leader." Since a group in Zurich consists of four men, the "mission" tactics result in a highly decentralized and potentially volatile police structure.

10. The directive was titled "Intervention Strategy and Intervention Tactics in a Non-peaceful Public Order Operation."

11. Prelicz-Huber of the Ecologist Party of May 15, 1991, demanded the prohibition of rubber bullets during public order operations following an incident during a demonstration on May 1, 1991, in which a demonstrator lost an eye. Despite a rather large majority vote in favor of the ban (58 to 49), Neukomm refused to bend to the pressure in the local parliament and defended the corporatist interest of police forces, who strongly opposed any such prohibition.

12. In Switzerland, control over coercive methods does not follow the stricter French model, which elaborates a separation of powers within the police administration: only an officer of the judiciary police can order the use of force in France.

13. Compare this with Zurich, where it is not rare to have between five and ten police officers in a police intervention structure.

14. Eidgenössische Kommission für Jugendfragen (1980).

15. For the use of these concepts, see Snow and Benford (1988) and della Porta (1997).

16. See, as an illustration of the late 1960s, the lead article in the *Neue Zürcher Zeitung*, which appeared two weeks before the Globus riot in Zurich, titled "Wehret den Anfängen" (June 17, 1968).

17. By way of example, let us mention two leading articles from the *Journal de Genève*. In the first, which appeared on the front page, columnist Jacques-Simon Eggly wrote that the "principle of permanent contestation proclaimed by students should be imposed on professors and politicians.... This does not mean a return to anarchy, but much more a revitalization of democracy" (May 20, 1968). The second, an editorial by Peter Haggenmacher titled "Illegal Initiatives: Brake or Stimulus for Democracy?" is in the same vein: "It is possible that

these illegal actions do have a sense that is not negative . . . they constitute attempts to give to a political system its vital principle, the democratic idea, which is threatened by a heavy legalistic machinery" (July 24–25, 1971).

18. Interestingly enough, while the *Rechtsstaat* notion in Germany includes an extensive codification of police action, we find that the legalistic culture has not fully penetrated the police domain in Switzerland. With the exception of firearms, the use of coercive means by the police is regulated in all Swiss cantons only at the administrative level (and is not controlled by the parliament). Further, the use of force in Switzerland is based on an "intensive principle," that is, of the "general police clause," which allows the police to use force if there is a concrete threat to police goods (see Reinhard, 1993). This contrasts sharply with the "extensive" legislation in Germany, which regulates in detail the use of force at the legislative level. Some Swiss cantons do not even have a police law (Basel, Bern, and Zurich, for example). In other words, there is a strong hiatus between the Swiss-German culture on protest and the state itself, which, in our view, reveals the low legitimacy of protest in this region.

19. This point was brought to our attention by Martin Winter. Urs Saxer (1988), a Swiss constitutional jurist, mentions the availability of direct democratic instruments in the political system of Switzerland as the main reason why the Swiss Federal Court has not adopted the position of the German Federal Constitutional Court on the right to demonstrate.

20. Ladner (1994) prefers to call this a "segmented interests style."

Chapter 5

Controlling Protest in Contemporary Historical and Comparative Perspective

P. A. J. Waddington

Controlling Protest

All states seek to control protest voiced by, and dissent among, their population. Otherwise, if protest gets out of control, rebellion and revolution might follow and the very existence of the state be jeopardized. *How* that control is exercised varies enormously from occasion to occasion and from one state to another. At one extreme, the Communist Chinese regime responded to student demands for greater democracy by the massacre of Tiananmen Square. Elsewhere, such protest would be treated by the authorities as both unexceptional and unexceptionable. But even in liberal democracies there are periods during "protest cycles" (Tarrow, 1989a) when the police react forcefully to demonstrations and protest. How can we account for these variations? In this essay I want to consider, first, how protest is controlled by nonconfrontational methods in London; second, to suggest why those methods may be abandoned in some circumstances, such as the yearlong miners' strike that was marked by repeated violent clashes between police and pickets; third, to apply that analysis to a society that was typified by the violent suppression of protest—apartheid South Africa. Throughout, the theme I will be developing is that styles of policing protest are contingent on the institutional context within which they take place.

Nonconfrontational Control

It may be necessary briefly to describe the organization of public order policing generally in Britain and particularly in London. Generally speaking, policing in Britain is unitary: that is, the police in any given locality have full responsibility for law enforcement, from littering to treason. There is no separate riot police, nor national gendarmarie with special responsibility for quelling public disorder. Public order policing is simply one of the many policing tasks with which local police deal. London's Metropolitan Police is responsible for policing the capital city apart from the square mile of the City of London. Scotland Yard records approximately 150 major public order operations annually. In addition to these protest marches, demonstrations, and rallies, there are literally hundreds of minor operations such as pickets of embassies, local residents campaigning for pedestrian crossings, and the like that go unrecorded and are policed as part of the routine tasks of local divisional officers. That figure also excludes major "ceremonial" functions, such as Trooping the Colour, Beating Retreat when troops parade before royalty, and the annual Service of Remembrance to the war dead attended by a bevy of VIPs, that involve the mobilization of possibly hundreds of police officers. Almost all these major public order operations are concentrated within central London and focus around established protesting sites, notably Trafalgar Square and Hyde Park. Responsibility for policing these operations is equally concentrated on a relatively small coterie of officers at the Public Order Branch of Scotland Yard and the Special Events Office at the headquarters of the police "area" responsible for central London. The Public Order Branch has responsibility for coordinating public order operations throughout the Metropolitan Police. "Special Events" deal with the routine public order operations in central London. Thus, although there is no separate public order force, the policing of public order is specialized both functionally, through the Public Order Branch at Scotland Yard, and territorially, because of its concentration in the center of London.

Protest demonstrations in London are characteristically peaceful and minimally disruptive. Arrests of protesters are rare and disorder is rarer still (for details, see Waddington, 1994b). This is not because protesters scrupulously observe the law—they do not. Indeed, it is difficult to imagine a protest worthy of the name that does not breach some law or other. Nonarrest is a formal policy adopted by senior officers and communicated to their subordinates through briefings. On some occasions, impediments to arrest will be deliberately introduced to restrain zealous subordinates. For example, the annual Gay Pride march through central London typically includes many acts of overt homosexuality likely to provoke homophobic reactions among accompanying police officers and bystanders. Public decency laws are rarely invoked, however, because senior officers dictate that any arrest must be sanctioned by an officer of the rank of inspector or above, and must be at the instigation of a bystander who is willing to testify in court—requirements that are very difficult to satisfy. Contingency planning typically excludes the use of arrest in response to mildly disruptive behavior that is nevertheless plainly illegal. Thus, officers are instructed that if protesters stage a sit-down on the highway, officers accompanying the march should encourage marchers to continue their march, and "sit-downers" should be allowed to remain sitting down until they weary of the tactic and rejoin the march. The fact that any such sit-down inevitably involves an obstruction of the highway is carefully ignored. Even when marches are held in clear violation of the law, police prefer to accompany them rather than to attempt to prevent the continuation of the march by force. Thus, on the evening of January 15, 1991, when the ultimatum to Iraq expired and the Persian Gulf war became virtually inevitable, a wholly illegal march from Trafalgar Square to Parliament Square was not only allowed to continue but traffic was diverted to facilitate the protesters' crossing to the central area of Parliament Square, where they held their vigil.

Indeed, the law is notable by its absence in policing protest demonstrations. Despite the passage of legislation considered by civil libertarians to be draconian and to presage an authoritarian suppression of dissent (Hewitt, 1982; Wallington, 1984; Greater London Council, 1985, 1986; Staunton, 1985; Thornton, 1985; Driscoll, 1987; McCabe and Wallington, 1988; Uglow, 1988; Robertson, 1989; Ewing and Gearty, 1990), these legal powers have been little used. The 1986 Public Order Act introduced powers to impose conditions on marches and assemblies, and greatly enhanced police powers to ban marches. Yet only a handful of marches have had conditions imposed on them, and none have been banned in London, a situation that seems to extend nationwide. The reason for this disinclination to use these powers is that it is deemed not to be "worth the trouble." The "trouble" that senior officers fear bears a striking resemblance to that which dictates much of the behavior of their subordinates involved in routine patrol (Chatterton, 1979, 1983; Norris, 1989). In patrol work it takes two general forms: "on-the-job trouble" refers to problematic encounters, incidents, and tasks that police officers are routinely called on to deal with, from quelling a disturbance to suppressing a challenge to their authority; "in-the-job trouble" arises from the officer's relationship with the police and criminal justice bureaucracies and usually entails the need to account for one's actions and avoid the possibility of "comeback." In public order policing these general forms of trouble take on specific characteristics. "On-the-job trouble" arises from the potential for disorder and violence that might result in damage to property and injury to participants, including the police. There is also the problem of maintaining control over the police operation: this is always perilous, but in the mayhem of disorder is usually lost completely (a prospect shared by senior officers in more para-military police forces [see Fillieule and Jobard, in this volume]). "In-the-job trouble" takes the form of official inquiries that inevitably follow any outbreak of disorder. Senior officers are well aware that such an inquiry will review the decisions they made in the "heat of battle" from a position of calm detachment and with the benefit of hindsight. Confrontation is, therefore, a "recipe for trouble": an arrest for a minor offense could spark a riot in which damage and injury result and an inquiry that threatens careers. Hence, confrontation is avoided.

Confrontation might be abjured, but the police cannot be disinterested in maintaining control. In fact, extensive control is exercised over demonstrations and marches; protest in London is not only peaceful, but also *minimally disruptive*. Protest marchers obligingly follow a set of unofficial "standard routes" and comply with police requests to minimize traffic dislocation. How, then, do the police effect such control? They do so, not by invoking their legal powers, but by mobilizing their social and organizational resources. The 1986 Public Order Act does impose an obligation on organizers of protests to notify police of forthcoming marches, but this does not seem to be the major incentive for organizers to enter negotiations with the police in anticipation of a demonstration. Virtually all organizers approach the police well in advance of the statutory six-day notification period. What they seek is police *assistance* with the demonstration, for without that assistance it is unlikely that any march would be able to proceed through the traffic-clogged streets of London. Moreover, police belong to a network of organizations that exchange information; thus, if the organizer of a protest approaches the government department responsible for managing Hyde Park or Trafalgar Square, or a local authority with responsibility for open spaces elsewhere, these agencies will routinely inform the police who will make contact with the organizer and seek to arrange a meeting. There is no requirement on these other agencies to inform the police (nor to refuse use of open space for a demonstration if the organizer is unwilling to negotiate with police), but the protest organizer confronts the social power of the police, who are enmeshed within an informal network of reciprocal obligations.

Once negotiation begins, the aim of the police is to "win over" the negotiator so that the demonstration is conducted as far as possible in accordance with police wishes. Thus, negotiations are conducted with the amicability and good humor that would seem more appropriate to arranging a loan from a bank. Organizers are greeted with smiles and handshakes, those present are introduced, previous experiences are reminisced and mutual acquaintances recalled, refreshment is offered, jokes are exchanged and favors done. Such amicability is not the product of genuine liking for or agreement with the organizers, the campaigns they represent, or their cause. It is a studied performance designed to dispel any tension, hostility, or antagonism that the organizer might harbor. Once negotiation begins, the police stance is one of proffering help and advice—"How can we help you?"—"help you," that is, to "do it our way." Many organizers are inexperienced and so the police "organize it for them." They recommend routes along which to march, provide the telephone numbers of officials in other organizations that need to be contacted, and suggest how difficulties might be resolved. Favors are routinely offered, such as refusing to enforce the prohibition on banners being displayed in Hyde Park (one of the prime termini for protest marches in London). Such assistance can reach enormous proportions: when the National Union of Mineworkers sought a hastily arranged protest demonstration to protest at the closure of thirty-one coal mines, the police virtually arranged the whole event, including prevailing on a reluctant government department to close Hyde Park for the day, and closing surrounding streets so that hundreds of coaches bringing protesters to London could be parked in the near vicinity of the rally.

"Winning over" protest organizers might even entail antagonizing others, including those in positions of authority. On March 31, 1990, a demonstration against a new form of local taxation unofficially labeled "the poll tax" degenerated into one of the worst riots to occur in central London this century. The organizers of that march sought to hold two further demonstrations against the tax in the year that followed. The first was held in south London and it too degenerated into disorder when a follow-up demonstration to Brixton Prison to protest against those imprisoned for their part in the riot turned violent. The second march was to be held to celebrate the anniversary of the riot itself. On both occasions, police were willing to circumvent political attempts to impede or ban the holding of the demonstration. Although they had plenty of legal grounds for applying for a ban and were pressed to do so by local authorities, members of Parliament, and the government, they refused to do so. Moreover, they actively assisted the organizers in staging their demonstration. For example, on the first occasion, the organizers lacked the funds to hire open spaces at both the assembly point and the terminus. The police closed a public road adjacent to a public park in which the march could assemble at no cost to the protesters. All this was done in order to minimize the likelihood of disorder, which was always considered high. Banning the march would simply increase the sense of grievance and marginalize the organizers. Resisting pressure to ban the march would give the protest a structure and focus that the police could use to minimize the threat of disorder (Waddington, 1994a). At least, knowing where protesters would assemble and from where they would disperse allowed the police to make their contingency plans.

Attempts subtly to extend maximum control over protest do not cease once prior arrangements have been made. On the day of any demonstration, senior officers seek to perpetuate a nonconfrontational style by overtly displaying bonhomie toward the organizer and the protesters generally, keeping riot police out of the view of protesters, and controlling the progress of the march by the careful orchestration of traffic flow around it. Senior officers commanding the operation often greet the organizer of the march in full view of other protesters: hand outstretched, they address the organizer by his or her first name from some distance away, advance smiling broadly, and warmly shake the organizer's hand. They eagerly accept any invitation to brief marshals, not only to explain the respective responsibilities of marshals and police, but also to emphasize the *collaborative* relationship they want to exist between them. Any action that threatens to disrupt the appearance of amicable relations is stoutly rebuffed. Thus, attempts by the Hyde Park authorities to enforce the prohibition against serving food by Sikh demonstrators were summarily dismissed by the officer in command of one march: "Threaten a riot just to stop them serving food? They must be mad!" Reserves of police are kept hidden from the view of protesters. The police who accompany the march are dressed in their normal uniform supplemented by a high-visibility fluorescent jackets to make them and the march conspicuous to passing motorists. Their task is to keep the march contained within a "neat and tidy" boundary. Control of the march actually rests with traffic patrol officers, whose ostensible task is to shepherd the marchers through the congested streets, but who actually surround the march with a "moving wall of steel" sufficient to dissuade demonstrators from departing from the agreed-upon route.

Not only must protesters be controlled, so too must the police operation, since the greatest threat is that some ill-considered action by an officer might spark an unwanted confrontation. There are two principal ways in which senior officers seek to reduce the threat of confrontation. The first is by minimizing any provocative feature of the operation itself. Hence, the insistence that tactical reserves be kept out of view of the protesters. Moreover, those officers are not allowed to dress in riot gear lest this give the impression to any bystander that the police are expecting trouble and thereby exposing the police to the allegation that any disorder that does arise was the outcome of a self-fulfilling prophecy. The second means of minimizing provocation is to ensure, so far as possible, that the behavior of individuals conforms with the overall strategy. Great care is taken in the appointment of suitable intermediate commanders, and the system of "strategy meetings" for the larger and more problematic operations in which policy options are discussed is designed to ensure that officers responsible for various sectors and functional responsibilities share a common perspective. A more significant problem lies in ensuring that constables and sergeants understand and accept what is expected of them. Large operations are preceded by a briefing for all those in charge of "serials" (the basic squad of police consisting of eighteen constables, three sergeants, and an inspector who is in charge). Even then, senior officers lament the tenuous control they have over subordinates, who are perceived as often reluctant conscripts with little interest in, or commitment to, the operation. Even if briefings are of doubtful utility as methods of ensuring the compliance of lower ranks, they serve an essential function of "covering the backs" of senior officers in the event of "on-the-job trouble." Throughout the entire planning phase, senior officers are conscious that they might need to demonstrate their competence to a subsequent inquiry.

Through the means just described, the police in London routinely accomplish extensive, nonconfrontational control over the conduct of protest demonstrations. This is all the more remarkable given the unavoidable conflict of interest that divides almost all protesters from the police. Presumably, the aim of protest is to bring a cause or grievance to public attention and, therefore, one objective must be to maximize exposure to the public. Hence, protesters marching from Hyde Park to Trafalgar Square would achieve their aims by proceeding along Oxford Street and Regent Street—streets that would be packed with shoppers on Saturdays. In fact, *none* of the protests that I observed took this route; instead they almost invariably proceeded along the "standard route" of Park Lane and Piccadilly where there are hardly any pedestrians to attend to their protest, only passing motorists for whom the demonstration is likely to constitute an obstacle designed to provoke annoyance rather than sympathy. There is no legal restriction on proceeding along Oxford Street and Regent Street; if the police wanted to impose conditions under the Public Order Act stipulating an alternative route, they might need to justify it in court and might have difficulty doing so. They achieve their aim of diverting marches from these congested shopping streets by a number of informal stratagems. First, the Oxford Street–Regent Street route is never mentioned by the police, and if it is raised by the organizer it is dismissed as wholly impractical. Second, the "standard route" of Park Lane and Piccadilly is suggested as the most obvious course to take, so obvious that it is unquestionably assumed. Third, all this is couched in terms of what the police will be doing *for* the protesters ("We will *escort* you along here and then *take* you along there"). Fourth, if protesters press to take the Oxford Street–Regent Street route, they are presented with all manner of "practical" obstacles. Fifth, if protesters remain undaunted, the police will appeal to the demonstrators' self-interest by pointing out that it will not help their cause if they antagonize bystanders by creating traffic chaos (congestion in these invariably congested streets is automatically elevated to the condition of "chaos"). Sixth, they might even appeal for the sympathy of protesters by pointing to how the police are duty-bound to balance the interests of everyone: protesters, motorists, bystanders, traders. Having succeeded in persuading the protesters not to take the Oxford Street–Regent Street route they might further dissuade them from diverting from the agreed-upon Park Lane–Piccadilly course by artificially creating intense congestion around Marble Arch, thus physically denying access to Oxford Street. They go to these lengths, rather than a legal prohibition, because it serves their interests: they avoid both "on-the-job trouble" and "in-the-job trouble."

Overwhelmingly, then, the pattern of protest policing in London is nonconfrontational and control is exerted through negotiation with protest organizers that echoes the contemporary situation as observed in Italy by della Porta, in Paris by Fillieule and Jobard, and in Washington, D.C., by McPhail, Schweingruber, and McCarthy (all in this volume). There seems to be widespread acceptance among police throughout the liberal democratic world that cooperation is better than confrontation.

Confronting Protesters

Nonconfrontation is not, however, an invariant strategy of the police. They remain "monopolists of force in civil society" (Bittner, 1970), and on some occasions are willing to confront protesters. They do so for the same underlying reason that they normally avoid confrontation, namely, the avoidance of "trouble." To counter the risk of "on-the-job trouble," senior officers invest heavily in what they call "insurance"—large numbers of reserves waiting on standby, sometimes equipped with riot equipment. On small operations, they will be deployed in minibuses, "shadowing" the demonstration from a distance. On larger operations, they may be held in "holding centers," where they wait, usually in vain, to intervene forcefully. For example, at the annual

Notting Hill Carnival—a Caribbean street festival that attracts huge crowds but has been associated with serious crime and disorder—hundreds of offi-cers are secreted away in premises in the heart of the Carnival area, equipped with riot gear, supported by specialists armed with plastic baton rounds (col-loquially known as "plastic bullets") and squads of fully armed officers, all waiting for serious disorder to erupt. Those officers will spend time at the Public Order Training Centre—a large complex that resembles a film lot with streets lined with "buildings" that consist only of frontages—practicing ma-neuvers and tactics. The police in London, like their counterparts elsewhere, remain willing to suppress disorder by force, if necessary by a significant measure of force (Waddington, 1991). Nevertheless, confrontation with pro-testers amounted to "dying in a ditch": a last resort to be contemplated only when all else had failed (Waddington, 1993b).

Police are willing to "die in a ditch" to suppress disorder, but more sur-prisingly they are equally willing to confront protesters who threaten the dig-nity of various state institutions. A good illustration of this is the enforcement of the so-called Sessional Area around the Palace of Westminster. At the com-mencement of each parliamentary session, the Houses of Parliament pass their respective "Sessional Orders" instructing the Commissioner of the Met-ropolitan Police to keep highways in the vicinity of the Palace of Westminster free from obstruction and disorder. This "Sessional Order" is enforced by the commissioner, who issues "directions," the violation of which constitutes legally petty offenses and for which the courts have, according to the police, shown little enthusiasm to convict. Nevertheless, the police vigorously en-force the "Sessional Order"; indeed, they prohibit forms of protest that ap-pear *not* to violate the strict letter of the law. Thus, even peacefully displaying placards within Parliament Square is likely to provoke police intervention. During routine protest demonstrations, the Palace of Westminster receives special and exceptional protection with relatively large of numbers of officers assigned to guard its exterior and the Thames Division detailed to patrol the river side of the building lest any water-borne protesters daub graffiti on the terrace wall. Thus, when the militant gay rights group OutRage! sought to march from Bow Street magistrate's court to the Palace of Westminster to lobby MPs, they found the police unswervingly opposed to their entering the "Sessional Area." Quite unlike other negotiations, the organizer of the march found that the police simply refused to accommodate his plans and threat-ened prosecution if any such attempt was made. Eventually, the organizer and the police agreed that the march would be escorted to the perimeter of the "Sessional Area" and once it entered, all protesters would be arrested.

Similarly vigorous action is reserved for the policing of official government buildings. Downing Street is routinely provided with a squad of officers who act as a last line of defense if protesters climb the gates that restrict access to the residence of the prime minister. Demonstrations held in protest at the actions of a particular government department are accompanied by special protection for the building in which the department is located. Likewise, foreign embassies—especially those of friendly powerful countries, such as the United States—receive special protection. Large numbers of police were assigned to guard the American Embassy during all of the demonstrations that punctuated the period leading up to and including the Gulf war. Contingency planning made it clear that any demonstration outside the embassy would be strictly controlled. On one occasion, a demonstrator who tried to set fire to the Stars and Stripes suddenly found that the flag was torn from his grasp and the flames extinguished in a singular departure from the generally tolerant style of policing that Gulf war protests received. It was explained to me immediately afterward that U.S. diplomats find the immolation of their flag particularly objectionable and the police did not want any complaints.

What is, perhaps, most unacceptable of all to the police is desecration of a royal ceremonial. The annual Trooping the Colour, Beating Retreat, Service of Remembrance, and State Opening of Parliament are not only secular state pageants, but also major policing operations. Although most attention is concentrated on preventing a terrorist attack on either the royal family or the assembled troops, the threat of terrorism also justifies an extraordinary level of enforcement. Spectators are placed under close police surveillance from closed-circuit television and snipers on rooftops; sections of the crowd lining the route are "adopted" by police officers stationed at intervals who use the appearance of friendly conversation to identify any behavior they consider suspicious; and spectators seeking access to the near vicinity of the ceremony itself are subjected to a search. Individuals with a suspected fascination with the royal family—so-called royal watchers—are placed under special surveillance and if seen in the vicinity of the event are subject to arrest. Any attempt at protest activity is vigorously prevented. Thus, a peace protester who tried to play a pennywhistle during the two-minute silence held in respect for the war dead during Service of Remembrance was hurriedly arrested and removed from the scene. When members of OutRage! sought to hold a protest during the State Opening of Parliament, their movements were monitored by intelligence officers. As the royal procession approached, squads of specialist public order officers moved in and arrested the protesters as they attempted to unfurl their banners. Likewise, when OutRage! members tried to conclude a routine demonstration by adjourning to St. James's Park to protest outside Buckingham Palace, the police mobilized a small army of officers to defeat them.

Why are the police prepared to "die" in the proverbial "ditch" to preserve the dignity of these places and occasions? It is because those whose dignity they preserve have the capacity to cause trouble. MPs are notoriously jealous of their privileges and are prone to complain to the home secretary if they perceive those privileges being breached. The home secretary will call for a report from the Commissioner of the Metropolitan Police who, in turn, will demand an explanation from the senior officer responsible for the operation. There will, in short, be a considerable amount of "paper" to be written and, as police officers are well aware, paper "bites" (Chatterton, 1987). Members of the royal household enjoy a reputation as "troublemakers," so much so that republicanism is quite rife, almost universal, among those senior officers experienced in policing royal ceremonials. I was told with bitterness of how a member of the royal family had complained of hearing a police radio transmission during the two-minute silence at the Service of Remembrance, when the "offending" officer was merely calling for an ambulance to attend a spectator who had suffered a heart attack. Ambassadors too are able to make trouble through the Foreign and Commonwealth Office. In other words, the threat of confrontation is outweighed by the trouble that would be caused if police tolerated even the mildest desecration of these sensitive places and occasions. The avoidance of "trouble" that normally encourages tolerance is thrown sharply into reverse and now dictates confrontation.

Institutions and Confrontation

Why are police willing to confront some protesters on some occasions, but not others on other occasions? It depends on the contingencies of trouble: if it is necessary for the police to "die in a ditch" to avoid even greater trouble, then "die in the ditch" they will. Otherwise, the avoidance of trouble dictates the use of nonconfrontational methods of control. But why does trouble take the form that it does? Compelling the police to "die in a ditch" seems a pretty naked expression of social and political power and "troublemakers" are those who occupy institutionalized positions of power. Government, Parliament, and the monarchy represent the center of political power. Foreign embassies too, especially if they represent powerful allies, occupy positions of entrenched influence. Protest demonstrations inconvenience and disrupt large numbers of people: motorists become irate as they are stranded in traffic jams caused by marches, bystanders might be antagonized by the opinions expressed by protesters, businesses might suffer from the dislocation of trade (as when shops close early from fear of disorder associated with a demonstration), but those who suffer in this way simply do not have the institutionalized power to cause sufficient trouble to the police.[1]

This is not to say that police action can simply be "read off" from institutionalized power relations, for although these relations set the scene within which police act, their actions retain a measure of interpretative autonomy. Peculiar circumstances might dictate special tolerance being shown to particular acts of protest. For example, on the evening that the United Nations ultimatum to Iraq expired, and again two days later when the bombing campaign began the Gulf war, large numbers of protesters illegally gathered in Trafalgar Square and marched down Whitehall to hold a demonstration in Parliament Square, the very heart of the "Sessional Area." Again, when the National Union of Mineworkers held its demonstration against the closure of thirty-one coal mines, some demonstrators were allowed to gather on Parliament Green, opposite the Palace of Westminster, to voice their grievances. On these occasions, the political sensitivity of the issue was thought to justify exceptional tolerance. Even then, the home secretary was informed of police intentions.

The extent of police autonomy was revealed by their response to what they perceived as the abuse of institutional power for noninstitutionalized purposes. For example, when the anarchists who opposed the holding of a general election notified the police of their intention to protest, negotiations and planning began in the usual way. Trafalgar Square, however, is notionally private property administered by a government department and that department exceptionally refused permission for its use by this group. Anyone using the square without formal permission commits a criminal (but petty) offense that the police would normally feel compelled to prevent. Despite the fact that the decision to refuse permission had been taken at ministerial level, the police first objected, arguing that the square had become a venue for all manner of protests, and when this failed to persuade they decided to take no enforcement action other than to report the names of the organizers to the government department and invite the latter to prosecute. The minister was unable to compel the police to "die in a ditch" because her actions were perceived as arbitrary and partisan, and therefore beyond the institutional structure that the police felt duty-bound to defend.

On the other hand, the police are routinely willing to risk confrontation with all manner of protest groups to prevent the slightest desecration of the

Cenotaph—the memorial to Britain's war dead that stands in the middle of Whitehall. Thus, even the attempt by gay activists to place pink roses at the foot of the memorial was physically prevented by a phalanx of officers. The police need no bidding to do this; the Cenotaph has an institutionalized symbolic significance that goes virtually unquestioned. The police anticipate that the trouble that would be heaped upon them if—horror of horrors—the Cenotaph were desecrated would be enormous, even if no such desecration has yet occurred. Thus, institutional power is refracted through the lens of how the police define their task. Power does not need to be wielded by those who occupy powerful positions because it is embedded in the structure of political institutions themselves (Lukes, 1973).

The police perception of their task includes recognizing the unquestioned right of citizens to protest, despite the fact that no such right is recognized by English law. The trouble that would arise if the police were seen to treat legitimate protesters in a heavy-handed fashion is believed to be enormous. Senior officers are intuitively aware that in the event of disorder the facts of who did what and when will be contested and there will be plenty of scope for accusations of overzealousness, provocation, and heavy-handedness to be leveled against them. Democratic institutions make the policing of protest intrinsically morally ambiguous: protesters are not criminals, but citizens participating in the political process; they are not motivated by willful self-interest but are expressing a grievance or altruistically pursuing the collective good; and thus any conflict between protesters and the police tends to be a battle of moral equals in which both sides are seeking the approval of bystanders (Waddington, 1995). Thus, apart from the "on-the-job trouble" of battling with rioters, the "in-the-job trouble" of justifying the policing operation is sufficient incentive to avoid needless confrontation.

Institutional pressures are reflected in the stereotypes and attitudes that police officers routinely express about protest and protesters. "Ordinary decent protesters" and "professional protesters" abide by the unwritten rules of institutionalized protest. As such, they can be relied on not only to be peaceful but to enter into dialogue with the police and arrive at a mutual accommodation. "The opposition" of hard left and anarchist groups not only threatens violence but rarely "plays the game" (see della Porta, in this volume, for an extended discussion of these stereotypes). Groups like OutRage! also belong to "the opposition" because, despite their commitment to nonviolence, they challenge the police and refuse to restrict their forms of protest to the parameters of institutional boundaries. In some respects, OutRage! is more trouble than the hard left, since its "stunts" are so innovative that the police find it impossible to anticipate what they might do next.

Not only do institutional pressures make themselves felt at the level of operational decisions, but those decisions in turn reproduce the boundaries of institutionalized protest. When protesters meekly assemble at one of the commonly used assembly places and proceed along one of the "standard routes" to a rally at a frequently used location, they confirm that this is what protest means in the contemporary British context. Their compliance further strengthens police expectations and encourages them in believing that their demands—for example, to minimize inconvenience to other road users—are reasonable. Moreover, the fact that "vulnerable premises" and sensitive occasions remain unsullied by protest merely strengthens their inviolability. It becomes increasingly unthinkable that protesters should express dissent at the State Opening of Parliament or the Service of Remembrance, even though both occasions are suffused with political significance.

The institutional influence is so compelling that there is a detectable strain toward institutionalizing protest on any issue and voiced by any group. Thus, when the anarchist group sought to hold its "antielection" protest referred to earlier, the police went to considerable lengths to facilitate the march, although they had little fondness for the anarchists, whom they believed to have been implicated in several episodes of disorder. Likewise, OutRage!, despite the difficulties it had caused police in the past, was facilitated once it began to conduct a more conventional campaign to inject gay rights issues into the general election campaign. For example, when OutRage! sought to "out" several of Britain's war heroes by hanging female garments on statues that had been erected by a grateful nation, the police negotiated with the Ministry of Defence (on whose property some of these statues stood) for the protesters to gain access. Statues erected in the middle of major roads were surrounded by crowd control barriers and road signs to ensure that the protesters would be kept safe from passing traffic while they committed their act of secular sacrilege. So long as OutRage! was willing to "play the game," the police were more than willing to accommodate them. It was not until OutRage! broke the institutional boundaries by staging an unannounced protest at the State Opening of Parliament and a subsequent demonstration outside Buckingham Palace that relations between it and the police became strained.

Police actively seek to institutionalize protest because that enhances control. The norms associated with legitimate protest minimize disruption: protest is expected to be merely *symbolic* and thus those whom the protesters oppose will not be attacked; protesters are assumed to be appealing for public support and, therefore, will abstain from actions likely to antagonize by-standers. They and the police can, therefore, share a common purpose: a successful and *peaceful* demonstration of dissent. This trend toward the institutionalization of peaceful protest is consistent with the longer British tradition in which no one was killed in such circumstances between 1919 and 1974 (Critchley, 1970). However, police are prepared to confront those who lie beyond institutional politics or who refuse to abide by "the rules of the game." Indeed, the shifts between tolerance and repression reflect the institutional standing of protesters.

Historical Patterns in Controlling Protest

Shifts in the balance of tolerance and repression can easily be seen in the history of industrial conflict. Geary (1985) has argued that in Britain picketing and its control were transformed from "stoning and shooting" at the end of the nineteenth century to ritualized "pushing and shoving" by the 1950s. Thus, in 1893 troops fired on striking coal miners, killing two people, but by 1910 the government was refusing to deploy troops against striking miners and dispatched officers of the Metropolitan Police instead (Vogler, 1991). Even the general strike of 1926 was accompanied by surprisingly little bloodshed. As confrontation and violence declined, the police began accommodating the legitimate demands of pickets, for example, by stopping vehicles entering strikebound premises so that pickets could put their grievance to drivers in the hope of persuading them not to break the strike. Geary attributes this tacit conspiracy by the authorities and the unions to "cool it" on the picket line to wider institutional changes, especially the growth of the labor movement. The growth of the parliamentary arm of the labor movement and the legitimation of "collective bargaining" between employees and employers institutionalized class conflict. As it did so, the labor movement had no incentive to become associated with violence and disorder that would compromise its electoral appeal, nor did the authorities have any desire to appear as oppressors of the working class.

However, as Geary notes and others have elaborated (Morgan, 1987; Weinberger, 1991), this was not a unilinear process. Where the state itself felt directly under threat, either from Bolshevism or the sheer power of the unions to paralyze the increasingly integrated national economy, it was willing to confront. Thus, amid fears of revolution arising from the police strike in Liverpool in 1919, the government ordered the battleship HMS *Valiant* into the mouth of the River Mersey as a direct show of force (Weinberger, 1991).

Likewise, the creation of the Triple Alliance of coal miners, railway staff, and dockers gave the trade unions enormous potential to dislocate the economy. It was a potential to which governments of all political parties responded by covertly creating an elaborate system of civil contingency planning designed to break any such strike (Jeffery and Hennessy, 1983). This planning not only involved the police in a fully integrated role but transformed the notionally fragmented policing system in Britain into a national organization directed by government (Morgan, 1987). Tolerance toward pickets was always contingent: if the working class decided to "play hardball" by threatening the basic institutions of the state, then the state was prepared to do likewise in the interests of self-preservation.

It was not only self-preservation that motivated confrontation, for where working-class protest was organized *outside* the institutional framework, the police showed much less tolerance and often displayed the mailed fist that was otherwise obscured by the velvet glove. Thus, during the early years of the Great Depression, the communist-inspired National Unemployed Workers' Movement organized a series of "hunger marches" from northern industrial areas that suffered acutely from unemployment. These marches were subject to close surveillance, official harassment, and not a little brutality from the police (Bowes, 1966). It was not until the Trade Union Congress adopted the tactic of "hunger marches" and they were incorporated within the institutional framework of class relations that policing reverted to the more tolerant and accommodating pattern that was being established between the police and the unions.

Not only was the transformation that Geary describes not unilinear, it was also reversible. By the 1960s, a cross-party consensus had emerged that the cause of Britain's relative industrial decline was due, at least partly, to its antiquated system of industrial relations. The 1964–70 Labour government attempted to legislate reforms of the trade unions and impose restrictions on industrial action, but it was defeated. The incoming Conservative administration did impose major reforms, but this prompted serious industrial conflict and eventually resulted in electoral defeat. The succeeding Labour government reversed many of these reforms and sought to incorporate still further the unions into economic policy making, but this too terminated in acrimony, industrial conflict, and electoral defeat. It was the overtly confrontational stance of Margaret Thatcher's government that finally defeated union power.

The policing of picketing reflected these institutional changes. As the unions came under progressively greater threat of legislative restriction and faced the destruction of their industries, institutional channels for resolving conflicts became less appealing. Even before Thatcher virtually excluded unions from any influence at all over government policy, unions had less reason to "cool it" on the picket line. The symbolic power of notional picketing was less effective on an increasingly fragmented and nonunionized trucking industry. Thus, new forms of picketing began to emerge that lay outside established institutional boundaries, most notably "mass picketing" during which strikebound premises were forcibly closed by the sheer weight of numbers. This tactic was initially, and very visibly, successful during the 1972 miners' strike when strikers and their sympathizers succeeded in blockading and closing the Saltley coke works in Birmingham. It was repeated, less successfully, during several disputes in the 1980s. It was not the sole innovation in picketing methods: during the construction industry strike of the mid-1970s, squads of "flying pickets" sought to bring building sites to a halt by the use of intimidatory tactics and for which the three pickets served prison terms. The capacity of uninstitutionalized forms of industrial action to defeat government policy was, perhaps, most dramatically demonstrated in Northern Ireland, where in 1974 the "power-sharing executive" was destroyed by the Loyalist workers' strike backed by intimidation.

The police did not stand idly by as these developments took place. Although antagonism between police and pickets should not be exaggerated (most picket lines during the miners' strike of 1984–85 were peaceful [McCabe and Wallington, 1988]), police operations no longer relied on the assumption that disorder was unlikely. They responded to the humiliation of Saltley by transforming erstwhile civil defense arrangements into a public order capability and created a centralized national system for deploying police officers to locations where they might be needed. The policing of public disorder shifted in a noticeably paramilitary direction in response to violent picketing and other episodes of disorder (Jefferson, 1987, 1990, 1993; Waddington, 1987, 1991, 1993a; Hills, 1995). When confrontation reached its peak in the mid-1980s, police and pickets reverted to a pattern of confrontation distinctly reminiscent of the earlier period of "stoning and shooting," except that there was no shooting. Nor was this a unilateral act of the police alone: other components of the criminal justice system responded to the breach of institutional expectations by imposing coercive restraints on picketing. Long before the miners began their strike, the High Court had supported police action to limit the number of pickets at any entrance to affected premises;[2] codes of practice issued under employment legislation both defined mass picketing as intimidatory and indicated that no more than six pickets should be present at any entrance; during the strike, magistrates colluded with police in setting bail conditions that effectively prevented those awaiting trial from participating in picketing; the High Court ratified the use of roadblocks positioned at some distance from coal mines to prevent mass pickets from assembling; and the civil courts were used to sequestrate the funds of the miners' union, thereby destroying its capacity to fight.

Mass picketing represented serious "on-the-job trouble" for the police. The closure of the Saltley coke works demonstrated their inability to control public protest. The police were *defeated* in their core responsibility of maintaining the Queen's Peace. But just as influential was the perception that strikes were not merely a tactic in industrial conflict but an assault on the institutions of the state itself. The threat posed to the institutions of the state was clearly apparent from the experience of the loyalist workers' strike in Northern Ireland. Many commentators have sought to identify the hidden hand of government influence over the policing of the strike (Coulter, Miller, and Walker, 1984; National Council for Civil Liberties, 1984; Fine and Millar, 1985; Reed and Adamson, 1985; Sunday Times Insight Team, 1985; Loveday, 1986; McCabe and Wallington, 1988), yet they ignore the very visible finger jabbing the police and reminding them of their legal duties. Statements by the attorney general and Home Secretary, and the tenor of the debate as a whole, made it clear that the government viewed the strike as an attack on constitutional institutions. By elevating the coal strike to a de facto, albeit not de jure, state of emergency, the government dug a proverbial mile-wide "ditch" in which the police felt obliged to "die."

It would be inaccurate, however, to portray the strike as one of uniform confrontation between police and pickets. In those places and on those occasions when the police were able to negotiate with union representatives, little violence occurred. In Derbyshire, for example, police donned riot equipment on only two occasions, because they and the local union representatives had established a modus vivendi (Leonard, 1985). When I briefly visited the area during the height of the strike I was amused to see pickets making their way through police cordons in order to occupy their designated positions from which to hurl abuse at strikebreakers. The cockpit of violence was the South Yorkshire area, in which the union seems to have been particularly unwilling to liaise with the police (Wright, 1985; Waddington, Jones, and Critcher, 1989). Denied the opportunity to exert control by nonconfrontational methods, the police resorted to coercive methods.

Thus, whether confrontational methods are employed or avoided by the police varies according to the contingencies of trouble. Normally, these contingencies favor nonconfrontation: there is a trend toward institutionalization.

However, the wider institutional framework within which the police operate may change, causing a shift in the contingencies of trouble and encouraging, if not obliging, police to "die in a ditch." Yet the oscillations of public order policing between benign tolerance and coercive repression have pivoted around a relatively tranquil center of gravity in Britain. The recent adoption of paramilitary tactics and equipment has only amounted to a modest step toward methods of riot control considered unexceptional throughout much of the world (Waddington, 1991). What, then, accounts for comparative differences between the general styles of public order policing to be found in different jurisdictions?

Habitual Confrontation: The Case of Apartheid South Africa

In some jurisdictions, the institutional framework is such that the contingencies of trouble are almost permanently skewed toward confrontation and violence. This seems to have been largely true throughout the British Empire, where the police had the task of imposing unwanted colonial authority on resentful and rebellious populations. They did so by consistently aggressive militaristic methods (Ahire, 1991; Anderson and Killingray, 1991, 1992). Brewer has argued that apartheid South Africa represented the last vestige of this style of policing—what he calls "internal colonialism" (Brewer, 1994). Nowhere was this repressive style of policing more apparent than in the control of political dissent (Steytler, 1989; Brogden and Shearing, 1993; Cawthra, 1993). As a succession of official inquiries confirms (see, for example, Kannenmeyer [1985] and Goldstone [1990]), police often chose to confront otherwise peaceful protesters and to resort to force at an early stage. Police evidence to the multinational panel convened by the Goldstone Commission (Heymann, 1992) indicated that they saw no alternative but to confront any demonstration that had not received official permission. The attitude seemed to be that they would use as much force as was necessary to prevent illegal protest from continuing: if protesters failed to disperse after a warning, CS smoke was used; if this failed to disperse the crowd, police fired birdshot; if this did not achieve the aim of dispersal, then resort would be made to high-velocity rifle fire.

No apparent attempt was made to negotiate with protesters or those who might be able to influence them. For example, in the immediate aftermath of the Boipatong massacre, rioting erupted as township residents attacked the police, who seemed more intent on preventing the residents from seeking revenge than on detecting the perpetrators of the murders. Early the following morning, a clergyman who was also a local representative of the African National Congress (ANC) arrived at the township and attempted to intervene to prevent further violence. According to police testimony at an international inquiry on behalf of the Goldstone Commission (P. A. J. Waddington, 1992), this "community leader" was unceremoniously told to depart. If he wished to intervene, he was told, he should do so through the established community relations channels. Thus, the police squandered the valuable resource volunteered by a "community leader."

This might seem like a gross, but all too common, lack of imagination on the part of a habitually authoritarian and repressive police force, but that would fail fully to understand how the South African Police (SAP) operated. For there were undoubtedly occasions when they could act with tact and sensitivity. Of course, tact and sensitivity were usually reserved for white protesters and members of the Inkatha Freedom Party, prompting accusations of naked discrimination. But there were occasions when protests by other sections of the population were dealt with in a comparably sensitive fashion. I witnessed one such occasion during the investigation of the policing of the Boipatong massacre (P. A. J. Waddington, 1992). A few days after the international investigation team arrived in the area, the residents of the township and squatter camp wished to march to the hostel whose occupants had apparently committed the massacre and to demand its demolition. The police, not unreasonably, feared a confrontation between the township residents and the hostel dwellers. They succeeded in negotiating an arrangement in which this illegal march terminated some distance from the hostel, whereupon a senior executive of the steel company ISKOR (the owners of the hostel) received a petition in front of the assembled world's press. This was, in other words, a nonconfrontational solution that would not have looked out of place in any liberal democratic nation. What this single instance demonstrates is that the SAP were able to negotiate nonconfrontational arrangements when they chose to do so; evidently, they *abstained* from doing so on many other occasions, not least when President F. W. de Klerk visited Boipatong and the police shot several demonstrators dead.

Why, then, did the SAP habitually confront protesters rather than negotiate with them? Again, the answer lies in the contingencies of trouble that reflect the wider institutional framework within which policing took place. Trouble, for the SAP, was of enormous proportions. If a demonstration in central London got out of hand, as did the protest against the poll tax in March 1990, the consequences would be a riot. Property might be damaged, people might injured, some might even be killed, but it was not conceivable that the government would be overthrown. This was not the case in apartheid South Africa (or the colonial regimes of the British Empire). Eight percent of the population held the remainder in subjection through unrelenting oppression. If that oppressive shield were allowed to slip, power might be wrenched from the grasp of the white minority, as had happened elsewhere in Africa. On the other hand, little trouble accrued from confronting members of the subject population. They were not citizens with rights to be respected; on the contrary, the ANC was an enemy engaged in a "total onslaught" against the regime. Protest, especially within the townships, was not an institutionalized expression of specific grievances but an integral part of the ANC's strategy of making the townships ungovernable. As analyses of killings by the police have repeatedly demonstrated (Haysom, 1987; Hansson, 1989; Weitzer and Beattie, 1994), the brutality of the SAP was matched only by the supine stance of the courts in those rare instances when they were asked to adjudicate on police conduct. During the state of emergency that covered the final phase of apartheid, police officers were actually indemnified if they used force in "good faith." The Boipatong inquiry discovered that police incident logs merely required officers to enter the number of shots fired, apparently without any further requirement to account for their actions. Hence, the failure to suppress dissent by force threatened the most enormous trouble, but the use of force—including lethal force—was virtually trouble-free.

In the absence of incentives to the contrary, members of the SAP did not develop competence in the peaceful management of public protest. For example, the SAP correctly anticipated that a funeral of six people killed by police during riots and to be held at Uitenhage would attract a large crowd of mourners and protesters. The police decided to prevent such a crowd from attending the funeral. Not only was this overtly confrontational, but, having decided to confront any crowd that might appear, the police operation was remarkable for its ineptitude. Only two large armored personnel carriers ("Casspirs") holding approximately twenty officers each and a Land Rover were deployed to intercept a predictably large crowd; one of the Casspirs was deployed without a functioning radio and was, therefore, unable to report on the mood of the crowd at an early stage; another squad was on patrol in the area but operated independently; the most senior officer in command of the operation held the rank only of lieutenant; and the officers had been denied the use of low-lethality munitions as a matter of policy made by the local commander. When the crowd appeared, the Casspirs blocked the road, and the lieutenant stood on top of one of the vehicles and ordered the crowd to disperse. When the crowd refused, the lieutenant fired a warning shot, which provoked a woman protester to throw a single stone; the lieutenant replied with the order to "Fire!" Twenty people were killed by the fusillade that followed (Kannenmeyer, 1985). The inquiry into the killings revealed the most appalling catalog of brutal incompetence, but it is only symptomatic of the general style of apartheid policing; for the most telling feature of the Kannenmeyer inquiry was its outcome—no police officers were prosecuted or disciplined. Detailed planning for public order operations was absent because, unlike the police in London, "backs" did not need to be "covered."

The SAP were not uniformly incompetent and confrontational, however. When the contingencies of trouble demanded it, they too could win over protesters and negotiate mutually acceptable arrangements. This was illustrated by the sensitive policing of the illegal demonstration held in the wake of the Boipatong massacre referred to earlier. The massacre and the subsequent collapse of the peace accord had focused international attention on this otherwise obscure township. The police themselves were under international investigation amid accusations of complicity in the massacre. The township residents enjoyed the status as victims of the massacre that, if it did not confer rights, at least attracted sympathy. The police had been severely criticized for their mishandling of President de Klerk's visit to Boipatong. To provoke yet another violent confrontation would cause considerable "on-the-job trouble," with which the SAP were singularly unfamiliar. With the reversal of the contingencies of trouble, the SAP reversed their habitual style and negotiated a mutually acceptable arrangement with the township dwellers.

It is pretty clear that in acting as they generally did, the police were reflecting the imperatives of the institutional framework within which they operated. The precarious hold over the subject population was maintained by coercive means, so it is little surprise that the police resorted to coercion in policing public order. In doing so, they were abiding by the institutions of apartheid just as assuredly as the London police abide by democratic institutions in habitually using nonconfrontational methods. Those whom the police oppressed had little opportunity to exert influence over their oppressors. The mass media did not publicize allegations of brutality and the white electorate seemed unconcerned at the oppressive activities of the police. The courts condoned violent oppression and the government supported it (Cawthra, 1993).

Conclusion

Public order policing in contemporary London seems to fit the pattern observed elsewhere in modern Europe and the United States and described by other contributors to this volume. The police seek to avoid confrontation by tactics of negotiation and accommodation. I am unpersuaded, however, that this is part of the secular trend toward a more democratic style of policing that della Porta (in this volume) hopefully detects. For, as Reiner (also in this volume) points out, the recent history of public order policing in Britain could be interpreted as a shift toward "paramilitarism." I would want to insist that styles of public order policing are *contingent* on the institutional context in which they take place. In liberal democracies, there is a preference for non-confrontational methods and a trend toward institutionalization because this is relatively trouble-free. The police are also competent in achieving their goals by nonconfrontational means. On the other hand, when the established social, political, and economic institutions are perceived to be under threat, institutional pressures will encourage more confrontational methods of public order policing, as happened in Britain during the miners' strike of 1984–85.[3] As Reiter (in this volume) notes, once the authorities in Florence defined communists as "the *enemy*," the local police reverted to the overtly repressive tactics from which they had abstained since the end of fascism. The police in authoritarian societies, such as apartheid South Africa, habitually confronted protesters because the precarious grasp on power by the white minority meant that the existence of the state was perpetually under threat and the institutional structure of apartheid excluded nonwhite protest, thus devaluing any harm that was inflicted on black opponents of the regime. The SAP did not need to be competent in how they dealt with public order because they could be confident that they could shoot their way out of any difficult situation with impunity.

The implication of this analysis is that confrontational or nonconfrontational policing is a reflection of the politics of inclusion and exclusion. Contrary to what Wisler and Kriesi (in this volume) argue, I would maintain that open democratic systems are *more* (not less) tolerant of public demonstrations. What is not tolerated is the threat or actuality of violence, or indeed of significant disruption. As Fillieule and Jobard (also in this volume) note, protesters are expected to abide by "the rules of the game." The reason that Britain succeeded in maintaining relative civil peace during the last quarter of the nineteenth and first three-quarters of the twentieth centuries was not because Britain enjoyed a "*police* advantage" (Bowden, 1978), but because of a *political* settlement between labor and capital. When a similar settlement was reached in the United States through New Deal legislation, the hitherto violent history of labor relations was likewise transformed (Taft and Ross, 1979). The challenge that faces all political systems is to incorporate groups and issues into institutional channels. In Britain, the exclusion of black people has exacerbated police race relations, a tinder that has ignited rioting on several occasions.

Inclusion is not a panacea, however. First, since most social movements arise from beyond institutional politics, it is likely that they will not benefit from institutionalization in their initial stages, nor might they wish to. Tarrow (1989a) has pointed to how "early risers" give the initial impetus to a protest cycle by the use of innovative methods of protest that catch the authorities unprepared and bring the cause that is being pursued to a wider audience. Reciprocally, it is unlikely that the authorities will respond to "early risers" with benign equanimity. Disavowal of institutional constraint is likely to be met with coercive suppression by the police. Second, there may be issues and groups that it would be wrong to incorporate into constitutional politics; for example, it would be quite wrong, in my view, to treat racism and racist groups as respectable participants in a liberal democracy. Third, issues and groups might also be irreconcilable: "pro-choice" and "pro-life" groups might find it impossible to compromise, just as ethnic groups might refuse to accommodate each other. It is unlikely that conflict, grievances, and causes will disappear. Whether liberal democratic states will continue to be able to incorporate otherwise excluded groups and issues is the most pressing issue confronting those who value democratic freedoms.

Notes

1. The particular sources of institutionalized power may be very context-specific. For example, provincial police forces may be far more susceptible to the influence of local businesspeople. For example, a firm transporting live animals for slaughter on the continent of Europe obtained a High Court injunction against the police, who had sought to limit exports in order to minimize the protests that it had occasioned (see *Police Review*, August 4, 1995). It is simply that in central London, the hub of government in Britain, political institutions are paramount.

2. *Piddington v. Bates* [1961] 1 W.L.R. 162; 105 S.J. 110; [1960] 3 All E.R. 660, D.C.

3. A similar process of oscillation between relatively tolerant and coercive policing strategies was evident in Germany and Italy from the 1950s to the 1990s (della Porta, 1995).

Part II

Policing Protest in Young Democracies

Chapter 6

Police and Public Order in Italy, 1944–1948: The Case of Florence

Herbert Reiter

This essay is based on a case study of the public order interventions of the police in the city and province of Florence in the immediate postwar years. Unlike the situation in the south of Italy, in Florence the resistance movement against fascism and the German occupation was a political and military reality. The consequences of the liberation of the city in August 1944, however, were not the same as those encountered later on in the north, in particular as far as political violence and the competition posed for the state police by a "partisan police" was concerned (Storchi, 1995). The central region of Tuscany and more specifically the province of Florence, however, did form a stronghold of the Communist Party during the postwar period. The archival sources used are predominantly the files of the *questura* (provincial police headquarters). For this reason, I deal with the national state police, which report to the Ministry of the Interior in Rome and are considered "the government's police." The carabinieri (see Oliva, 1992), as the traditionally royal national police force, form part of the regular army, and are dealt with only inasmuch as they are referred to in the *questura* files.

During the transition period from a fascist dictatorship to a democratic republic, the Italian police maintained a very high level of continuity in their organization, personnel, tasks, and powers of intervention, the latter defined in the police laws of 1926 and 1931, which stayed on the books until the mid-fifties.[1] Although it did not prevent adaptations to the new situation, the fact that the Italian police had inherited a great part of their personnel and legal dispositions from the old regime undoubtedly influenced police response in public order cases. Additional influences were certain characteristics of the long-term Italian traditions in the field of public security, as well as the overall political situation. In a first phase of disorientation (1944–45) the police were largely conditioned by the weight of their fascist past and visibly unsure about how to react to public protest. Police intervention during the second phase of transition (1946) was determined by the internal contradictions of the governments of "antifascist unity," which proved too heterogeneous to indicate clear objectives in the face of growing social unrest. These clear objectives were defined during the third phase of "cold" civil war (1947–48), when the police were deployed as a fighting force in order to defeat an internal political enemy, if need be in a situation of "hot" civil war. This development was determined by the political situation, but also in keeping with the traditional Italian police style. The difficulties of the police in the first and second phases can be explained in part by the fact that the type of intervention they were capable of providing was not the one asked for by the political power.

The Traditional Police Style and the Organization of the Police Forces in Italy

During the transition period, the high level of continuity of the Italian police with the old regime was accompanied by an almost complete absence of a reform effort in the field of public security on the part of the responsible Italian politicians and administrators.[2] Consequently the dominant police style in Italy was not questioned. The tradition of the "forces of order" in Italy was characterized by centralization and militarization, following the model of a "state police" dominant on the European continent. Even within the logic of this police model, however, it is surprising to what extent the Italian police privileged the maintenance of public order over the protection of the safety of the citizens. The Italian police literature of an official or semiofficial character theorized about a "general public order," relative to the "primordial goods necessary for the cohabitation of the collectivity," which was supposed to find its concrete expression in a "public order in the strict sense," that is, in the "defense of the normal course of the everyday life of the collectivity," in public safety, public morality, and public health (Roddi, 1953, 7). In theory, public order was not to be imposed by force, nor was it to suffocate "customs, religion, national spirit, rights of the citizens." Significantly, the main reason given was not that such intervention might infringe on the human and democratic rights of the citizens, but rather that "in such a case public tranquillity would be ephemeral and precarious and society in permanent unrest" (Salerno, 1952, 600).

Behind this verbosity stood a highly politicized practice of internal security policies. Even before fascism, the Italian police were known more for being the police of the government in a political sense than for effective crime control. The methods foreseen for the defense of the "general public order" were primarily "observation" and *vigilanza* (surveillance). The Italian police were in fact convinced of their ability to recognize and eliminate all potential causes of danger for public order with a perfect and inconspicuous control of all aspects of public life. Consequently, a large part of police activity was devoted to the gathering of information, especially political information, rationalized as an emphasis on prevention (Roddi, 1953, 59). This large-scale surveillance was accompanied by a massive deployment of policemen for guard duty at public buildings—the official term for the rank-and-file policeman in Italy was in fact *guardia*, and not an equivalent to the English "patrolman," a term that indicates an emphasis on patrols.

Contrary to official and semiofficial literature, police action for the maintenance of public order was far from restricted to "prevention." Postunification Italy endured a high degree of political and social tension, with its governments and security forces reacting with exemplary harshness to popular protest (Canosa, 1976, 27ff., 83; Fiorentino, 1978; Jensen, 1991). Within this framework, however, the state police accumulated a largely selective and therefore limited experience in the handling of demonstrations, concentrated on "preventive" measures (e.g., the large-scale provisional arrest of the known "subversives") and the command functions of their functionaries. Before World War I, the dominant role in the control of public order continued to be played by the army. This indicates that the process of professionalization of the Italian police was not very advanced (Dunnage, 1989). Despite the growing reluctance of the army to fulfill internal security functions—the deployment of soldiers for public order duty hampered their own professionalization—the situation changed only after World War I, when drafted soldiers were no longer deemed politically reliable. During the few years up to Mussolini's march on Rome, a reorganization of the police was undertaken, in order to prepare them for the exclusive responsibility in the control of public demonstrations. This reorganization emphasized centralization and militarization (Donati, 1977). In the twenty years of fascist rule, the police force was undoubtedly one of the pillars of the regime, but it largely maintained its traditional style without degenerating to the extent of its German counterpart.[3]

Only in the postwar period did the control of public demonstrations become the exclusive responsibility of the Italian police forces and a very important aspect of their work. Confronted with this challenge, they referred back to their specific tradition, reinforcing both centralization and militarization, that is, two organizational characteristics that tend to facilitate "harsh" interventions in the control of protest.[4] Certain aspects of the resistance movement and of the war of liberation also contributed to this development. The push toward centralization was reinforced by the forces contrasting the national government, those of a political character, for example, the Committees of National Liberation (CLN), but also by those of "superior force," for example, the confusion and the contradictions of war and civil war. The strengthening of the military aspects of the police was favored by the tradition of the rival police force of the carabinieri, but also by the military characteristics of the resistance movement. The fact that the police, for example, after the liberation of Florence, were immediately integrated into the war effort had the same effect. Even more important in the long-term perspective was the ceiling set by the Allies for the strength of the Italian army in the armistice and later the peace treaty. It is also important to emphasize that the centralization and militarization of the police could appear as a necessity in the confused situation following September 8, 1943—this, in fact, was the argument used by the Italian governments to counter the perplexities of the Allies—and that it could be framed as a modernization of the old police corps.[5]

The concrete response of the Italian police in their public order interventions was also influenced by other organizational characteristics. Especially in the first and second phases indicated earlier, some of these characteristics were revealed as weaknesses, in contrast with the image of force transmitted by terms like "centralization" and "militarization."

1. The dominant role of the political aspect in the daily work of the police on all levels emerges clearly from the monthly reports on the general situation by the police stations to the *questore* and by the *questore* to the prefect. Together with the high degree of submission to the political powers characteristic of the Italian police, it made a strong political prejudice in the public order interventions more than likely. For a police force of these characteristics, however, the absence of clear political directives seems to have had a paralyzing effect in the field of public order interventions.

2. Numerous problems were inherent in the very structure of the public security system in Italy, the main one consisting in the coexistence of a strong centralization with multiple conflicts of competence within the state police and between them and the other police forces, especially the carabinieri. These problems emerge in an exemplary way if one looks at the position of the *questore*.[6]

3. In its specific Italian form, the military organization of the Corpo delle Guardie di P.S., at least up to 1946, constituted an element of weakness rather than of strength. Characterized by a considerable hierarchization and by a deployment of personnel more oriented toward service in a military fortress than in a modern city, it resulted in tension inside the corps and a chronic lack of personnel. Police leaders tried to explain both, not very convincingly, by pointing to the high number of auxiliary policemen and presumed Communist infiltration. The situation provoked by the organizational deficiencies was further aggravated by the material privations of the state administration as a whole, which, however, were more an Italian tradition than a consequence of the war.

The reaction of the government to these organizational weaknesses consisted not in a reform, but in an impressive rise in the number of personnel, which in fact managed, at least in part, to camouflage them.

The Police and Public Order in Florence

As the concept of "public order" affirmed in the official and semiofficial literature was very extensive, so was the one applied in practice (Corso, 1979, 133ff., 213ff.; Canosa, 1976, 142ff.). The files of the Florentine *questura* show that *ordine pubblico* served as a justification for police intervention for a variety of reasons. Intervention was resorted to not only for "incidents" of a legal or illegal nature, but in principle for all occasions where a crowd, organized or not, gathered. For example, each year on November 2, the day of the commemoration of the dead, policemen were deployed for surveillance of all Florentine graveyards.[7]

In the following, I will concentrate on police intervention during demonstrations, many of which were spontaneous. The immediate postwar period saw numerous protest marches in the city of Florence. Already in the autumn of 1944 the scarcity of food and fuel had led to protests, to a large extent carried out by women. From the spring of 1945, with the return of the soldiers, partisans, and prisoners of war, the unemployment problem became more and more pressing. Throughout the postwar period this problem led to numerous demonstrations, organized by official organizations like the trade unions and by informal associations. From the summer of 1947 onward, the political debate became increasingly heated, a tension that made itself felt during demonstrations and that reached a peak with the general strike following the assassination attempt on Palmiro Togliatti, the leader of the Communist Party.

Phase 1 (1944–45): Disorientation

After the fall of fascism, signs of a material, organizational, and personnel crisis were evident in all Italian internal security forces, including, although in a minor way, the carabinieri (Sannino, 1985, 431). In Florence, the disorientation of the police—which could, as other situations in Italy show, also degenerate into interventions of excessive harshness—translated into a considerable tolerance toward protest events. Above all, the parties and movements connected with the fight for the liberation of the city enjoyed a great degree of freedom, which would not repeat itself in the postwar period. During the months following the liberation in August 1944, the *questura* issued numerous ordinances regarding conferences and assemblies of these groups, which contained the order to escort spontaneous marches, should they form, that is, not to intervene in a repressive way against demonstrations that, on the basis of the law, were illegal because they lacked the necessary authorization by the *questore*. At the same time, the self-representation of the *questura* tried to project an image of the Florentine police as part of the resistance movement, for instance, by underlining the contributions of the police to the liberation of the city at the annual *festa della polizia* in October 1944.[8]

The tolerance of the *questura* toward demonstrations of the parties and movements of the resistance (i.e., those who in an opportunistic way could be interpreted as the "new bosses") was, however, not without ambiguity and did not extend to all protesters and all forms of protest. In all the different police forces, for instance, anticommunism was deeply ingrained.[9] In its interventions against spontaneous protests, without known and politically legitimated organizers, the Florentine *questura* already in the autumn of 1944 revealed two fundamental aspects of its public order philosophy, which were clearly radicated in the Italian police traditions: a profound mistrust toward demonstrations in general, and a tactic based on extensive surveillance in order to suppress protest at an initial stage (*sul nascere*).

The *questura*'s understanding of demonstrations was based on the conviction that protests were legitimate only if they were meant to draw the attention of the government to a problem it had overlooked. The protests against the scarcity of staple commodities that were multiplying in the city and province of Florence during the autumn of 1944 could be interpreted in this way only initially. With reference to the "hunger marches," the *questura* in fact affirmed in a communiqué dated November 20, 1944, that the competent organs, in agreement with the Allies, were doing their best to remedy the shortage of indispensable goods. "In order to achieve this goal, however, the population must cooperate, keeping the most perfect tranquillity and conserving complete trust in the authorities that have assumed such a heavy burden."[10]

After one of the "hunger marches" in October 1944 had managed to reach the *prefettura* building without any intervention on the part of the police forces, the *questore* issued a general order concerning demonstrations.[11] The ambitious demands he made on the police developed logically from the application of the traditional Italian protest policing style. The police leadership expected perfect control of the territory and of its citizens, repeatedly insisting on the importance of this point in its correspondence with the police stations. This "complete" information on all risks to public order was intended to enable the suppression of all potentially dangerous situations at an initial stage. The available forces were to be used *in massa*. If they failed to disperse the crowd, the police were to concentrate on the defense of government buildings.

The order of October 1944 set down the principles of the tactic, which was to be practiced by the Florentine police against demonstrations in the coming years. During the first phase, however, the police were not able to satisfy the demands of their leadership. They did not manage to prevent further "hunger marches," and even in numerically favorable circumstances failed to disperse the crowd. There were several reasons why the expectations of the police leadership were not realistic. With the liberation of the city, still a very recent event, the atmosphere of resistance remained strong, even dominant. The protest group (Florentine housewives) and the reason for the demonstration (an undeniable shortage of food and other essential items) were also significant factors. We may assume that individual policemen felt sympathy for or solidarity with the demonstrating women. However, the most important element in explaining the initial tolerance of the Italian police toward demonstrations may be traced to their delegitimation because of their fascist past and their disorientation regarding their role in a democratic society. Even though the police were officially integrated into the coalition against Nazifascism, in practice they were on probation. Their delegitimation is already perceptible in the attempts to project an image close to the resistance movement at the *festa della polizia* in 1944: the date of the celebration, October 18, referred to the renewed foundation of the state police by Mussolini.[12] In the months immediately following the liberation of Florence, any sanction or physical coercion—for instance, the use of batons—inevitably led to protests and provoked the unanimous condemnation by all political parties and local newspapers, which attacked the police for using "fascist methods." The few cases of "energetic" intervention against demonstrators had direct negative consequences on the relationship between the public and the police, thus intensifying the disorientation within the police ranks. The considerable tolerance of the Florentine *questura* toward demonstrations, which we have observed for this first phase immediately after the liberation from fascism, therefore has to be defined as a tolerance out of weakness.

The long-term effects of the disorientation of the police were limited, however, because public criticism of single episodes, although harsh, was not combined with a fundamental critique of the Italian police system. The political parties of the resistance movement stigmatized these episodes as a relapse into fascist methods, but attributed the causes exclusively to an inadequate *epurazione* (purge of the state apparatus of fascist personnel). They did not criticize the tactic used by the police in public order interventions, nor did they discuss their relationship to the population, nor did they demand a profound reform of the system of public security, if not with very generic slogans.[13] It is important to stress, however, that large parts of the population, and in the immediate postwar period also the majority of politicians and the press, routinely made the connection with the fascist system when clashes between the police and the public occurred. The possibilities of success for the attempts of the Florentine *questura* to project the image of the police as a significant part of the resistance were therefore scarce. These attempts did not last long, in any case: already in the spring of 1945 the Ministry of the Interior intervened against those functionaries who, according to its own interpretation, were too closely linked to the resistance, that is, with the Comitato Toscano per la Liberazione Nazionale (CTLN).[14]

Phase 2: Transition (1946)

The most active protest group by far in the second phase was the unemployed. Starting in the second half of 1945, increasingly frequent and disruptive demonstrations took place, which put the police under pressure simply by their frequency. Repeatedly, the local commands of the police and the carabinieri proved unable to put the requested number of men at the disposition of the *questore*. Initially, the intervention of the police forces was still conditioned by disorientation, clearly indicated by the reports of the responsible *funzionari* on single demonstrations, so different one from the other as to make it impossible to reconstruct the chain of events. This continuing disorientation resulted in continuing moderation.

The development of a demonstration of the "common" unemployed in Florence on May 2, 1946, which finished with the invasion of the prefecture, demonstrates the persistence of organizational, operative, and tactical problems, only some of which were connected with short-term material deficiencies. Although the police had collected sufficient information to foresee a violent demonstration—the "common" unemployed had been excluded from certain programs in favor of unemployed partisans and veterans and on this day were expecting a reply to their requests by the prefect (who, however, had left for Rome)—no adequate measures were taken. Both the police and the carabinieri command sent fewer men as a reinforcement to the prefecture than requested by the *questore*. The organization of the riot squad (*reparto celere*) of the police was so superficial that its intervention was delayed until after the invasion of the prefecture: the officer in command had to assemble all the men he could find in the barracks, including those who had just gone off the night shift. Even though the *questore* did sent repeated requests, the carabinieri refused to send their mobile squad as a reinforcement.[15]

During the year 1946, however, there was a visible shift toward a less tolerant attitude toward demonstrations. The public order interventions of the police indicate that the *questura* was trying to put into practice a policy of normalization and legalization. By doing so, it followed the instructions of the governments led by Alcide De Gasperi, who had promised a firmer policy against crime but also against political and social unrest. A first "decisive" intervention on the part of the Florentine *questura* against the unemployed dates, in fact, from January 31, 1946, when the police attempted to disperse a demonstration with armored cars mounted with 20 mm machine guns. This intervention failed, however, and public order in this case, as in similar ones during the "transition" phase, was reestablished not by the police, but by the intervention of leading members of the trade unions and the Communist Party who managed to calm the crowd.[16] To these failures the police did not respond with a revision of their tactic, which on the contrary was confirmed by interior minister Romita, but with an increase in the number of men and the deployment of heavy equipment, increasingly put at their disposal.[17] This supply of heavy equipment of a military type was judged unnecessary for police purposes by the Allied Commission and led it to discuss whether the Corpo delle Guardie di P.S., the state police, was to be considered an integral part of the army as far as the limitations on its size set by the peace treaty were concerned.[18]

It was due to a lack of political cover if, even after this strengthening of the police, their public order interventions remained mostly unsuccessful. The governments of the great coalition that dominated Italian politics in this period—with a Christian Democratic Party (DC) for which the restoration of public order was of great importance, and a Communist Party (PCI) with a far more uncertain position (Canosa, 1976, 114, 122)—was too heterogeneous to indicate clear objectives. Although the official policy of the government was to check political and social disorder, this heterogeneous political constellation seems to have discouraged especially the local administrators and police officers from issuing clear orders for an "energetic" intervention to the police, given the risk if not the certainty of criticism from influential members of the coalition. With the passing of time, however, the grand coalition entered into a crisis, and public order was one of the problems dividing the coalition partners. The official organizations of the working-class movement proved increasingly less able to control the radicalized unemployed, who were more and more organized in an autonomous and spontaneous way. At the same time, the clientele of the DC expressed increasing exasperation at the continuing unrest. In this situation, the police and the political leadership at both the local and the national level blamed the public order problems on agents provocateurs, who were described as *facinorosi* (ruffians), common criminals, black marketeers, and, above all, fascists.[19]

It was against the autonomously organized "common" unemployed, stigmatized as undemocratic by the theory of the fascist agents provocateurs, that the Florentine *questura* reinforced the military and offensive aspects of its tactic. The de-escalating contents of its ordinances were in fact progressively contradicted by a massive deployment of men (to be used *in massa*) and by an increasing use of heavy equipment of a military type.[20] As a logical consequence of this offensive deployment, the police increasingly had to choose between the alternative to limit themselves to the defense of government buildings or to break up demonstrations forcibly. If they intervened with any intention other than that of dispersing the crowd, they provoked violent incidents.

An example of this dilemma is a demonstration in Florence on July 20, 1946, by the "common" unemployed, from which the official workers' organizations had dissociated themselves. Throughout the morning, the police restricted themselves to the defense of public buildings, giving the demonstrators free reign of the city center, one reason being that the initial appearance of armored cars ordered out to patrol the streets had provoked violent reactions. Only after a warning from the prefect (communicated to a delegation of the demonstrators in the presence of the local leadership of the trade unions) and an appeal by the (Communist) mayor had remained without effect was the order given to disperse the crowd. The intervention of the police, however, provoked violent incidents, and public peace was reestablished only after the intervention of the secretary of the local Communist federation, who promised a united demonstration of workers and unemployed people for the near future, thus pointing out to the "common" unemployed a possibility of overcoming their isolation. If at first sight the development of this demonstration and the police intervention seem to have followed a known pattern, a closer look reveals important changes. The attempt on the part of the demonstrators to occupy the trade-union headquarters and the failure of the mayor's appeal clearly indicate the growing difficulty of the organizations of the working-class movement to combine their presence in government with a control of social protest. On the other hand, the articles in the local press reflect the exasperation of one area of public opinion, especially the shopkeepers, with the continuous disturbances of normal life. Moreover, the harsh intervention of the police was not criticized in the terms used since the liberation—that is, as a relapse into fascist methods—but because of its failure: the police had intervened too late, and then with too much violence and without making distinctions.[21]

The development of the demonstration on July 19, 1946, and the criticism of the police produced an immediate and definite hardening in the attitude of the Florentine *questura* toward demonstrations. The *questura* further increased the military and offensive aspects of its tactic for public order intervention. For the protests of the unemployed it issued practically identical orders, which indicate the following model: groups of uniformed policemen with the task of suppressing acts of violence were concentrated in several public buildings. Plainclothes policemen, who were to patrol the city and to refer all suspicious movements, were assigned to these groups. Also, all police stations and the political office received the order to collect information. Large units of the police and the carabinieri, armed with automatic weapons and armored cars or tanks with heavy machine guns, were kept in reserve for eventual serious disorders. The invitation to "intervene with tact" and to avoid useless confrontation vanished from the orders of the *questura*. Apart from the collection of information, the tactic of the *questura* foresaw only direct confrontation with the demonstrators, and in this context its orders presented the whole city as a possible enemy.

The move toward a "cold civil war tactic" during 1946 is evident not only with regard to groups like the unemployed, who might have been seen as particularly dangerous, but also with regard to those who earlier could count on special consideration, such as the housewives. In September 1946, together with firmer action against the black market, the police intervened in a massive way against the protests denouncing the rising cost of living, indicating that no further disturbance of public tranquillity would be tolerated. Highly significant in this context is an order by the *questura* according to which the policemen were to intervene not only to reestablish public order, but also "anyway, in order to give them (the demonstrators) the sensation that the police forces are watchful."[22] In this context, the massive deployment of police forces on the markets and the patrols throughout the city with heavily armed policemen assume the sense of a collective warning against the population of Florence. The intimidatory spirit of the police action can be deduced from the *diffida* (written and signed warning of an official character, served by the police) directed against single demonstrators. On September 24, 1946, the police stopped two women, "who, during the demonstrations in protest against the rising prices that took place today, had given signs of being among the most agitated demonstrators." The women were kept in the *questura* until 7 P.M., that is, until dark, and then released with the *diffida* "to not perform again otherwise ill-advised deeds, or to participate in demonstrations hazardous to the public peace."[23] For a complete realization of a "cold civil war tactic," however, a change in the national government was necessary.

Phase 3: Completion: The Police in a Cold Civil War

The "ditching of the left" in the summer of 1947 (i.e., the end of the "grand coalition" governments of antifascist unity) provided a clear signal for the completion of the move toward a "cold civil war tactic" in the public order interventions of the police. At the local level, the relationship between the left-wing parties and the Florentine *questura* immediately and substantially worsened.[24] The minister of the interior, Mario Scelba, gave the police a clear political direction against the political parties and the associated organizations of the working-class movement, with a growing repressive attention toward the trade unions and strikes.[25] In the second half of 1947 the accusations against the trade-union organization CGIL mounted.[26] As the prefect and the *questore* repeatedly affirmed in their monthly reports, the trade unions tried to impede the work of the government or to make it downright impossible through orchestrated industrial action. This strongly ideological position against the organizations and political parties of the working-class movement was also rampant among the police. In his *Enciclopedia di Polizia*, Luigi Salerno (1952, 786) claims that under the influence of Karl Marx (from which, according to him, they tried to escape at first) the trade unions changed from a defensive to an offensive organization and became the instrument of political parties and of class struggle, also giving themselves up to manifestations of violence with the characteristics of revolt.[27]

In the practical work of the police, this shift in policy was translated into continuous police intervention in labor conflicts in order to safeguard the *libertà di lavoro* (freedom to work). Each side felt increasingly provoked by the other. Clashes between the police and demonstrators or strikers became more and more "physical." In a general climate of polarization, an ever clearer political positioning of the police went hand in hand with physical confrontation. Images dear to the left-wing parties, which found themselves more and more on the defensive, were soundly refuted. When four policemen, wounded in clashes during a general strike in the province of Florence in January 1948, were interviewed in the hospital, their first reaction was: "Don't say the usual phrase 'blood flowed between brothers'; that's crap, anyway, that nobody believes anymore."[28]

The final showdown, for which both sides prepared, was to take place with the political elections scheduled for April 1948.[29] Although Scelba himself was very skeptical about the existence of insurrectional plans (Marino, 1995, 118), the government acted on the assumption that some kind of "surprise" by the Communists before, during, or after the elections was to be feared. It probably felt its fears confirmed by the international situation, especially the Communist coup d'état in Czechoslovakia in February 1948, and by alarming reports about the internal political situation. Even accepting the hypothesis of the existence of secret structures inside the PCI, the reports of the police, the carabinieri, and the secret services, many based on *fiduciari* (informants) of dubious reliability, were improbable (ibid., 129). According to the information received by the *questura* of Florence, in the region of Tuscany alone, thirty thousand Communist partisans, completely armed and equipped, stood ready to march; the PCI had put into practice various schemes to falsify ballots and electoral lists; "subversive elements" planned attacks against isolated polling stations and on the transport of the ballot boxes; especially in the bigger cities, the popular front (the united electoral list of Communists and Socialists) had organized the throwing of small and harmless hand grenades in order to create panic and abstention from voting. Nothing of this nature did happen, nor are there indications that similar actions were actually planned, but the preparation of the police for the electoral period was conditioned by this climate.

Compared with the elections for the constitutional assembly in June 1946, the specific aspects of police intervention in 1948 did not lie in a stronger pronounced partisanship. A climate hostile to the left-wing parties was certainly evident, visible, for instance, in the net refusal of any collaboration from their side. At the order of the *questura*, even the offers of refreshments for the policemen on duty at the polling stations were refused. However, the most significant characteristics in 1948 were the concrete preparations for a civil war. At the local level, the dispositions of the central government translated into a reduction of normal police services to an absolute minimum; an elaborate collection of information, with the explicit order to all *funzionari* (and not only those of the political branch) to build up a net of *fiduciari*; massive guard services at public buildings and polling stations, for which the *questura* drew on all national and local police forces, on the private *vigili giurati*, and on the army; continuous motorized and heavily armed patrols of the whole territory of the province, which were aimed above all at the psychological effect of intimidating the "subversive elements" and encouraging "the healthy part of the population." Together with detachments from the army, strong units of the police and the carabinieri with an entirely military armament stood in reserve at a regional level. Their deployment was facilitated for the strongholds of the left in Tuscany and Emilia-Romagna. The correspondence between the *questura* and the regional military command moreover demonstrates that the *questura* had developed plans for the exigencies of a "hot" civil war situation, and that it had realized defensive construction work at the police barracks, ordered the construction of mobile roadblocks, and so on. The heavy patrols of the province and all other "preventive" measures continued throughout the months of April and May.

Although the type of intervention exercised by the heavily armed police units during the election period of April 1948 was restricted to patrols of the territory and standby duty, they were undoubtedly prepared for deployment should a "hot" civil war situation develop. This is evident from an episode in March 1948. In talks with British politicians about the Italian police, the Italian defense minister, Randolfo Pacciardi, expressed the hope that the Western powers would not press the Soviet satellite states, principally Bulgaria, for information regarding their paramilitary organizations with a view to accusing them of violations of peace treaties. Pacciardi feared that if these states were accused, the Soviets would undoubtedly retaliate by making accusations regarding the Italian police. He himself defined the Italian police as an effective and well-equipped fighting unit with battle training appropriate for the quelling of civil disturbances. In February, the American embassy in Rome had already arrived at the same definition.[30]

Only a few months after the election, the riots provoked by the assassination attempt against the Communist leader Palmiro Togliatti on July 14, 1948, led to the intervention of the police along the lines of the tactic for a cold civil war that it had developed. The Italian government, in fact, saw behind the popular protest the insurrectional plans of the PCI and interpreted the proclamation of a general strike in defense of democracy by the CGIL and the call for the resignation of the "government of civil war" by the PCI as the first steps in this direction. In a telegram, Minister of the Interior Scelba ordered measures of extreme rigor to contain any kind of reaction to the assassination attempt.[31] The reference made by the left, on the other hand, was to the assassination of the Socialist member of parliament Giacomo Matteotti by the fascists in 1924.

In Florence, police units were immediately commanded to protect public buildings, the offices of the political parties in government and those of the extreme right, radio stations, power stations, and so on, and to form patrols of the same type as those organized for the electoral period. Independently from specific tasks, the *questura* expected the customary "complete" collection of information from all its offices. The order of the *questore*, which defined the general lines of the police intervention, demonstrates that the tactic adopted was based on the scenario of a possible civil war. Already in the first hours of the crisis the police tactic was not restricted to a purely defensive position: "The concept is to always maintain considerable forces at disposition for maneuver and attack, without scattering the force in ineffective peripheral services, which could expose the small numbers of policemen to unpleasant aggressions on the part of eventual predominant forces" (order of the *questura,* July 14, 1948).

As soon as possible, the police started their offensive against the general strike, which was supposed to last until 12 o'clock on July 16. On the morning of July 16, the *questore*—who, according to his report dated August 5, 1948, had had "the clear sensation" that the great majority of the workers and clerks were tired of striking—ordered the "resolute" intervention against strikers and pickets, which led to the provisional arrest of forty-eight people. He thus could report to Rome that the strike had practically ceased at 10 o'clock, that is, two hours before it was supposed to end. By employing proactive repression techniques against picket lines, the police had put into practice yet another element of their "cold civil war tactic."

There are several indications, however, that public order was never really in danger in Florence.[32] Violent incidents were few and of limited importance. By July 24, 1948, only seven people had been arrested in connection with the general strike; thirteen more had been charged without arrest. Most of these legal proceedings were for unauthorized meetings and unauthorized distribution of leaflets. No policeman had been seriously hurt. More incidents seem to have occurred in the surrounding province, but none of them created problems for the police. Even there, violent acts and roadblocks were isolated and individual affairs, without any coordination. This is implicitly acknowledged in the monthly report of the prefect, even though he also expounded on the impressive organization and presumed paramilitary structures of the Communist Party. According to him, the police forces in the province had been sufficient to deal with the situation in the city of Florence, but that certainly in the case of an insurrectional movement, well prepared and carried out simultaneously everywhere, they might be insufficient to keep ahead of well-trained masses, perhaps even sustained materially and morally from abroad. Implicit in this report is the admission that the July events in the province of Florence lacked all characteristics of a revolutionary uprising or insurrection.[33]

It was not the real situation in Florence July 14–16, but national if not international politics that decided further developments, as they had determined the police intervention on the days of the strike. Minister of the Interior Scelba ordered rigorous punishment for the serious crimes committed, according to him (unlawful imprisonment, roadblocks, attacks against the "freedom to work" and the freedom of the press, as well as against the circulation of trains), "whatever may have been the trade-union position or qualification covered" of those responsible. On August 10, 1948, ninety men and twenty-two women were in Florentine prisons in connection with the general strike. Repression was diffuse and could be provoked by minimal causes. In the days and months after the general strike, the Florentine police used a mimeographed *diffida*, which threatened those cautioned with "more rigorous measures against him, save the charge for crimes for which he might make himself responsible, if on the occasion of future disorders he were again arrested for having a provocative attitude or for incitement to disobedience of the law or for attacks against the 'freedom to work,' also on the occasion of strikes."

In one concrete case this *diffida* was issued against a man whose friend had twice made a *pernacchio* (deprecatory noise) at a cinema, first when De Gasperi was shown at the mass in honor of the two policemen killed at Abbadia San Salvatore, and a second time when police cars were shown in action. According to a local newspaper, later the two friends and a third person were officially charged with vilification of the armed forces.

The shift in the public order interventions of the police toward a fully developed "cold civil war tactic" was accompanied by a growing politicization of police action and a corresponding polarization of public opinion about police intervention. This is perceptible in the case of protests already before the general strike of July 14, 1948, and in relation to groups that earlier could count on a special tolerance. An example are the protests of the tuberculosis patients of the sanatoriums of Careggi in June and July 1948, which led to the "firm" intervention of the riot squads inside the hospital.[34] As had been the case in the preceding years, the protests were officially directed against the quality of the food, but according to the director of the sanatorium the real reason was his efforts to transfer the women to another hospital, especially those with "marked sympathies for the [male] patients." Against these attempts to restore order and morals, the members of the *commissione interna* (the elected commission representing the interests of the patients) organized the protest, which the director and the prefect interpreted as a rebellion, possibly against the national government.

In the atmosphere of the summer of 1948, several different versions of reality existed about the mobilization of the tuberculosis patients. Contrasting accounts can be found in newspapers with conflicting political orientations, as well as in different police reports. Not only the legitimacy and justification of the protests, but even the immediate causes, were presented differently. Depending on the political alignment of the newspapers, these were attacks of subversives against law and order and moral values, protests of ill people against neglect, or acts of resistance against the "bosses" of the sanatorium organized by the representatives of the proletariat. The higher the position of the reporting police office, and therefore the closer it was to the political center, the more dominant was a purely political interpretation of the events, within the ideological terms of the Cold War.

Conclusion

In just three years the Italian police developed from a delegitimized and disoriented force uncertain about their role in a democracy and the tactic to be employed for public order intervention into a force with strong paramilitary elements, ready to intervene without hesitation in a "harsh" way, notwithstanding the criticism of a consistent part of the population, consistently employing a "cold civil war tactic": strong central control; constant surveillance, which increasingly lost all pretense at de-escalation and routinely utilized espionage methods focused on the internal political enemy; the deployment of heavily armed paramilitary units for intimidation, and proactive as well as reactive repression. The decisions regarding equipment and training of the police were made with the scenario of a "hot" civil war constantly present, and with the police being considered an integral part of the armed forces.

This rapid transformation was possible because all elements of this tactic, partly in a less-developed form or fully operational only in concord with other corps of the armed forces, were all part of the Italian tradition of public security. For this reason, the police adapted easily to the situation of the Cold War, as it had to fascism before. As the fascist secret political police, the OVRA, had been the logical supplementary element for the particular needs of Mussolini's dictatorship, the *celere*, a paramilitary unit for the control of the piazza, was the logical supplementary force for the needs of the "protected democracy" of the Cold War years. The high number of civilians killed by the Italian police forces during their interventions at public demonstrations—at least 109 in the period of Scelba's tenure as minister of the interior from 1947 to 1954 (Marino, 1995, 169)—should, however, not be blamed only on the political line of the minister or on certain traditions in the state response to popular protest.[35] An additional reason was the organizational and operational weaknesses of the Italian police system, clearly evident after the fall of the fascist regime, to which defects in training and equipment must be added.[36] Even after the considerable strengthening of the police, operated by interior minister Scelba exclusively in terms of manpower and material, these weaknesses remained visible behind the image of strength transmitted by the *celere*.

These weaknesses find their expression also in the tension within the self-image of the police between the explicitly paramilitary way in which they presented themselves to the public (more than evident in *Polizia Moderna*, the official monthly of the Italian police) and the professed conception of police work concerning the protection of public order as consisting of observation and prevention, with few acts of repression (Roddi, 1953, 59). In the Cold War years, this tension did not produce open contradictions, because more than at the service of a "protected" democracy, the police found themselves at the service of a "limited" democracy. Against the internal political enemy, all police forces routinely used a "preventive" approach based on the traditional possibility of using a large number of administrative measures on the basis of pure suspicion (Canosa, 1976, 83), further extended by the public security law of 1926. On the basis of this fascist law the police enjoyed extensive powers of intervention, which they could use at their discretion in order to prohibit leaflets and posters, rallies and demonstrations of the PCI.[37] These powers were also activated against social protest. A particularly problematic instrument used by the police forces in this context was the *diffida*, with clear intent to intimidate, pronounced against activists who had managed not to break any law or administrative rule.[38] Political tension certainly existed, on both a national and an international level, which explained special precautions. However, as Scelba's methods on the national level bordered on an attack on the democratic freedoms and fundamental rights guaranteed by the Italian Constitution (Marino, 1995, 155), so did certain methods used by the police at the local level to control public order.

The "energetic" intervention of the police force and its ever more evident one-sidedness led to a growing polarization of opinion within the population. The leadership might even have approved of this development. In the period immediately after the liberation of Florence, the police had found themselves in the awkward position of trying to present themselves as and being officially celebrated as part of the resistance movement, only to be attacked as fascists when problems with the public arose. After the intervention during the general strike in July 1948, the police were lauded and criticized by the "right" people. In his monthly report of July 31, 1948, the prefect reported that the open and widespread manifestations of sympathy toward the police revealed complete trust in the police forces and that their prestige was growing ever stronger.[39] In the weeks following the general strike, donations of more than five hundred thousand liras were made in Florence for the families of the two policemen killed in the nearby province of Siena.[40] Initially, the left had tried to contribute to this movement with a subscription for all victims of the general strike. Following the negative reactions, in the government press, for instance, the name for this subscription was changed to *Pro vittime di Scelba*.[41] Within this political subculture, the image of the police as an enemy of the working-class movement and a tool of the Christian Democratic government, based on numerous experiences with the kind of "preventive" measures mentioned earlier, was cemented for the coming years, if not decades. This image also infected the perception of the police in activities that had nothing to do with politics, but reflected a "social" role.[42]

Notes

The material used in this essay was collected as part of a research project, "Reform or Restoration? The Police in Italy and Germany 1943/45–50," financed by the Harry Frank Guggenheim Foundation, New York, to which my special thanks are extended. For a more detailed account of the events and richer references to the archival sources, see Reiter (1997b).

1. The police law was changed only after the intervention of the Constitutional Court in 1956. On earlier reform projects, see De Fina (1959) and Canosa (1976, 152ff.).

2. On the attempts of the Allied Commission to push the different Italian governments

toward a comprehensive reform of the Italian police system, see Reiter (1997a). The impact of the initiative of the Socialist minister of the interior, Giuseppe Romita, to incorporate partisans into the police forces remains uncertain, especially because the competition to fill the posts was also open to all deportees and veterans of the war of liberation, including the members of the royal army, some of whose units had all but democratic traditions.

3. Mussolini had dissolved the *guardia regia*, the new paramilitary police corps founded after World War I, but shortly afterward reconstituted a national state police force. The fact that the Italian police did not sully itself with infamous crimes like the German police (not only the Gestapo, but also the Ordnungspolizei, i.e., the corps of uniformed policemen) was an important factor contributing to the continuity of the postwar period. The "benevolent" aspects of the Italian police during fascism should not be overestimated, however, as frequently occurs. Among the scarce scientific literature on the Italian fascist police, see Carucci (1976). On the involvement of the police and the carabinieri in the fascist violence in the early twenties see Canosa (1976, 61). On the local level, not only parts of the police, but also of the carabinieri intervened directly in favor of the fascists, mainly in the provision of weapons and transport, but also in the participation in "punitive actions" (Snowden, 1989, 96f., 198ff., 202f.). See also Dunnage (1992).

4. See della Porta and Reiter, in this volume. For the Allies, (i.e., the United States and Great Britain), this consideration had to be the basis of any police reform (Reiter, 1997a). For the practice of their reform efforts in the case of the German police, based (apart from denazification) on demilitarization and decentralization, see Kempner (1953); Werkentin (1984).

5. For the Germany of the Weimar Republic, this interpretation has been developed by Bessel (1992).

6. The *questore,* as the highest ranking policeman in the province, had the role of coordinating the work of the different police forces within each province. He was answerable to the Ministry of the Interior, and also to the prefect. The carabinieri, however, conserved not only a complete organizational independence, but also a wide operative autonomy. The *questore,* for instance, did not have direct authority over certain units of the carabinieri, which were of great importance for public order interventions. For the uniformed members of the state police, a separate command existed, in a different building from the *questura,* through which all orders to the uniformed policemen had to pass, and which did not always follow the orders of the *questore* to the letter (Reiter, 1997b).

7. AS (Archivio di Stato) Firenze, Questura 414, file *Defunti Commemorazione.*

8. AS Firenze, Questura 431, file *Festa della Polizia.* In Florence, the celebrations of the *festa della polizia* up to 1943 had followed a fixed program, culminating in a parade to the fascist sanctuary in Santa Croce, where a police honor guard wearing the uniform of the Fascist Party was positioned (ibid., file *Festa della Polizia e Rivista del Corpo*).

9. At the end of 1944, without a direct order from the Allies, and based on their directive to control the politically dangerous people in the just-liberated territory, which was clearly directed against fascists and collaborators, the carabinieri investigated the Communists at Borgo San Lorenzo (NA [National Archives] Washington, D.C., RG 331, 10802/143/45).

10. AS Firenze, Questura 342, file 152. With the growing political polarization of the following years, this attitude of the *questura* led to the suppression of criticism.

11. Ibid., *ordinanza* dated October 6, 1944. As the local symbol of the central government, the *prefettura* was of equal importance for the police and the demonstrators. It was the destination and target of most protest marches. For the demonstrators it was paramount to force the prefect to take notice of their requests. The police had to defend the *prefettura* building as the symbol of the authority of the state against any attack.

12. An interior ministry telegram dated October 11, 1946, suspended the celebration for

that year and announced that a different date would be fixed for the future. In the coming years, however, the *festa della polizia* was again celebrated on October 18. AS Firenze, Questura 431, file *Festa della Polizia*.

13. This attitude emerges clearly from two cases in Florence. In the first one, policemen on public order duty at the central market, while intervening against protests connected with the scarcity of food, fired into the air in order to disperse the crowd, killing one woman and wounding a second. In the second case, a journalist, who had attributed the arrest of the war criminal Pietro Koch to information given by the public and not to the investigation of the police, was maltreated in the offices of the *questura*. In both cases, criticism of the police was harsh, but the concrete requests were limited to a more incisive *epurazione* and a raise in the rations of the policemen. AS Firenze, Questura 449, file *Mercato centrale—vigilanza*; Questura 370, file 24. See also Volpi (1983), who points to the lack of attention by the Constituent Assembly to questions of administrative organization and analyzes the scarce influence that the general principles proclaimed in the Constitution had on the actual structure of the police system.

14. A letter of the ministry dated March 4, 1945, for example, defines the *vice questore* Soldani Benzi, who had led the Florentine *questura* in the critical months after the liberation, as a creature of the CTLN, incapable of guaranteeing public order and responsible for considerable Communist infiltration of the police. NA Washington, D.C., RG 331, 10000/143/532.

15. AS Firenze, Questura 414, file *Disoccupati manifestazioni*.

16. Ibid. Also, in the case of this demonstration the reports of the different *funzionari* are contradictory. The water pumps of the firemen who had been commanded for public order duty were not put to use because of the refusal of the firemen to use their pumps against demonstrators and not against fire.

17. In a telegram of March 25, 1946, Romita ordered the collection of all possible information on the unemployed, in order to be able to suppress their protests at an initial stage. However, he tried to avoid an escalation of violence, and for this reason ordered, for example, the use of the water pumps. AS Firenze, Questura 414, file *Dimostrazioni di protesta contro la disoccupazione—identificazione elementi estranei perturbatori dell'ordine pubblico*.

18. See NA Washington, D.C., RG 331, 10000/105/577, correspondence of summer 1946; Reiter, 1997a.

19. See, for example, a telegram by minister Romita dated March 25, 1946. AS Firenze, Questura 414, file *Dimostrazioni di protesta contro la disoccupazione—identificazione elementi estranei perturbatori dell'ordine pubblico*.

20. As an example of the de-escalating intent of the Florentine *questura* during the first half of 1946, see the order of March 22 concerning a demonstration by the unemployed announced for the following day: "I strongly recommend that all leaders of the services use the necessary vigor and maximum tact in order to prevent any act of violence and at the same time avoid serious conflicts between the police and the demonstrators, which could degenerate into dangerous disorders." AS Firenze, Questura 414, file *Disoccupati manifestazioni*.

21. For newspaper cuttings and police reports, see ibid. The disorders in general, but especially the attempted occupation of the trade-union headquarters, were attributed, by the police and by the left-wing parties, to fascist agents provocateurs. However, a first report of the police on provisional arrests is in clear contrast with this version. The reasons given for the arrests range from having criticized the work of the police to having called single policemen "fascist." More than on facts, the hypothesis of the fascist agents provocateurs seems to have been based on the need to pin the unrest on a scapegoat that was acceptable to all. For this role the fascists were the lowest common denominator between the DC and the PCI.

22. Order dated September 24, 1946, AS Firenze, Questura 450, file *Panettieri—Sciopero*.

23. Ibid., report of the *funzionario* in charge to the *questore*, September 24, 1946.

24. The *questura* prohibited displaying a wall poster critical of the new government because it "sounded offense" to the ministers in office. Monthly report of the *questore*, July 31, 1947, AS Firenze, Questura 536, file 8, *Situazione politica ed economica della provincia*.

25. For a political biography of Mario Scelba, see Marino (1995). As far as the organization of the police was concerned, Scelba was not an innovator—the *celere*, the famous riot squads, were organized by his Socialist predecessor Romita—with the exception of having constituted the first *corpo speciale* of the republic in the fight against the Sicilian bandit Salvatore Giuliano (ibid., 104). Scelba was, however, responsible for the impressive growth of the Italian police forces, especially in the years 1947 and 1948 (Canosa, 1976, 132). On the "radical anti–trade-union culture" of Scelba, see Marino (1995, 138). Prime Minister De Gasperi saw strikes as a crime against the economy and considered the fact that he had to accept their legality as the fatal consequence of an error of the Constitution (ibid., 139).

26. The Confederazione Generale Italiana del Lavoro (CGIL) at that time was still a unitary trade union, but the internal divisions had become increasingly evident after the "ditching of the left." The split finally occurred in the wake of the general strike after the assassination attempt on PCI leader Palmiro Togliatti. The Christian Democratic trade unionists formed the CISL (Confederazione Italiana Sindacati Lavoratori), their laical colleagues the UIL (Unione Italiana del Lavoro), and the Communists and Socialists remained within the CGIL.

27. On the importance of this work for police training, especially for officers and *funzionari*, see Lehner (1978, 33ff.). A similarly hostile attitude toward the working-class movement was displayed by a semiofficial manual for the *guardia regia*, the Italian police corps of the early 1920s (Donati, 1977, 494 n. 95).

28. Interview of the Christian Democratic daily *Il Mattino dell'Italia Centrale*, January 11, 1948, AS Firenze, Questura 486, file *Bonelle di Pistoia—Incidenti fra polizia e dimostranti*. The clashes took place when the police tried to remove roadblocks near Pistoia.

29. For the archival material used in the following, see AS Firenze, Questura 001, 30/I, *Pezzo 1–3, Elezioni politiche 1948*.

30. NA Washington, D.C., RG 59, 865.105, London to Secretary of State, March 24, 1948; ibid., Embassy Rome to Secretary of State, April 2, 1948.

31. For the archival material used in the following, see AS Firenze, Questura 477, file *Attentato all'On. Togliatti—Manifestazioni*.

32. On the general situation, see Di Loreto (1991, 291ff.), who speaks of an Italy on the brink of armed conflict; Marino (1995, 126ff.) emphasizes a maximum state of tension that remained close to a revolutionary explosion. Exaggerated seems the image presented by Jenkins (1988, 147) of tens of thousands of workers, many of them armed, attacking a police force rapidly disarmed by the insurgents. It must be stressed that the popular reaction to the assassination attempt was spontaneous, defensive in character (the shooting was interpreted as the beginning of an attack on the left), and restricted to the north. However, the response was not uniform and spectacular action was restricted to Genoa, Turin, Venice, and Abbadia San Salvatore in central Italy. Not only the national leadership of the PCI but also its local leaders seem to have tried to control the protest and did not move to exploit it. For the province of Livorno, see Grillo (1994), who in the case of Piombino also shows how the initial appreciation of the "authorities" for the de-escalating intervention of representatives of the PCI and the CGIL after indications from the national government transformed itself into an indictment for "armed insurrection against the powers of the state." Throughout Italy, six policemen and eleven demonstrators were killed during the general strike.

33. Monthly report of the prefect, July 31, 1948, AS Firenze, Questura 536, file *Relazioni mensili del Prefetto 1946 ott.—1948 dic.*

34. AS Firenze, Questura 479, file *Careggi—sanatorio—agitazione fra i ricoverati.* The endemic protests of the tuberculosis patients of Careggi had already started in 1945, and on September 20 of that year even led to the occupation of the *prefettura* building.

35. For government dispositions that authorized the use of firearms also against unarmed demonstrators, see Corso (1979, 57–58) and Canosa (1976, 143–48).

36. See Sannino (1985, 471ff.), for instance, on the fact that the carabinieri were (and are) not supplied with batons and therefore exclusively relied on their guns.

37. In August 1950, for example, the Florentine *questura* refused the "authorization for the posting of leaflets, printed by the PCI, on the subject of price increases, which had an alarmist and propagandistic content aimed against the government." Monthly report of the prefect to the ministry, September 1, 1950, AS Firenze, Questura 525, file *Situazione in generale della Provincia. Relazione mensile.* For the month of September 1950, on the occasion of the celebrations for the "month of the Communist press," the *questura* prohibited fifty-six marches and three assemblies "for reasons of order and security" (*ibid.*, report of the prefect to the ministry, September 26, 1950). The Florentine *questura* also repeatedly censored or prohibited leaflets in which the collateral organizations of the Communist Party, for example, the women's organization Unione Donne Italiane (UDI), called for contributions to their charity activities such as winter help or assistance to the unemployed. Police measures of this character were routinely upheld by the courts (see, e.g., Canosa and Federico, 1974, 186ff.).

38. For examples, see Reiter (1997b, 59). A report of the *compagnia esterna 1ª dei carabinieri* dated May 5, 1949, contains the information that the subsidiary carabinieri stations had always charged all those responsible for attacks against the "liberty to work" and had in this way achieved a far less numerous participation in strikes. AS Firenze, Questura 525, file *Difesa della libertà sindacale.*

39. AS Firenze, Questura 536, file *Relazioni mensili del Prefetto, 1946 ott.—1948 dic.*

40. AS Firenze, Questura 488, file *Offerte—elargizioni e premi ad agenti di PS (o familiari) feriti e caduti in servizio.* In its communications to the press, the *questura* especially mentioned small contributions by "the people," for example, by "a modest worker" or by a seven-year-old child. See ibid., newspaper clippings from July 21 and July 28, 1948.

41. See AS Firenze, Questura 477, file *Attentato all'On. Togliatti—Manifestazioni, sottofasc. 6,* especially *Il Mattino dell'Italia Centrale* of August 28, 1948.

42. Reporting on the flood of November 1949, the Communist daily *L'Unità* accused the police of having hindered the distribution of food and clothing organized by the Communists and their organizations. *La Nazione Italiana*, on the contrary, lauded the police for their heroic work, saving widows and children and staying in their offices with the water up to waist level. See AS Firenze, Questura 512, file *Allagamenti in Provincia causati da straripamenti fiumi*, newspaper clippings of November 28 and 29, 1949. The reporting reflects the clear division within the country. Except for blaming the government for negligence, the Communist daily centered all its attention on the work of the "democratic" municipal governments and the collateral organizations of the PCI, for instance, the Unione Donne Italiane. The "heroic" and "human interest" stories had as protagonists workers and Communist activists. *La Nazione Italiana*, on the contrary, reported on the efforts of the prefect and the government bureaucracy, of the police and the army, that is, the "authorities," and on the voluntary initiatives of Catholic organizations.

Chapter 7

The Policing of Social Protest in Spain: From Dictatorship to Democracy

Oscar Jaime-Jiménez and Fernando Reinares

In analyzing the evolution of the police model in Spain during the country's shift from dictatorship to democracy, the approach employed in this essay is grounded on the premise that *police knowledge* is conditioned by the professional culture of the police—in other words, by the image the security forces themselves have of the functions they fulfill, and by the cultural environment, which is made up of the perceptions they have of the external reality (see della Porta and Reiter, in this volume). In this respect, one would expect to find tangible differences between democratic and nondemocratic systems in relation to the formation of police knowledge.[1] In the latter case, the functions carried out by the police are of an explicitly political character. Their main objective is the surveillance of social groups that could represent a threat to the survival of the regime. The state does not seek to institutionalize or integrate those groups that challenge, to a greater or lesser degree, the established power, but simply to eliminate them, or at least to control them. The police model in this case is, to a large extent, comparable with the ideal model of the *Staatspolizei* (the king's police) and characterized by a mentality wholly concerned with the maintenance of "law and order" and the supreme interests of the state. Any unrest or criticism, no matter how moderate, is perceived as a threat to the very foundations of the state and is met with a disproportionately harsh response. Demonstrations are regarded with suspicion and distrust because they disrupt harmonious relations between the state and society. In short, the police force in a nondemocratic state is specifically molded by the state to defend its own interests and rulers. On the other hand, tolerant political systems, characterized by a broadening of participation and depending to a greater extent on public cooperation, tend to facilitate the development of a *Bürgerpolizei* (citizens' police); namely, a force that is closer to the citizen, whose primary objective is not to protect the state's interests but rather to defend the basic rules that ensure the existence of democratic society.[2]

This essay focuses on the evolution of a police model—the shift from a model characterized by its principal task of defending the interests of an authoritarian state controlled by a narrow range of elites toward one that is at the service of a significantly broader range of political elites dependent on a greater number of interests. We shall look at how police knowledge has evolved within those units of the security forces that represent the state's last resort for the imposition of public order. For certain social groups, these units embody the true face of the state's structural violence in its purest form. In many cases, the citizen's image of state action is determined by contact with these police units. In social protests, these units represent the oppressive power of the "system." For this reason it is important to understand how this part of the state structure views the citizenry and tries to live up to its expectations. Likewise, we shall focus our attention on the evolution of police knowledge within a framework of the continual interaction that takes place between the security forces and the citizenry at a critical time, that is, the profound political transformations in Spain during the transition period (1976–82) and the subsequent democratic consolidation.

The Spanish Police and Franco's Dictatorship

In the evolution of police responses to social protest from the time of Franco's victory in the civil war (1936–39) until the present day, it is possible to distinguish four different stages. The first period, from the end of the war in 1939 until 1960, was, socially, a time with no significant disturbances. The second period, from 1960 until Franco's death in 1975, was marked by a weakening of the regime's iron grip on society as a result of the emergence of significant social groups that began to dissent openly from the political principles on which the regime was based. The intensity of protest increased until the breakdown of the regime, which occurred formally in 1976. A dynamic of progressive political change, intertwined with residual elements of the former regime, began in the following period. Uncertainty about the immediate future characterized this third period, and there is no doubt that it not only conditioned police perceptions of the external environment but also their actions in various fields. This period of democratic transition ended in 1982 with the victory of the Socialist Party at the general elections, from which moment we may consider democracy to have become consolidated. Thus began a period of progressive accommodation of the security forces to the new sociopolitical reality. Any threat of regression had been practically eliminated.

With the end of the civil war, a new political regime emerged, characterized by the authoritarian and personal power of General Franco.[3] The most reactionary sectors of Spanish society had contributed to Franco's victory and subsequently enjoyed a privileged relationship with the new regime, although bitter confrontations, which were difficult to conceal, divided the different elites. During the first years of the regime, close ties were maintained with fascist countries. However, the end of World War II and the consequent defeat of the fascist regimes brought a distinct cooling in relations with fascism. Within Spain, the regime displayed a marked hostility toward any kind of political dissent. This animosity was logically translated into the development of security forces whose main concern was to combat threats to the regime. Postwar repression was severe and, in many cases, indiscriminate. Between 1939 and 1944, nearly two hundred thousand people were executed because of political reasons.[4] The political opposition initially chose to fight the regime by means of guerrilla warfare, a strategy that was successfully and pitilessly defeated by the state security forces. With the realization that this strategy was a costly mistake (4,500 guerrilla fighters had been killed without having achieved anything), the opposition developed a new set of tactics at the beginning of the 1950s based on political activity in the workplace. During this period, the population was either too afraid or too passive to initiate a revolt. In fact, broad sectors of Spanish society were satisfied with the principles of the regime. Until the end of the 1950s, the dictatorship did not experience any real threat, either from the weak internal opposition forces or from external actors.

Historically, the first national police force was the Guardia Civil (the Spanish civil guard), created in 1844 by an army officer. As part of the army, its structure was militarized, but some small differences kept the institution as a differentiated corps inside the army. Following the civil war, the Guardia Civil underwent profound changes as a result of the role assigned to it, namely, that of a surveillance agency with the maintenance of public order as its first and principal function, mainly in the countryside. This paramilitary force took a very active part in the fight against the political opposition. Gradually, however, the importance of the Guardia Civil in the fight against the political opposition declined. The golden days of the struggle against the communist and anarchist guerrilla maquis belonged to the past. With increasing urbanization, the importance of the rural areas diminished in favor of the cities, where the growing population became a potential source of political and social unrest. Thus, the role of the new urban police force rapidly grew in significance.

After Franco's victory, the civilian police system settled in the urban areas and controlled by the Ministry of the Interior was radically changed. At the beginning of the 1940s, the republican Guardia de Asalto (urban nonmilitary police force) was renamed the Policía Armada, and more and more personnel were employed and resources spent in response to a presumed latent social unrest and the fear of leftist activism. Public order in large cities was so important to the dictatorial regime that in 1959 the armed traffic police was dismantled in order to increase the number of policemen deployed on the streets. Having become part of the armed forces, the Policía Armada, like the Guardia Civil, had a militarized structure. This new force was made up largely of civil war veterans, who were aware of its repressive political function and who developed a deeply authoritarian organizational culture.

Franco's repressive system was highly effective during the first decades. After the war and during most of the 1950s, social protest was almost nonexistent. Neither the Policía Armada nor the Guardia Civil was used to confront social protests or strikes in the streets. Public protests were forbidden and heavily punished. In a situation of potential unrest, the usual procedure was for the Guardia Civil to send a *pareja* (pair) of civil guards to the site; if the unrest had already abated, the mere presence of the pair of men should have been enough to deter any further action. If this did not suffice, the *pareja* could always use their regulation weapons to reestablish public order. This procedure was highly effective (Martín Fernández, 1990, 75).

During the 1950s, the working class began to organize to defend basic social and economic rights, though this proved to be very difficult due to the initially low level of organization. The former trade unions and political parties had been dismantled and the regime's control over the official trade unions was strong. There was no real need for the government to develop sophisticated means of control of public order during these years; the whole decade was extremely peaceful. The regime no longer felt threatened by the international community as Franco believed that he was a necessary arm in the Western fight against the communist world; moreover, the internal communist threat was not strong enough to present a real problem.

The 1960s marked the beginning of a very important period of economic development, which, however, did not so much favor the emergence of a widespread political consciousness as an individualistic desire for economic improvement. Nevertheless, it was only from the 1960s on, when the impact of the civil war and the postwar period had been partly surmounted and new generations who had not experienced the war were appearing in the political arena, that the regime's overwhelming control began to be defied by small intellectual groups at the universities, with a serious attempt to undermine the old values and the power of the political elites. Real problems for the regime in terms of public order started as the 1960s opened. At the end of the fifties, the workers' organizations, well organized and led by efficient and experienced communist leaders, rocked the apparent peacefulness of the regime. Moreover, a significant number of students began to voice their disaffection with the lack of public freedom and the absence of freedom of speech (Maravall, 1978). This sudden source of unrest had not been foreseen by the government.

In order to defend the continuity of the political system, the regime's repressive strategies and tactics had to be adapted to the new situation. Several important measures were thus introduced. First, in 1959, the Public Order Law, which detailed the procedures to be employed in confronting public demonstrations, was passed. This law remained in force until 1992. Second, some specific units of the Policía Armada received training in antiriot tactics in urban areas. Franco's dictatorship was aware that Spanish society was changing very rapidly and that the opposition was developing new strategies to fight against the regime. In order to meet the new public order challenges more efficiently, the Compañías de Reserva General (general reserve companies) were created in 1969 as antiriot force units. They were based throughout the national territory but were concentrated in the most critical urban areas. The values, discipline, and structure as well as the administration of this new force were a copy of those of the army. Despite the use of the new units and antiriot defensive and offensive equipment, the number of deaths caused by the police at demonstrations remained very high. The reason for the deaths was sometimes the inappropriate use of the new equipment and sometimes simply the brutality waged against demonstrators during the suppression of unrest. Third, aware of the advancing age of police officers, the government developed a recruitment program aimed at young people for the Policía Armada. Fourth, in 1964, the TOP (Public Order Court), a special court to deal with issues relating to public order offenses, was established. A few years later, this court would demonstrate its full capacity when thousands of people appeared before it. Fifth, the articles of the penal code relating to social and political offenses were modified to increase the severity of punishments. Sixth, the Guardia Civil received antiriot equipment, although only after the Policía Armada had already been so equipped, as its use was considered less important in the rural areas. Finally, the well-developed information service network of the Guardia Civil was increasingly focused on detecting political opposition organizations and, more specifically, their leaders. In this specific field, its activity was not restricted to the rural areas.

The main preoccupation of the Spanish police forces during the 1960s was the fight against growing social unrest. Serious public order problems began for the police in 1962, when the workers' groups started to display a high level of activism and organization. As a consequence, the government rapidly increased the members of the Policía Armada. During the last years of the regime it was the main force used to deal with social protests on the streets of the industrialized urban areas. The increasing number of riots were one of the prime concerns of the dying regime during the 1970s, leading to further increases in the number of Policías Armadas in the middle of the decade—a doubling of the ranks from thirty thousand to sixty thousand occurred over a short period of time. Attitudes within the hard-core regime elite demonstrated that powerful sectors, such as the Falangists and the army, were not ready to allow a peaceful political transition. Some public statements issued by high-ranking army officers encouraged the elite's most conservative sectors to resist and the police to exercise tough control over the political opposition.[5]

Some changes in the behavior of the security forces did begin to slowly take place from 1976 on, during the period of political transition. The police forces withdrew from the universities and intervened less frequently in labor conflicts.[6] However, despite these changes, the antiriot units continued to respond to breaches of public order in almost exactly the same way as before: between 1975 and 1979, the police caused the deaths of thirty-six people in street confrontations (Ballbé, 1985, chap. 13). Not even the approval of the new democratic Constitution in 1978 proved a definite turning point. The concept of public order as an issue relating to the internal security structure was absent from the text, but there was still a confusion between the concepts of public order and *seguridad ciudadana* (public safety). The constitutional text, based on a broad consensus about the structure of the police forces, allowed for a broad interpretation by the political forces (Jar Couselo, 1995, 21).

It was only in the 1980s, and especially after the Socialist victory, that the antiriot forces became less harsh in their actions and demonstrations began to be conducted in a more moderate manner. The largest Socialist trade union tried by every means to decrease pressure on the new Socialist government. Furthermore, the student movement almost completely disappeared. In response to this new public order situation, which was closer to that of the Western democracies than to the former dictatorial and post-Franco period, the structure of the antiriot forces changed. Deployment of these forces had been a response to a critical political and social situation that no longer obtained. In addition, it was increasingly clear that the average age of this specialized police force was too high for them to perform their functions properly (policemen were assigned to these special units and remained there for the rest of their professional lives). The last reason for the transformation was that the Basque terrorists changed their patterns of action. The violence of the Basque terrorist organization ETA (Euskadi ta Askatasuna) decreased in the Basque country and increased in Madrid and Barcelona. The new deployment of these antiriot forces made it possible to better surveil these large cities and reduce the units' presence in the Basque country. The new Basque autonomous police force (Ertzaintza) would perform the task of riot control. Thus, in 1989, new units, known as the Unidades de Intervención Policial (police riot squads), were formally created.

The Characteristics of the Spanish Transition to Democracy and the Evolution of the Police

The model of political transition seized upon in Spain and the way it unfolded in different phases are issues that remain subject to diverse interpretations. Debate has turned on the specific quality of the Spanish transition, that is, whether it was characterized by a radical break with the past or by a reform of the essential structures of the previous regime in order to adapt them to a new sociopolitical context. With regard to the phases during which the transition occurred, we shall opt for an operative approach, highlighting the political rather than the institutional aspect. In the following, we take July 1976, when the king dismissed the last prime minister of the Franco regime, Carlos Arias Navarro, as the starting point of the transition; and we consider it to have been concluded in October 1982, when for the first time a change of government was brought about by electoral means with the victory of PSOE (Spanish Socialist Workers' Party).

The dictator's death in 1975 ushered in a period of intense political and social uncertainty. In 1976, a process of political change was set in motion. Favored by a public opinion inclined toward moderate political change and the positive influence of democratic countries, the different political camps—those surviving the decay of the old regime and those of the opposition—achieved a tenuous consensus (see Tezanos, Cotarelo, and de Blas, 1989; Cotarelo, 1992). While this consensus gave rise to a stronger tendency toward change, at the same time it limited more resolute and profound progress in some areas (O'Donnell and Schmitter, 1986). Initially, the situation

that emerged was characterized by the attempt to rehabilitate the old structures, adapting them to the new political necessities. The most important opposition parties implicitly accepted this situation, subjecting themselves to a
set of ground rules despite the fact that they had not participated in their formulation. Subsequently, the apparent stalemate—the opposition forces were
unable to provoke radical political change and the political establishment was
no longer able to keep broad sectors of Spanish society under control—led
the most moderate political sectors of the former regime to negotiate with the
most significant opposition parties in order to give shape to a new political
regime for the post-Franco era.

Progressively, the transition took the form of an "agreed rupture": on the
one hand, the political rules changed radically, political parties and trade
unions were legalized, and a parliament was established that could foster a
standard Western democracy; on the other hand, the monarchy remained
and the administrative structures were left practically untouched. The state
bureaucracy, including the army and the old security structures and agencies, remained practically unchanged. Even during the transition period, former members of the state official unions and the traditional fascist organization, Movimiento Nacional (an evolved form of the earlier Falange Española y
de las JONS), were incorporated into the civil service (Tezanos, 1989). The
elites of the Franco regime continued to play an important role in the political
decision making of the state. Their presence, legitimized by their new affilia-
tions to parties of the right and center and/or by their royal appointment
as senators, thus conditioned the evolution of the new regime.[7] During the
period of political change, highly placed politicians in the Ministry of the Interior were constantly overreached by formerly influential politicians of the
previous regime.

The army had been one of the props of the former regime, which made
it credible for a large part of the most reactionary sector to shelter within it.
Although difficult to quantify, this sector undoubtedly wielded a very real
power and was clearly dissatisfied with the initiation of a process of openness.
The army was the power that most patently showed its hostility to the democratic process; indeed, military authorities inhibited the government on many
occasions with their attitude of open challenge to the civil powers.[8] Rumors of
a military coup d'état constantly circulated during the first years of the transition, leading up to an actual attempt in February 1981. Its eventual failure was
largely due to the lack of real objectives and coordination within the rebel
forces, and because of the widespread loyalty maintained by the military

authorities to the crown as the only prevailing institution legitimized by Franco's regime.

Although the police forces were similarly suspect, they did not undergo any changes in the first part of the transition period. As Rodolfo Martín Villa, minister of the interior from 1976 to 1979, later acknowledged, reform of the security forces did not begin until 1979 because of fears of a possible rebellion (Martín Villa, 1984, 150ff.). The security forces created during Franco's regime were composed of a dense network of loyal officials whose main task was to ensure the perpetuation of the existing political system. The police were modeled on a military ethos, according to which the maintenance of public order prevailed over other police functions. During the first years of the transition, police officers who had taken part in the harsh political repression of the opposition remained in their posts. Even those officials who had committed obvious abuses during the course of their work, such as police chiefs suspected of having participated in plots to destabilize the new regime, kept their positions.[9] Nor were significant changes introduced during the first years of the transition in terms of the methods employed to suppress demonstrations; things continued by inertia from the last period of the previous regime.

The information services had played a very important role during Franco's time in the detection of opposition groups, and they did not completely cast off this function during the transition years. Likewise, they collaborated at different levels with groups of extreme right-wing foreigners that had been allowed to establish themselves in Spain, supposedly as a reward for certain "dirty services" carried out by them for the Spanish security forces during the transition years (the "dirty" war against the ETA, actions against left-wing groups).[10] Some of these groups even began to collaborate with the security forces only after Franco's death in 1975 (Rodríguez-Granero, 1988). Furthermore, a certain passivity could be perceived on the part of the security forces in the investigation of crimes perpetrated by extreme right-wing groups, while actions of the extreme left wing were answered immediately and forcefully.[11] Finally, some small changes began to take place beginning in the 1980s when the government sought to keep under control and discipline the police units in charge of surveillance and investigation of ultraright gangs (Reinares, 1990, 389).

However, the new sociopolitical situation, together with the generational change, favored the emergence of a new society, one that was profoundly different to the one that had existed twenty years earlier. During the final years of the Franco regime, a moderate political attitude on the part of the public could already be perceived, and this was clearly at odds with the principles of the regime (López Pintor and Buceta, 1975). This was to be a decisive factor, one that undoubtedly contributed to smoothing the way for the transition and to avoiding serious social convulsions.[12] Even before the death of the dictator there was a move toward developing a more open, pluralistic kind of press. Various periodicals began to be published that attempted, as far as possible, to be free of the influences and conditioning imposed by the regime. In part, this was made possible with the Press Law of 1967, which, by imposing self-censorship, made each publication responsible for its own content. The democratic press had backed a smooth change of regime and already possessed a certain degree of savoir faire. During the last years of the regime, and especially during the first years following Franco's death and the initial years of the transition, the press helped to bring to the public's attention issues that were delicate and sensitive for the governments of the time, particularly issues concerning internal security and terrorism. The press reported the excesses of the security forces and any actions or attitudes on the part of the administration or nostalgic groups that recalled past times. Likewise, the press played an important role in helping public opinion adapt to the new political situation, assuming to a large extent the functions of political interpreter and educator.

The political parties had remained underground since the end of the civil war. Throughout the following decades, their presence was very weak and their position precarious in Spain. With the end of the dictatorship and the subsequent appointment of Adolfo Suárez as prime minister, a slow process of political accommodation began, involving the opposition parties that had been most active in the struggle against the Franco regime. Among these, the Communist Party stood out as being the largest and best-organized political force of the time. Nevertheless, other minor political forces that would later achieve considerable importance, as well as figures from the former regime known for their liberal and democratic tendencies, joined in this process. In this way, a series of solid links was sought, with the aim of developing implicit agreements between the different political sensibilities. It was intended that these links would create a propitious climate to facilitate the process of moving on from that politically critical phase. After the general elections of 1977, the main political forces signed an agreement establishing the conditions for a set of immediate political, economic, and social rules that would help solve the deep-seated political and economic problems besetting the country. This agreement, known as the *Pactos de la Moncloa* (Moncloa Agreements), set down some vague foundations for a reform of the police forces, which, however, lacked far-reaching goals. Indeed, the primary and immediate objective of the political opposition was to weed out those members of the police forces who had played a direct role in the political repression. With only some "minor" specific changes, almost the entire structure and personnel remained. Only a few officials who had been involved in suppressive actions against the political opposition were actually dismissed.

The reform of the police forces following the Moncloa Agreements was to a large extent the result of agreements between different political sensibilities. However, the military sector and, most significantly, conservative members of parliament retained a strong influence and acted as a decisive factor in holding back and postponing a restructuring of the police forces. Changes were effected slowly and without great conviction since no target model of what a police force should be had been defined. In the new legislation, innovative elements showing a willingness to change were combined with others that merely served to perpetuate the militarized nature of the police force. This resulted in the drafting of legal texts that were difficult to interpret or, in many cases, contradictory.

With the new Police Law, passed in 1978, the influence of the army on the police structure decreased, but nonetheless remained very important.[13] Prior to this basic reform, most of the officers of the Policía Armada came from the army. After the 1978 law, most of the new officers came from a specific police academy; only a few military officers selected by the Ministry of the Interior had access to the police structure, though training continued to be largely military-based and was given by army personnel. The most immediate significant change with the new law was that military courts no longer dealt with cases relating to citizens' free expression and the police forces ceased to be protected by military legislation. In 1986, new police legislation, the *Ley Orgánica de Fuerzas y Cuerpos de Seguridad del Estado* (state police law), was approved. Finally, thanks to this law, the nonparamilitary police forces rationalized their organization. But one of the most important outcomes of this new law was the creation of the Cuerpo Nacional de Policía (CNP), which from the beginning became a fully civil corps, abandoning military status. A few years later, in 1992, the Public Order Law of 1959 was abolished and replaced by the *Ley de Protección de la Seguridad Ciudadana* (protection of public safety law).

The future model of the police force was shaped during the years of transition and democratic consolidation, and formed within an ongoing interaction of forces, which favored a dialectic between continuity and innovation. Unity within those forces that were hindering change broke down with the slow decomposition of the elites of the old regime during the years leading up to the death of Generalissimo Franco. As a consequence, the conservative nuclei appeared as an uncoordinated front with very limited credibility as a political alternative. Each of the political sectors had different aims and plans, and the military sectors did not even have viable projects of any specific nature. They were merely trying not to lose the power they had enjoyed up until then. Nor, however, were the opposition groups unified and coordinated. Each shade of political sensibility sought to ensure that its point of view held sway over the rest. Nonetheless, a positive attitude prevailed with regard to the development of a new political regime. The political organizations and those powers that had backed the process of change, as well as the greater part of the public, pushed together toward a political transformation without too much tumult.

The Evolution of Police Knowledge during the Transition and Democratic Consolidation[14]

In this section we will analyze the evolution that has taken place in police perceptions of the outside world. We will also compare the self-image of the present-day police forces as they carry out the functions with which they have been entrusted and that of former units charged with the maintenance of public order during the transition period. This analysis is based on in-depth interviews using semistructured questionnaires and conducted among high- and medium-ranking officers of the Unidades de Intervención Policial of the Cuerpo Nacional de Policía.[15]

Police Perceptions of the Past

Most of the members of the riot squads are young people who took up their posts in the 1980s and 1990s. Indeed, one of the purposes of the creation in 1989 of the Unidades de Intervención Policial was to enable a renewal of staff so that it would be better suited to the objective necessities of the functions that personnel must carry out. The structure of the Brigadas de Reserva was hampered by a series of basic limitations (no age limit for service, policemen had to live in barracks, and there were no permanent training programs), which severely impaired their abilities when faced with immediate necessities. The generally young medium-ranking policemen and chiefs (group and unit chiefs) belong to generations that were socialized within a sociopolitical context postdating the dictatorship. Some of the high-ranking chiefs, on the other hand, did serve in those units during the 1970s, although they remain a minority since the 1989 reform affected all levels of the unit's organization.

There is consensus among the officers of the riot squads, regardless of when they joined, that significant changes have taken place, not so much in police mentality as in the sociopolitical and legal environment. They recognize, however, that this has to a great extent determined the character and form of their behavior. These changes are perceived very clearly, as a medium-ranking officer commented:

> There was anxiety among the citizens. . . . During the previous years, large gatherings were not possible, there was a bit of rowdiness, but not now. Everything is much calmer, more controlled on their part, more experience on ours. We anticipate events. Anyway, there is much greater freedom; now much more is allowed than before. Now, in Madrid there are collectives that can block a road like the M-40, they authorize it and everything's all right. A few years ago that was unthinkable. . . . It's also true that it was much easier for the police, orders were much clearer: it's prohibited and we're going to break it up. . . . Before, it was more violent, but I don't think it was more difficult. It was a different method. (Interview no. 6)

This opinion expresses a widely held feeling; although most of the interviewees did not experience the earlier period firsthand, they consider that there is a marked difference between that sociopolitical time and today. The public's attitude during those years is not openly criticized, but a link is constantly made with the present. The intolerance of those days is contrasted with the permissive character of today's society. Most of the interviewees regard the turbulent 1970s at arm's length, and not without a certain relief that those times now belong to a relatively distant past in people's minds as well as in years. The nostalgia betrayed in certain interviews by Italian police for the time when the actors had "comprehensible" goals (della Porta, in this volume) has not yet appeared in Spain, due fundamentally to the fact that the past decades, characterized by a high level of confrontation and manifest hostility on the part of many sectors of the public, are still very present in the inherited collective consciousness of these units.

Notable differences are also perceived between the 1980s and the present, as may be seen in the following remarks:

> [In comparison with the 1980s, control of public disorder today] is easier, above all because of the great experience we now have, and it's also true that the level of aggressive confrontation has diminished. There are more demonstrations, more public shows, but there is less violence. It's easier to control it, and there are clearer delimitations about what people can do within the bounds of legality.

Now everybody knows the rules that apply. . . . We have acquired experience
and so have the citizens. (Interview no. 5)

In comparison with the 1980s, the 1990s have displayed notably less aggressive confrontation in society. The fact that the actions of these units are,
from a legal point of view, more restricted means that officials are freed from
the obligation of taking decisions, thereby diminishing the likelihood of mistakes. Legislation on public order dating from 1959, with only minor changes,
remained in force until 1992, which meant that legal texts had not been fully
adapted to the new sociopolitical circumstances. This was clearly perceived
by the interviewees. They also observed that the public has moderated the
expression of its grievances, conforming to legality and to what "good demonstrations" and the "demonstration culture" from a police point of view ought
to be.

However, these transformations, particularly in relation to the 1970s, are
perceived very differently by the high-ranking chiefs interviewed. They are
much more reluctant to acknowledge that significant changes have taken
place in police behavior. As these high-ranking officers were members of this
type of unit in the 1970s, their caution points to a need for self-justification.
They find it necessary to show that no important changes have occurred in
the unit's way of operating and that they themselves have not changed in the
way they carry out their duties. By the same token, it must be pointed out
that some officers who were in service during the earlier period did recognize that certain changes had taken place in police control of social protests
after the death of Franco: In the second half of the 1970s "a certain disorientation developed. Unions and political parties were given authorization. And
police principles underwent a transformation now that their main activity was
to protect demonstrations. This period was a difficult one for the police" (interview no. 4). Those interviewees who served in these units during the
1970s particularly establish a direct connection between their interventions,
the relevant legislation, and political power, and thus avoid making the security forces responsible. This form of argument continually cropped up during
the interviews.

According to other officers interviewed, a significant change occurred in
1982 when the Socialists won the general election. A high-ranking officer observed: "In 1982–83, a more important change took place. The provincial gov-
ernors and the politicians told the brigades that they had to be more tolerant.
So, for example, an unauthorized demonstration was then treated with great
respect. During the UCD government, the law was interpreted more strictly"

(Interview no. 5). A further difference, relating to operational deployment and its criteria, may also be detected in the officials' comments, as the following illustrate:

> Their form of deployment was not always the same, but it was very similar. It's also true that demonstrations were broken up more than they are now. . . . It's true that we, the police, have become increasingly permissive, and it's also true that the groups are much less radical than before. The demonstration culture has entered into demonstrations more than before. We've all advanced, the police and the demonstrators. (Interview no. 9)

> Before, the old reserve units stayed in their barracks and only left them when there was already a rumpus to sort out. . . . As the demonstration was developing, there were police from that city there, and when it began to get out of hand, the reserves were called out and acted forcefully. The technique they use now is preventive deployment. When the demonstration is developing, the police are already deployed and they control the situation by means of that preventive deployment. (Interview no. 7)

A clear distinction is established between reactive and preventive forms of control over social protests. The handling of protests prior to 1985 (approximately) is considered purely reactive, whereas since that time it has been mainly preventive. This assertion explicitly establishes a clear distinction between two very different police models: one belonging to an authoritarian regime whose only objective is the maintenance of public order, and a preventive model that is gradually being introduced into all areas of police administration. This latter model denotes an appreciable change in attitude with respect to the past. Greater forcefulness is acknowledged in those police interventions where the reactive model prevailed.

The tactics employed by these units indicate to a large extent which model of police control a state has decided to apply. These tactics stamp relations between police and citizens with a very specific character, serving, in the Spanish case, as a reliable indicator of changes in police attitudes within the new sociopolitical context, as well as its adaptation to the European context. The following comments provide a clear example:

> Nowadays containment is practiced more than penetration. Ninety per cent of the interventions we carry out are a matter of waiting patiently, covering an area, and saying, "You can't go further than this." Then you see who can stand it longer. . . . In Cádiz we didn't go into the docks. Before, we would have gone into the docks and got them out. But on this occasion we limited ourselves to being there and preventing them from blocking the road into Cádiz. And waiting, waiting for hours. (Interview no. 5)

Now, we are increasingly moving toward massive intervention. . . . Increasingly, they try to send more police to this type of confrontation so as not to have to act with greater harshness. (Interview no. 4)

Total tolerance. Now we carry the idea in our heads that we've got to try to avoid a worse evil. There have even been times when we've known something illegal is going on in a demonstration. And we think about it and see that it's better at that moment to ignore it, because intervening would mean a bigger problem that would then be more difficult to resolve. And so we tolerate it. (Interview no. 8)

The tactics employed are typical of a police force that tends to exercise a gentler control over social protests. The use of forceful and aggressive means has fallen into disuse. The foreign models that most appeal are those that display a more tolerant attitude toward citizens' grievances. The police are aware that forceful methods may have counterproductive effects that would be difficult to predict.

There have also been appreciable changes in the actual methods used, judging from the remarks of police officers:

The baton is what is most used because, in the long run, it causes less harm. The first thing we do is carry out a full-scale police deployment to try to dissuade people. Firing rubber bullets is very problematic because they are not weapons with a precise aim. Tear gas is problematic because it can cause serious injury. You don't know whether some person has a respiratory condition. That's why we try not to use it. What we use most is police presence, massive deployment, and, as a last resort, the baton; in other words, hand-to-hand fighting. (Interview no. 8)

Water cannons. People associate them with South American dictatorships— Chile, for example. And here we say, if I use the water gun they're going to bracket me with those regimes. . . . perhaps that's why we don't use them. (Interview no. 9)

Horses are the last resort. They haven't been used in recent years because it's a risky business. In Spain, the cavalry hasn't been used, and using it now would attract a lot of attention. (Interview no. 5)

Those elements most associated with the past have been relegated to the shelves of history as far as possible and are only employed when absolutely necessary. The use of pressurized water or horses fosters an aggressive and violent image in the public mind, and for that reason utilization is eschewed. The advantage of batons is that they are inexpensive, their use can be easily controlled, and the consequences are predictable. Although there may be a general feeling within the public that the use of batons can lead to bloody scenes, the advantages easily outweigh the drawbacks. In general, techniques considered to be most harsh or shocking for the public tend to be used less.

Police Perceptions of the Opponent

The police force as an institution dedicated to the defense of the state's interests and to the peaceful coexistence of its citizenry develops a perception of the environment that is conditioned by the functions it carries out and by its own experience. Analysis of this perception is of special interest in the case of Spain. It will allow us to gain an understanding of the extent to which the perception of the opponent has evolved from the repressive 1970s to the present day when an attempt is being made to emphasize the predominantly social function of the security forces. Most of the interviews highlight the problems these units have had to face in the Basque country and in labor conflicts.[16] A medium-ranking officer explained the situation, without much enthusiasm:

> You're in Cádiz and there are HB people there, and now here in Madrid there's been a demonstration of conscientious objectors and there were advisers there who were pals of Jarrai.[17] The violent methods they use are the same: you find a device in Gijón, and you see the same one in Cádiz two months later. A Molotov cocktail is made with the same technique; a set of spikes for puncturing the tires of police vehicles: you find one in Galicia and then another in Sagunto [Valencia County]. There is a connection there. (Interview no. 3)

There is an idea, as the officer's remarks illustrate, of a sort of "Spanish International," with Basque groups helping the most troublesome sectors to oppose the state.

In general, differences are established within the police perception between "good" and "bad" demonstrators:

> Workers' conflicts are the same as they were a hundred years ago, with the same tactics, the same organization, the same problems. They are peaceful people, normal run-of-the-mill people who, at a given moment, get angry, organize themselves, use the methods they can, which are always the same. . . . They become very radical. Someone whom they're going to dismiss has lost everything and refuses to accept it, and it's logical that he refuses to accept it. For us, these are the cases we most dislike, because often you see these people's situation and you say, hell . . . what are these men supposed to do if all they've got left is the right to protest? But, well, it's got to be done, and we do it. But they're the most disagreeable cases, and they're the people who become most radical. (Interview no. 9)

The "good" demonstrators are those who protest about labor-related matters. Great sympathy is shown toward them, despite the harshness of the confrontations. Grievances of a political-nationalist nature, however, are decried, as clearly expressed by a medium-ranking officer: "Normally, someone who demonstrates . . . unless it's a question of ideologies, as in the case of the Jarrai lot, because they, well, they're not right about anything. But normally someone who demonstrates does so for strong reasons" (Interview no. 8).

This statement, which reveals a latent attitude, points to a clearly political element in the police evaluation of demonstrators as they deny the validity of collective grievances of a political nature or on the part of Basque radicals, with whom they have traditionally had very harsh confrontations. This tendency shows a net contrast with other European cases, such as that of Italy, where political protests are considered "positive," especially in relation to "nonpolitical" protests, because the latter usually involve violent behavior (della Porta, in this volume). Nevertheless, in both Spain and Italy protests are more readily legitimized by the police when the demonstrators make claims about matters that directly affect them. In the case of Spain, this rule tends to hold regardless of the level of violence generated by the protest. Violent demonstrations motivated by specific grievances and with specific objectives—generally of a material nature—are more likely to be tolerated, whereas those of an ideological nature are most despised by the security forces. This is possibly because of the fact that in a context of economic crisis, material grievances are more readily understood by the policeman-citizen, and at the same time they are less disturbing and threatening to the status quo.

"Low-intensity" confrontations with other groups elicited fewer comments from the interviewees:

> The problem with the students is that 90 percent of them don't know why they're in the demonstration. There is a tremendous lack of information. Ninety percent go because they know there's going to be a lot of larking about. The thing is that students are young people who enjoy having a good time. (Interview no. 3)

> The thing is that these groups are always the same, that is, the squatters are conscientious objectors and they are anarchists and they are anticapitalists and they are ecologists, and when we go to the demonstrations, they are the same. All those groups are the same people. (Interview no. 7)

The students are discredited by the police on the grounds that most of the demonstrators do not know what the objective of their protest is. A generally deprecatory attitude toward opponents is expressed here since all the groups are considered to be almost always the same: fringe youth groups.

At the same time, in some cases the police establish links between young

groups and organizations with more subversive targets, as explicitly recognized in the following statement: "[Behind the squatters] there are well-
constituted organizations. They are given respectability by lawyers who attempt to misrepresent the illicit activity and focus on the possible irregularity
of police activity. . . . They exploit every mistake we might have made in the
inquiry in order to set the media at our throats" (Interview no. 9). A conspira-
torial environment is perceived by the police, one that perhaps harks back to
earlier times when any sign of opposition to the regime was seen as the fruit
of a conspiracy. In any case, the enemy's image is very clearly profiled.

In contrast to the assertion by some experts in the field that there is a natural tendency on the part of the police to display sympathetic attitudes toward
ideologically right-wing positions (Lipset, 1971), no clear tendency of this
kind—nor, indeed, of the opposite—surfaced in these interviews. This was
also confirmed in the Italian case (della Porta, in this volume).

Thus, in the interviews with police officers, the way in which police perceptions have evolved in relation to their functions and to the surrounding
social environment can be observed. Although a few perceptions survive in a
partly altered form from earlier nondemocratic times, it may clearly be seen
that the preoccupations and tactics of these units do not greatly differ from
those of other European countries. It is also possible to conclude that there
is an overt tendency to use methods and tactics appropriate to what might
be called "soft" control of public order, characterized by the adoption of an
attitude of tolerance, generally speaking, by these units during outbreaks of
violence.[18]

Conclusion

As we have observed, the Spanish transition during the second half of the
1970s was characterized by a process whereby significant political and social
elements from Franco's regime were combined with new forms of political organization. These latter were mainly demanded by an emergent political elite
and by a society that had undergone a marked structural transformation
throughout the preceding decades. This linking of the mentality, the forms of
organization, and the interests of certain sectors of the former regime with
new ideas about how the state and society should be reorganized brought
with it, in many cases, new forms and hybrid structures. Depending on the
particular circle in which this process of combination took place, the resulting new structures either inclined back toward the old forms or toward a
break with them. In this sense, it may be seen that the administration was one

of the areas that experienced a slower pace of transformation. Indeed, both its structure and its personnel remained practically unchanged throughout the entire transition period. Within the administration itself, the armed forces, the judiciary, and the security forces, in comparison with other institutions, underwent the least significant transformation.

The police forces—independently of the pressure that the recently legitimized political forces were able, or wished, to bring to bear—underwent minimal personnel changes, affecting only certain members of the security forces who had been especially and directly important in the repression of the emergent political elite. With regard to police mentality, and particularly the structure of the forces, the transformations foreseen from the political Moncloa Agreements did not begin to take noticeable effect until well after the transition. When they came, it was largely as a consequence of the generational turnover that was progressively taking place during that period. Despite the evident differences between postwar Italy and the Spanish transition, clear parallels are evident in relation to the evolution of the security forces.[19] The initial conditions as regards their assigned sociopolitical role and the police "ethos" were significantly similar, largely as a consequence of the disadvantaged position of the progressive forces during the period of change—in the Spanish case, from the beginning of the transition; in the Italian case, particularly from 1947, when the progressive parties were removed from government.

It should be stressed here that, during the years of transition and democratic consolidation, the speed with which change occurred at the heart of the political organization varied significantly from one context to another. From what can be observed, we may deduce that those police sectors that were most closely linked with and committed to the former regime, those most impervious to external control (for example, the intelligence services), continued during the transition and the following years to carry out tasks that did not fully correspond to the functions assigned to the police in a democratic regime, displaying attitudes and conducting activities that, in many cases, escaped political control.[20]

In other parts of the police forces, certain transformations, albeit at a slow pace, began to be observed in operations, as in the case of the police units assigned to the control of social protests. Although it was not until the 1980s that such changes became noticeable and that they translated into a smaller number of victims in protests, it is true, judging by the officers' statements, that members of these police units began to feel the changes during the first years of the transition. These changes can only be explained within a three-tiered structural perspective. First, as social protest began to be seen as a legitimate form of expression of dissatisfaction on the part of citizens in a democratic state, the political elites gradually shifted toward adopting a more permissive line. Politicians were not willing to accept the high political cost of disproportionate police interventions. Second, the modernization of police personnel and methods, together with a progressive demilitarization of their perception of the environment, led the security forces to moderate their interventions and the forcefulness of their conduct. Third, the social demobilization advocated by the parties of "the masses" and the subsequent victory of the Socialists in 1982 resulted in a diminution of the intensity of social protests. The election victory contributed to a moderation of demands on the part of broad sectors of workers. From the beginning of the 1980s, all of these factors undoubtedly worked together to favor an abatement in the virulence of confrontations. In turn, this development translated into a significant decline in injuries and deaths, which became rare events from that time on.

Notes

1. We refer to the ideas of authoritarianism and democratic systems proposed by Lipset and Raab (1978) and O'Donnell and Schmitter (1986, chaps. 2 and 3).

2. The distinction between *Staats-* and *Bürgerpolizei* (Winter, in this volume) does not automatically correspond to the functions assigned to the police in a repressive state and a tolerant one, respectively. Rather, it corresponds to the degree of openness of the political elites in relation to new sociopolitical demands and the institutionalization of excluded political elites.

3. On the nature of the Francoist period, see Linz (1974).

4. After the civil war, two hundred thousand people were executed by the new regime (Preston, 1987, 223) after a trial or killed by fascist squads. Figures provided by official statistics of Franco's regime recognize implicitly that 105,000 people died violently after the war, but probably the final figures are higher (Tamames, 1973, 353).

5. In 1974, Lieutenant General García Rebull declared to the press: "As a Falangist, I do not accept any kind of associations. Associations are a dangerous evil for the whole of society." Quoted in Ballbé (1985, 452).

6. Ballbé, 1985, 455. There is no evidence that this change of attitude was ever the result of tacit agreements between the police force and demonstrators, as seems to have occurred in Hungary at the end of the 1980s (see Szabo, 1995).

7. In 1979, 20 percent of the members of parliament came from the elite of the Franco regime. UCD (Unión de Centro Democrático) members (center-right) belonging to this elite accounted for 23 percent, while for the AP (Alianza Popular; conservative) the figure rose to 82 percent. Similarly, 70 percent of the senators directly appointed by the king had been members of Franco's elite. As Baena and García Madaria (1979, 15) remark: "It is clear that the continuity in respect to the former regime has been propitiated by the person [the king] whom we must consider to be the engine of change."

8. For the attitude of the civil powers toward the army officers, see Preston (1986, chap. 5).

9. Some commentators consider it plausible that members of the state security services

were involved in certain terrorist actions that were carried out at crucial times during the transition period against high-profile individuals (Reinares, 1990).

10. As the Florentine judge Pier Luigi Vigna affirms: "The Spanish secret services used radical and violent exponents of the Italian groups in the extremist provocations of the first years of the transition" (Sánchez Soler, 1993, 167).

11. Between December 1975 and June 1976, for instance, more than fifty attacks were carried out by the extreme right, but the police did not make a single arrest (*El País*, July 20, 1976, 6). This state of affairs began to change in February 1983 as a result of the imprisonment of certain Italian, French, and Spanish ultraright-wingers involved in international terrorist attacks (Sánchez Soler, 1993, 202).

12. In fact, significant social convulsions did not take place either in favor of or against the change of regime. According to some authors (e.g., López Pintor and Buceta, 1975), anomie (in terms of a subject's attitude when faced with an environment he or she is powerless to influence) prevailed among the Spanish population. Subsequently, during the transition, the public's passivity favored the premeditated strategy of political "normalization" practiced by the elites (Benedicto, 1989). These elites became practically the only actors to define the evolution of the new regime.

13. The effects of this law have been discussed by Ballbé (1985, 471ff.), López Garrido (1987, 14), and Macdonald (1985).

14. We would like to thank the Área de Prospectiva del Gabinete de Estudios y Prospectiva de la Secretaría de Estado de Interior, as well as the Jefatura Central de las Unidades de Intervención Policial, for their help with this part of our research.

15. The interviews were carried out by Oscar Jaime-Jiménez between March 15 and December 19, 1995.

16. The police riot squads are no longer deployed in the Basque country, having been replaced by the mobile brigades of the autonomous Basque police (Ertzaintza). However, they still operate in Navarre, where the radical Basque collective is also strongly represented.

17. HB = Herri Batasuna, a legal political organization considered to be the political arm of the ETA. Jarrai is the youth branch of HB.

18. On the different styles of protest policing, see della Porta and Reiter (in this volume).

19. In both Spain and Italy, the police were characterized by the militarization of their structures and the adoption of primarily surveillance functions. Officers came from the army, so they had only minimal experience in civil matters. The similarities between these two cases are surprising (see Reiter, in this volume).

20. Again, significant parallels can be established between Spain during the transition period and Italy in the decades following the fall of the Mussolini regime (de Lutiis, 1993).

Chapter 8

Police Philosophy and Protest Policing in the Federal Republic of Germany, 1960–1990

Martin Winter

Problem Definition, Concepts, Hypotheses

How did the political self-image of the German police, and particularly that of high-ranking police officers, change during the period from 1960 until the German reunification in 1990? In which direction did police protest control strategy move during this period? What kind of interdependence exists between police conflict strategy in the context of public protests and police self-definition? This essay attempts to respond to these three questions by means of a chronological history of the police debate on the self-definition of the police and on police interventions during public protest events. The empirical basis of the essay lies not in police action but in *police knowledge* of their action.[1] One of the implicit premises of this essay is that cognitive structures are of significant relevance to action (Malinowski, 1975, 61). The type of police knowledge that is relevant to the questions above consists in interpretative models on the social and political macrolevel as well as on the mesolevel of conflict that have a direct bearing on protest policing.[2]

Two fundamental categories may be distinguished on the level of conflict knowledge: first, *protest diagnosis*, defined as the police assessment of protesters, their action patterns, and their action motives. In addition, protest diagnosis takes account of the police interpretation of conflicts involving the police themselves as actors and their political perspective on the conflict; second, *policing philosophies* favored by high-ranking police officers, that is, the conceptual principles and guidelines underlying police operations during protest events. The policing philosophy determines the method of protest policing resorted to in the case of specific forms of protest—that is, whether the police opt for offensive or defensive, tolerant or repressive, hard or soft, cooperative or confrontational tactics (see della Porta and Reiter, in this volume). On a second level, the macrolevel of police knowledge, I deal with general patterns of interpretation. On the one hand, this involves the *social diagnosis* of police officers, including their reflections on or perceptions of society, the state, and the political system, and, on the other hand, it takes in their definitions of the role of the police in the state and society. This is where the term "police philosophy" comes into play, which became an established term in police literature in the mid-1980s. "Police philosophy" expresses the normative (i.e., also the political) and factual self-image embedded in the social diagnosis, that is to say, the view of society and the conception of the police, the state, and democracy. In short, the term relates to views on the function and position of the police in the state and society. The categories of police knowledge—"police and policing philosophy" and "social and protest diagnosis"— may be regarded as legitimation theories (Berger and Luckmann, 1966), which provide both justification and explanation for police behavior.

We can construct a *typology of police philosophy* in two (ideal) basic patterns of police self-image: *Staatspolizei* (police serving the interests of the state) and *Bürgerpolizei* (police serving the interests of the citizens). In the *Staatspolizei* conception, the police protect the existing legal order, the *status constitutus*.[3] In their strictly legalistic thinking, highest priority is given to law enforcement, criminal prosecution, and the principle of legality. The safeguarding of the state and its monopoly on the use of force, seen as the greatest cultural achievement of civilized mankind, and the maintenance of the legal order are the core duties of the *Staatspolizei*. The state and its monopoly on the use of force are not only means to an end, but the end per se. The cornerstones of the self-image of the *Staatspolizisten* are centered on lines of argument based on a "well-fortified democracy"[4]—a democracy that is able to protect itself, which should fight its enemies, if necessary by restrictions on their fundamental rights—or on the police as the personification of the state and as the institution responsible for the protection of the state. Radical critics and disturbers of public order thus become personalized enemies of the state, and hence also of the police. This results in rigorous repressive police action against such activities considered to be hostile to the state. The threshold of police intervention (i.e., the adoption of "immediate coercion") is quite low in order to ensure that any threats to (public) order might be nipped in the bud. The protesters—the objects of police action—are ostracized as being deviant. Their existence contradicts the dominant conviction regarding the identity of the state and citizens. It is for this reason that dissidents are thought to come from outside the state (preferably from the Communist Eastern bloc, at least while it existed). The phenomenon of demonstrations meets with fundamental mistrust. It is perceived as an irritating, even alien, element in the harmonious concord between state and society, the governing and the governed.

The policing philosophy of the *Bürgerpolizei* model is grounded on the basic idea that the police must protect the democratic framework of opportunities for change. The underlying understanding of democracy and the state emphasizes the changeability of the legal system. The *status constituens*—defined as the "state-generating *Rechtsstaat*" (Denninger, 1978a, 117)—has constitutional status, its protection is of higher significance than mere law enforcement.[5] The advocates of this police philosophy set their value-conscious "constitutional legalism" against the formal juristic legalism of the *Staatspolizei*. They attach the highest importance to the Constitution and its values. The *Bürgerpolizisten* do not envisage the police force as an institution of the government, but rather of the Constitution and the republic. "To serve the people rather than the state" is the motto underlying this philosophy, which originated in the Anglo-Saxon police tradition (Busch et al., 1990, 18). The citizen is the subject of political change rather than the object of state actions. The public welfare orientation of the *Staatspolizei* is replaced by an individualized and citizen-centered self-image within this model. Typical lines of argument pertaining to this republican police philosophy include a continuous emphasis on the primacy of politics and on the primacy of political solutions over operative-tactical "substitute actions" on the part of the police. In particular, the police are required to protect demonstrations as an expression of the people's sovereignty in order to safeguard the opportunity for democratic change. Their intervention methods are thus characterized by the claim of civility. Language and communication are considered the major tools of action of the *Bürgerpolizei*. The use of force must remain the *ultima ratio*.

As this outline of the two types of police philosophies has shown, determination of the role and function of the police in state and society is embedded in the understanding given to democracy and the state. The image of the state and democracy and the self-image of the police are thus inseparably linked.

This essay has a historical-analytical character and is based on an evaluation of statements made by high-ranking police officers and ministerial officials in nationally published specialized police journals over the period from 1960 to 1990. Such semiofficial or official professional organs are used by police or ministerial officials to communicate with the professional public, that is, a group of people with similar status. In a qualitative contents analysis, I examined thirty-one volumes (1960–90) of the monthly *Die Polizei* (hereafter *DP*), fifteen volumes (1976–90) of the quarterly *Schriftenreihe der Polizeifüh-*

rungsakademie (hereafter *SPFA*), and four seminar reports produced by the Polizei-Führungsakademie (police staff college).[6]

The results of this analysis may be condensed into four hypotheses. First, the police force as a single entity does not exist. There are different schools of thought in the higher echelons of the police hierarchy regarding the position and functions of the police in state and society, and there are differences in opinion concerning "appropriate" methods of protest policing. Despite this plurality, however, the range of opinions among the police is relatively narrow;[7] many patterns of argumentation and interpretation as well as the essential frameworks within which conflicts are perceived and processed belong to a general repertory of high-ranking police officers. Continual calls by authors for consensus on internal security policy reflect the desire for concord and conformity.[8]

The second and third hypotheses concern developments in the debate within the police forces over the three decades under review. First, the prevailing police philosophy shifted from a state-focused, executive-oriented, and thus authoritarian *Staatspolizei* model toward a republican *Bürgerpolizei* conception, supportive of basic rights. Second, on the level of protest policing, an extension of police tolerance toward unconventional forms of protest can be detected. However, the extent to which these tendencies are actually manifest in the practice of protest policing and hence verifiable can only be ascertained through observation of police interventions.

The fourth hypothesis is the most significant: from 1960 until the German reunification in 1990, the police defined their position and functions within the state through their protest policing duties. Police philosophy and the philosophy of protest policing are therefore mutually dependent—the development of police philosophy (hypothesis 2) cannot be separated from the development of protest policing philosophy (hypothesis 3).

Phases and Developments in the Police Discourse between 1960 and 1990

Phase 1: The "Era of Good Feeling," 1960–67

The first phase in the development of the discourse within the police can be subdivided into two periods: a first period of public peace and order until 1961, and a second one, from 1962 to 1967, during which the first signs of political unrest could be felt. Fairchild (1988, 43) defines Phase 1 as the "era of good feeling": economic growth and internal peace characterized this period of stability in the history of the Federal Republic of Germany (FRG) and in the history of the police self-image. This is reflected in the satisfaction with state and social order expressed in journal articles. In comparison with later phases, the police view of society during 1960–67 was largely homogeneous. The social world of the high-ranking police officers was (still) in order and they identified themselves with the state. During this time there were no political protests of any import out on the streets. The previous major wave of protests in 1957–58, aimed at putting a stop to the nuclear armament of the Bundeswehr (the German army), had long since subsided.[9] Gradually, however, the first signs of cracks in this structure appeared: youth riots, in particular the so-called Schwabinger Krawalle in July 1962, and later on the nascent student protests.

A debate on the combatant status of the police gradually developed from 1961 on (most heated from 1961 to 1963), centered on the issue of the protection of the police under international law according to the Hague Land Warfare Convention. The issue was whether the police force was a military institution, with its members consequently enjoying combatant status, or whether it was a civil administration. At its core this discussion on combatant status was a dispute about the military versus the civil character of the police; the cue for the debate was: the "deployment of mortars by the police" (*DP* 9, 1961, 257).[10] Particularly the troops of the *Bereitschaftspolizeien* (barracked standby units) of the *Länder* (federal states) and of the *Bundesgrenzschutz* (federal border police) had a paramilitary character.[11] In particular, the reform-oriented Gewerkschaft der Polizei (the strongest police trade union in Germany) came out strongly in favor of a civil police force. The debate focused not only on the profile, job content, equipment, and armament of the police, but also on the internal leadership style, the "internal structure" (*DP* 12, 1961, 357) and esprit de corps (*DP* 9, 1961, 258), the institutional independence of the police, and thus on their role and position in state and society (i.e., on a police philosophy). A number of conferences were held on themes relating to a mental reorientation of the police. This debate on the military character of the police began to subside in *Die Polizei* in 1963.

From 1962 to 1965, the police were forced to deal on a large scale with the youth riots, that is, with masses in the streets who were neither "orderly" nor firmly led. The disproportionate nature and brutality of police interventions, especially during the Schwabinger Krawalle, proved to be highly controversial. The massive public criticism and a flood of charges brought against the police gnawed at the police self-image.[12] As a consequence of their violent overreaction, the police moved to the center of public attention. In turn, the strong criticism from outside initiated a debate within the police force on appropriate tactics for dealing with such new phenomena: the "traditionalists" (the advocates of a state-oriented police philosophy clinging to the status quo) demanded that decisive action be taken in order to "nip anarchistic excesses in the bud and to set further deterring examples" (*DP* 3, 1964, 74); the "reformers" pleaded for a "soft wave," a flexible and less confrontational concept of police action, in order to avoid an escalation of violence. This debate also took up general issues of police philosophy, and of the position of the police in the state and society, as central themes.

On the whole, the experiences in Schwabing greatly influenced the learning process within the police on a national level. The Schwabing example shows, incidentally, the degree to which the police learned by experience, that is, reactively. The organizational and tactical consequence of the Schwabinger Krawalle was the development of the *Münchner Linie* (Munich line) by the local police chief, Manfred Schreiber. This line of thought advocated a method of protest policing better suited to the events, with greater tolerance toward unconventional behavior by young people and less spectacular employment of force, which had to be justified in the eyes of the public. A mobile press office for public relations work and, very importantly, a police psychological service were institutionalized. The "occurrence" of the riots was described by Schreiber as a "mass psychotic event" (*DP* 2, 1965, 33); as a consequence, police psychology for the first time received the order to provide consultation in leadership and operational issues (Trum, 1981, 701). In the fields of deployment, leadership, and personnel, measures were taken to increase police efficiency and to improve technical resources. The fierce clashes between the police and crowds led to the development of a long-term and central debate on the issue of acceptance of police measures against public protesters.

In Phase 1 the police self-image was strongly state-focused; the traditionalists, "policemen of the old school," dominated the discourse. The police identified themselves with the state and equated the authority of the state with the authority of the police. Authors in the specialized journals spoke of a "state consciousness" which needed to be instilled in citizens as a bulwark against egoism, which was detrimental to public welfare and disturbed the harmony between state and society. The executive power was exalted as the core of the state; by analogy, the police saw themselves as a "meta-institution," as an authority that stood above social affairs. The major duty of the police was seen as the protection of the community—and this meant the state order, according to the dominating view. Therefore, in Phase 1 the police, according to their self-image, can be classified as a *Staatspolizei*. However, even in this first phase forces already existed that demanded a departure from the military traditions toward more civilized police structures and patterns of action.

Phase 2: Radical Change and Reform, 1967–72

As was the case with Phase 1, this second phase can be subdivided into two periods: the period of unrest and upheaval from 1967 to 1969 provoked by the student revolt, and the reform era from 1970 to 1972. The "good feeling" that marked Phase 1 was replaced by a certain dissatisfaction with the state and society on the side of the traditionalists; a system of order was collapsing. Rockers, hippies, beatniks, and political "provos" were destroying their harmonious worldview, with its assumption of consensus between the governing and the governed, between state and society. The identification of the police with the state and its society—an essential element of the police self-image in the first phase—was suffering a severe crisis.

The new phase began in June 1967, marked by the fatal shooting of a student, Benno Ohnesorg, by a policeman, Karl-Heinz Kurras, during a demonstration against the visit by the Shah of Iran to West Berlin on June 2.[13] Suddenly, the discussion within the police changed; a controversial dispute between the reformers and the traditionalists flared up. Profound differences between the two camps became visible in their general approaches to protest policing (the policing philosophy) and in police philosophy. The tone of the debate became more and more aggressive, particularly on the part of the traditionalists, who fought a dogged rearguard action. Whereas only a small number of reformers had held their ground in Phase 1, this new phase saw them gradually become dominant.

The main stimulus for the intense debate derived from the student protests. The conflicts caused by the student revolt and the Außerparlamentarische Opposition (extraparliamentary opposition—hereafter, APO) in 1968 provoked the most profound break in police discourse in thirty years, and paved the way for the further development of the police. A fundamental right was discovered! "Until the beginning of the sixties, the heading 'Demonstration' was not to be found in the textbooks on politics and constitutional law" (*DP* 7, 1970, 213). The phenomenon of (political) demonstrations took the police by surprise and became the central topic in police discourse because, as had happened at the time of the Schwabinger Krawalle, the police and their operations became a focus of public attention. This time, however, the public scrutiny occurred to an extent previously not believed possible. Problems concerning police image and legitimation resulted from severe public criticism of the brutal policing methods during student demonstrations (Hoffmann, 1968, 1268f., 1281); the debate on the definition of the position of the police reached its climax. The number of contributions to police journals increased accordingly.

The first articles published in 1968 were concerned with the methods used by the police to deal with the protests; the debate between traditionalists and reformers concentrated on the issue of a repressive versus a flexible tactical line. The first signs of this debate could already be observed in Phase 1. Owing to its success in Munich, and probably also to the change in the general political climate (there was a change of national government to a Social Democrat–Liberal coalition in 1969), the *Münchner Linie* prevailed. Parallel to the dispute on operational conceptions, a controversy developed around political assessments of the protesting students. The following two quotations reflect the range of opinions on the protest diagnosis among the participants in the discussion: "The student youth constitutes an extremely strong democratic potential in the population" (*DP* 12, 1969, 377); "When the demonstrators today shout 'Away with Huber' [the minister of culture] or 'Ami, go home,' with this message of salvation they are not very far away from the SA who shouted 'The Jews are to blame for everything'" (*DP* 7, 1970, 214f.).

Not least among the repercussions of the emerging demonstrations, which during Phase 2 became a part of normality in the FRG and an important component of the range of police duties, was the change they provoked in the concepts of democracy and of the role of the police. Social conflicts made the discrepancy between state and society apparent to police officers; the traditionalists' belief in the harmonious identity of state and citizens was proven to be mistaken by the practice of protest policing. Massive crowds were even associated with communist attempts at a coup d'état and equated with a revolutionary danger for the state. Following Le Bon's *Mass Psychology* (1982, first published in 1895), mass gatherings were seen as irrational and animalistic and hence potentially dangerous (*DP* 4, 1964, 103).

It was with this understanding of extraparliamentary protests that the police faced the student revolt. Strict injunctions, such as the requirement for demonstrators to walk in rows of three, curtailed the freedom of protesters. Any transgression was met with harsh and violent action by the police; the threshold for the use of police force was very low, the police were liable to interfere even if the demonstrators deviated from the preannounced march route. The level of violence was also an expression of the perplexity and sense of impotence on the part of the police, who did not know how to assess or handle this new phenomenon of "disorderly" and spontaneous demonstrations—all they had experienced in the past were disciplined rallies, parades, and Corpus Christi processions.[14] Because of this feared inadequacy, the political aversion of the police leaders and, in case of doubt, an order-dominant (i.e., violent) solution determined police actions.

The implementation of the *Neue Linie* ("new line," as I call this new operational concept) in the late 1960s marked a turning point in police thinking from "paramilitary" insurrection combat to "police-style" protest policing. With this new line, the police actually recognized the freedom to demonstrate as a fundamental right deriving from the Constitution (Article 8). Police action was thus supposed to be directed not against a demonstration as a whole, but against the troublemakers and violent activists among the demonstrators. The protection of the gathering was one of the duties of the police force. The freedom of assembly enshrined in the Constitution obliged the police leaders to approve of demonstrations—even if the political motives of the demonstrators seemed incomprehensible to them. In retrospect, a seminar of the Police Staff College came to the following conclusion:

> The police were forced to realize that the conventional principles of police deployment often did not meet the psychological requirements during this phase of demonstration activities. Especially in this period of time, the police had to learn "the hard way" because they offered themselves time and again as an aggressive partner and in their efforts to safeguard obsolete concepts of law and order they very often provoked conflicts that could have been avoided. (Polizei-Institut Hiltrup, 1971, 4)[15]

The debate progressively moved away from protest policing to more general topics, such as the predominant commitment of the police to the Constitution and the proximity of the police to citizens; discussion on the police self-image, a police philosophy, thus reached a first peak (Boldt, 1992, 34). Until its gradual decline, following the fall of the grand coalition (1969), the student revolt provided much tinder to the debate within the police force. In the wake of the students' radical drive for change, the larger society as well as parts of the police were infected by a mood for reform: on the one hand, the police feared impending revolutionary machinations; on the other, the general reformatory euphoria was contagious and led to demands from within the forces for democratic reforms of the state and the police. Once again, the discussion focused on the demand for a more civil character of the police. Calls were made for police actions to be demilitarized, police competences and duty profiles were to be shifted toward "social engineering," and, last but not least, a debate on the function and role of the police in the political process developed.

After calm had returned to the demonstration events and the police had slowly drifted from the center stage of public discussion, more extensive reform aspirations going beyond a mere increase in the efficiency of police work faded from the debate. This was also the case with regard to the duties of protest policing: the *Neue Linie* became generally accepted in 1969 and guidelines issued by the Ministries of the Interior vested it with an authoritative character. The dysfunctional ballast of the protest policing course of the traditionalists, which only created problems in terms of public acceptance and the image of the police, was abandoned. The conception of the *Neue Linie* can only be judged, however, as ambiguous: on the one hand, it followed the line of argument of the reformers in defining the fundamental right of freedom to demonstrate as an object of police protection; on the other hand, it moved away from the reformers' sociopolitical demands aimed at a democratization of the state and the police, which, for instance, were fervently made by the commanding officer Tonis Hunold (1968). The political open-mindedness shown by the reformers toward protesters was replaced by an instrumental-tactical opposition to "troublemakers," who were to be "fought" by means of flexible, efficient operational tactics, improved equipment (water cannons, tear gas, etc.), and with the support of psychological methods.[16] This approach was significantly strengthened during Phase 3.

From this point on, political demonstrations became a regular aspect of practical police work. Many high-ranking police officials, however, continued to harbor a negative attitude toward this phenomenon. The association of demonstrators with troublemakers remained vital, as reflected in the markedly instrumental views of police leaders on protesters and their actions. Their attention was focused on the troublemakers, who were to be separated from sympathizers and other participants in protest events. Disturbing the peace and nonadherence to the "rules of the game" in political conflicts were punished by disciplinary measures. By projection, it was assumed that the troublemaker, as an opponent of the police, followed an instrumental strategy and tactic, which the police themselves adopted toward the troublemaker. This instrumental thinking contained a fundamental distrust toward protesters, who, under the disguise of "spontaneous" demonstrations, were suspected of following a strategy of strict leadership with an elaborate preparation of events and adopting aggressive tactics in order to provoke the police (*DP* 5, 1969, 102).

The limits of the police reform in the areas of centralization, expansion of police competences, and degree of autonomy were drawn at the political level. The commitment to law and order was and remained the supreme maxim of the police; this meant the rejection of an overly far-reaching preventive orientation of police work. The reform debate died down in 1972;

from then on there was once again political consent on the police issue. The result on paper of the police reform efforts was the "Programm für die innere Sicherheit" (Program for Internal Security), adopted in 1972 by the Conference of the Ministers of the Interior, and modified in 1974. The reform covered the organizational structure, police law, training, equipment, personnel, and duties. It consisted above all in modernization (e.g., the entire technical equipment of the *Bereitschaftspolizei* was modernized), specialization, standardization, (limited) "defederalization," and financial and personnel expansion of the security forces (see Busch et al., 1985, 69ff.).

The police reform of Phase 2 must be described as exclusively technocratic-organizational; there was no reform of the contents. The democratic reform demanded by some police reformers did not materialize; what was left was an "improved bureaucratic efficiency" (Busch et al., 1985, 441). The police reform did away with the dysfunctional remnants of police thinking and action—for instance, in the area of protest policing, where it abolished counterproductive strategies and operational principles (massive use of force at a low intervention threshold)—and created the material preconditions for the *Neue Linie* by bringing about a demilitarization of the police armaments: CN gas, water cannons, helmets, and shields were introduced, while mortars and machine guns (which had never been used in the context of demonstrations) were scrapped.

The *Neue Linie* in protest policing was certainly based on democracy-friendly principles. However, like the general police reform, it detached itself from the democratic understanding of the reformers. By bringing strategic and tactical factors to the fore, the instrumental perspective denied the political character of the demonstrations. The result was limited to an increase in efficiency and to the adaptation of police measures to the practice of protest policing. The conventional methods of protest policing damaged the image and acceptance of the police within the public; the frequent use of seemingly arbitrary force had high costs for the police in terms of legitimation. The understanding that protest policing not only takes place during a police intervention but also in the public discourse on such interventions was gradually accepted. "What matters for the police is not that they win a battle but that they avoid one" (Polizei-Institut Hiltrup, 1971, 7). Violent conflicts and battles were considered counterproductive not only for democracy, but also for the police image; the threat remained that public criticism of coercive police interventions would undermine the legitimation of police action.

Phase 3: Consolidation, 1973–79

Once again, this phase can be subdivided into two periods: a period of stabilization of the reform and consolidation from 1973 to 1974, and a period dominated by the fight against terrorism from 1974 to 1979. Following the troubled period of the student revolt and the waning of the debate within the police in 1972, the 1973–79 period can be described as relatively calm. The police were not exposed to a critical public—a statement that requires qualification, however, from 1975 on.

The continuation and 1974 amendment of the "Program for Internal Security" and the considerable increase in state spending on internal security hardly constituted reasons to debate police philosophy. The 1970s reform of the internal organization of the police toward greater efficiency was accelerated by the "supportive thrust of terrorism for police reform" (Busch et al., 1985, 440): politicians declared that decisive resistance would be put up against left-wing extremist terrorism (i.e., the Revolutionäre Zellen, the Bewegung 2. Juni, and, above all, the Rote Armee Fraktion). The fight against terrorism as the outstanding duty of the state became the priority task of the police; the improvement of efficiency of police actions was now at the center of police reform. In the debate (1974–78), the fight against terrorism eclipsed all other facets of protest policing interventions. During this "state under threat" period, the new priority role of the police as the institution mandated to protect the order of the state brought sufficient legitimation and acceptance among the population.

The fight against terrorism did not shake the police self-image, which explains why there was virtually no controversial debate during these years on police philosophy. Owing to the existence of an external enemy—the terrorists—the police were united internally. During this phase, an extraordinarily large number of contributions by the highest-ranking politicians were published in the specialized police journals under review. Police and politicians seemed to move closer under the impression of danger they perceived as threatening the state.

Some of the participants in the police discourse even launched a political "rollback": the liberalization of society was blamed for the emergence of terrorism; in the opinion of police leader Georg Wolf, for instance, it caused "a dismantling of the *Rechtsstaat*" (*DP* 6, 1978, 195). Driven by the terrorist threat to the state, argumentative figures in favor of a "state police" emerged. This led to a renaissance of arguments for a strong state that must defend itself against attacks from both the left and the right, pleas for a stronger "constitutional militancy," and opposition to tendencies for social liberalization, which were fervently put forward during Phases 1 and 2, as is illustrated by the following remark: "A *Rechtsstaat* that is not able to defend itself is incapable of surviving and risks the danger of soon ceasing to be a state and hence a *Rechtsstaat*" (*DP* 6, 1978, 195).

Phase 4: 1979–90, Evolution of a New Police Philosophy?

Phase 4 can be subdivided according to a number of "milestones," mainly created by the activities of protesters and protest groups. The main points of emphasis in the police discourse triggered a gradual evolution of the police self-image, which makes it difficult to draw lines between the different periods.

The first focus of public debate, beginning in 1979 but especially during 1980–82, concerned police treatment of protesters—participants in the so-called youth protest,[17] the alternative movement and, in general, the new phenomenon of *Bürgerinitiativen* (civic action groups). Articles on protest policing proliferated in the specialized journals during 1981, reaching numbers similar to the time of the first protest wave in 1968. Once again clashes between the police and social protest movements and their strong public resonance stimulated a lively debate on the position of the police, although it did not seem to shake their very foundation as had been the case in 1968. Problems relating to political guidelines and the political aspects of police interventions became the main topics in the police discourse, which reached its peak in 1982. The controversy was sparked by the eviction of squatters; its legal peg was the dilemma faced by the police between carrying out their duties to enforce the law and fending off dangers. This debate on the toleration of violations of the law, on "law-free" areas (*rechtsfreie Räume*), and on the principles of legality, appropriateness, and proportionality in the context of squatting and other protest actions led to the gradual delineation of different tactical lines. Further protest waves were shaking the police: the period of the peace movement saw leading police officials grappling with issues concerning methods of civil disobedience—nonviolent methods, but relevant under criminal law.

The second important "milestone" during this phase was the change in October 1982 on the national political level in West Germany, with the coming to power of a conservative-liberal coalition. This swing, according to Werkentin (1988, 99), did not have a significant impact on the internal security policy of the federal government. However, following the shift in power on the national level, the *Länder* governed by the Social Democrats moved toward a citizen-centered police philosophy. The politicization of security policy was dividing the *Länder* into two camps: the so-called *A-Länder* and the *B-Länder*, the former were governed by the SPD (Social Democratic Party), the latter by the CDU (Christian Democratic Union). Responsibility for this split lay principally with the politicians, not the police. However, it was also reflected at the highest police levels, where, parallel to the political level, two camps had formed. The rupture of the (informal) grand coalition over police policy translated into a crisis within the police from the early 1980s on regarding basic concepts. Regardless of whether there was a general split or merely differences of opinion on individual points, divergences in the evaluation of protest movements (protest diagnosis), in the police "management" of protests (policing philosophies), and in the conceptions of police philosophy now existed.

The third "milestone," a crucial event in the evolution of the political self-image of the police, was marked by the 1985 decision of the Federal Constitutional Court (*Bundesverfassungsgericht*) on the prohibition of a demonstration against the nuclear power plant at Brokdorf in 1981. In its judgment, the court underlines the important constitutional role of the freedom of assembly; consequently it claims that the authorities have to act in an assembly-friendly way. The degree to which this judgment in favor of basic rights dominated further debate is quite astonishing: the definitive ruling can be judged as confirmation of the arguments put forward by the police reformers of Phases 1 and 2. This decision also influenced ideas concerning protest policing in the *Länder* governed by the conservatives.

The fourth "milestone" during Phase 4 was the new antinuclear power movement (1986), the last big protest wave of the 1980s. Triggered by the reactor disaster at Chernobyl, demonstrations were held across the country in the FRG. Energy policy became the center of a nationwide public discussion. The crest of this wave was the violent clashes between protest groups and the police around the building site of a reprocessing plant for spent nuclear fuels at Wackersdorf and the demonstrations at Wackersdorf, Brokdorf, and Hamburg. As a result of their interactions with protesters, which escalated into violence, the police were again pushed into the hot spot of public attention.

Chernobyl and the "Battle for Nuclear Power" (as a series by the news weekly *Der Spiegel* [nos. 30, 31, and 32, 1986] was headlined) proved to be the catalysts for the subsequent discourse on police philosophy, which for the first time was conducted *expressis verbis* under this name. The foundations for this discussion were laid by Kurt Gintzel and Hermann Möllers in 1987 with an article on their basic rights-friendly *Neue Polizeiphilosophie* (new police philosophy) (*DP* 1, 1987, 10), as they themselves called their programmatic statement. The debate on police philosophy lasted from the mid-1980s to the early 1990s, with an intensity unparalleled in the thirty years under review. This debate was dominated by representatives of the constitution- and citizen-oriented new police philosophy (the director of the *Bereitschaftspolizei* in North Rhine-Westphalia, Kurt Gintzel, and Bonn's police chief, Michael Kniesel). No other diverging outlines of a police philosophy were put forward.

Why were police leaders explicitly demanding a police philosophy? Several lines of argument emerge from the police journal articles:

- When police work increasingly suffers acceptance problems, a police philosophy acts as an antidote to legitimacy and identity crises among the police. A police philosophy serves to explain police measures to the outside world, also in view of changed (legal) opinions (*SPFA* 4, 1989, 50).

- The discussion on police philosophy also has an internal effect, serving to "consolidate a self-image of the police" (*SPFA* 4, 1989, 6). The creation of a police philosophy aims to distance the police from daily politics and to immunize them against populistic and opportunistic behavior (*DP* 5, 1990, 100). In particular, during legally delicate interventions, the police have to avoid giving the impression of exercising *vorauseilender Gehorsam* (anticipating obedience, i.e., police in a given protest policing situation act as they assume their superiors would like them to), or actual or apparent political opportunism (ibid.). A police philosophy as a clarification of the police self-image is linked with calls for greater self-confidence and independence of the police from politics (*SPFA* 4, 1989, 98), especially because there is "a relatively high degree of disappointment and anger toward politics" among the police in the late 1980s (*SPFA* 4, 1989, 97).

- A common police philosophy functions as a unifying bond within the police and strengthens them in relation to the outside world. The deficit concerning a unified conception of the role and duties of the police results in differing assessments of situations and differing attitudes during police interventions (*SPFA* 4, 1989, 107f.). In order to be better armed for the "challenges during violent events" (*SPFA* 4, 1989, 5) and for increasingly aggressive crime, agreement on the issues involved in the definition of the position of the police is a necessary condition. Finally, the demand for a unified police theory includes a call for consensus in security policy (*SPFA* 4, 1989, 116).

Within the general development toward a new police philosophy, however, more conservative lines of thinking remained clearly visible in the discussion. State-focused and legalistic elements of a *Staatspolizei* program permeated (still permeate?) the interpretation patterns of police leaders, as reflected in the frequent statements concerning the identity of state and police, of the police as "the state power personified" (*DP 2*, 1984, 38). Until well into the 1980s (and partly even in more recent discussions), the discussants' concepts of democracy were chiefly grounded in representative parliamentarism and the majority principle. Authors showed suspicion toward plebiscitary and participatory elements, such as the collective articulation of political demands on the streets. They presumed that decisions taken by a majority in parliament should be accepted by the population. Police leaders reacted with incomprehension and disapproval not only to calls for militant resistance but also to calls for civil disobedience. They saw such actions as a violation of the basic "rules of the game" of the democratic political process and of law and order. In their *protest diagnosis*, actions of this nature lost their credibility and legitimacy. In a polarizing manner, authors separated constructive criticism from destructive criticism: politically credible protests that adhered to the "rules of the game," from politically illegitimate protests that disregarded the "rules." The *Rechtsstaat* and democracy were seen in black-and-white terms—yes or no; any intermediate level of "more" of democracy or "less" of *Rechtsstaat* was unimaginable within this either-or perspective. This "magnetic field" of bipolar "friend-foe" thinking meant that even less radical critics of the state order fell into the category of opponents of the system to be fought. Troublemakers, according to the line of argument commonly used to this day, abuse the right to demonstrate as they commit criminal offenses under the cover of this fundamental right. For this reason they should be prosecuted under criminal law. Demonstrations continued to constitute an irritating, even potentially threatening, issue for public order, as can be gathered from articles published in Phase 3 and early Phase 4. The evaluation of demonstrations as a positive element of democracy only gradually gained momentum in the consciousness and the published texts of the police leaders.

As far as the *policing philosophy* is concerned, the central ideas of the *Neue Linie* remained valid in the 1980s. However, the gap between their claim (protection of the right to demonstrate) and the actual acceptance of plebiscitary forms of action on the part of protesters was narrowed only slowly. A decisive step in this direction was the Brokdorf decision of the Federal Constitutional Court. This decision strengthened the positive evaluation of the right to demonstrate by emphasizing its democratic functions and confirmed the basic principles of the *Neue Linie*. Its impact on the police discourse should not be underestimated; participants in the discussion simply could not sidestep this decision. The argumentation of the Constitutional Court became the mainstream line—also in the *Bundesländer* governed by the conservatives.[18] The police discourse and the practice of protest policing were now concentrated on violent troublemakers and militant activists. The differentiation ruling of the Federal Constitutional Court supported the consistently harsh action taken against violent troublemakers: they were to be arrested on the basis of secure evidence, while the police were to assist and help peaceful demonstrators. The judgment narrowed the instrumental perspective of the *Neue Linie* to the militant core of demonstrations; the police concentrated their tactical efforts on the *Schwarze Block* (black block) formed by the black-dressed Autonomen activists during demonstrations. The court decision also increased tolerance by its broad definition of demonstrations, which included spontaneous ones. Acceptance of spontaneous demonstrations was not new for the *Neue Linie*, but the authority of the Federal Constitutional Court gave this point additional weight. One indicator of the increased tolerance toward assemblies was the more relaxed handling of mass demonstrations involving tens of thousands of participants. The police of the 1980s ceased to fear any threat to the state, nor even the danger of revolution, as they had twenty or twenty-five years earlier.

A shift toward greater tolerance should also be noted in police dealings with nonviolent civil disobedience, cultivated in particular by peace movement activists in blockades of military installations between 1982 and 1984. In accordance with a 1969 decision of the *Bundesgerichtshof* (Federal High Court, hereafter, BGH),[19] the police condemned such actions as coercive violence. The commentary on the police service regulation *PDV 100* of July 1986 (3.4.3.1, 6) argues along the same lines. However, the nonviolent nature of the peace movement's sit-in blockades made it unthinkable for the public to place them in the militant "corner," nor did it seem appropriate from a police tactical point of view. Thus, evaluations of this phenomenon developed from a categorical rejection of blockaders and condemnation of blockades as acts of violence toward a differentiated view that, however, was not shared by all police officers. Some of the authors, particularly the supporters of the *Neue Polizeiphilosophie* (for whom the state monopoly of force is not jeopardized by sit-in blockades), began to make a distinction between blockaders committing an offense and violent activists and warned against the criminalization of peaceful blockaders. Yet, uncertainty remained among the police as to the legal situation of sit-in blockades.[20]

Supported by the Brokdorf judgment of the Federal Constitutional Court
and driven by the debate over police actions during the antinuclear power
protests, the police discourse from the mid-1980s on saw an increasing tendency to align the police self-image less with state-focused and more with
republican ideas: "The citizen is superior to the state. . . . From this it follows that police intervention as a matter of priority must serve neither the
furtherance of some ominous reason of state nor of the collective good of
public welfare or the public interest, but the protection of the individual"
(Kniesel, 1987, 26f.). For the citizen-oriented police philosophy, "more" of
civil society meant "less" state in the political process: "Democracy is not
an event controlled by the police with the citizen as a participant in the
state" (Alfred Dietel and Michael Kniesel, in *DP* 11, 1985, 337). Legitimation
for police intervention was provided by reference to the Constitution, its
principles and fundamental rights, which the police were to protect. Advocates of this constitution-oriented police philosophy came predominantly
from North Rhine-Westphalia. Distinct from the traditional, state-focused
police philosophy, they argued for the police to be regarded as a *Bürgerpolizei*, a police force serving the people: "Because of this position as a guar-
antor, the police cannot be qualified as the mere preserver of the status quo,
as a repressive instrument wiping off political protest. In this respect, it is
not a *Staatspolizei* but a *Bürgerpolizei*, as it has to guarantee the chances of
the minority—which, according to Article 1, Paragraph 1 *Grundgesetz*, as a
subject of political change is a majority 'in being'—to become a majority, as
long as it keeps itself within the framework of the Constitution" (Kniesel,
1987, 28).[21]

If the police philosophy supported by high-ranking police officers has
moved away from concepts of a police force serving the state and toward concepts of the police serving the citizens, and if the philosophy of policing has
developed along the lines of greater tolerance toward forms of protest—if,
therefore, profound changes have occurred—we need to pinpoint the factors
that brought about these changes:

- Personnel changes at the highest executive, political levels (ministers
  of the interior, secretaries of state, high-ranking ministerial officials)
  and in the police hierarchy brought about by election changes or retire-
  ment: only a new generation of top-level police officials could facilitate
  a general change in police philosophy. Individuals within the police
  hardly change their self-image over the course of time; they adapt it, if
  at all, to the prevailing linguistic usage.

- The authority of the Federal Constitutional Court, which is capable of cementing turning points in protest policing by the legal force of its decisions.

- Changes in the assessment of forms of protest by the population: representative opinion polls have shown a tendency toward growing acceptance of unconventional forms of action among the population (Kaase and Neidhardt, 1990).

- The actions of protesters: it may be assumed that the actions of protesters have positively influenced the public climate in relation to the use of unconventional forms of protest (as well as the attitudes of the Federal Constitutional Court and of the police).

The Interdependence of Policing Philosophy and Police Philosophy

During the thirty years under review, the police were marked by "chronic" identity and legitimacy problems, as the discourse among officers in the highest echelons of the police hierarchy illustrates. Why did the police require continuous clarification of their self-image throughout these years? This question can be answered by linking police philosophy and policing philosophy in the police discourse.

It is striking that the controversy over protest policing reached a peak of intensity during the same periods as the debate on police philosophy, as may be seen at the time of the student revolt in the late 1960s and the youth protest in the early 1980s. Discussion within the police climaxed in each of these cases a few months after the heyday of protest events and the maximum public reception.[22] Thus, it would appear that discussants among the police are always reacting to protests, they never succeed in anticipating them.[23] Debate is sparked within the police as a consequence of police interventions during demonstrations and public reactions.

This interconnection between police philosophy and protest policing is confirmed by the authors themselves. The high-level police officials writing in the specialized journals continually established a link between a general definition of the position of the police and the debate on protest policing. Starting from general statements on the role and position of the police in the FRG, authors often concentrated on the political sphere of police action, on the issue of demonstrations and of violent actions during demonstrations. Even in articles on the general crime situation, discussants focused particular attention on politically motivated criminality during protests, squatting events, and so on. During periods of intense protest activity this connection became even more apparent, with frequent calls for a (re)definition of the position of the police in state and society. From the viewpoint of the top police officials, protest policing constitutes a significant range of tasks for police action for the following reasons:

- The police, who define themselves as the personification of the state and as an instrument for the protection of the state, feel challenged by protests that criticize the state, particularly in terms of their potential delinquency.

- Protest policing constitutes the most publicity-effective field of police action. In the wake of coverage of (spectacular) demonstrations and police interventions, the police were drawn into the center of public debate. In the confrontation with protesters, the dilemma of legality and legitimacy in police intervention was brought to light.[24] If their leaders deemed the use of "immediate compulsion" appropriate, the police revealed their "ugly," because violent, face during demonstrations. Police leaders felt responsible for possible conclusions drawn by the public, from the police as the "'visiting card' of the state" (Hunold, 1968, 128) to the state itself, since general legitimation and acceptance problems of the state also touched the identity of the police given that they identified themselves with the state. The use of force by the police is both the trump card (as a legally usable resource) and the Achilles' heel of police tactics. Violence, even if legally used, has to be publicly justified; the legal justification does not (any longer) suffice for its legitimation in public opinion. Continuous legitimation deficits of police interventions in public opinion result in general identity crises of the police, who feel stripped of the basis of trust within the population.

- Further dilemmas of police actions are especially reflected in the concrete police intervention. The police find themselves in a strained relationship between protection of the existing legal system and protection of the emerging one, between *status constituens* and *status constitutus*, between security and freedom, between state and society, between neutrality in the political process and political responsibility. Confrontation in the streets with people who are critical (of the state) thus becomes a test case for the self-image of the police, particularly in situations where the law is violated.

Protest policing forms an essential component of the political self-image of the police, with the result that the police philosophy is mainly defined through protest policing. On the other hand, police conceptions of the state and democracy become manifest in their treatment and control of protest movements. It thus follows that there is a mutual feedback process between police philosophy and policing philosophy.

How does this interconnection between the police philosophy discourse and protest events come about? One major "battle" between demonstrators and police may not necessarily shake the basis of acceptance of the police by the public; indeed, a number of impressive protest events were not taken up in the sources.[25] It is only the public (political) discussion on an event and the relative police intervention, the controversy over the question of blame, responsibility, and legitimation, that establishes the important link between protest and police discourse. In almost all reports on concrete police interventions in the specialized journals, the authors attempted to refute any blame placed on the police and to legitimize police actions. The internal police debate was therefore especially intense if the public debate caused a stir and if this was perceived by the police. Analysis of the journal articles shows that the frequent occurrence of protest events, accompanied by intense public attention, over a certain period, as was the case at the time of the APO and the youth protest, created stronger repercussions than any single action.

Police philosophy and policing philosophy cannot be viewed separately. The actual as well as the discursive and the cognitive dealing with extraparliamentary protest reveals the authors' conceptions of democracy and the police. Analysis of the specialized police journals reveals a far-reaching, chronologically shifted parallel between the history of new social movements, especially their publicity-achieving actions, and the self-image of the police. The evolution of the police self-image is, then, a (distorting) mirror history of political conflict "in the streets" of the FRG. Roughly generalizing, this means that the history of the police should be viewed in relation to the history of new social movements.[26]

The following diagram presents an idealized illustration of the linking process between protest movement, public, and police self-image:

> Protest event
> Police action
> Public criticism
> Police perception of the criticism
> Identity crisis of the police
> Discussion of police philosophy

External criticism of the police, and particularly criticism of police interventions during demonstrations, causes a crisis of legitimation and thus of meaning and identity among the police for it is perceived as a lack of trust by the people in the police. The deeper the legitimation and identity crisis of the police, the more urgent is the demand for a police philosophy. Thus a police philosophy functions as a remedy on the part of the police to counteract the complaining power of the sensitized public, both as a means of strengthening police "self-confidence" and as an argumental aid in the face of public criticism. Thus, in addition to the determinants of law, tactics, resources, and political leadership, the public is a further factor influencing police action. Protest policing takes place on two stages: on the one hand, the police intervention itself (the event on the action level) and, on the other, the public discourse on the intervention.

The thesis of a reciprocal connection between police philosophy and policing philosophy is confirmed by the tendencies on these two stages over the thirty years of history of the political self-image of the police: the shift in police philosophy from a *Staatspolizei* toward a *Bürgerpolizei* is manifested in policing philosophy by an extension of tolerance toward unconventional forms of protest. Further studies will need to be carried out in order to ascertain whether the results of this analysis of the specialized police periodicals can be verified in the practice of protest policing. However, the high rank of authors and the official character of the sources reviewed would appear to suggest that it is true.

In conclusion, we might stress that for the years up until the accession of East Germany to the FRG the police defined their function and role in the state and society to a large extent through their protest policing duties. There is, however, no easy answer to the question of whether this new police philosophy represents a "genuine" reformatory step for the police or merely provides ideological material for a "legitimation lining" of police work and for improved public relations. On the one hand, the citizen-oriented police philosophy appears to be serious about the claim for democratic adequacy and a civil character of the police; on the other hand, in the late 1980s, as was the case after 1960, reformatory efforts were separated from their democratic demands and the instrumental component (particularly the rule to distinguish between violent and peaceful demonstrators) became dominant (e.g., *DP* 10, 1987, 290–97). Therefore, it has to be stressed that the extension of police tolerance in the policing philosophy does not necessarily have to be combined with an explicitly democratic claim; it may also be based on merely pragmatic policing motives, for example, the aim to avoid an escalation of conflict.

Notes

For an earlier and more detailed version of this chapter, see Winter (1997).

1. For a definition of "police knowledge," see della Porta and Reiter (in this volume).

2. "Protest policing" is defined as police interventions during protest events; more generally, police "treatment" and control of protesters. The term was introduced into the discussion by della Porta (see, e.g., 1995, chap. 3). For a definition of "protest policing," see also della Porta and Reiter (in this volume).

3. For a definition of *status constitutus*, see Denninger, 1978a, 117.

4. The principle of a "well-fortified democracy" is based on constitutional norms: Art. 5 Para. 3, 9 Para. 2, 18, 21 Para. 2, 79 Para. 3 *Grundgesetz* (see Jaschke, 1991).

5. The *status constituens* "goes far beyond the right to vote and eligibility; it also consists, for instance, in the freedom of information and speech, the right of assembly, the freedom of association, and the freedom to form a coalition, as well as the right to a hearing and the right to participate in administrative proceedings, participation in self-governing bodies, and so on" (Denninger and Lüderssen, 1978, 9f.).

6. The complete titles of the seminar reports are given in the bibliography (Polizei-Institut Hiltrup, 1971; Polizei-Führungsakademie, 1986a, 1986b, 1987). Apart from these sources, other specialized journals were also used in a random sample way in order to check the results of my interpretations. These include *Bereitschaftspolizei-heute*, *Kriminalistik*, and the *Polizeidienstvorschrift "Einsatz und Führung der Polizei"* (Police regulation on "deployment and leadership of police forces") (hereafter, *PDV 100*). For the text of the *PDV 100* with a commentary, see Altmann, Bernhardt, and Ehrlich (1975).

7. It goes without saying that this may be largely due to the semiofficial nature of the sources, which apparently allows for only a limited range of opinions.

8. In the Federal Republic of Germany, the police are a sovereign issue of the federal states, not of the federal government; that is, the federal states are responsible for their police forces, including police organization and police law. Exceptions are the federal border police (*Bundesgrenzschutz*) and the central criminal investigation department (*Bundeskriminalamt*), which belong to the federal Ministry of the Interior.

9. See Brand, Büsser, and Rucht (1986, 52ff.) for the "Kampf dem Atomtod-Kampagne" (fight nuclear death campaign).

10. Following a resolution adopted by the Conference of the Ministers of the Interior in 1969, mortars were no longer to form part of the armament of the *Bereitschaftspolizei* (Busch et al., 1990, 26). This decision was facilitated by the 1968 emergency legislation. Because the Bundeswehr now could serve as a military safety anchor in domestic politics, the police formations could be demilitarized and turned into a purely civil police force (Schneider, 1986).

11. Werkentin (1984, 211ff.) gives a survey of the training scenarios of the *Bundesgrenzschutz* and the *Bereitschaftspolizei*. The dreaded enemy was represented by the Communist bloc in the East and its supporters and partisans in the West.

12. One hundred and forty charges were brought against the police officers involved in the Schwabing events; however, these charges resulted in only four convictions (*DP 2*, 1965, 34).

13. This date is of great significance for the development of the student movement: "June 2, 1967, marks the leap from local protest to nationwide revolt" (Scheerer, 1988, 262).

14. See Narr (1983) on the changing forms of demonstrations and on the evolution in perceptions of demonstrations.

15. In their paramilitary maneuvers, the police rehearsed antiguerrilla warfare, with a backdrop of communist subversive scenarios. It is for this reason that unconventional stu-

dent actions during demonstrations often carried the police, with their rigid confrontational policing philosophy, into the role of a brutal, heavy-handed Goliath. "The fighting method of committing nonviolent breaches of the rules proved exceptionally useful, in particular in view of the rigid, easily provocable institutions they challenged. The overreactions came with absolute certainty. And with the same, almost mechanical certainty these clashes brought an ever-increasing part of the bourgeois-liberal sympathy potential over to the demonstrators' side" (Scheerer, 1988, 257).

16. However, consideration should also be given to the fact that demonstrations tended to be more militant than before 1967–68.

17. The three cornerstone topics of the youth protest were housing policy (squatting), nuclear power, and peace.

18. With the new version of the commentary on the chapter "Unpeaceful Demonstrative Actions" dated October 1991, the guidelines of the Brokdorf decision are inserted into the *PDV 100* (3.4.1, 7ff.).

19. The decision was published in *Neue Juristische Wochenschrift* (1969, 1770ff.).

20. The stalemate of the Federal Constitutional Court in the sit-in blockade decision of November 11, 1986, did not remove the uncertainty surrounding this issue. The decision states that sit-in blockades do not necessarily fall outside the scope of the fundamental right of the freedom of assembly. Nevertheless, police leaders were in agreement with the court that blockaders must be prosecuted under criminal law, as coercion or because of the infringements committed. With the new decision of the Federal Constitutional Court dated January 10, 1995 (published in *Neue Juristische Wochenschrift* (1995, 1141ff.), actions of civil disobedience cease to be punishable coercive force (according to § 240 *Strafgesetzbuch*). This decision corrects the Mutlangen decision and puts a stop to the broad interpretation of violence.

21. Phase 4 also saw a reemergence of the attitude patterns of the traditionalists from Phase 1—including the public welfare concepts and doubts about the maturity of citizens to participate in politics. Such ideas were put forward by some police leaders, without, however, violating the linguistic conventions of the *Neue Linie* (e.g., the recognition of the right to demonstrate as a fundamental right). A state-focused attitude was also revealed in the strictly formal legalistic thinking of some high-ranking police officials. At this point it was the *Rechtsstaat* (and its laws) and no longer the state per se that the police had to protect (*DP* 8, 1988, 218; *DP* 1, 1982, 5).

22. See Winter (1991, 233) for statistics concerning articles on police philosophy and protest policing in the periodical *Die Polizei*.

23. This circumstance is also interesting because the prevention of social conflicts by scientifically supported police prevention corresponds to the conceptions and targets of several "police philosophers."

24. For example, evictions of illegally squatted houses by the police, while the housing shortage and large number of unoccupied houses provide political legitimacy for the squatters.

25. For this reason, the interdependence hypothesis requires some qualification: the protest may not be the only driving force of a discussion; other decisive factors are the general mood and sensitivity of the public toward the police, which in turn depend on the police actions and their public reception. Despite public criticism of the police interventions during the antinuclear power demonstrations in the second half of the 1970s (Brokdorf, Grohnde, Kalkar, Whyl), no discussion in the periodical *Die Polizei* followed these events. One explanation is that the balance in the police's legitimation account showed a credit. The police saw themselves as sufficiently legitimized and accepted by the population because of their fight against terrorism. The surplus of legitimacy compensated the legitimation deficits resulting from their disputed actions against nuclear power protesters.

26. It is obvious that this process also develops in the other direction, though this is not the topic of this essay. Accordingly, this would mean that the history of protest movements has to be viewed in connection with the history of the police. Haupt (1986) confirms this general hypothesis in his comparative historical examination. Police measures had a significant impact on the formation of the workers' movements in Germany and France in the second half of the nineteenth century. See also Willems et al. (1988, 20) and Harrach (1983, 171).

Chapter 9

The Policing of Hooliganism in Italy

Rocco De Biasi

Police and Public Order

Both from an institutional point of view and from the point of view of practical
knowledge gained and used by the Italian police, the term "public order" has
a very specific meaning. My intention here is not to discuss the issue of the
collective representation of public order in the common sense, but to investigate the meaning that Italian police give to this term.[1] For this reason, "public
order" will be given a rather different meaning than that usually employed by
the social sciences.

Some examples of definitions found in interviews conducted with police
officials will clarify this point:[2]

> The problem is that public order may have a wider meaning or a strictly techni-
> cal one. We say "public order" when we speak about demonstrations. The *Digos*
> [political bureau of the divisional police station, the *questura*] is essentially con-
> cerned with demonstrations. Public order is the stadium and mass demonstra-
> tions. (Interview, Milan, December 29, 1994)

> There are many shades and facets here. With public order, we always mean a
> service in the open, in the piazza. Public order is demonstrations, concerts, sta-
> diums. The grounds take up a big share of our time. These are the main "public
> order" issues: concerts, demonstrations, stadiums, and whenever people as-
> semble in masses . . . participating in political or sporting events. (Interview,
> Milan, October 18, 1994)

> For us, in a technical sense, public order is the control of demonstrations that
> assemble a great number of persons. I don't make scientific distinctions; my dis-
> tinctions are practical. In the police, when we say public order we are speaking
> of demonstrations, marches, and soccer matches. (Interview, Florence, Novem-
> ber 17, 1994)

If we go looking nowadays for people who are a dangerous threat to public order, they can be found in the world of sport. I'm talking about the problems linked with soccer matches, where we find both large numbers of people ... and special features that depend on the game being played. ... However, it is a fact that between the problems of the 1970s and those of the 1990s, there is, as far as I can see, a difference in the type of disorders involved. ... The problems then were essentially connected with political protests of "opposition," whereas now they are above all connected with sport. (Interview, Florence, November 10, 1994)

Although the tension and uncertainty typical of the "Italian case" have recently shifted our attention to more strictly political problems, it should not be forgotten that violence connected with the "ultras" phenomenon has been, and remains, one of the principal public order problems; for, although mass demonstrations pose a thorny set of problems, particularly given the political repercussions they may provoke, the violence of soccer fans at the stadium—or the "ultras," as they are called—regularly requires large numbers of men and intense activity by the police forces every week. This phenomenon is often underestimated by observers because it is not related to great economic and political processes. However, when we refer to public order in research on the police forces in Italy, we have to keep in mind that the most frequent experience of crowd management, including violent engagements with crowds, takes place on the soccer grounds, with the ultras. Soccer hooliganism has also resulted in deaths, which has not occurred for a long time in the context of mass demonstrations of a political nature. Thus, the phenomenon of violence in soccer is one of the major public order problems, not only from the perspective of observers or sociologists but also in the opinion of the police force itself. To understand the scale of the problem, we need only think about the large numbers of police deployed each Sunday just to check supporters going in and out of the soccer grounds: in the 1993–94 championship, police reinforcements (*reparto mobile*) assigned to the *questure* numbered, on a national level, more than eighty-eight thousand persons (more than 150,000 when the carabinieri and *Guardia di Finanza* are included).[3] The total cost for one championship amounts to 8 billion Italian liras, at the expense of the state. In England, where the hooligan problem first appeared, the costs involved in protecting public order are much lower and a large part of the expense is charged to the soccer clubs. In Italy, in contrast, each day of a championship costs the state 2 billion liras (to which transport costs and lost workdays due to injuries should be added).

Police forces at the stadium are organized on the basis of the same criteria that are used for other public order activities. In each province, the *prefetto* has the basic responsibility for public order, while the *questore* is the senior police official with technical responsibility.

For operations of a public order nature, the *questore* deploys his policemen as well as officers of the *reparto mobile*, the carabinieri and the *Guardia di Finanza*, who are assigned to the *questore* from the Ministry of the Interior. An official from the *questura* has responsibility for police actions and interventions during each specific public order operation. This pattern of institutional organization, well tested in the context of mass demonstrations, is also applied to the policing of soccer grounds.

Although public order duties in the stadium—and investigation and prevention activities aimed at controlling ultras groups—are not the main task of the *questura* (because this structure deals more specifically with the political consequences of problems relating to public order), soccer matches represent for the *reparto mobile* their most exacting activity and the most frequent and risky occasion of crowd management. In comparison with mass demonstrations, soccer matches frequently require recourse to means of forcible intervention, such as batons and tear gas. Added to this high level of potential and actual violence are problems relating to safety in the stadium, a closed and crowded place, where the police have the tricky job of protecting ordinary spectators while controlling the ultras.[4]

As some of the interviewed police officers remarked:

About the stadium, I can say, if I think about the past years, that public order duties have radically changed. At one time only a few policemen were needed because nothing happened. The fans watched the match, enjoyed their team's performance, and then went home. Now there's the match and the aftermatch! Because now there are these ultras. (Interview, Milan, November 10, 1994)

In terms of frequency, the situations that can most easily give rise to trouble are certainly soccer matches. There's always a risk factor and we try to prevent problems as much as possible. (Interview, Milan, November 9, 1994)

Every three days we are at the stadium. On Sundays we know that we have two matches because the *reparto mobile* takes care of public order throughout its territorial area, which is all of Lombardia; so we keep public order in Bergamo, and in Brescia, Como, Monza. . . . We have five teams for the first and second divisions. This means that last Sunday, for instance, we had thirty men in Monza, which is a third division team. . . . It is the stadium, essentially, that accounts for 90 percent of the public order problems we usually cover: that's 80 percent stadium work and 20 percent public demonstrations. (Interview, Milan, October 19, 1994)

In order to analyze the policing of soccer hooliganism in Italy, it is necessary to clarify that Italian ultras represent a very specific case of *organized*
aggressive spectators. Sociologists from other European countries often find
it difficult to understand the Italian case because they do not have sufficient
ethnographical information about the specific context of soccer-related disorders. Thus, the first part of this essay describes the distinctive identity of
Italian hooligans, before going on to examine the relationship between police
and ultras. The second part offers a critical assessment of the problem of
negotiation and the policing of soccer grounds.

The Ultras

Although soccer hooliganism is a universal phenomenon in Europe, it as-
sumes different forms in each country. The picture I shall draw of Italian
spectators is quite different to the analysis of soccer and popular sports carried out by renowned scholars such as Norbert Elias and Eric Dunning. For
these scholars, the social roots of English hooliganism lie in the male aggressiveness of small gangs of the lower working class.[5] Perhaps soccer is today
an important prism through which we can view *different* societies. In my
opinion, however, the main difference between English and Italian soccer cultures does not lie in the social class distribution of supporters, but rather in
the presence or absence of a strongly structured form of association. The Italian soccer culture is not only locally based and independent of social stratification, but is also tightly organized.

In Italy, there are two kinds of supporters' associations: the official supporters' clubs and the ultras. From the very beginning, groups of ultras
(wrongly considered the equivalent of English hooligans) reflected a more
heterogeneous youth movement than that which populated the British terraces. According to several sociologists, when English hooliganism was at its
peak, the fans in the stands were linked by a common social class or lifestyle
as well as by shared youth subcultures.[6] In Italy, the ultras support has never
been dominated by any particular social stratum or any specific youth style.
The unifying element for the Italian youth in the *curva* (the rounded end of
the stadium) has always been support itself, and not social consumption, or
class status, or political belief, or musical fashions, and so on. Thus, in the
case of Italian ultras, it is crucial to investigate the peculiar autonomy of the
cognitive *frame* of rituals inside the stadium.[7]

The ultras style of support is based on visibility, and this is also of significance in terms of hooliganism. If we consider that in England, several years

ago, some hooligans even traveled incognito to an away match (by train and well dressed) so that the police could not identify them, Italian ultras, on the contrary, want to be visible. The issue of visibility is very important from a sociological point of view, and, of course, for the police as well. Ultras travel in large groups and, in the case of any trouble, often adopt very similar strategies to the types of fighting evident in political riots.

In order to understand the social dimension of Italian "hooliganism," it is necessary to consider Italy's political protest movements and disorder during the 1970s. The incidence of political riots led to the introduction of more powerful equipment and more severe repression techniques used by the police and carabinieri. In turn, the intensification of police control inside and outside of the stadium led the ultras to adopt a military mode of organization and a warlike attitude against the police. As a result, soccer hooliganism as a social problem must be regarded as the legacy of such political policing. Some of the tactics that police normally adopted against political extremists during the 1970s are now employed against the ultras.

This legacy of political conflict also influenced the associations of young supporters occupying the *curva* of the Italian stadiums, but only in a formal sense. I am not referring here to the political symbols displayed on supporters' banners. Such symbols and emblems, in the cognitive *frame* of the *curva*, assume another meaning and lose their original reference (I am using the term "frame" as defined by Erving Goffman, 1974; a frame is the interpretative schema that determines the meaning of messages and symbols). In the early years, ultras groups did not take any political commitment with them to the stadium. However, there has been a transposition of the firmly structured organizational dimension of some extremist political youth associations, as many of the characteristics of these groups illustrate: the presence of a *direttivo*, a sort of political bureau; the assembly-like or democratic style of decision making in the ultras groups; the strong commitment of some members during the week (meetings, preparation of banners and choreography, distribution of leaflets); and even the use of flagpoles as weapons. These are all elements that formed part of political extremism. This is not to imply that those political riots have moved from the schools or the factories into the stadium. It is indeed worth underlining that the political groups of the extreme left or right have constituted a *form* of association that, despite the crisis in political commitment among young people in Italy, tends to present itself again in new contexts.

So too the pattern of fighting among rival groups or between ultras groups and the police recalls to some extent the political violence linked to the extremism of left or right. Among the types of transgressive behaviors witnessed in Italy, it is true that there are phenomena (including vandalism, machoism, exhibitionism) that are typical of youth mobs rather than of political groups. However, in the Italian case, those elements that are typical of the British experience blend in with other dimensions of group life, which, at least initially, remind us of the political movements of the 1960s and 1970s.

Today, not even the soccer clubs themselves can ignore the importance of the ultras and the influence they exert on the game. Relations have been established between the soccer clubs and ultras groups, which necessarily lead to negotiation. It does not appear that English hooligans, in the past, had this sort of relationship with the club.

The general *frame* or dominant metaphor of the ultras culture in Italy is that of war. A general war, mainly symbolic and theatrical but sometimes real and bloody, is fought by organized groups of young soccer fans. It is a war in which temporary or permanent alliances (*gemellaggi*, from the Italian word *gemello*, "twin") are formed, maintained, or broken, a war that has been going on since the 1960s, when the first ultras groups were created, and that will probably last as long as soccer remains the main interest for large strata of Italian teenagers and youngsters.[8]

Politics and Soccer Hooliganism

In various European countries (such as England in the 1970s and Germany later on), a convergence between right-wing political extremism and hooliganism has appeared. The peculiarities of the ultras phenomenon in Italy means that interferences between "political extremism" and soccer hooliganism extend in different directions, even though the relationship between soccer hooliganism and the extreme right wing has been emphasized the most. To claim that the ultras culture is "of the right" would be a serious error. The vulnerability of the ultras culture to penetration or to political exploitation is a known fact—which, however, has nothing to do with the specific, original matrix that produced a phenomenon involving such a large number of young, as well as older, people since the early 1970s.[9]

Apart from the gravity of the episodes of violence, the associative reality, the rituals, and the aggressiveness of soccer hooliganism are, for the most part, unpolitical or, within a certain perspective, metapolitical phenomena. The ultras culture has its own particular autonomy, its own definite rules, specific rituals, and codes that go beyond, or "above," the ideological orientation of a minority number of supporters or really politicized militants. It forms a universe into which opposing and extremist political values can circulate from time to time, while the unifying factor remains supporting soccer—or a certain mode of intending support that is common to all the ultras in the stands and is *beyond* any sense of political belonging. All the ultras militants, who in the majority of cases are scarcely politicized, know the repertoire of rules to be followed by fans supporting any club, are socialized to certain values—including the acceptance of violence or of physical fighting with opponents—and have learned specific forms of behavior and expressive rituals that can be observed in the stands during matches. In sociological terms, it may be said that each ultras militant has specific role expectations defined by the situation.

Now, all of these specific characteristics of the ultras universe precede any political drift—real or presumed—of the phenomenon. The large-scale political vulnerability of soccer hooliganism is, without a doubt, a recent fact and this vulnerability is not exclusively political. Ultras organizations are experiencing a process of fragmentation: created in the 1970s, and well established in the 1980s as highly structured organizations, they are now in a state of deep crisis. Symptoms of this crisis include the absence of a generational turnover of the old leadership, fragmentation, and splitting into different groups,[10] the emergence of violent "nonofficial" groups that elude the control of the recognized leadership, predominance of physical engagement with opponents (increasingly less ritualized and more "acted") in comparison with other associative activities (such as the choreography, emotional involvement in the match, playful aspects of the stadium rituals, etc.).[11] Ultras organizations risk becoming weaker and more changeable and, precisely for this reason, more dangerous. In the opinion of a *Digos* officer in Milan:

If these groups of fans come together under a particular flag or label, under a symbol of some significance, and if there are people at the head of this group who are recognized as leaders, let's just say it all makes our life much easier. If, on the other hand, it can be seen, as has been the case in recent times—at least this seems to be the tendency—that there is a splintering of groups and gangs, our police work becomes more difficult. This is because these groups and gangs can move around and hide during the course of a season, and you then have difficulties in your police operations staying on top of these continual developments. Whereas when the phenomenon was more structured and more stable, it was much easier for us. When you talk to the people, and intervene when it is necessary to intervene, and therefore keep things stably within the limits of certain possibilities, then that is a situation that is evolving in a positive manner. That is, try to speak to these people, to make them sensitive to the situation, and do it in a way that makes them understand that Sunday is a day for entertainment, not for fighting. But when you start to see groups and gangs of all kinds forming, that are difficult to mark out because they move around and hide, then your work, when there is splintering, becomes more difficult. And that's true whether you are talking about mediation, confrontations, investigations, or interventions. (Interview, Milan, December 5, 1994)

During the debate on appropriate norms against violence, sparked by the killing of Vincenzo Spagnolo, a young supporter of the Genoa team who was stabbed by an ultra on January 29, 1995, even the SIULP, the main police trade union, asserted that dissolving ultras groups would be a dangerous mistake, as it would mean dissolving the already slight "endogenous" control that these associations still have on the extremist fringe groups or on the *cani sciolti* (stray dogs).

What gave strength to the ultras culture for two decades was precisely its unpolitical or metapolitical nature, and what makes it so weak nowadays is precisely the deterioration of the organizations and associative realities that embodied it. There has been an escalation in the level of violence (from simple fights to knives, and then to the hooliganism of spontaneously formed small groups, which is more dangerous and similar to the English hooligans);[12] in addition to this type of violence, *internal* to the *extremist tifo* (soccer fanaticism) but still part of the culture of the terraces, episodes of violence have recently occurred as a result of well-defined political plans of the subversive right wing. The most significant of these episodes took place in Brescia on November 13, 1994, during a match between Brescia and Roma when a *vicequestore* was knifed and a police inspector badly injured. From the judicial acts, it appears that the assault was premeditated and directed against the police force itself (and not against other hooligans, as is normally the case). Some of the youths who went to Brescia for the day were not regular match-goers, but rather members of extreme right-wing groups. A similar episode occurred two weeks later in the north end of the Olympic stadium of Rome, during the Roma–Lazio match. In this case, again, the trouble was not simply a fight between ultras hooligans, but instead took the form of a cold-blooded attack against the police force.

In Goffman's terms (1961, 20), social situations "place a 'frame' around a spate of immediate events, determining the type of 'sense' that will be accorded everything within the frame."[13] Now, if we consider soccer a phenomenon that is not reducible to a single *frame*, we can observe that at the stadium, as in the collective representations of soccer that transcend the match event, there exists a kind of interference between provinces of meaning, or realms of being, since the dominant playful cognitive style is menaced by events that can, to use an expression coined by Goffman, "poke through the thin sleeve of immediate reality" (1961, 81). In other words, the *frames* are not rigid or firm, and can fail to constitute a barrier by means of which participants in a social situation can cut themselves off from external matters. This metaphoric membrane, enclosing the playful reality of the soccer spectacle and the stadium as a social universe, may turn out not to be a barrier, but something frail instead. In this sense, the barrier, in its external attributes, is more like a sieve than a solid wall, and this sieve not only selects, but also modifies, what it filters. This is also true in the case of political symbols that can assume another meaning and lose their original reference.

The ultras universe, apart from the exploitable presence of radical right-wing elements with definite political plans (that in the final analysis destroy the ultras logic, breaking the *frame* somehow or realizing actions outside the *frame*), experiences an equivocal and conflictive relationship with politics. The dominant logic, then, still appears to be a conception of the *gratuitous* or unpolitical conflict, involving the symbolic opposition between competing ultras groups in the context of stadium rituals. From this point of view, the phenomenon of soccer hooliganism is considered by the police leadership to be not "politically motivated." In this way, ultras became part of the worst class of "bad" demonstrators (see della Porta, in this volume). Soccer hooliganism is seen as a pure problem of vandalism, or "violence pure and simple."

The Problem of Negotiation

Although the phenomenon described here presents some analogies with political disorders, the fact that soccer hooliganism is not the result of *serious* motivations led the police for a long time to underestimate the importance of mediation, dialogue, and negotiation with the ultra groups.[14] For the *Digos*, at least, the presence of extreme right-wing infiltrators in the ultras groups certainly constitutes a complicating element in the hooliganism problem; but from the general point of view of the police force, the issue seems to remain that of "violence pure and simple."

The difficulty in accepting—or simply understanding—the existence of unpolitically oriented forms of organized and mass violence delayed police efforts to institute precautionary measures. Nevertheless, in Genoa, a successful experiment was tried out for a short period—namely, extending to the stadium those precautionary measures usually employed in the political context. As a *Digos* officer in Genoa explained:

The first typical thing about a sporting demonstration is that supporters are usually always the same. I'm speaking of course about ultras supporters. . . . The second rule we set ourselves was to enhance the internal hierarchies of the group. This is a phenomenon that also tends to happen when there's a mass meeting. When we follow a march or demonstration of a political or trade-unionist nature, we [the police] guarantee the maintenance of public order first of all by contacting the leaders, the factory delegates, the trade-union representatives. Now, all this doesn't usually apply to ultras because there's a moral prejudice that says that the ultras are not worth this kind of consideration. Ultras are something negative and the police tend to simply resort to authority with them. We decided to set aside those moral values; anybody can make his own, but in the specific reality it was our responsibility, and it still is, not to do that. We thought instead that it was important to appreciate the leaders of the ultras but not, I repeat, to obtain information from them . . . only because we believed that they were able to control the phenomenon directly, so that we could control it through them. This is for me a basic rule: to reduce to a minimum the need for *manu militari* interventions, to really keep armed intervention as an ultimate resource. If a minor fight erupts in the stands, two plainclothes policemen find the leaders of those ultras, accompany them to the place of the fight and try, with them, to calm down the opponents. (Volta, 1994, 73)

In Genoa, the negotiations with ultras groups became problematic again when the officer who had promoted this type of intervention was transferred. Innovative ideas are seldom assimilated by the police structure and generally remain the property of the individual officer. This model, as described by a police officer, works for political demonstrations but is rarely used for stadium troubles. In Florence, for instance:

Yes, the ultras belong to organized groups, but when problems arise they distance themselves from each other and all become like stray dogs. Theoretically, there are many organized groups of supporters, all professing their willingness to collaborate. But these groups are made up of people who can leave the fold at any time, and when they do, nobody will assume responsibility for them. (Interview, Florence, November 10, 1994)

The Policing of Soccer Grounds

The problem of controlling ultras groups first emerged at the beginning of the 1980s. At that time, control was mainly needed *inside* the stadium and the principal police task was to segregate the home and away supporters. In England, where these problems appeared earlier, stadiums are usually built on a quadratic plan and the stands are structurally separated (often different parts of a stadium are separated because they were built at different times.[15]) In Italy, the soccer stadiums are nearly always multisports arenas constructed on an elliptical plan (thus the term *curva*—curve—to describe the ends), and structural barriers do not exist. Consequently, the police had to compensate for this deficiency by deploying lines of men. The first problem to be confronted was to prevent physical contact *inside* the stadium between rival ultras groups. Ultras permanently occupied a territory in the stadium (the *curva*) and considered it "sacred" and inviolable. One of the main duties of the police was, and still is, to prevent rival ultras from invading the opposing *curva*.

It is important to mention that the police surround the *curva* but avoid entering that territory as much as possible. The entrance of police in a *curva* usually provokes a highly combative reaction from the ultras, the consequences of which are unpredictable. The *curva* becomes, within its own boundaries, a place for tolerated transgressions: fireworks are employed in choreographies, banners insulting the enemy team are waved, light drugs are consumed, and the police themselves are offended with abusive songs.[16] Objects smuggled in are often thrown on the field or against the police. But the rule is to tolerate as much as possible in order to avoid incidents in a place as closed in and potentially dangerous as the stadium. Television cameras are still seldom used, but should theoretically have a deterrent function: in the Milan stadium, for instance, before the beginning of the match, and during the break, a giant screen projects footage taken by the police television camera as a warning to ultras that they can be easily identified.

During recent years, due also to the massive deployment of policemen, the risk of fights arising in the stadium has significantly decreased.[17] As in the English case (and notwithstanding the great differences), the most violent ultras learned ways of escaping police control and provoking trouble outside the stadium. Consequently, for the police, the hardest part of their work shifted from that of controlling the crowd during the match to keeping a close watch on visiting supporters for the entire length of their stay in the town: from their arrival at the railway station to the stadium, and from the stadium back to the station or the highway. From the police observations I gathered, it appears that these are the trickiest moments in police activities. Police duty in the stadium may be for as long as eleven to twelve consecutive hours, to the great annoyance of the trade unions. It is during these moments that clashes similar to political riots may occur, during which the police use tear gas (which cannot be used in the stadium), or baton charges, to scatter the ultras.[18] But unlike the case of public demonstrations, control in this situation is very up close, never at a distance. In addition, there are occasions when the ultras organize protest demonstrations (for instance, against the transfer of a player from one club to another). These demonstrations usually take place during the week, in the streets of the town, and are very similar to political demonstrations. For some years, the only urban guerrilla warfare episodes in Italy that the newspapers reported on were of this type.[19]

Hooligan control remains, especially for the *reparto mobile* operators, the main opportunity the police have to test their forcible intervention techniques. This is not to say that the stadium has become a sort of military training field; but there is no doubt that the experience of violent clashes—just like the learning of self-control in difficult situations—is related to the frequency of conflicts with the ultras. Finally, the fact that up to twelve hundred policemen can be deployed during a single soccer match is in itself indicative of the type of commitment required by the ultras phenomenon.

Some Critical Observations on Soccer Crowd Disorder and the Italian Police

The relatively widespread notion of a continuous shattering of public order occurring in the *curva* of Italian stadiums is definitely misleading. Events that take place in the stands depend not so much on a failing within the social order but on a meaningful action structured by a set of rules. These rules are often hidden but become at least partly visible in practical experience. In a well-known essay (criticized by some scholars for being too indulgent toward hooligans), Marsh, Harrè, and Rosser (1978, 170) showed how a hidden social order governs events that are traditionally defined as "dangerous" and "anarchical": "We find it more reasonable to seek for the actual possibilities of controlling the violence mechanisms instead of simply hoping that they will dissolve. If we accept the existence of *rules* in the disorder, we can develop control strategies certainly more effective than those adopted so far."

It is true that the police had to develop a tacit knowledge of the rules governing and marking the different types of situations in the stadium. But the process has been slow, largely due to the belief that experience in the field is more important than a theoretical coding of knowledge on public order.

In the second half of the 1980s, in a period of relative social peace, the stadium became the main public order emergency situation. For some time, soccer hooliganism generated a new form of "moral panic" in public opinion (this term was coined by Cohen, 1972). From the postwar period on, English society has experienced a certain variety of "moral panics," each one with a specific "object" (Teddy Boys, Punks, Skinheads, etc.). The same process occurred in relation to hooligans, described by the mass media as a senseless and destructive phenomenon. So too in Italy it may be seen that the absence of a "serious" motivation for violence led the police to consider the ultras phenomenon in these terms. Some of the police interviews express acknowledgment of a certain dignity inherent to the political extremism of the 1970s, motivated as it was by specific ideals. In that period, political demonstrations were often extremely dangerous for policemen themselves, and resulted in some very serious incidents. However, in the opinion of many of the persons interviewed, the present time is definitely worse.

As a *Digos* officer from Genoa commented, a "moral prejudice" within the police force for a long time prevented the possibility of seeing the ultras as an organized subject, as had earlier occurred with extremists in political organizations. Thus, they did not develop, as had been the case with political extremists, appropriate repressive techniques as well as negotiation and dialogue strategies. This type of mediation strategy could be acknowledged nowadays by the police (and to some extent it has been), but the change of context and the deterioration within the ultras organizations themselves now make this form of negotiation more difficult.

The escalation has been symmetrical: as the control measures and physical presence of the police were strengthened, so too was the aggressiveness of the ultras and their ability to outwit protection measures. Violence in the stadium became violence outside the stadium. This type of confrontation, referred to as "symmetrical schismogenesis" by Gregory Bateson (1972, Part II), produces a potentially unrestrainable escalation unless external factors intervene to modify the relationship.

In conclusion, although foreign observers are usually shocked by the massive militarization of Italian soccer stadiums, for Italian spectators, and police officers too, this is a matter of simple routine, a part of the event. From an ethnographical perspective, this event reveals a highly theatrical and dramatic element. We could describe soccer—the match event, and the function of the public in the stadium—as a "deep play," to use the expression coined by Geertz (1973). In this *frame*, some forms of behavior may seem useless or irrational because the prize at stake is symbolic to such an extent as to not be rationally justifiable. As in the Balinese cockfight described by Geertz, during a soccer match in Italy all the actors involved seem to perform a sort of ritually dramatized self-portrait. And the police are also part of the drama or *sceneggiata*.

This interpretation may appear overly anthropological. Yet it is true that in the symbolic, or ritual, behavior of the young supporters in the *curva*, the playful dimension does not necessarily exclude violence. The police also consider this context not as serious, but equally as dangerous and tricky as a political riot. As Triani (1994, 61) remarks:

> It becomes almost legitimate to think that there is not a real will after all to reach a real conclusion on hooligan violence. Perhaps this happens because in a hidden and unconfessable way, disorders, devastations, injuries, and a few deaths represent a reasonable and acceptable cost when they are ascribable to a sporting event, that is, to a definite context that is not critical to the integrity of the social system. "Better to be violent there than somewhere else," wrote Raymond Aron.

But let us take this analysis one step further by situating our results in the general context of public order in Italy. Having moved on from the *consociativismo* phase, the general climate is now one of heavy political tension, and the country seems to be split in two.[20] This tension is undoubtedly of considerable concern to the senior police officers responsible for public order, more so than soccer hooliganism is. Moreover, the *reparti mobili* are now faced with new forms of disorder, due, for instance, to the influx of large groups of *extracomunitari* immigrants in the big cities. Control duties in the territory have taken the place of more traditional tasks, such as protest policing. Changes such as these in the larger cities produce forms of disorder whose underlying rules are still unknown.

If the stadium constitutes a lesser concern than other control-related problems, but at the same time its policing remains such a difficult and costly job, we may wonder whether the Italian police have not at least partially failed in the slow process of learning the rules of soccer-related disorders.

Notes

1. On the collective representation of public order related to citizens' demands for safety, see Palidda (1993, 1995).

2. In the case of Florence, interviews were carried out with seven officials from the *questura* (police headquarters); in Milan, interviews were conducted with five officials from the *questura* and ten from the *reparto mobile* (police action force), as well as the head of the center of study and research into the police run by the SIULP (the largest police trade union). The interviews in Florence were conducted by Donatella della Porta, those in Milan by Rocco De Biasi.

3. Small villages normally only have carabinieri. The *polizia di stato* (state police) are found in larger towns and cities. For an analysis of the historical duality of the Italian police forces, see Collin (1985). See also Canosa (1975, 1976) and Corso (1979).

4. One of the main concerns of the police during soccer matches is to avoid the involvement of ordinary spectators in incidents, particularly as the outbreak of panic in a crowd can have disastrous results. A dramatic example of this type of situation was the Heysel disaster of 1985, where English hooligans came into contact in the *curva* (the rounded end of the stadium) not with the ultras but with normal civil Italian supporters. Seized with panic, the Ital-

ians tried to run away. Tragically, unable to find a way to escape and pushed back by the police, thirty-nine spectators died from being crushed or by suffocation.

5. For further details, see Elias and Dunning (1986); Dunning, Murphy, and Williams (1988).

6. See, for instance, Dunning, Murphy, and Williams (1988).

7. See Dal Lago (1990, chap. 2); Salvini (1988).

8. The general frame of the ultras world is analyzed in Dal Lago and Moscati (1992), chaps. 6 and 7.

9. Not all soccer fans of the *curva* are teenagers. For the main part, ultras groups aggregate youths in the fourteen to twenty-five age group, but there are still, especially among the leaders, many over age thirty-five.

10. See Roversi (1992).

11. On the distinction between and relation between violence and aggressive ritual, Marsh, Harrè, and Rosser (1978) is still a key essay. See also Salvini (1988).

12. See Dunning, Murphy, and Williams (1988) and Murphy, Williams, and Dunning (1990).

13. See also Bateson (1972, Part II).

14. In contrast, as is well known to the *Digos*, the soccer clubs have always sought to negotiate with the ultras groups, and to develop a good relationship in order to obtain their consent and support.

15. See Englis (1983).

16. The police confiscate banners before a match begins only in the extreme case that they bear racist messages. In the English stadiums, on the other hand, no banners are allowed.

17. TV news programs often show images of brawls in the *curva*, but these are usually short-lived ritual clashes, after which order is soon restored. The most serious incidents take place outside of the stadium after the match.

18. Some policemen complained during interviews that their colleagues, the carabinieri, did not have appropriate uniforms for public order duties (they are forced, for instance, to use their rifle butt instead of a baton).

19. Disorders provoked by the ultras in cases such as the transfer of Roberto Baggio (1990 in Florence) or Luigi Lentini (1993 in Turin), even though directly motivated by the transfer, proved to be more exacting for the police than many demonstrations organized by the extreme left wing.

20. On the concept of *consociativismo*, see Pizzorno (1993).

Chapter 10

Police Knowledge and Protest Policing: Some Reflections on the Italian Case

Donatella della Porta

One of the most delicate functions taken on by the police is the control of public order. Indeed, for people involved in demonstrations, the police represent the very face of state power (Lipsky, 1970; see also Muir, 1977). Direct interventions by the police to restore public order, moreover, put the police on the front pages of the press and increase the likelihood of public criticism (della Porta, 1995, 1997). It is likely, then, that because of this particular delicacy, the strategies of the police concerning the question of public order are multiple and ever-changing, so much so that important changes in the police organization often follow periods of political turmoil (e.g., Geary, 1985; Morgan, 1987; Reiner, in this volume), while a weakening in the repressive capacity of the state has been considered as a precondition for cycles of protest (e.g., Tilly, 1978; Skocpol, 1979; McAdam, 1982).

In Italy, as well as in other Western democracies, following the great wave of protest that came to a peak in the late 1960s, the strategy of control of public order has been profoundly transformed. While the right to public protest has tended to be broadened during this period, strategies of intervention have become distanced from the coercive model of policing that had predominated until then. During the course of the 1970s and 1980s, despite some setbacks and reversals, it is possible to trace a growing tendency to tolerate certain violations of the law that are now considered minor offenses. During these two decades, the public debate concerning police interventions into protest demonstrations followed a fixed scheme, between the left's "coalition for civil rights," which criticized any harsh repression, and the right's "coalition for law and order," which supported a tougher approach. By the 1990s, this situation seems to have changed. Whereas the movements of the left have little by little abandoned the most violent forms of protest that some-

times sparked a spiral of conflict with the police, violence connected with soccer fans and racist skinheads has grown. In particular, on certain occasions
involving attacks on immigrants, the police have been accused—and not only
in Italy—of being excessively tolerant, this time by the left.

A variety of conditions influenced the strategic choices of the police facing
protest. The study of collective movements suggests that state reactions to
challengers are influenced by specific characteristics of the political opportunity structure: in particular, the existing dominant culture and institutions
(Kitschelt, 1986; Kriesi et al., 1995; Tarrow, 1994). The political "complexion"
of a government is (or at least has been) another decisive variable in explaining strategic choices concerning public order. Another element intervenes,
however, between the "reality" of the situation and police action: the perception that the police have of disturbances, of the techniques at their disposal,
and of the requests that come from outside their ranks. These perceptions
make up part of what can be called *police knowledge*, a term that refers to the
images held by the police about their role and the external challenges they
are asked to face. We may assume then that, as in other spheres of social life,
the activity of the police to control public order is influenced, first, by the *professional culture* of the police, that is, by the images the police hold about their
own role—or, put another way, by the "totality of assumptions, widespread
among actors, relative to the 'cause' to which they must be committed" (Worden, 1989, 674)—and second, by the *environmental culture* of the police, that
is, the totality of assumptions they hold about external reality.

In the course of my research, I have sought to reconstruct this *police knowledge* through in-depth interviews, following semistructured questionnaires,
conducted with police officials in two Italian cities: Florence and Milan. This
essay draws on illustrations taken from around thirty interviews,[1] integrated
by close observations of certain police interventions in situations concerning
public order, and interviews held with actors who are "challenging" public
order. In the first part of this essay, I describe police officers' perceptions
about the strategies available for reestablishing order, singling out four different models of police control. In the second part, I try to explain police choices
on the basis of the police's images of the kinds of actors who create potential
disturbances to public order, and the role of the police themselves.

The Control of Public Order in the 1990s

Studies on the evolution of police styles have presented a complex image,
describing at the same time a militarization of the police, but also a growing

attention to de-escalation, the increase of technological means for the use of force and at the same time the development of a sophisticated bargaining. How does the Italian case fit into this framework? What is the central model of control of public order in present-day Italy?

The Police Force and Public Order in Italy: The Organizational Structure

In Italy, as elsewhere, an intervention to reestablish public order involves various institutional actors. At a local level, the political duty to maintain public order falls to the *prefetto* (who represents the central government at the local level), whereas technically the *questore* (the head of the police) is responsible. When potential disturbances to public order arise—when, in particular, a gathering of a large crowd or political initiative is foreseen—the *questore* orders the police to become involved, delegating an official to command the forces in action. The principal police corps that may intervene are the *Digos* (branch for general investigations and special operations, a political policing unit), and the *reparto mobile* (forces for rapid reaction). The plainclothes *Digos* have responsibilities for information gathering; the uniformed *reparto mobile* is available for forcible intervention. Whereas the *Digos* forms part of the *questura*, the *reparto mobile* is under the direct command of the national head of the police: the *questore* must therefore ask the head of the police to assign a certain number of men or women in uniform, who may be taken from various units of the city under the *questura*'s control, or from other units. In the sphere of public order, the *questore* also commands the carabinieri (militarized police), who are expected to cover half of the policing duties in the case of large-scale police interventions. In exceptional circumstances, the army may also be mobilized. In certain situations, the *squadra mobile* (mobile squad) may sometimes also intervene, a squad that is composed mainly of agents in civilian dress who are responsible for judicial policing, as may the *volanti* (flying squad), a uniformed patrol, and the *polizia scientifica* (scientific police), plainclothes agents and officials who are responsible for gathering evidence on possible crimes.

In the words of a Florentine official, a police intervention over public order is hierarchically organized, with police agents responding only to their direct superior:

> Every action concerned with public order ... starts with the communication [by the organizers] to the *questura*, three days before the demonstration. On this basis the *questore* get informed on the demonstration, makes an evaluation of the route, the size and the type of the march, and then sends out orders on this

basis that indicate the following: what type of demonstration it will be, who is directing the forces of public order, who is being given duties, the size of the force to be assigned, and possible special assignments relative to the particular demonstration. (Interview, Florence, November 10, 1994)

Other actors, external to the police, may be involved in the management of public order, if only in a consulting capacity. For more significant interventions, the *prefetto* may make use of the suggestions of the Provincial Committee for Public Order and Safety, in which representatives of different political parties may participate in addition to the *questore* and the chief of the carabinieri. After hearing the opinion of the committee, the *questore* makes the order requesting the minister for a certain number of men and women from the *reparto mobile* and the carabinieri to be assigned. Only after this will the chief officers of the *reparto mobile* be contacted (Interview, Milan, October 10–11, 1994).

Coercion, Containment, Consensus: The Use of Force in the Control of Public Order

The most prevalent perception among the police is that their presence is oriented primarily toward the *defusing of a situation*.[2] Nearly all the officials interviewed agreed on defining the strategy used in recent times as a strategy designed to seek a consensus through "dialogue" with protesters:

> On each occasion a dialogue is sought with whichever go-between comes forward. We always look to avoid incidents. All demonstrations, of whatever kind or type, are normally preceded by direct contacts with police headquarters or the officials of the *Digos* or other forces to agree on the course of the march, in order to know whom we should speak with, to see what kind of situation we will be faced with, to understand what the real issues of the march are, so that we can prepare a possible dialogue with the people who are organizing the demonstration. In this sense, the tactics, particularly during the 1980s, have changed the style of interlocution, that is, demonstrators do not find themselves in front of masked men with helmets and batons: there is always some attempt at mediation. (Interview, Florence, November 10, 1994)

The choice of dialogue seems to have come with a limitation on the type of coercive tactics considered appropriate to face public order problems: the use of firearms is stigmatized; "tough" techniques (such as jeep charges or the water cannon) have fallen into disuse; the shortcomings of the baton charge and tear gas are often emphasized.[3] Recourse to a repressive intervention is, in general, considered to be a failure in policing terms. According to the officials, the primary objective of a police intervention in defense of public order is to avoid "upsetting the balance of the situation," and hence producing disturbances to the peace. For this reason, especially when there are more radical groups of people within a larger peaceful demonstration, a strategy of "underenforcing the law" and "containment" prevails, which, however, takes on different characteristics according to the different actors that are "threatening" public order.

In spite of the often-quoted principle of "neutrality," by which the police claim that "the reaction of the police is always the same," in reality responses to a range of challenges to public order reveal diverse models of *protest policing*, each formulated with regard to the particular problem posed. As a young vice superintendent of the *reparto mobile* observed:

> Clearly, when we are talking about Leoncavallo, that is, demonstrations with a particularly high political element, then we always keep our distance. With the ultra [radical] soccer fans, the opposite is the case: we get right in among them. With the ultras, if you give them fifty meters, they start throwing stones at you. When we want to show our muscles, especially with the Leoncavallo people [a radical "autonomous" group], the policy of the *questura* in the last few years has usually been to send a massive and highly visible police presence, of a size such that it is made very clear that the balance of forces is tipped strongly in our favor. With such a visible presence, they can see that if they misbehave, we are going to be there en masse. . . . For the demonstration of May 1, we had a purely passive presence. With the workers on May 1, it's almost like it was our celebration, our presence is purely a formality, with the idea that we are there simply to demonstrate our own presence. Obviously, we are always alert, and on the spot (even if, maybe, more hidden), because you never know when someone might get into the crowd and cause a disturbance. However, we never put on our helmets on May 1; we just walk along quietly at the front of the march, with the utmost calmness. And it's really because there is no longer that sense of opposition with the workers' movement nowadays. (Interview, Milan, November 24, 1994)

For large demonstrations organized by the trade unions or political parties, a *cooperative* model of managing public order seems to predominate. This is based on collaboration between the organizers and the police force, with policing oriented toward protecting, in equal measure, demonstrators and potential "targets of risk." As one official from Milan observed:

> Demonstrations by workers, civil servants, whatever, we're there for all of them. Also, because we are no longer a force opposed to them. In fact, people see us as workers ourselves, who are there to guarantee everyone's security . . . *we are not there to stop them from causing a riot, but rather we now accompany the demonstration to make sure they can demonstrate without being disturbed themselves.* (Interview, Milan, November 24, 1994; emphasis added)

In these situations, the perceived danger is the infiltration of violent groups. A forcible intervention is considered to be inappropriate because it could cause peaceful demonstrators to get involved. Thus, a policeman explained, for instance, the reason for the "soft" handling of a demonstration during the Gulf war:

> There were some stones, money, bottles, and so on, thrown at a church. . . . In the center of the demonstration, there was a small group from one of the social centers, with bad intentions. We were lined up in front of the church, fixed and immobile, and then these stones, bottles, and stuff are thrown. We didn't react in any way because these people, in the middle of a big demonstration of four to five thousand people, well, we would have immediately created a panic and disturbance among all the others. Or we might have got ourselves hurt, or others, confronting people who had nothing to do with it. For four people who were throwing stones. It wasn't the right time to intervene. You understand that to go and arrest a protester in the middle of a demonstration, even with an enormous deployment of officers, that would just create more disorder rather than restore public order. So the officials were right not to order us to arrest a protester who was writing graffiti on a wall; that is, those responsible for public order prefer a wall to be written on than a big disturbance in the streets. And, in my opinion, I think they are right. (Interview, Milan, October 18, 1994)

Peaceful demonstrators are seen in these cases as the police's best allies in the face of violence: "When the Milanese [radical] 'social centers' were protesting in the middle of certain other demonstrations, they were marginalized, not by us, but by the other demonstrators themselves! . . . our biggest help . . . were in fact the marshals of the demonstrators themselves" (Interview, Milan, November 24, 1994). In concrete terms, the common interest is that the "peaceful demonstrators" take the head of the march: "If the head of the march is made up of peaceful people, whom we can trust, then the march unfolds normally" (Interview, Milan, October 18–19, 1994).

In contrast, a more *negotiated* intervention of the police characterizes more disruptive protests—roadblocks or rail blocks, for example—of workers, the unemployed, homeless, and so on. In these cases, the police see themselves as a mediator who must make visible a certain presence to the protesters, at the same time reducing inconveniences for other citizens:

> We try to plan alternate routes for the traffic, by collaborating with the head of the *vigilanza urbana* [traffic squad]; we thus try to avoid exactly what the protesters are aiming to do—that is, paralyze the traffic, create problems for everyone—by blocking the traffic coming in one direction or the other, deviating it for a while, creating alternative routes around the streets as far as possible. (Interview, Milan, December 27, 1994)

The police, intervening in this case in a "visible" way, often interpose themselves to avoid direct conflict between the demonstrators and drivers who might try and force their way through the roadblock. The roadblock is thus tolerated, at least for a period of time judged sufficient to "express" the protest: "Generally, we find a way of mediating; that is, by telling them, 'OK, we won't intervene, if you're here for a quarter of an hour, we can tolerate the roadblock, but more than that, I ask you, no!'" (Interview, Milan, October 18, 1994).

A third model, which is based on a kind of *ritualized standoff,* appears to be the dominant approach to protests by the youth clubs associated with the autonomous groups. In many of the demonstrations by autonomous groups the forces of order are present in numbers judged sufficient to discourage any violence. Their equipment is, in general, "combat gear": with a helmet under the arm and a baton (just putting the helmet on can be a good means of dissuasion). Large cordons are deployed to defend "sensitive targets," and to prevent the march deviating from its planned route. As one officer of the Milan *reparto mobile* affirmed:

> With the autonomous groups, it is a question, let's say, of maximum attention. . . . You see, you feel, that at any moment something could break out. The way of approaching this, generally speaking, is always clear in this case, that if they are going past certain parts of the city, public buildings, or offices, and so on, they are all covered by forces of order to avoid them becoming the target of various attacks. (Interview, Milan, November 21, 1994)

Sometimes, however, the presence of the police might be less visible, as a way of "calming the mood" of the protest: "Quite often, and voluntarily, it is a good idea to hide ourselves. They don't see us, and so they stay calm. Because they see us as the ones who cause trouble" (Interview, Milan, October 18, 1994).

A fourth model is based on the *total isolation* of "troublemakers." It foresees a complete control over the area at risk and the movement of persons considered "dangerous" for public order. The principal application of this model of police control is during soccer matches, above all those that involve some kind of traditional rivalry between the fans:

> In my opinion, all in all the situation that creates the most worries for us, from the point of view of public order, is the soccer stadium. In the sense that you get so many people at an event like that. In Milan, that means seventy to eighty thousand people; in Bergamo, thirty thousand. They stay in the stadium, they meet up, they go wherever they want, on the underground, for example . . . for us, for sure, it's the hardest job we do. It's the most tiring work, it's the thing that takes the most time, because a day at the stadium begins in fact at 8 A.M., with the service that goes to check the inside of the stadium, to see if they have

hidden any sticks or blunt objects, anything that could be used to hurt the opposing fans. That's eight o'clock in the morning, and the match is at half past
three in the afternoon. . . . We have to meet up, assemble, get our equipment together, set off, and so on. And sometimes we finish at eight in the evening. And
then maybe there is the escort for these people. We have to wait until the train
leaves, see that everything is peaceful. . . . Often we are deployed to take the
people from the trains. A train arrives—usually it would never arrive in the center of Milan; for security reasons it arrives at Sesto San Giovanni, making use of
the fact that there is an underground station there—so therefore they take the
underground, without stopping, and they are accompanied directly to the stadium, that is, in Piazzale Lotto. It's a kind of special train. The journey is quite a
long one: thirty-five to forty minutes, with us in helmets standing in the underground. It's a heavy situation. Especially the return journey. You've already
done six, seven, eight hours of service. (Interview, Milan, October 18–19, 1994)

As has been confirmed by our eyewitness observations at the stadium, a
total isolation is maintained both outside and inside the stadium. Inside
the stadium, the two groups of fans are kept apart, often by creating open
spaces (segments of empty stadium seats) that separate the two potential
adversaries. Police cordons form close to the fans of the home team and on
the edges of the field. The officers are overtly equipped for the defense of
public order, with helmets, batons, and protective devices. The police involvement is designed to prevent contact between the two groups of fans, although they do not stop the throwing of various types of objects (money,
plastic bottles full of water, and objects taken from the toilets). The concern
with separating the two groups of fans is also evident outside the stadium,
both before and after the match. Here, police officers and carabinieri, present in large numbers and equipped for combat duty, collect the fans of the
visiting team from the railway station and bus stops, surround them with a
police cordon that closes the group in on all four sides, and escort them to
the visitors' entrance, where the fans have to go through a brief search. At
the exit to the stadium, the supporters of the visiting team have to wait until
their rival home fans have been moved on. Before the doors of the guest
fans' section are opened, the police create what one official defined as a
bonifica or "reclaimed space," distanced from the spaces where the other
fans and onlookers are standing. The guest fans are then surrounded by a
police cordon once again, and reaccompanied to the trains and buses. In the
case of the police intervention for the Fiorentina versus Roma match, which
we observed at close range, one official later explained the reasons for an
intervention that was criticized in some newspaper commentaries as too
"heavy-handed":

Here is why we need twelve hundred officers: it's necessary to cover all eventualities. There was an escort all the way during the train journey. . . . On the train there was also the escort from Rome, which accompanied them all the way to Florence, and here in Florence there was a large force of order deployed. . . . At the end of the match, the same thing—in general, the technique, even for matches where there is no risk but where there is a presence of visiting fans, it's always the same. First we let out the mass of local people (around twenty-five thousand spectators). We wait fifteen to twenty minutes, enough that the zone around the stadium begins to clear a bit. After that we do an operation to reclaim space with the officers that we have at our disposal, and we ask people to move away from the path that has to be made with the opposing fans; then we surround them and accompany them to the train or buses. In general, this is the technique that we use for operations at the stadium. (Interview, Florence, December 12, 1994)

The Mediators of Public Order

The more "cooperative" the method of control, the more important a particular figure becomes: *the mediator.* The relevance of mediation, underlined continually in our interviews, has also been explicitly recognized in the highest ranks of the police. For example, in an information note of March 7, 1990, the head of police Vincenzo Parisi advised *prefetti* and *questori* to make "contacts with the organizers of the demonstrations in order to ensure that they unfold peacefully," suggesting, moreover, that they "avoid incidents and limit direct interventions to concrete cases of danger to public order and security, and where there is a need to avoid serious damage being done."

Other research on public order in Europe has already stressed the importance of the negotiation phase between the police force and demonstrators.[4] In Italy as well, the communication to the *questura* of demonstrations—a formal act required at least three days before the demonstration—is followed, in the case of the largest ones, by negotiations on the route of the demonstration, its duration, and how it will disperse. As one interviewee observed:

For better or worse there is a great deal of work spent on planning. . . . We pay particular attention to the route that is going to be followed. . . . There is a lot of work done on the route, through informal contacts, at the level of "we won't go that way when you go that way"; in the end what's allowed is a small protest that won't degenerate further than that. There is a lot of work of this kind. There are persons, also on the other side, who . . . make direct contact with our senior officials. (Interview, Milan, November 24, 1994)

The negotiation phase is presented as being oriented toward facilitating the realization of a common goal: the peaceful unfolding of the demonstration. When the participation of groups considered as a source of potential danger to public order is foreseen, the police officials may make an agreement with the organizers in order to avoid any escalation. According to one chief officer of the *Digos*:

> We are also able in some way to give suggestions and ask for clarifications and give them help. We say, 'Look at these people who might create a bloody mess, excuse the term, either you isolate them or we'll have to think about doing it ourselves'; that is the technique we use. *This works every time, because when a sizable part of the demonstration are workers, then it is in fact the workers who want everything to go well, otherwise the demonstration fails. These days, well, the degeneration of a demonstration is now seen as a failure of the demonstration it-self.* . . . you have to isolate the virus. (Interview, Florence, November 14, 1994; emphasis added)

Mediation activities can go as far as offering informal "services" to the demonstrators. In order to deal with all kinds of protest, from squatting to road blocks, the police may "use the intervention of social and political authorities" (Interview, Florence, November 14, 1994). The taking on of this role of mediator seems now to be a police routine in the control of public order:[5] "in certain cases—when, for example, demonstrators say that they want to speak with counselor so and so—in effect, we undertake this task through our own channels; we contact the secretary of these political figures and tell them that they have asked for them to get involved. Ninety percent of the time they come" (Interview, Florence, December 12, 1994). Moreover, since demonstrators usually want to make a certain audience aware of their problems, thus exerting pressure on the ruling powers—given that "in the end all these people here are interested in is the photographer arriving, or that the television people arrive; they make their interview or take their photos, then they pack up and go home" (Interview, Milan, November 24, 1994)—police officers may assume an active role in contacting the journalists and organize a press audience, in exchange for a reduced disturbance.

Unlike other countries, however, in Italy the figure of the mediator, although present informally, has not been institutionalized. It is thus a role covered, according to the circumstances, either by the police official who is directing the operation or by the chief officer of the *Digos* present at the demonstration. Again in contrast to other countries, there is in Italy also a lack of official rules, and action is therefore based predominantly on individual initiatives by the police officers in command of the intervention. This informality brings with it a mixing up of roles that can have potentially negative effects. As an example, the *Digos* officials, who are responsible for negotiation, are the same ones who press charges; and the official of the *questura* is the one in charge of possible cases of custody. Contrary to the British case, where the formality of the agreement facilitates a certain respect, the informal Italian culture may favor an opportunistic approach in which, particularly in situations of uncertainty, both parties might be tempted not to conform to the agreements they have made.

Information Work and the Control of Public Order

Dialogue and mediation are accompanied, in the strategic conception of the police, with an important element of "control" of demonstrators through the collection of information.[6] The strategy that is defined as "dialogue" goes hand in hand with the development of certain *information techniques*, in particular those allowing for surveillance at a distance, such as television cameras in stadiums and interventions from above with helicopters during marches.[7] As regards the control of stadiums, one official explained:

> We are advising the use of cameras that have tremendously good zoom lenses for all sections of the stadium. You can really see a person's face well, with the possibility therefore of photographs and the registration of images at any moment in time. Thus, during the match there are two or three permanent operators; we have the chance to follow exactly what is happening . . . we can fix the image, then we can go and print the photo immediately. [Troublemakers] can be photographed immediately in ten seconds through a Polaroid system . . . now in some matches this system with video-cameras is allowed to be screened on the announcement board that they have at the stadium for results and advertisements. When there are moments of particular tension or brawls, the image is projected on the largest screen. We write on it: the police are filming you. Then they can see for themselves that we are filming them and underneath it is saying: these images will be taken, and examined as evidence, and so on. This might also work as a deterrent. (Interview, Florence, December 12, 1994)

The gathering of information with audiovisual technology is usable in the event that charges are pressed, but it is necessary that there be interventions prior to crimes being committed, in particular the identification of people who may participate in disturbances to public order. As another official observed, in the case of the soccer stadium, this form of control can be implemented through keeping records on file of those who buy tickets to follow their team in away matches:

> The matches that are particularly at risk are prepared in the minutest detail. As for yesterday's match, there was a considerable amount of work put in by the *questura* in Rome. Already from Rome it had been signaled in great detail who were the people leaving to come, they had been identified, given tickets—I am talking about official departures here, some of them come in their own cars. But

for those on the train and the buses, that is the majority, nearly seventeen hundred people, they had been identified, given tickets, and signaled to us. (Interview, Florence, December 12, 1994)

Because it happens in advance of any crime being committed, this type of police intervention cannot be defined as a criminal investigation, nor does it have the character of prevention. It is instead oriented to make repressive action possible.

The trend toward an increase in intelligence work, which appears to be common to several countries, can be summed up in Italy with the peculiar conception of the *Digos* as an information service that operates above all in political terms. In distinction from the *squadra mobile*, which has the function of judicial policing for "everyday" crimes, the *Digos* deals with "political" crimes—that is, according to the definition given by its own chief officers, of crimes "known to have political ends"—and, in addition to the criminal investigations, it also has the function of information gathering, for which no authorization from the magistrature is needed.[8]

The "omnipresent" conception of the information-gathering powers of the *Digos* is reflected in its organizational structure, with sections specialized in the collection of information on the sources of social and political tension. For instance, in Milan: "The first section deals with political parties and trade unions. Then there is a second section that deals rather with movements of the radical left, the extreme left. The third section is the antiterrorist section. The fourth section . . . deals with movements of the extreme right, the radical right, you might say" (Interview, Milan, December 27, 1994). The gathering of information even about parties and movements that are perfectly legitimate is justified through a distinction—that frequently reemerged in the interviews—between "investigating" and "collecting information." The *Digos* thus portrays itself as a genuinely "epistemological" organ of the state. Its activity reflects a conception that has taken root over time, of policing oriented toward the total knowledge of a particular territory (see also Reiter, in this volume):

In practice, we follow events, in a journalistic way, that is, with reports and memos, and also with research, news that is in advance of that which is given to the public, therefore with the same kind of input that a journalist might have. I deal with parties, institutional parties, and the political parties that are now registered, and all the trade unions. . . . *The Digos, as part of a questura, is a kind of observatory of Milan and its region in the service of the minister of the interior, to know what is going on in the country in substantive terms.* So, what do we do, myself or my colleagues? We go to find out about these parties. We go and attend meetings of the party sections, we try to develop relations with the trade unionists, with the members of parliament, with the local secretary, or with the representative of the local area. . . . I go to the branch meetings, I go to the party congress, I present myself as an official of the Milan *Digos*, I tell them who I am, and I am the person who is known to them, of course. For them, I am the face of the *questura*. . . . My work is often exactly the same kind of thing as the work of those whom I refer to as my journalist colleagues. (Interview, Milan, December 29, 1994; emphasis added)

Similar to this, and equally interesting, is the image presented by a Florentine official, who compares the functions of the *Digos* to those of a research center: "Our activity is about making reports on the progress of social, economic, political, and criminal events. These are reports that go the minister, that go to the *prefetto*. . . . You know, *we are the information eye of the Repubblica, without that meaning that we are questioning or fighting against what we see in the purview of law and social rules*" (Interview, Florence, November 14, 1994; emphasis added).

This model of control based on not making an immediate coercive intervention, together with the gathering of information that allows charges to be pressed with the magistrate, is an explicitly strategic choice that is reproduced through training and instruction at police school.[9] As one young officer of the Milanese *reparto mobile* recalls:

They trained us to not repress all violations of the law during the demonstration, that's right, not in public. Various instructors on public order told us that to repress a violation of the law during a demonstration at which there are thousands of people present can cause the whole situation to degenerate. During the course, we followed a program that was designed by the Higher Police Institute, in which . . . there were a certain number of hours dedicated to the question of public order. On this subject, during the course on public order, it was in fact a great surprise and very confusing to learn that during demonstrations in which thousands or tens of thousands of people are converging on a certain street or square, it was absolutely forbidden to the police force to intervene in order to suppress open violations of the law. . . . In these cases, in order to prevent the demonstration from degenerating, the chief of service, the chief of the section in charge of the operation in the street, will have to look for these violent individuals, the people who are breaking the law, by identifying them so that we can pick them up later, instead of intervening then and there. Identify them perhaps with the help of the scientific police, with the right equipment, video cameras, and that kind of thing, individuate the people who are the authors of crimes, and look to arrest them later on, when the demonstration is over, perhaps when these people go home after they have been filmed by the helicopter or cameras or video recorder. (Interview, Milan, October 10–11, 1994)

Subsequent training is oriented toward reinforcing these instructions given during the police course.

Police Knowledge and Police Strategies

The Actors Who Produce Public Disorders: Bad and Good Demonstrators

Police reactions to demonstrations are linked to the knowledge police have about the disturbances, as well as their role and the role that other actors, notably political power and public opinion, play. The sociological literature on the police emphasizes the diffusion of stereotypes on the origins of disorders, and of those who are considered to be responsible for breaking the rules (Lipsky, 1970, 4). Some recurrent themes have been singled out in the police definition of potential troublemakers as mainly *young, "outsiders"* (immigrants, ethnic minority members, or "agents provocateurs"), deviants, and *disadvantaged socioeconomic groups* (Lacey, Wells, and Meure, 1990, 71). More specific to political disorders are the stereotypes related to "conspiracy" theories—such as the "masked man," the "rotten apple," or the communist agitator (among others, McClintock et al., 1974, 127–30; Kettle and Hodges, 1982, 20). One of the first questions that we asked ourselves, therefore, was whether similar stereotypes were held by the leadership of the police concerning people who potentially threaten public order. As we will see, our research uncovered a different classification, based on the twofold distinction between demonstrators who are either "good" or "bad" by nature (for a similar point, see Waddington 1994b; Willems et al., 1988).

The interviewees are in agreement, above all, on an image of profound change in the nature of challenges to public order. In the words of one official from the *questura* of Florence, there has been a *qualitative* transformation of the question of public order: "The problems of public order of the 1970s and early 1980s . . . were essentially problems linked to political demonstrations: by the Autonomia Operaia [autonomous workers], opposition groups, or the extreme right. The problems then were essentially connected with political protests of 'opposition,' whereas in this period now they are above all connected with sport" (Interview, Florence, November 10, 1994). Nowadays, the principal source of public order problems "is the stadium, essentially, which accounts for 90 percent of the public order problems that we usually cover" (Interview, Milan, October 18–19, 1994).

According to a commonly held perception, in contrast to the past when political *motivations* were uppermost, whoever creates problems of public order today does so because they want a fight. "Above all, it's young hooligans who throw themselves into these acts of violence for the taste of violence alone. . . . What they want to do is get in a fight either at the stadium or with the immigrants" (Interview, Florence, November 17, 1994). The perception prevails, therefore, of a distinction between "political" protest, seen as "positive," and "nonpolitical" protest, seen as "pure acts of vandalism, outbursts, violence pure and simple" (Interview, Milan, July 15–27, 1994). Hooligans do not have motives:

> It is the high-risk soccer matches that really put public order most at risk. There's no motive for it. It's just soccer hooliganism let loose, people going crazy for their team, their passion. They go there because they have to. *Above all, they enjoy a fight with the police. Because they want to challenge us. In other words, they want confrontation with public institutions, with the state.* (Interview, Milan, November 21–22, 1994; emphasis added)

The lack of "politicization" of public order problems gives rise to a particular problem, which was referred to frequently in the interviews: the difficulty of "predicting" the actions of the crowd. While politically motivated demonstrators, with their instrumental logic, are perceived as relatively easy to deal with, irrational hooligans are more difficult to control, precisely because of the lack of an understandable logic behind their actions:

> In the 1970s there were many demonstrations, all of them of a political nature— and for this reason easy to deal with in an instrumental manner. Whereas, let's say for about ten years now, demonstrations no longer have this kind of nature, they are simply demonstrations of intolerance, by people who, above all in the case of stadium violence, have found a way of releasing their own internal tensions. (Interview, Milan, November 21, 1994)

This is also true for a second group of troublemakers, apparently of a more political nature. A distinction between disruption that is comprehensible and genuine because it is "motivated" and the more dangerous violence that is "violence for the fun of it" is also used to distinguish among the politically motivated demonstrators, between "good" and "bad" ones (see also Waddington, 1994b, 112–13). Good demonstrators are above all those who protest for their own direct interests, often dangerously under threat: workers defending their jobs, unemployed people who cannot find work, people who have been evicted and cannot find a home, or people who live on a particularly busy and chaotic street. Bad demonstrators are those who protest about issues that do not concern them directly, and themes that are more "abstract" and easily "manipulated." Protests in the eyes of the police are also more legitimate the more those who participate in them are directly concerned with the issue that they are mobilizing around:

> Nowadays, for the policeman who is involved in the protection of public order, but also in other duties, one thing is clear: he can recognize exactly the different kinds of people who go on demonstrations—maybe this wasn't true in the 1960s, but today it certainly is. And, I would say on many occasions, faced with people who have lost their jobs, and who are protesting in a calm and dignified manner, then there is even an emotional involvement with them, that is, we felt close to these people. We were there to protect public order because we had been sent there. *Therefore, we don't have a predetermined negative attitude against people who are protesting, because on many occasions people are protesting to safeguard a certain right or their jobs, which is essential in order to survive.* Nowadays, before we go out on a public order assignment, we often have a chat with our chief and in some cases with the leaders of the demonstration, during which, therefore, before we go out on service, we ask what are the motives and scope of the demonstration. *That is to say, we go out into service knowing who we are going to meet. We know whether we are going to encounter family men in the streets, or people who are likely to cause trouble.* (Interview, Milan, December 5, 1994; emphasis added)

In this case too, the instrumentality of the action gives predictability to the actors and pushes them to avoid escalation. "Just" motives legitimate forms of protest that were once considered illegal, through definitions that differentiate specific types of illegality. Thus, repeatedly, the officials interviewed underlined the difference between a peaceful obstruction of traffic and a violent roadblock:

> When we talk about roadblocks, we mean something different: these are when people put themselves in the middle of the road to protest, although, if you think about it, any demonstration is a kind of roadblock. No, with these people, what I mean is they take the trash can, they throw it down in the middle of the street, they make barricades; in that case, we are talking about something that is against the law. (Interview, Florence, November 10, 1994)

The recognition of a certain legitimacy to a protest permits the justification of actions that are more radical, perhaps even involving a certain aggressiveness toward the police:

> One has to evaluate the mood of the demonstrators: For sure a demonstration by *cassa integrati* [people on unemployment benefits] who come to carry out illegal acts against the officers who are there to show their presence and manage public order—and I don't just mean acts of violence, but also mention other things that are much more widespread, which are generally not pursued, like spitting or verbal abuse—now, obviously these things could be pursued, but clearly they are made by people who are angry and exasperated . . . it must be

seen in a, let's say, wider perspective; that is, *because the police officer at that mo-ment has offered a service, in a practical sense, in fact a moral service, you might say, that is why we must try to tolerate, if you like, even the most angry demonstra-tions, because they might be people who have genuine motives for this. Certainly, the same behavior by soccer fans, or young people who just want to provoke us, that's a standing order, that is certainly a different thing altogether.* (Interview, Milan, November 19, 1994; emphasis added)

Not only the workers, however, but even the autonomous protest groups (anarchists) of the past—of the 1970s in particular—would now be preferable to today's protesters, according to current police perceptions, because of their "higher ideals":

With these autonomous groups these days—we might even ask whether they really are "autonomous groups," because I used to know the autonomous groups of the past. And I know these people we have now. And in my opinion, they are two completely distinct and separate things, for generational and ideo-logical reasons: once these people used to put themselves personally at risk and weren't afraid to put themselves at risk. They weren't afraid to go and take re-sponsibility for their actions before the state, which they considered to be the principal target of their action. *Yet they were people that had a strong idea of social justice, even if they were perfect delinquents, by God! These others, however, I think of them more as hooligans.* The hooliganism of the soccer stadium, that's what it is. Their political ideology is purely nostalgic, because they have to prove some-thing, I say. But they are completely anachronistic. *In contrast, the autonomous groups of the past, they were an integral part of society, because they were a move-ment that had very precise demands, it was something completely different. There was also a worker's movement that was particularly active at the time. . . . A lot of the people in the autonomous groups were people who would then go off to work in a factory. Some of them were also university students. . . .* What they were talking about, in effect, were values. *They wanted to make a revolution! Completely wrongheaded, but at least they were talking about something concrete. . . .* Nowa-days, why do you think these people talk about social centers? Because it's a business, that's why! (Interview, Milan, November 24, 1994; emphasis added)

Moreover, the control of public order becomes more complex the less there is any structured *organization*. The control of stadiums, therefore, be-came more difficult when the traditional structure of organization of soccer fans weakened. As one interviewee observed:

If these groups of fans come together under a particular flag, or label, under a sym-bol of some significance, and if there are people at the head of this group who are recognized as leaders, let's just say it all makes our life much easier. If, on the other hand, it can be seen, as has been the case in recent times—at least this seems to be the tendency—that there is a splintering of groups and gangs, our police work becomes more difficult. This is because these groups and gangs can move around and hide during the course of a season, and you then have difficulties in your police operations staying on top of these continual developments. *Whereas when the phenomenon was more structured and more stable, it was much easier for us.* (Interview, Milan, December 5, 1994; emphasis added)

Also, for the more political form of disorders, the interviewees underline the difficulties that derive from "unorganized" violence:

Nowadays we do have difficult problems to face, and they are caused by exactly the same political fringes that are sprouting again; that is, today there is a return of the kind of violence that was always characteristic of the political extremes of left and right, but whereas before these people also followed a doctrine, their violence was organized; nowadays there is no longer this organization, there is no longer a school where they learn like anyone else how to exercise violence. *Violence today, therefore, can break out in isolated episodes, which are very violent, however, because sometimes not even they understand why it is happening....* When they don't have that school for violence, then when someone decides to be violent and says "Today, I want to be violent," more often than not they don't control the violence that they set off, which is therefore an unpredictable violence; that is, a group that comes out into the streets nowadays might immediately use means and arms that we are not expecting, and we are therefore unprepared in the face of this kind of violence.... *Less organized groups are more difficult to manage: the best example of all that I have been saying is violence in the stadium, which is really very hard to handle.* (Interview, Florence, November 28, 1994; emphasis added)

The Conception of the Role of the Police: Police of the Citizens or Police of the King?

The strategic choice about protest policing is related not only to the image of demonstrators, but also to police self-understanding of their role. In general, the police tend to present themselves as a neutral actor, constrained by the law. As we have seen, however, the police have a high degree of discretion in the use of their power, a discretion that the strategy of "dialogue" tends to increase. The police need therefore other sources of legitimacy. In historical studies one can trace two main lines of thought, more or less opposed to each another: one sees the police as a body created from below, or by civil society, the other as a body created from above, by rulers. Both of these conceptions have some basis in history (Robinson and Scaglio, 1987). In the creation of the police, the requests for security and protection by the citizenry were certainly important—above all, by those who were not rich enough to be able to buy these services on the private market. On the other hand, the institutionalization of the police as a function of the state was linked above all to moments of social tension, in which the state needed an instrument in order to impose respect for its laws, even on those social classes and organizations that did not recognize themselves as under its rule. During the evolution of the police, the two functions of defending the citizens and protecting the order of the state coexisted, with a fluctuating dominance of one or the other according to different phases of history. The combination of the two functions creates a dilemma for the police, given that the defense of political order often alienates the sympathy of a good part of the citizenry, and this in turn undermines the police capacity to fight criminality.

To each of the two models, or functions, there correspond two modes of self-legitimation: a political legitimation in the first case, a social legitimation in the second. Conceptualizations of the role of the police oscillate between the two poles of the state police (*Staatspolizei*) and the citizens' police (*Bürgerpolizei*) (see Winter, in this volume). In Italy, ever since the formal creation of the police, the conception of "state police"—a function of the government—has dominated. Also in the first decades of the Italian Republic, the prerogative of public order and political control prevailed over the fight against criminality (Canosa, 1976). Various documents (for example, Fedeli, 1981; Medici, 1979) indeed portray a police isolated from the population and close to political power. From the 1970s on, nevertheless, there seemed to be a tacit emergence within the police of a larger consideration for the opposite conception of policing. In particular, the struggle against terrorism, seen as a national emergency, and the progressive legitimation of the political opposition contributed to a process of legitimation of the police "from below." In some of the interviews, a self-definition of the police as "people among the people," who "work for the citizens," "full part of the social fabric," a "citizens first of all" emerged. In the words of one interviewee:

> Nowadays the police are democratic, aware, and conscientious. There is an internal culture that many years ago didn't exist. The *questore* was an eternal father figure. Now, he is a civil servant like the rest of us, a high-ranking official with certain responsibilities. The mentality of the absolute authority figure has been lost; it's absolutely right that we are here in the service of everybody . . . now, there's more of a consensus, we are well integrated. (Interview, Florence, November 28, 1994)

According with the picture often presented in our interviews, up until the 1970s there was a sharp division between the police and the citizens. The principal turning point was in fact singled out in the 1980s, with the police and union reform. In the police perceptions, one of the most important effects of this reform was the rapprochement of the citizens and the police, and the resolution of those tensions that, in the eyes of many of those interviewed, were connected to the past "tough" interventions in defense of public order.

> As far as I'm concerned, from the point of view of social relations, for certain, the 1960s with all the battles in the streets and the killing of people, of demonstrators, *we arrived at the low point of relations between the people and the forces of order, who were thus seen in a negative way, as if they were operating with an iron fist.* This, particularly in Emilia, and the north, was felt as a real problem. The changes of 1981, with the reform of the police, aimed at reestablishing contacts with the people in which we tried to re-create, to found what were the basics of police work and its activities, looking to pursue more concrete activities, more in the social context, to go in the opposite direction and try and make the people understand that the point of police operations is that it is a service, developed to manage and guarantee certain values, such as individual liberty. (Interview, Milan, November 19, 1994; emphasis added)

The need for support in public opinion may explain police choices in the control of public order. Our interviewees admitted, in fact, the role that anticipating the reaction of public opinion has in the choice of strategies taken by the police leadership. For instance, the growing tolerance in police interventions seems related to the perception that public opinion would criticize police behavior if an escalation should occur. As a chief officer of the *Digos* in Milan put it, *"We don't want to see violence anymore*; the state now tries to avoid getting into physical conflicts with demonstrators, but instead tries to have control of the demonstrators" (Interview, Milan, July 15–27, 1994; emphasis added). According to one official with considerable experience in the management of public order, police response takes into account "who is creating a problem for public order. *You cannot adopt the same coercive methods if, for example, the Union of Blind People goes out into the streets and someone then starts behaving strangely, compared with two thousand Lazio fans who arrive as an organized group on a train. . . . You have to think about public opinion"* (Interview, Florence, November 10, 1994; emphasis added).

The police in fact feel constantly "under fire" for possible errors—as one interviewee defined it: "We respond one way or another according to whether there is a decision to intervene or not to intervene. In the first case, people ask, Why didn't you intervene? In the second case, they ask, Why did you intervene if you could have contained what was going on?" (Interview, Florence, November 28, 1994). It is interesting to note that, in general, the less "political" the actor causing public disorder is, the stronger the perceived pressure on the police to "intervene":

> At the stadium, so often we hear people say, "Look what's happening over there! Go get involved! Intervene!" . . . so many times you hear "Isolate the trouble-makers," "Throw them out of the stadium . . ." In a demonstration, this is more difficult, but at the stadium I've heard them say this. Many times. Perhaps they want to see more decisive action on our part. And maybe criticize us later on for that. (Interview, Milan, October 18–19, 1994)

According to widely held opinions, the control effected by public opinion is achieved through the intervention of the mass media.[10]

> Public opinion is neither deaf nor blind. The citizens are people who face their own problems with public order and so you can't hope that the press won't see or hear anything. So then you have to weigh up the fact that certain interventions might even get you on to Japanese television—for example, what happened in Vicenza [where neo-Nazis demonstrated], they even showed it on the TV news in Germany. While if I start beating up the Jewish community during their march, well, probably I'll be on the air in Tel Aviv. (Interview, Florence, November 10, 1994)

From this point of view, our research seems to confirm in the Italian case the widespread perception of the press as a filter between the police and citizens—and therefore the importance of enjoying "good press," given that "if the citizen doesn't have faith in the police force, they won't even turn to us when they need us" (Interview, Milan, November 11, 1994).

Even when public opinion acquires a more and more important role, however, the police remain, at least to a certain extent, "king's police." And in fact, as Wisler and Kriesi documented in this volume, the political power often intervenes in the strategic choice on law and order.[11] In Italy, where various studies have documented a blind obedience of the police to the government of the day (among others, Canosa, 1976; Reiter, in this volume), our interviews have put into clear relief the important role that is still attributed to the ruling political powers in making decisions about which styles to privilege in the maintenance of public order. To cite just one example, concerning the decision to intervene in a public demonstration, an official of the *questura* of Florence observed:

> It depends a lot on the orders that come from above. . . . The center of the power is political, the minister responsible, and the chief of the police. We get the information on the front line; and then the *questore* relays what the situation is; he is the carrier of information, which means to say that it makes known what is happening on the ground, that, for example, in Florence a week from now the workers from Hantarex are going to occupy the motorway. And so he then asks the minister what to do: do we keep the motorway closed for an hour, with the repercussions that that can have nationally on traffic, or do we instead break them up immediately? (Interview, Florence, November 28, 1994)

Police choices in public orders are therefore influenced also by the actual and expected reaction from the political system. To end up appearing on the television news or in the newspapers because of a public order intervention not only risks losing the public's sympathy, as we have already pointed out, but also increases the probability of creating what the literature on the police defines as "in-the-job troubles," that is, problems linked to political and administrative investigations into their behavior:[12]

> There are things that we do, or certain mistaken interventions ordered by chiefs, that get censured by the administration. When we manage to contain a public order problem, well, then when public order is protected, that isn't much of a news item. When, on the other hand, public order is not maintained, either through some fault of our own or because the intentions of the protest are particularly extreme, in these cases, if there are brawls, clashes, violence, in these cases, then not only is it going to be in the press, but it will end up in a ministerial inquiry, it will end up with the political parties making parliamentary and ministerial interventions. There are always further consequences. There are always inquiries, that go this way or that way, that say you did right or you did wrong. (Interview, Florence, November 28, 1994)

Especially when "political" demonstrators are involved, the police acknowledge in fact a particular potential of "in-the-job troubles." As Waddington observed on the London case, "Protesters were regarded [by police officers] as archetypal 'challengers' or 'assholes,' that is people who are difficult to control because they are vocally knowledgeable of their roles. They were seen as having influential supporters amongst journalists, campaigners and MPs, who would join in protesting about any police action that might have been construed as infringing freedom of speech" (1994b, 51).

Summary

The object of this study has been to reconstruct some of the aspects of police knowledge relative to the control of public order in Italy. As we observed in the first part of this essay, the strategy used during the course of the 1980s and to date appears to be dominated by three principles: avoid coercive intervention as much as possible, mediate with the demonstrators, and perfect the instruments for information gathering. This strategy is similar to the one adopted by other police forces in continental Europe, although, differently than in the Anglo-Saxon world, the practice of negotiation remains rather informal. Another characteristic of the Italian case is the weak presence of limits and controls on the activity of information gathering by the Digos, which, as we have seen, functions as an "epistemological" organ of the state, given its role of collecting information on all the political actors and interest groups. Within this general sketch, we distinguished four models of control of public order: a model of *cooperation*, based on a collaboration between the police forces and demonstrators, and an inconspicuous police presence; a model of *negotiation*, based on a more active presence by the police, with the objective of mediating between the demonstrators and "nondemonstrators" who suffer the disruptive effects of protests; a model of *ritualistic standoff*, based on a more "aggressive" police presence, but often at a distance; and a model of *total control*, based on a massive presence and close involvement of the police forces. The principal example of the application of the first model is the large trade-union demonstrations: of the second, direct action by unemployed or homeless people; of the third, demonstrations by the youth social centers; and of the fourth, the control of soccer fans.

In the second part of the essay, we looked at the effects of police knowledge on public order control. The principal actors who provoke disorders in the 1990s are, according to a widespread perception of the police, actors who are moved not by political motives, which are considered to be "noble" ends, but by an impulse for "hooliganism" that reflects social problems—"good" demonstrators who protest with ends that are understandable, and "bad" demonstrators who are just "troublemakers." Among the former category are "workers," or "family men"—according to the definitions of those interviewed—who demonstrate in defense of their jobs or union demands, and who have both long experience in demonstrating and a noteworthy capacity of "self-control." Among the second category are soccer "ultras" and the young people from autonomous social centers, whose motivations appear at best "confused," and whose behavior often appears to be "unpredictable."

Police strategies are a function not only of the images the police have of the actors involved in a protest, but also of police conception of their own role. As far as the police are concerned, we found a growing search by the police for legitimation in the eyes of the public. In this sense, the Italian police seem to have acquired some of the characteristics of a citizens' police (or *Bürgerpolizei*)—at least insofar as the search for legitimation in public opinion is concerned. On the other hand, however, the organizational structure itself of the police, as well as their self-definition of their societal role, assign to politicians a larger degree of control than that accepted by the police in other countries. In this respect, the Italian police retain many of the characteristics of the king's police (*Staatspolizei*), characteristics evident above all in the acceptance by the police of methods of control exercised through the activity of information gathering about social and political actors.

Moreover, it remains an open question to what extent the new conception of police involvement based on "dialogue" has been internalized, and to what point this conception is still a pure reflection of requirements that have come from elsewhere. It is probable that to stabilize the evolution that has been observed during recent years, a legislative reform is necessary in order to redefine the tasks and duties of the police and the rights of the citizens in respect to these.

Notes

The author wishes to thank Alessandro Pizzorno for his conceptual contributions to her research on the police. The support of the European University Institute, the A. v. Humboldt Stiftung, and the Consiglio Nazionale delle Ricerche is gratefully acknowledged. This essay was translated by Adrian Favell.

1. In the case of Florence, seven officials from the *questura* (police headquarters) were interviewed; in Milan, five officials from the *questura* and ten from the *reparto mobile* (police action force) were interviewed, in addition to the head of the center of study and research on the police, run by SIULP (the largest police trade union). The interviews in Florence were conducted by Donatella della Porta, those in Milan by Rocco De Biasi.

2. Similar tendencies are stressed elsewhere in this volume, not only about long-lasting democracies—such as France (Fillieule and Jobard), Great Britain (Waddington), and the United States (McPhail, Schweingruber and McCarthy)—but also about recent democracies, such as Spain (Jaime-Jiménez and Reinares). Moreover, on Italy and Germany, see della Porta (1995, chap. 3).

3. As regards tear gas, the police officers underline the technical limits of its use: atmospheric conditions, when there is a downwind; logistical conditions, which require escape routes for those trying to get away; and the general problem of the large numbers of uninvolved persons present. As for baton charges, two limits are indicated: first, although the point of intervention is, according to the police manuals, to stay compact and together, during the charge the officers enter into direct "combat" with the protesters, with the risk of injury; second, the baton charge creates the risk of "direct contact," with a consequent loss of control of chief officers over individual policemen (see also Waddington, 1991).

4. This point on the importance of negotiation for public order is also made in this volume by Waddington on Great Britain; Fillieule and Jobard on France; McPhail, Schweingruber, and McCarthy on the United States. See also Winter (1991); Fillieule (1995a).

5. By mediating with the political authorities, the police enter into a strategy of mutual exchanges with the demonstrators: "By doing favors, they expected organizers to offer compliance in return" (Waddington 1994b, 86).

6. Those interviewed were, however, in general against interventions aimed at "outlawing" groups that systematically provoke disorder and incite violence—a solution they judged to be counterproductive and antidemocratic.

7. On the influence of technological development on police techniques of information gathering, see also Donner (1990).

8. As far as interventions in demonstrations are concerned, personnel from the *Digos* participate in civilian clothes, and without any official identity badge. The presence of plainclothes officers among demonstrators has often caused arguments and criticisms about their possible role as "agents provocateurs."

9. The role of training in the diffusion of the protest policing style is emphasized in this

volume by McPhail, Schweingruber, and McCarthy. Also in this volume, Martin Winter suggests that this choice is linked to the debate on the police understanding of their own role.

10. On the relationships between media, protesters, and the police, see, among others, Sumner (1982); Murdock (1984); Geary (1985); Fielding (1991); Green (1990, chap. 3).

11. On this point see, for instance, Goldstein (1978, 1983); Reiner (1991).

12. As P. A. J. Waddington observed in his research on the policing of public order by the London Metropolitan Police: "Arrests were regarded by the police as the last resort, for they risked escalating on-the-job trouble by sparking a greater confrontation" (1994b, 54–55).

Afterword

Some Reflections on the Democratic Policing of Demonstrations

Gary T. Marx

Three decades ago when the American Kerner Commission (President's National Advisory Commission on Civil Disorders, 1968) studied questions of the police and civil disorders, there was very little social science research to inform the analysis.[1] We have fortunately come a long way in our understanding since then, as the articles in this volume make clear. Within Western democracies, we have also come a long way in the institutionalization of a more tolerant and humane response to those forms of organized protest that stay broadly within the realm of nonviolence.

I first became aware of this ethos as applied to crowds in a conversation with a high-ranking member of the Chicago Police Department shortly after the police violence during the 1968 Democratic Convention in Chicago. He indicated how unprofessionally the department had behaved. He said that as a commander in a protest situation he is willing to listen, to negotiate, to tolerate minor infractions, and to keep a low profile. He felt strongly that saving lives should be more important than protecting property or symbols. He believed that demonstrations could actively help create, rather than undermine, political stability (at least relative to not permitting or responding violently to them). The extensive media coverage of Chicago police attacking protesters was a public relations disaster and such behavior made the police job much more difficult. At that time, his views were heretical and he left the police soon after, but in the decades since (as the articles in this book make clear), they have become widely shared among police leaders both in the United States and beyond.[2]

The views expressed by this officer contrast markedly with those found in totalitarian regimes, which blur or erase the line between politics and crime; any oppositional politics may be defined as crime. But they also contrast with the creation of the first modern police department in Paris at the end of the seventeenth century in which the protection of public order was also equated with the protection of the political order. Indeed, for many observers the connection has been reversed; that is, protecting the right to protest against the political order is defined as the best way of protecting it—at least if the political order is broadly defined to involve a set of democratic principles, rather than the particular persons or groups in power.

This book is particularly welcome in that it involves scholars from countries with varied traditions and languages exchanging ideas and dealing with a common set of theoretical and social concerns. The conditions under which democracies can accept nonelectoral political challenges and yet remain democracies is an issue of enduring importance.

A central argument of most of the articles in this book is that there has been a leavening of police response to protest, regardless of the country. Rather than taking an adversarial and intentionally violent approach, police seek a more neutral stance. The policing of protest has become more normalized.[3] Although police hardly welcome mass demonstrations, in general they no longer arouse the degree of hostility or fear they previously did. To a greater extent than ever before, police view their job to be managing, rather than repressing, protest, protecting the right to demonstrate, and guaranteeing (even to those whose views they may find intolerable) due process of law. The more repressive European control behavior of the 1960s and 1970s, reflecting fears that a weak state response in the face of mass demonstrations could lead to a rebirth of fascism, has given way to increased acceptance of mass protest.

To be sure, there are many exceptions to this trend (which itself involves a series of interrelated developments) and it may not continue in the face of wrenching social changes or grave provocations. Nor is it unilinear across dimensions, groups, time periods, or contexts—as any venture into marginalized, ethnically diverse, lower-income areas, or discussions with those who have been injured in demonstrations will attest. But viewed in comparative and historical terms in which the standard police response was, and in many countries still is, to prohibit demonstrations or to fire on or charge into crowds, the trends noted in these articles are worthy of note. In this concluding comment, I relate this development to some broader trends in social control and note some areas for future research.

Pacification

The relative decline in police and demonstrator violence during mass protest situations can be located within wider social currents. One of these involves the decline of internal violence associated with the rise of the modern liberal state and the continuing elaboration and institutionalization of the idea of citizenship. The state has not only come to have a greater monopoly over the means of violence, but it has also been more restrained in using that violence against its own citizens.

In the United States, for example, we have fortunately not seen a repeat of massive state violence as a response to crowd situations that was responsible for hundreds of deaths in the 1960s (e.g., Watts, Detroit, Newark, Kent State University, Orangeburg).[4] Of course, there is an element of reciprocity and interaction here (and it is difficult to say which came first), but mass protests have also generally become more muted. Perhaps this is partly out of fear of repression and memories of the police violence of the 1960s. It is also related to strategic beliefs regarding the need to avoid a backlash. The protests of the 1960s were followed by the election of presidents Nixon and Reagan and more conservative governments in France and Britain. But a more tolerant approach is also related to lessened police provocation and more ritualized, formulaic expressions of protest crafted for the mass media.

Considering this decline in violence more generally, in the United States (and I suspect in Western Europe) relative to earlier periods, there has been a decline in the police use of violence in traditional criminal contexts and in the interrogation of suspects (Leo, 1992; Chevigny, 1995); the practical disappearance of whipping and flogging as punishments; the abolition of capital punishment in Europe and restrictions and greater controversy over it in the United States; the decline of corporal punishment in the home and in schools and a decline in the homicide rate. The growth of paramilitary police units with much of the paraphernalia and rhetoric of war might suggest the opposite. Yet, even among these burgeoning units the motto for most is "not to kill or be killed" and "less-than-lethal" technologies are favored (Kraska and Kappeler, 1996).

The reverence for life expressed in the peace, environmental, animal rights, and related movements touch similar cultural themes. Looking not just to changes in recent decades or at this and the last century but across several centuries, the work of Norbert Elias (1982) on the rise of civility would also seem to apply. The work of Thomas Humphrey Marshall (1950) on the gradual extension of economic, political, and social rights implied in the idea of citizenship is also relevant.[5]

The changes reported in this book relate to broad changes in social control and to a degree of convergence across national police systems in which there has been a general softening of social control, as the velvet glove increasingly comes to replace, or at least cover, the iron fist. [6]

There appears to be an "Americanization of social control" relative to the strong state traditions of Europe.[7] Dario Melossi (1990) has argued that American conceptions of authority broke with the European tradition of the need for a strong Leviathan state. In the United States, the emphasis came to be placed on the public and on communication as the key to effective societal control, rather than on an all-powerful centralized state. Emphasis was also placed (following the English tradition) on law as a factor controlling *both* elites and those they were to control.

Following World War II, the Allies sought to institutionalize democratic ideas and weaken strong national governments by reintroducing a federal system (e.g., in Germany) and creating conditions that would favor the emergence of interdependent, cross-European entities such as the European Economic Community and the Council of Europe at the expense of the nation-state. The many ways that the victors sought to introduce their version of a democratic society to the vanquished in Europe and Japan has yet to be studied adequately and is an issue of great contemporary signficance given the changes in Eastern Europe and Asia.

But regardless of its origins, there is an emerging ethos or philosophy of modern social control that to varying degrees permeates Western democracies.[8] Central to this is a particular relationship of police to law, a value on human dignity, communication, and the idea of citizenship, and rational analysis as filtered through science and technology. This applies to traditional criminal investigations as well as to the tasks of maintaining order. But with respect to the latter, a flexible and humane response has received increased value, as has the task of managing behavior as distinct from enforcing the law. As the public expression of an *ideal*, this ethos involves basing police actions in demonstrations on seven overlapping ideas.

(1) *Police are servants of the law, not the private army of whomever happens to be in power.* Although they are agents of the state in one sense, they are not the personal agents of those running the state. The state or society is no longer the king, nor even the prime minister or president.[9] Police are not loyal soldiers in a war, but civil servants whose allegiance is to the law. This is central to the Anglo-American police, who were created in opposition to a military model of policing. The differentiation of police from the absolute control of the executive and rejection of the military model is more pronounced in the United States and Great Britain than in Europe, but even in Europe the trend applies.

(2) *The law and policy are being extended to tactics that had once been ignored and unregulated.* There is a broad twentieth-century move toward legitimat-

ing police activities according to law and nonjuridical rules and the strengthening of the belief that police means have a moral component as well as ends. Indeed, this is an important idea of democracy. Max Weber's general observations about bureaucracy and modern society apply here, but take a contemporary twist in sanctifying the use of discretion. What started with efforts to legally and organizationally control how police regulate traditional criminal behavior has in recent decades been extended (to a degree) to the relatively less regulated "high policing of politics," including demonstrations.[10]

There is an interesting paradox and potential minefield here involving official police discretion—we see moves toward both bureaucratization and antibureaucratization. The rationalization of crime control need not mean subjecting it to rigid rules—quite the opposite. The move toward rule-based policing also acknowledges the importance of discretion to police activity. Ironically, it seeks to legitimate discretion by regulating it (rather than ignoring or denying it, as in the past). This is particularly important to the fluid and emergent crowd situations but applies much more generally as well.

(3) *The law must be viewed flexibly and a broad pragmatic view of the likely consequences of police action needs to be taken*, rather than a moralistic or political view based on police attitudes toward demonstrators and their goals or on whether or not the law is violated. Beyond repression, police acknowledge the presence of multiple (and often conflicting) goals, as well as a variety of alternative means for reaching goals. This has been aided by a police force more representative of those to be controlled and perhaps with better understanding of the needs that lead them to protest.

In asking how best to maintain order and minimize harm (whether material or symbolic/political), police may conclude that rigidly enforcing the law through use of overwhelming force will be counterproductive, whether in the short or the long run. Maintaining order as broadly defined may take precedence over enforcing the law. The presence of the mass media is an important factor here serving to moderate police behavior. The symbolic importance of always being in control is given lesser importance than the harm that might befall police, demonstrators, and third parties and the longer negative consequences that might flow from media accounts of police violence.[11] Maintaining a semblance of order (even if at a "cost" of not intervening as forcefully as technical and legal means permit) is seen to be better than rigid law enforcement.

(4) *The primary goal of police in conventional crowd situations is to manage them to see that they do not get out of hand.* Police may serve as mediators and interpreters. They may protect demonstrators and counterdemonstrators

from each other and irate citizens, as well protecting the property and representatives of the state. There is an emphasis on communication and procedural means for resolving conflicts. One of the bargaining chips police have is underenforcement, or nonenforcement, of the law. To become law enforcers via the use of force and arrest can be seen as evidence of failure.

(5) *There is an emphasis on prevention rather than on responding after the fact.* If possible, the latter, which often involves relying on the use of force and/or arrest, is to be avoided. It is simply more efficient to avoid problems of disorderly crowds and invariably messy coercive responses. To do this involves planning and anticipation and is dependent on the empirical analysis discussed in point 7 below. But it may go beyond this to active police involvement in helping to resolve problems that might lead to escalated crime and disorder. Solving problems is seen as superior to forever dealing with symptoms. Rather than simply serving as the representatives of established interests, as buffers between them and challengers, police may serve as referees, liaisons, interpreters, and even advocates for protesters to ensure that their claims are heard. In such situations, police not only avoid criticism for overreacting, they may be praised for problem solving, or at least helping an aggrieved group put forth its claims. This is an important strand of the community-policing model popular in the United States. Citizen involvement is an important element of prevention.

(6) *There should be a "coproduction of order" involving a decentralized and delegated reliance on citizens to mobilize the law and to control themselves and others,* rather than relying exclusively on external and imposed state agents to do this. Police legitimacy in a democratic society is seen as requiring popular support through active citizen participation, whether in setting policy, negotiating the terms of a protest demonstration, or using marshals from the protest group during a demonstration. This is not only legal but practical. Because police are denied (at least formally) the draconian measures of police in totalitarian states, they must work harder to cultivate goodwill among the public. When this is done, the police job is much easier because citizens are actively involved in both self-control and the control of others. In an age of mass communication and the ascendancy of democratic ideals, a strong state that acts negatively and coercively, imposing censorship, restricting the expression of grievances and opinions, and viewing citizens as objects to be controlled rather than as a partners, is a vulnerable state.

(7) *There is an emphasis on science and technology involving (a) relatively dispassionate intelligence gathering and analysis and (b) efforts to engineer physical and social environments.* The former involves interest in broad cate-

gories of potential problems beyond particular individuals or events. There is emphasis on general problem solving and intelligence about systems and networks, as well as individuals. This also involves the development of contingency plans, empirical analysis of various scenarios, and the likely costs and benefits of various police actions (including nonaction) and after-the-fact analyses by police of their own and others' behavior. More sophisticated intelligence activities permit greater selectivity in response to protest activities. Rather than stereotyping all demonstrators, authorities are better able to discriminate and can be more selective in their strategies, as some of the articles suggest. Thus, should the use of force and arrests become necessary, they can be focused on those groups thought most likely to behave violently.

The engineering of physical and social environments (e.g., fences or separate zones to keep supporters of rival soccer teams or social movements apart) may lessen disorder and the need for arrests, or, if that is not possible, it may make the identification of violation and violators automatic and less fallible (e.g., through video cameras or electronic location monitoring). The availability of protective clothing, helmets, and shields and improved communication may make police feel less threatened and less vulnerable. The development of intermediate crowd-control and dispersal technologies (beyond firing regular weapons or charging into crowds) reduces the need to use force should arrests be necessary. With video identification, arrests may also be made at a later time apart from a potentially explosive crowd setting. An array of more exotic technologies is also available ranging from Russian "acoustic psycho-correction" devices that claim to be able to remotely alter behavior, to immobilizing nets propelled at demonstrators favored by the Japanese police, to a slippery goo sprayed onto streets. Efforts to engineer control will likely become more important in the future.[12] They stand in marked contrast to seeking it through self-control, meetings with demonstrators, and the establishment of ground rules as discussed earlier.

Of course, the development of a democratic policing ethos is not without contradictions, challenges, risks, and trade-offs relative to other models. There is no perfect solution or free lunch. There are instead optimal solutions that must be continually reexamined given changing conditions and strategic actors. In the case of efforts to regulate discretion, the trick, of course, is in finding the right mix such that honoring discretion does not put police beyond the law and responsible political control, while regulating discretion does not introduce undue rigidity. Police discretion can be abused, and taken too far can mean a lack of police accountability and legitimacy, as well as citizens taking the law into their own hands.

The other developments discussed earlier, such as negotiation, planning, prevention, citizen involvement, and engineering, also carry other risks. They can be expensive and time-consuming. In periods of fiscal austerity, they may be deemed a luxury. With self-policing and cooperation with authorities, protesters risk co-optation and manipulation. There are also equivalent (if less likely) risks for police. They may be accused of not doing their job and of being partial to, or captured by, the protesting group. A tolerant response may be exploited by those wanting to create maximum disorder. There is a threshold or tipping point in which underreaction may provoke just as overreaction may. Police are likely to face political pressures from less dispassionate leaders and groups for repression and getting tough with challengers.

Well-developed intelligence systems may chill political expression, although that concern is stronger in the United States and Germany than in France and Italy with their well-established agencies for gathering intelligence on all political actors, not just those prone to protest. Rational planning and efforts at prevention must continually encounter surprises and unintended consequences. In addition, once whetted, the cognitive appetite is insatiable. Information begets the need for more information and one can never be fully sure of its validity, nor with the movement of time, its currency. Engineering solutions may appear as undemocratic, deceptive, and manipulative, given their low visibility and the absence of choice on the part of actors.

Certainly these developments have not occurred evenly over time or within or between countries: the United States has taken the lead in police-citizen cooperative ventures and in the formalization of negotiations; Germany has gone far in using analytical techniques based on large databases; Great Britain makes the most extensive use of engineered solutions, including video surveillance; police in France and Italy seem to have the most aggressive (or at least less formally restricted) political intelligence collection and they seem to have greater discretion in crowd settings than is the case with the more legalistic police in Germany (these trends in general have come more recently to Italy and Spain). But the overall trend in recent decades is clear. A systematic accounting and explanation for the differences between countries, as well as for the broad convergence, are needed.

New Research Problems

Let us consider some themes for future research. Of particular salience is how social developments involving the increased importance of information technology and enhanced globalization and regionalization are likely to affect police and protest behavior.

One important area is the changing role of physical space. A possible reduction of public space and increases in private and quasi-private places such as malls and industrial, educational, and entertainment centers suggest new legal issues and, in many countries, new, private police organizations with different goals and means than public police. The generalizations made by the authors in this volume refer to public spaces and would not necessarily hold for these new settings and groups in which property is likely to take precedence over citizenship rights.

A less-noted aspect of space is a possible decrease in the relevance of physical copresence to human affairs (this, of course, began with the letter, the newspaper, and later, the telegraph and the telephone), but it is taken to qualitatively new levels with recent developments.

What, for example, will be the role of new communications technologies in protest? It is possible that, with the widespread availability of faxes, cell phones, the Internet, and other remote means of communication, citizens will find new ways of expressing their concerns that do not require the presence of a large group gathered together at a fixed location and particular time. We can imagine flextime protest suited to the work and family and travel schedules of protesters. Freed from traditional logistical constraints, protest could significantly expand and show increased creativity.

Traditional forms of disruption such as the sit-in and blocking of an entrance or destruction of physical property involve the risk of negative sanctions. But if such disruption were possible remotely and with anonymity, would it increase in scale and destructiveness? These traditional "physical" forms may be replaced by new, more remote, electronic tactics. The U.S. government is so concerned about this that it has appointed a presidential commission to study the dangers of "info wars." Many political leaders in the United States now have Internet addresses and Web sites and attend to discussions on computer bulletin boards.

In one of the first instances of a social movement gaining a goal via computers, widespread protest over the Internet against a new privacy-invading product by Lotus Corporation that would have invaded personal privacy led to its withdrawal. One can also imagine various "flooding," "hacking," and quasi blackmail tactics in which the communications lifeblood of a target of protest is attacked more directly. Police are already developing new strategies for responding to crime and protests in cyberspace. On the other hand, it is also possible that the ease of communication will help coordinate and increase physical space-based protests as well.

A related theme is the implications of increased economic, political, and cultural interdependence among nation-states and the weakening of a variety of traditional borders. There is an increased regionalization and even globalization of protest with respect to issues such as the environment, indigenous peoples, gender, and peace (e.g., international organizations such as Greenpeace and Amnesty International and various new rights groups). In the same way, there is increased cross-border cooperation and integration and even some merging among police. This raises important social and sociological issues with respect to police accountability and cultural and legal differences.

Comparative Research on Democratic Policing

As important as recent research has been, our knowledge now is still largely descriptive, historical, and observational. Although the social sciences will never match the natural sciences in quantification or hypotheses testing, we can go much further.

It may be true, as a U.S. congressman said at a hearing in which he did not like the data being presented, that "everbody's entitled to his own statistics," but it is also the case that a systematic body of data from a representative sample will take us a step further than argument by way of illustration. Systematic analysis requires variables to be more precisely defined and measured. Given different national contexts, this is challenging, but not impossible.

Building on the good beginnings offered by the essays in this book, I see at least three major conceptual and empirical tasks:

1. further conceptualization and measurement of variables relevant to classifying police responses to protest demonstrations;

2. conceptualization and measurement of variables relevant to other types of protest events;

3. locating the policing of protest within broader frameworks for understanding democratic policing.

Demonstrations

I would suggest finding ways to operationalize the ideal type of "democratic policing of demonstrations." As noted earlier, this has seven broad components. These are inclusive of the three tendencies characterizing protest policing in the 1990s noted by della Porta and Reiter in the Introduction (underenforcement, the search to bargain, and large-scale information collection). More broadly relative to the past, the enforcement ethos is soft, tolerant, selective, preventive, consensual, and flexible, as della Porta and Reiter argue (see figure 1 in the Introduction).

In addition, della Porta and Reiter suggest formal-informal and professional-artisanal dimensions. These are of a different nature and, I think, less determinant in their relationship to the democratic policing of demonstrations. They are, however, important factors and under different conditions may either support or undermine democratic policing. I would add to the list of less determinant factors (of democratic policing) a high- or low-tech variable (this refers to the sophistication and breadth of crowd-control means).

Five additional variables in the more determinant range likely to be associated with democratic policing are:

1. representative versus unrepresentative police (refers to the degree to which police are representative of those protesting)

2. high or low visibility of police and demonstrator actions (refers to the demonstrators as well the presence of mass media)

3. identifiable versus anonymous police and demonstrators (refers to the ease of identifying particular individuals)

4. administrative procedures for reviewing police behavior and means for citizens to express grievances (present or absent and fair or unfair)

5. cooperative versus adversarial demonstrators (refers to the degree of cooperation/provocation from protesters)

Adding these factors offers a fuller picture. In adding dimensions of demonstrator behavior that are the reciprocal of police behavior, we can more fully take account of the interactive nature of the event. We can also theorize whether nonviolent and nonprovocative (if sometimes disorderly) demonstrator behavior is explained by the same factors as a nonviolent and nonprovocative police response.

In principle, these factors and those shown in the Introduction (figure 1) can be viewed as analytically and empirically distinct dimensions, even though in practice certain clusters are likely to occur together. Thus all seven factors would not have to be present in equal degrees for us to characterize a setting as an example of democratic policing. However, the more they are present, the more the ideal type is approached.

We might try to predict either police or demonstrator behavior based on behavior by the other, or we might link them to broader clusters of factors such as those discussed later in this essay.

Given the ongoing nature of social life, variables can be viewed as either independent or dependent. They are often complexly intertwined with other variables such that making causal statements is ill-advised. Yet, even then, identifying the factors helps to direct our attention and spurs thought.

Other Types of Protest Events

Although this book is concerned with the "police handling of protest events," in general attention is devoted to only one type of "protest event"— relatively nonviolent demonstrations.[13]

It would be useful to devote equivalent research attention to responses to other types of protest events such as holding meetings, circulating petitions, publishing articles, lobbying, raising funds and making contributions, posting signs, wearing symbols, and engaging in various forms of civil disobedience (e.g., a refusal to pay taxes or to follow an unpopular law). In democratic societies, how generalizable is a tolerant police response to demonstrations?

Police response to one protest activity may be highly related to response to others. As a visible and dramatic example, police response to demonstrations may be taken as a shorthand indication of their more general response to other forms of protest behavior. One would expect a degree of consistency; that is, regimes that were tolerant of demonstrations would also be tolerant of a free press, would restrict surveillance of political dissidents, and would subject police to stringent legal requirements for eavesdropping and searches. But that should be subject to empirical documentation and there is certainly variation.

Many protest events do not require a physical gathering. The behavior may be hidden and so too may the response, thus potentially reducing accountability on both parts. In that sense, a police policy of toleration in the face of public demonstrations can certainly coexist with a policy of covert dirty tricks. A regime may indirectly seek to restrict other forms even as it accepts the freedom to organize and collectively demonstrate.

A related question is how responses to nonviolent protest relate to police responses to terrorism and other threats to state security. One hypothesis is that states that are tolerant of protest will be less likely to face terrorism since grievances can be legitimately expressed, but that ignores the role that international conflicts now play in domestic terrorism (e.g., expressions of the Algerian struggle in France). Since all states will respond to such threats, the issue here is to what extent the police and secret service agencies are given a free hand, as against facing restrictions (whether prohibitions of some actions or procedural requirements). Variation here may or may not relate to how tolerant police are of demonstrations.[14]

Policing in Democratic Societies

Another major task is to locate the policing of protest within broader national comparisons of policing in democratic societies. Although there is a growing literature to inform this, in general (with a few notable exceptions) it is not very analytic and most often focuses on only one country.[15] Or, if more than one country is considered, this is most likely done in parallel, rather than in a truly comparative and integrative fashion. There is a need to locate the policing of protest within a broader family of dimensions of democratic policing. We need better ways of conceptualizing and measuring this. The next task would be to explore the correlates of this.

Among factors whose correlates for democratic policing more generally should be explored:[16]

- a civil or common-law tradition
- an adversarial or inquisitorial legal process
- a national or federal criminal justice system
- significant or minimal role for judicial review of executive and judicial actions
- clearly codified Bill of Rights
- a single or multiple police system
- the degree of police officer heterogeneity within systems
- police as part of a civil or military bureaucracy
- an Anglo-American community or a strong-state model of policing—Mediterranean Catholic or Northern European Protestant traditions
- imposed or indigenously developed democracy (and recency of authoritarian rule)
- a colonial power or not
- feudal tradition or not
- monarchy or republic
- greater or lesser importance placed on citizen actions to mobilize the law

- greater or lesser role for private-sector social control for both individuals and organizations
- greater or lesser importance placed on anticipatory police actions

Some standard sociological variables that should also be considered:

- degree and types of inequality
- degree and types of heterogeneity and homogeneity
- degree of differentiation
- degree of legitimacy granted authority
- degree of consensus on the rules
- degree of self-control
- degree of expectation and willingness of citizens to control one another
- population size and density
- degree of geographical mobility and ease of creating new identities

Having once defined what we wish to account for from the variety of dependent variables relevant to protest policing and democratic policing more generally, we can explore the implications of clusters of these causal variables.

Yet, even if we had very clear measures of what we wanted to explain and of possible causal variables, we would, of course, note continuing significant variation between and within countries with their very different histories, cultures, and social structures. I think we would also find, however, as these essays and other recent research suggest, a movement, if halting, toward convergence and amalgamation in the form of a standardized, democratic, industrial policing model. The pace and contours of this vary and the reasons for it are diverse, but it is a vital topic for future research. It is exciting to see the collaborative efforts among scholars from different countries and perspectives on this topic and I look forward to continuing to learn from them.

Notes

1. In working for the commission, I had the opportunity to study police and disorders (Marx, 1970).

2. I do not wish to suggest that police have become converts to civil liberties values and to causes seeking class, gender, and racial equality or environmental protection and other goals (although police may share many views with those in their generational cohorts and the more representative police departments today are more understanding than were older, more homogeneous police confronting the 1960s protests). To a significant de-

gree, current, more restrained police behavior is political and strategic, as well as a result of technical innovations. It is political in that in the current political climate it will help individual careers and protect and help their organizations grow. With the mass media ever present, heavy-handed repression of crowds is not publicly acceptable in today's democracies. In addition, on pragmatic grounds contemporary softer approaches are seen to be more effective. They can be seen as a countermove in the face of some activists' strategy of trying to provoke police. Another very important factor in the United States is the fear financially strapped governments have of lawsuits from citizens claiming that they have been mistreated.

3. One might more easily speak of protest policing. But that suggests police as protesters, an interesting topic, to be sure, but not the subject of this book.

4. Lack of preparedness, tactical errors, and inappropriate strategies have led to state violence in the United States in response to hostage and resisting arrest situations, as with the Waco, Texas, case. But those situations are very different from the organized public protests studied by the authors in this volume. Even then there appears to be a learning curve and the response to Waco had few defenders, even among police. The contrast with the peaceful resolution of the Freemen case in Montana a short time later, in which authorities negotiated and waited and waited at great financial cost, better illustrates the argument developed in this Afterword. Beyond the absolute amount of harm done, we can also note the amount of harm done given the potential destructiveness of the technology. In that regard, the ratio between the amount of domestic violence and the potential of the technology appears to have declined. One could also argue that the availability of less lethal means, beyond any more humane esprit, is central. Given the technology, it is not now necessary for authorities to be as violent in controlling groups. However, the development of such technologies for domestic use is driven by that ethos.

5. Of course, the continuing violence in interpersonal relations, crime commission, and the policing of low-income, minority, and colonial-like areas, and in prisons, and the indiscriminate and massive destructiveness of modern warfare warn us against any premature celebration of nonviolence's triumph. The increased availability of information (e.g., through the Internet) about, and the resources to make, explosives are also a counterfactor.

6. Within Western democracies, there may be an inverse relationship between domestic and external violence. As Tilly (1990) notes, with the rise of the nation-state over the last century wars have become more frequent and lethal.

7. Of course, roads permit travel in multiple directions. Thus European practices also come to the United States. For example, in recent decades the U.S. Supreme Court extended police powers with respect to warrantless searches, narrowed the exclusionary rule, and broadened the police ability to interrogate absent the presence of counsel.

8. I do not argue that this trend characterizes all police behavior or all police. Even when it is the officially expressed view, that does not mean that it is privately accepted or that it is necessarily linked to behavior. Yet, in recent decades these ideas have become more prominent.

9. This raises an interesting issue characterizing many of these papers regarding the extent to which police can be "neutral" and guardians of, and controlled by, the law versus manipulators of the law and protectors of power and privilege who seek legitimacy via a slick and deceptive public relations gloss of universalism. Zola's remark about the rich and the poor being equal before the law in having the right to sleep under bridges certainly applies. The law, of course, on balance reflects the inequality of social interests, but it does not only do that. Some laws protect all citizens and laws guaranteeing the right to protest hold out the hope that, at least in principle, the balance might be legally changed. It is easy to dis-

268   MARX

parage that, as Marcuse and others have done, but the horrors of Tiananmen Square and continuing struggles for basic rights of political expression in China and much of the world offer a striking contrast.

There are several issues here: (1) Does a given law serve all members of society or favor some over others? (2) Is a law equally enforced? The best situation is equal enforcement of a law broadly serving all segments of the public.

10. See, for example, Brodeur (1983, 507–20). Ironically, covert policing and the harder to regulate forms of high policing have now also been extended in some ways to the "low policing" of everyday activities.

11. A little-noted fact is that this can cut both ways. For example, the videotaping of the Rodney King beating by police (and the subsequent jury finding that the police involved were not guilty) triggered massive violence in Los Angeles. Yet, during that incident the capturing on video of a white truck driver being dragged from his truck and brutally assaulted created sympathy in the other direction.

12. Marx (1995a) considers the varied forms and consequences of this. In the case at hand, is a well-prepared and well-equipped police force with strong legal grounds for harsh interventions more or less likely to do so? The iron fist has hardly disappeared. This suggests some ironic hypotheses in which repressive potential (1) serves as a deterrent making the actual resort to extreme force less necessary, (2) permits initial soft responses because authorities know that they can fall back on harder responses (the ace-in-the-hole argument), (3) by repressing the more violence-prone elements, the power of the moderates is increased and authorities have less need to resort to extreme force. Although there is a danger of doublespeak here (e.g., calling missiles peacekeepers), this also was the logic of a strong military during the Cold War. Of course, one can hypothesize in the other direction as well. Where there is a way, there may be a will. Power is often a hungry and insatiable beast. A strong repressive potential may feed on itself. It may provoke, whether intentionally or unintentionally, the very things that (according to its public goals) it seeks to avoid. The distancing of seemingly anonymous helmeted police wearing visors that hide their faces has often been commented on. Rubber bullets are another interesting example. As a potential they are certainly preferable to real bullets in response to unarmed demonstrators. Yet does their availability mean that police are more likely to fire given their presumed nonlethal character? The situation may be similar to the net widening that becomes possible with the development of intermediate sanctions such as electronic location monitoring in lieu of imprisonment. There are large questions here to which empirical answers are absent. It would be useful to explore the interconnections, patterns, and consequences of the development of "hard" and "soft" technologies over time. Under what conditions do they develop in tandem in some kind of an equilibrium as against cyclically as alternatives? Given the variety of techniques and of agents of control (including those from the private sector) and objects of control (including those favoring violence and those more moderate), empirically untangling this is a challenge.

13. Some attention is also devoted to "issueless" (at least with respect to conventional political ideologies) events such as the policing of soccer crowds. Interesting comparative questions appear in contrasting these forms and the responses to them. Another important issue involves more systematic study of demonstrators, as well as police, during an event. The essays in this volume devote most of their analysis to the police. They note the importance of the *interaction* between police and demonstrators, yet devote much less time to the behavior of demonstrators.

14. In Italy, for example, where police appear to have greater discretion and tolerance for disorder in facing demonstrations, its secret service in contrast is alleged to make use of

agents provocateurs, plot coups d'état, protect neofascist groups, and even to have been involved in murders.

15. Some exceptions to this include Miller (1977); Punch (1985); Brewer et al. (1988); Bayley (1985, 1994); Mawby (1992); and della Porta (1995).

16. These factors, of course, can be related (e.g., feudal, Catholic, strong state, national, inquisitorial or common law, civil bureaucracy, community, federal). Elsewhere (Marx, 1995b) I have speculated on how these factors might relate to another aspect of democratic policing—the use of covert tactics.

Bibliography

Ackroyd, Carole, Jonathan Rosenhead, and Tim Shallice. 1980. *The Technology of Political Control.* London: Pluto Press.

Adamek, Raymond, and Jerry Lewis. 1973. "Social Control, Violence and Radicalization: The Kent State Case." *Social Forces* 51 (3): 342–47.

Ahire, Philip T. 1991. *Imperial Policing: The Emergence and Role of the Police in Colonial Nigeria 1860–1960.* Milton Keynes: Open University Press.

Altmann, Robert, Helmut Bernhardt, and Horst Ehrlich, eds. 1975. *Handbuch für Führung und Einsatz der Polizei—Polizeidienstvorschrift 100 und Kommentar zur PDV 100.* Stuttgart: Boorberg.

American Civil Liberties Union. 1982. *Demonstrating in the District of Columbia.* Washington, D.C.: ACLU of the National Capital Area.

An, Mildred. 1991. "Free Speech, Post Office Sidewalks, and the Public Forum Doctrine." *Harvard Civil Rights-Civil Liberties Review* 26 (2):633–48.

Anderson, David M., and David Killingray, eds. 1991. *Policing the Empire: Government, Authority and Control, 1830–1940.* Manchester: Manchester University Press.

———. 1992. *Policing and Decolonisation: Politics, Nationalism and the Police, 1917–65.* Manchester: Manchester University Press.

Applegate, Rex. 1969. *Riot Control: Material and Techniques.* Harrisburg, Pa.: Stackpole Books.

Ascoli, D. 1979. *The Queen's Peace.* London: Hamish Hamilton.

Baena, Mariano, and José María García Madaria. 1979. "Elite franquista y burocracia en las Cortes actuales." *Sistema,* no. 28: 3–50.

Bailey, Victor. 1981. "The Metropolitan Police, the Home Office and the Threat of Outcast London." In *Policing and Punishment in the 19th Century,* edited by Victor Bailey, 94–125. London: Croom Helm.

Baldwin, Robert, and Richard Kinsey. 1982. *Police Powers and Politics.* London: Quartet Books.

Ballbé, Manuel. 1985. *Orden público y militarismo en la España constitucional (1812–1983).* Madrid: Alianza.

Bateson, Gregory. 1972. *Steps to an Ecology of Mind: Collected Essays in Anthropology, Psychiatry, Evolution, and Epistemology.* New York: Ballantine Books.

Bayley, David H. 1985. *Patterns of Policing: A Comparative International Analysis.* New Brunswick, N.J.: Rutgers University Press.

————. 1986. "The Tactical Choices of Police Patrol Officers." *Journal of Criminal Justice* 14.

————. 1994. *Police for the Future.* New York: Oxford University Press.

Benedicto, Jorge. 1989. "Sistemas de valores y pautas de cultura política predominantes en la sociedad española (1976–1985)." In *La transición democrática española,* edited by José Felix Tezanos, Ramón Cotarelo, and Andrés de Blas, 645–78. Madrid: Editorial Sistema.

Benyot, John. 1984. "The Policing Issue." In *Scarman and After,* edited by John Benyot, 99–113. Oxford: Pergamon Press.

Berger, Peter L., and Thomas Luckmann. 1966. *The Social Construction of Reality: A Treatise in the Sociology of Knowledge.* Garden City, N.Y.: Anchor Books.

Berlioz, J. M. 1987. "Les manifestations." *Revue de la Police nationale,* no. 126: 6–15.

Bessel, Richard. 1992. "Militarisierung und Modernisierung: Polizeiliches Handeln in der Weimarer Republik." In *"Sicherheit" und "Wohlfahrt." Polizei, Gesellschaft und Herrschaft im 19. und 20. Jahrhundert,* edited by Alf Lüdtke, 323–43. Frankfurt/Main: Suhrkamp.

Bittner, Egon. 1970. *The Functions of the Police in a Modern Society.* Washington, D.C.: U.S. Government Printing Office.

Black, Donald. 1980. *The Manners and Customs of the Police.* New York: Academic Press.

Blasecki v. Durham. 1972. 456 F. 2d 87 (4th Cir.).

Boldt, Hans. 1992. "Geschichte der Polizei in Deutschland." In *Handbuch des Polizeirechts,* edited by Erhard Denninger and Hans Lisken, 1–39. Munich: Beck.

Bowden, Tom. 1978. *Beyond the Limits of the Law.* Harmondsworth, England: Penguin.

Bowes, Stuart. 1966. *The Police and Civil Liberties.* London: Lawrence and Wishart.

Branch, Taylor. 1988. *Parting the Waters: America in the King Years 1954–63.* New York: Simon and Schuster.

Brand, Karl-Werner. 1985. "Vergleichendes Resümee." In *Neue soziale Bewegungen in Westeuropa und den USA. Ein internationaler Vergleich,* edited by Karl-Werner Brand, 306–34. Frankfurt/Main: Campus.

Brand, Karl-Werner, Detlef Büsser, and Dieter Rucht. 1986. *Aufbruch in eine andere Gesellschaft. Neue soziale Bewegungen in der Bundesrepublik.* Aktualisierte Neuausgabe. Frankfurt/Main: Campus.

Brandenburg v. Ohio. 1969. 395 U.S. 444.

Brewer, John, Adrian Guelke, Ian Hume, E. Moxon-Browne, and Roger Wilford. 1988. *The Police, Public Order and the State.* London: Macmillan.

Brewer, John D. 1994. *Black and Blue: Policing in South Africa.* Oxford: Clarendon Press.

Brodeur, Jean-Paul. 1983. "High Policing and Low Policing: Remarks about the Policing of Political Activities." *Social Problems* 30 (5): 507–20.

Brogden, A., and Mike Brogden. 1982. "Postscript. The Toxteth Riots, 1981." In *The Police: Autonomy and Consent,* by Mike Brogden, 238–50. London: Academic Press.

Brogden, Mike. 1982. *The Police: Autonomy and Consent.* London: Academic Press.

————. 1987. "The Emergence of the Police: The Colonial Dimension." *British Journal of Criminology* 27 (1): 4–14.

Brogden, Mike, and Clifford Shearing. 1993. *Policing for a New South Africa.* London: Routledge.

Brothers, John. 1985. "Communication Is the Key to Small Demonstration Control." *Campus Law Enforcement Journal* 15 (5) 13–16.

Bruneteaux, Patrick. 1993. "La violence d'État dans un régime démocratique: les forces de maintien de l'ordre en France. 1880–1980." Dissertation, Université de Paris-I.

Bunyan, Tony. 1977. *The History and Practice of the Political Police in Britain.* London: Quartet.

Bunyan, Tony, and Martin Kettle. 1980. "The Police Force of the Future Is Now Here." *New Society* 21 (August): 351–54.

Burden, Ordway P. 1992. "Peacekeeping and the 'Thin Blue Line': Law Enforcement and the Preservation of Civil Rights." *The Police Chief* 59 (6):16–26.

Burfeind, Thees. 1993. "Polizeiliche Maßnahmen gegen gewalttätige Demonstranten." Göttingen: Ph.D. dissertation, University of Göttingen.

Busch, Heiner, Albrecht Funk, Udo Kauß, Wolf-Dieter Narr, and Falco Werkentin. 1985. *Die Polizei in der Bundesrepublik.* Frankfurt/Main: Campus.

Busch, Heiner, Albrecht Funk, Wolf-Dieter Narr, and Falco Werkentin (CILIP). 1990. *"Nicht dem Staate, sondern dem Bürger dienen." Für eine bürgernahe Polizei.* Berlin: Alternative Liste.

Cain, Maureen E. 1973. *Society and the Policeman's Role.* London: Routledge and Kegan Paul.

Canosa, Romano. 1975. "La legislazione eccezionale sull'ordine pubblico in Italia, tra storia e cronaca." In *Ordine pubblico e criminalità*, edited by Lotta Continua, Organizzazione Comunista Avanguardia Operaia, Partito di Unità per il Comunismo, 15–39. Milan: Mazzotta.

———. 1976. *La polizia in Italia dal 1945 ad oggi.* Bologna: Il Mulino.

Canosa, Romano, and Pietro Federico. 1974. *La magistratura in Italia dal 1945 a oggi.* Bologna: Il Mulino.

Carucci, Paola. 1976. "I servizi di polizia dopo l'approvazione delle leggi di pubblica sicurezza nel 1926." *Rassegna degli archivi di stato* 26: 83–114.

Cawthra, Gavin. 1993. *Policing South Africa.* London: Zed Books.

Chandler, C. Lee. 1986. "The Role of Law Enforcement in Student Confrontations." *Law and Order* 34 (10): 74–75.

Chatterton, Michael R. 1979. "The Supervision of Patrol Work under the Fixed Points System." In *The British Police*, edited by Simon Holdaway, 83–101. London: Edward Arnold.

———. 1983. "Police Work and Assault Charges." In *Control in the Police Organization*, edited by M. Punch, 194–221. Cambridge: MIT Press.

———. 1987. "Front-Line Supervision in the British Police Service." In *The Crowd in Contemporary Britain*, edited by G. Gaskell and R. Benewick, 123–54. London: Sage.

Cherry, William. 1975. "The Military: A Source of Equipment and Training." *The Police Chief* 42 (4): 53–55.

Chevigny, Paul. 1995. *The Edge of the Knife: Police Violence in the Americas.* New York: New Press.

Chicago v. Mosely. 1972. 408 U.S. 92, 95.

CILIP. 1981. "Berlin, Zürich, Amsterdam-Politik, Protest und Polizei. Eine vergleichende Untersuchung." *Bürgerrechte und Polizei (CILIP)* 4 (9/10).

Cohen, Phil. 1979. "Policing the Working Class City." In *Capitalism and the Rule of Law*, edited by Bob Fine, Richard Kinsey, John Lea, Sol Picciotto, and Jock Young, 118–36. London: Hutchinson.

Cohen, Stanley. 1972. *Folk Devils and Moral Panics.* London: Paladin.

Collin, Richard O. 1985. "The Blunt Instruments: Italy and the Police." In *Police and Public Order in Europe*, edited by John Roach and Jürgen Thomaneck, 185–214. London: Croom Helm.

Collins v. Chicago Park District. 1972. 460 F. 22d 746 (7th. Cir. 1972).

Corso, Guido. 1979. *L'ordine pubblico.* Bologna: Il Mulino.

Cotarelo, Ramón, ed. 1992. *Transición política y consolidación democrática.* Madrid: Centro de Investigaciones Sociológicas.

Coulter, J., S. Miller, and M. Walker. 1984. *State of Siege: Miners' Strike 1984*. London: Canary Press.

Covell, Howard V. 1963. "Detailed Police Planning Key to Orderly Rally: The March on Washington." *FBI Law Enforcement Bulletin* 32 (11): 3–22.

Cox v. New Hampshire. 1941. 312 U.S. 569.

Critchley, Tim. 1970. *The Conquest of Violence*. London: Constable.

Dahrendorf, Ralph. 1959. *Class and Class Conflict in an Industrial Society*. London: Routledge.

Dal Lago, Alessandro. 1990. *Descrizione di una battaglia. I rituali del calcio*. Bologna: Il Mulino.

Dal Lago, Alessandro, and Roberto Moscati. 1992. *Regalateci un sogno. Miti e realtà del tifo calcistico in Italia*. Milan: Bompiani.

De Biasi, Rocco. 1992. "Il post-hooliganismo. Le nuove culture del tifo in Inghilterra." *Ludus* 2: 62–76.

De Fina, Silvio. 1959. "Testo Unico di Pubblica Sicurezza e Costituzione." *Giurisprudenza Costituzionale* 4: 964–93.

De Lutiis, Giuseppe. 1993. *Storia dei servizi segreti in Italia*. Rome: Editori Riuniti.

della Porta, Donatella. 1995. *Social Movements, Political Violence and the State: A Comparative Analysis of Italy and Germany*. Cambridge: Cambridge University Press.

———. 1996. "Social Movements and the State: Thoughts on the Policing of Protest." In *European/American Perspectives on the Dynamics of Social Movements*, edited by Doug McAdam, John McCarthy, and Mayer Zald, 62–92. Cambridge: Cambridge University Press.

———. 1997. "The Political Discourse on Protest Policing." In *How Movements Matter*, edited by Marco Giugni, Doug McAdam, and Charles Tilly. Minneapolis: University of Minnesota Press.

della Porta, Donatella, and Mario Diani. 1997. *I movimenti sociali*. Rome: Nuova Italia Scientifica.

Denninger, Erhard. 1978a. "Polizei in der freiheitlichen Demokratie." In *Polizei und Strafprozeß im demokratischen Rechtsstaat*, edited by Erhard Denninger and Klaus Lüderssen, 102–26. Frankfurt/Main: Suhrkamp.

———. 1978b. "Polizei und demokratische Politik." In *Polizei und Strafprozeß im demokratischen Rechtsstaat*, edited by Erhard Denninger and Klaus Lüderssen, 143–67. Frankfurt/Main: Suhrkamp.

Denninger, Erhard, and Klaus Lüderssen. 1978. "Einleitung." In *Polizei und Strafprozeß im demokratischen Rechtsstaat*, edited by Erhard Denninger and Klaus Lüderssen, 7–66. Frankfurt/Main: Suhrkamp.

Department of the Interior. 1965. "National Park Service Memorandum (P8615=OR) Regarding Public Assemblies and Demonstrations." June 7. Retrieved from the National Archives.

Department of Justice. 1970. *Demonstration and Dissent in the Nation's Capital*. Washington, D.C.: Department of Justice.

Di Loreto, Pietro. 1991. *Togliatti e la "Doppiezza". Il PCI tra Democrazia e Insurrezione 1944–49*. Bologna: Il Mulino.

Donati, L. 1977. "La guardia regia." *Storia contemporanea* 8: 441–87.

Donner, Frank. 1990. *Protectors of Privilege*. Berkeley: University of California Press.

Driscoll, J. 1987. "Protest and Public Order: The Public Order Act of 1986." *Journal of Social Welfare Law*: 280–99.

Dunnage, Jonathan. 1989. "Istituzioni e ordine pubblico nell'Italia giolittiana. Le forze di polizia in provincia di Bologna." *Italia contemporanea* 177: 5–26.

———. 1992. "Ordinamenti amministrativi e prassi politica. Le forze di polizia a Bologna di fronte al fascismo 1920–1921." *Italia contemporanea* 186: 61–89.

Dunning, Eric, Patrick Murphy, and John Williams. 1988. *The Roots of Football Hooliganism: An Historical and Sociological Study.* London: Routledge.

Eisenhower, Milton. 1969. *Report of the National Commission on the Causes and Prevention of Violence.* Washington, D.C.: U.S. Government Printing Office.

Elias, Norbert. 1982. *The History of Manners.* New York: Pantheon.

Elias, Norbert, and Eric Dunning. 1986. *Quest for Excitement: Sport and Leisure in the Civilizing Process.* Oxford: Basil Blackwell.

Englis, Simon. 1983. *The Football Grounds in Great Britain.* London: Willow Books.

Escobar, Edward J. 1993. "The Dialectic of Repression: The Los Angeles Police Department and the Chicano Movement, 1968–1971." *Journal of American History* 79: 1483–1514.

Etzioni, Amitai. 1970. *Demonstration Democracy.* New York: Gordon and Breach.

Eurispes. 1994. *Ultrà: Le sottoculture giovanili negli stadi d'Europa.* Rome: Koinè.

Ewing, K. D., and C. A. Gearty. 1990. *Freedom under Thatcher.* Oxford: Clarendon Press.

Fairchild, Erika S. 1988. *German Police: Ideals and Reality in the Postwar Years.* Springfield, Ill.: Charles C. Thomas.

Favre, Pierre. 1990. *La manifestation.* Paris: Presses de la Fondation Nationale des Sciences Politiques.

———. 1993. "Où l'on voit les acteurs sociaux ignorer la règle de droit et le législateur ignorer que les acteurs ignorent la règle, où l'on entend parler brièvement du droit de la manifestation et où l'on apprend comment on le réforme au Parlement, et où l'on est amené à conclure que le juriste et le politologue peuvent continuer à suivre chacun de leur côté leur petit bonhomme de chemin." *Cahiers du CURAP,* 187–94.

Favre, Pierre, and Olivier Fillieule. 1994. "La manifestation comme indicateur de l'engagement politique." In *L'Engagement politique, déclin ou mutation?* edited by Pascal Perrineau, 115–39. Paris: Presses de la Fondation Nationale des Sciences Politiques.

Fedeli, Franco. 1981. *Da sbirro a tutore della legge.* Rome: Napoleoni.

Federal Bureau of Investigation. 1967. *Prevention and Control of Mobs and Riots.* Washington, D.C.: Department of Justice.

Fielding, Nigel. 1991. *The Police and Social Conflict.* London: Athlone Press.

Fillieule, Olivier. 1995a. "Le maintien de l'ordre en France. Éléments d'un modèle de gestion des conflits manifestants par l'État. Rapport de recherche." Florence: European University Institute (manuscript).

———. 1995b. *Methodological Issues in the Collection of Data on Protest Events: Police Records and National Press in France.* Working paper of the Schuman Center of the European University Institute, Florence.

———. 1997. *Stratégies de la rue: Les manifestations en France.* Paris: Presses de la Fondation Nationale des Sciences Politiques.

Fine, Bob, and Robert Millar, eds. 1985. *Policing the Miners' Strike.* London: Lawrence and Wishart.

Fiorentino, Fiorenza. 1978. *Ordine pubblico nell'Italia giolittiana.* Rome: Carecas.

Flam, Helena. 1994. "Political Responses to the Anti-Nuclear Challenge: Democratic Experiences and the Use of Force." In *States and Antinuclear Movements,* edited by Helena Flam, 329–54. Edinburgh: Edinburgh University Press.

Foucault, Michel. 1977. *Discipline and Punish: The Birth of the Prison.* London: Penguin.

Funk, Albrecht. 1990. "Innere Sicherheit: Symbolische Politik und exekutive Praxis." In *40 Jahre Bundesrepublik* (Special issue of *Leviathan*), edited by B. Blanke and H. Wollmann, 367–88.

García Madaria, J. M. 1979. "Elite franquista y burocracia en las Cortes actuales." *Sistema* 28: 3–50.

Garret, David. 1981. *The FBI and Martin Luther King Jr.* New York: Norton.

Gatrell, Vic, and Tom Hadden. 1972. "Nineteenth Century Criminal Statistics and Their Interpretation." In *Nineteenth Century Society*, edited by E. Wrigley, 336–96. Cambridge: Cambridge University Press.

Geary, Roger. 1985. *Policing Industrial Disputes: 1893 to 1985.* Cambridge: Cambridge University Press.

Geertz, Clifford. 1973. *The Interpretation of Cultures: Selected Essays.* New York: Basic Books.

Gentile, Thomas. 1983. *March on Washington: August 28, 1963.* Washington, D.C.: New Day Publications.

Giddens, Anthony. 1973. *The Class Structure of Advanced Societies.* London: Hutchinson.

Gilbert, Ben W. 1968. *Ten Blocks from the White House: Anatomy of the Washington Riots of 1968.* New York: Praeger.

Giugni, Marco. 1991. "La mobilisation des nouveaux mouvements sociaux en Suisse 1975–1989." *Travaux et communications* (University of Geneva), no. 2.

Goffman, Erving. 1961. *Encounters: Two Essays on the Sociology of Interaction.* Indianapolis: Bobbs-Merrill.

———. 1974. *Frame Analysis: An Essay on the Organization of Experience.* New York: Harper and Row.

Goldstein, Robert J. 1978. *Political Repression in America.* Cambridge, Mass.: Schenkman.

———. 1983. *Political Repression in 19th Century Europe.* London: Croom Helm.

Goldstone, Richard J. 1990. *Report of the Commission of Enquiry into the Incidents at Sebokeng, Boipatong, Lekoa, Sharpeville and Evaton on 26 March 1990.* Johannesburg: South African Government.

Goldthorpe, John, Catriona Llewellyn, and Clive Payne. 1980. *Social Mobility and Class Structure in Modern Britain.* Oxford: Oxford University Press.

Gora, Joel M., David Goldberger, Gary M. Stern, and Morton H. Halperin. 1991. *The Right to Protest: The Basic ACLU Guide to Free Expression.* Carbondale: Southern Illinois University Press.

Graham, Hugh G., and Theodore R. Gurr. 1969. *The History of Violence in America: Report of a Task Force of the National [Eisenhower] Commission on the Causes and Prevention of Violence.* New York: Praeger.

Greater London Council. 1985. *Public Order Plans: The Threat to Democratic Rights.* London: Greater London Council.

———. 1986. *The Control of Protest.* London: Greater London Council.

Green, Penny. 1990. *The Enemy Without.* Milton Keynes: Open University Press.

Gregory, Frank E. C. 1985. "The British Police System." In *Police and Public Order in Europe*, edited by John Roach and Jürgen Thomanek, 33–72. London: Croom Helm.

Grillo, Andrea. 1994. *Livorno: una rivolta tra mito e memoria. 14 luglio 1948 lo sciopero generale per l'attentato a Togliatti.* Pisa: Biblioteca Franco Serantini.

Gruber, Charles. 1990. "The Lesson of Cedar Grove." *The Police Chief* 57 (9): 12–15.

Hague v. C.I.O. 1939. U.S. 496, 515–16.

Hansson, D. S. 1989. "Trigger-Happy?: An Evaluation of Fatal Police Shootings in the Greater Cape Town Area from 1984 to 1986." In *Acta Juridica*, edited by W. Scharf, 118–38. Cape Town: Faculty of Law, University of Cape Town.

Harrach, Eva-Marie, Gräfin von. 1983. "Grenzen und Möglichkeiten der Professionalisierung von Polizeiarbeit." Dissertation, University of Münster.

Haupt, Heinz-Gerhard. 1986. "Staatliche Bürokratie und Arbeiterbewegung. Zum Einfluß der Polizei auf die Konstituierung von Arbeiterbewegung und Arbeiterklasse in

Deutschland und Frankreich zwischen 1848 und 1880." In *Arbeiter und Bürger im 19. Jahrhundert: Varianten ihres Verhältnisses im europäischen Vergleich*, edited by Jürgen Kocka, 219–54. Munich: Oldenbourg.

Haysom, Nick. 1987. "Licence to Kill Part II: A Comparative Survey of the Law in the United Kingdom, United States of America and South Africa." *South African Journal of Human Rights* 3: 202.

Heffron v. International Society for Krishna Consciousness. 1981. 452 U.S. 640.

Hewitt, Patricia. 1982. *The Abuse of Power: Civil Liberties in the UK*. Oxford: Martin Robertson.

Heymann, Philip. 1992. *Towards Peaceful Protest in South Africa*. Pretoria: Human Sciences Research Council.

Hills, Alice. 1995. "Militant Tendencies." *British Journal of Criminology* 35: 450–58.

Hirst, Paul Q. 1975. "Marx and Engels on Law, Crime and Morality." In *Critical Criminology*, edited by Ian Taylor, Paul Walton, and Jock Young, 203–32. London: Routledge.

Hobsbawm, Eric John. 1959. *Primitive Rebels: Studies in Archaic Forms of Social Movement in the 19th and 20th Centuries*. Manchester: Manchester University Press.

Hoffmann, Rainer-W. 1968. "Staatsgewalt und Demokratie." *Blätter für deutsche und internationale Politik* 13: 1268–87.

Holdaway, Simon. 1984. *Inside the British Police*. Oxford: Basil Blackwell.

Hunold, Tonis. 1968. *Polizei in der Reform. Was Staatsbürger und Polizei voneinander erwarten können*. Düsseldorf: Econ.

International Association of Chiefs of Police. 1992. "Civil Disturbances." *The Police Chief* 59 (10): 138–45, 149.

Jar Couselo, Gonzalo. 1995. *Modelo Policial Español y Policías Autónomas*. Madrid: Dykinson.

Jaschke, Hans Gerd. 1991. *Streitbare Demokratie und Innere Sicherheit*. Opladen: Westdeutscher Verlag.

Jefferson, Tony. 1987. "Beyond Paramilitarism." *British Journal of Criminology* 27: 47–53.

———. 1990. *The Case against Paramilitary Policing*. Milton Keynes: Open University Press.

———. 1993. "Pondering Paramilitarism: A Question of Viewpoints." *British Journal of Criminology* 33: 374–88.

Jeffery, Kenneth, and Peter Hennessy. 1983. *States of Emergency*. London: Routledge and Kegan Paul.

Jenkins, Philip. 1988. "Policing the Cold War: The Emergence of New Police Structures in Europe 1946–1953." *Historical Journal* 31: 141–57.

Jensen, Richard Bach. 1991. *Liberty and Order: The Theory and Practice of Italian Public Security Policy, 1848 to the Crisis of the 1890s*. New York and London: Garland.

Jessen, Ralph. 1995. "Polizei und Gesellschaft. Zum Paradigmenwechsel in der Polizeigeschichtsforschung." In *Die Gestapo–Mythos und Realität*, edited by Gerhard Paul and Klaus-Michael Mallmann, 19–43. Darmstadt: Wissenschaftliche Buchgesellschaft.

Joshua, Harris, and Tina Wallace. 1983. *To Ride the Storm: The 1980 Bristol 'Riot' and the State*. London: Heinemann.

Kaase, Max, and Friedhelm Neidhardt. 1990. *Politische Gewalt und Repression. Ergebnisse von Bevölkerungsumfragen*. Berlin: Dunker and Humblot.

Kannenmeyer, D. D. V. 1985. *Report of the Commission Appointed to Inquire into the Incident Which Occurred on 21 March 1985 at Uitenhage*. Pretoria (manuscript).

Katscher, L. 1878. "Die blauen Männer von London. Eine Skizze aus dem Polizeiwesen." *Die Gartenlaube*, 285–87.

Kempner, Robert M. W. 1953. "Police Administration." In *Governing Postwar Germany*, edited by Edward H. Litchfield, vol. 2, 403–18. Ithaca, N.Y.: Cornell University Press [Port Washington, N.Y., and London: Kennikat Press, 1972].

Kerner, Otto. 1968. *Report of the National Advisory Commission on Civil Disorders*. New York: Dutton.

Kettle, Martin, and Lucy Hodges. 1982. *Uprising*. London: Pau Books.

King Movement Coalition v. Chicago. 1976. 419 F. Supp. 667, 674 (N.D. Ill.).

Kitschelt, Herbert. 1985. "New Social Movements in West Germany and the United States." *Political Power and Social Theory* 5: 273–342.

———. 1986. "Political Opportunity Structures and Protest: Anti-Nuclear Movements in Four Democracies." *British Journal of Political Science* 16: 57–85.

Kleinknecht, G. H., and Gerald Mizell. 1982. "Abortion: A Police Response." *FBI Law Enforcement Bulletin* 51 (3): 20–23.

Kniesel, Michael. 1987. "Polizei im demokratischen Verfassungsstaat." In *Schlußbericht über das Seminar "Polizei im demokratischen Verfassungsstaat - Bürgerrechte und Staatsgewalt" vom 3.–5. Juni 1987*, edited by the Polizei-Führungsakademie, 13–35. Münster: Polizei-Führungsakademie.

———. 1995. "Keine Strafbarkeit von Sitzdemonstrationen als Nötigung." *Polizei-heute* 24: 120–24.

Kraska, Peter, and Victor Kappeler. 1997. "Militarizing American Police: The Rise and Normalization of Paramilitary Units." *Social Problems* 44 (1): 1–17.

Kriesi, Hanspeter. 1989. "The Political Opportunity Structure of the Dutch Peace Movement." *West European Politics* 12: 295–312.

———. 1991. *The Political Opportunity Structure of New Social Movements*. Discussion Paper FS III, 91–103. Berlin: Wissenschaftszentrum Berlin für Sozialforschung.

Kriesi, Hanspeter, and Dominique Wisler. 1996. "Social Movements and Direct Democracy." *European Journal of Political Research* 30: 19–40.

Kriesi, Hanspeter, Ruud Koopmans, Jan Willem Dyvendak, and Marco G. Giugni. 1995. *New Social Movements in Western Europe: A Comparative Analysis*. Minneapolis: University of Minnesota Press.

Kritzer, Herbert. 1977. "Political Protest and Political Violence: A Nonrecursive Causal Model." *Social Forces* 55 (3): 630–40.

Lacey, Nicola, Celia Wells, and Dirk Meure. 1990. *Reconstructing Criminal Law: Critical Perspectives on Crime and the Criminal Process*. London: Weidenfeld and Nicolson.

Ladner, Andreas. 1994. "Lokale Politik und der Einfluß lokalpolitischer Akteure." *Revue de sociologie suisse* 20: 303–28.

Le Bon, Gustave. 1982 [1895]. *Psychologie der Massen*. Stuttgart: Kröner.

LeGrande, J. L. 1967. "Nonviolent Civil Disobedience and Police Enforcement Policy." *Journal of Criminal Law, Criminology and Police Science* 58 (3): 393–404.

Lehner, Giancarlo. 1978. *Dalla parte dei poliziotti (con un intervista di Riccardo Lombardi)*. Milan: Mazzotta.

Leo, R. 1992. "From Coercion to Deception: The Changing Nature of Police Interrogation in America." *Crime, Law and Social Change* 2: 33–60.

Leonard, Tony. 1985. "Policing the Miners." *Policing* 1: 96–102.

Linz, Juan José. 1974. "Una teoría del régimen autoritario. El caso de España." In *La España de los años setenta*, vol. 3, *El Estado y la política*, edited by Manuel Fraga, Juan Velarde, and Salustiano del Campo, 1467–1531. Madrid: Moneda y Crédito.

Lipset, Seymour Martin. 1971. "Why Cops Hate Liberals—and Vice Versa." In *The Police Rebellion: A Quest for Blue Power*, edited by William J. Bopp, 23–39. Springfield, Ill.: Charles C. Thomas.

Lipset, Seymour Martin, and Earl Raab. 1978. *The Politics of Unreason: Right-Wing Extremism in America 1790–1977.* Chicago: University of Chicago Press.

Lipsky, Michael. 1970. "Introduction." In *Law and Order: Police Encounters,* edited by Michael Lipsky, 1–7. New York: Aldine Publishing Company.

López Garrido, Diego. 1987. *El aparato policial en España.* Barcelona: Ariel.

López Pintor, R., and R. Buceta. 1975. *Los españoles de los años setenta: Una versión sociológica.* Madrid: Tecnos.

Loveday, Barry. 1986. "Central Coordination, Police Authorities and the Miners' Strike." *Political Quarterly* 57: 60–73.

Lüdtke, Alf. 1992. "Einleitung: 'Sicherheit' und 'Wohlfahrt'. Aspekte der Polizeigeschichte." In *"Sicherheit" und "Wohlfahrt": Polizei, Gesellschaft und Herrschaft im 19. und 20. Jahrhundert,* edited by Alf Lüdtke, 7–33. Frankfurt/Main: Suhrkamp.

Lukes, Stephen. 1973. *Power: A Radical View.* Oxford: Macmillan.

Macdonald, Ian R. 1985. "The Police System of Spain." In *Police and Public Order in Europe,* edited by John Roach and Jürgen Thomaneck, 215–54. London: Croom Helm.

Malinowsky, Peter. 1975. "Polizei-Kriminologie und soziale Kontrolle." In *Die Polizei—eine Institution der öffentlichen Gewalt,* edited by the Arbeitskreis Junger Kriminologen (Manfred Brusten, Johannes Feest, and Rüdiger Lautmann), 61–87. Neuwied and Darmstadt: Luchterhand.

Manning, Peter K. 1979. "The Social Control of Police Work." In *British Police,* edited by Simon Holdaway, 41–65. London: Edward Arnold.

Manwaring-White, Sarah. 1983. *The Policing Revolution.* Brighton: Wheatsheaf.

Maravall, José María. 1978. *Dictatorship and Political Dissent: Workers and Students in Franco's Spain.* London: Tavistock.

Maravall, José María, and Julian Santamaría. 1985. "Crisis del franquismo, transición política y consolidación de la democracia en España." *Sistema* 68–69: 79–129.

Marino, Giuseppe Carlo. 1995. *La Repubblica della Forza. Mario Scelba e le passioni del suo tempo.* Milan: Franco Angeli.

Marks, Gary. 1989. *Unions in Politics: Britain, Germany, and the United States in the Nineteenth and Early Twentieth Centuries.* Princeton, N.J.: Princeton University Press.

Marsh, P., E. Harrè, and E. Rosser. 1978. *The Rules of Disorder.* London: Routledge and Kegan Paul.

Marshall, Thomas Humphrey. 1950. *Citizenship and Social Class and Other Essays.* Cambridge: Cambridge University Press.

Martín Fernández, Manuel. 1990. *La profesión de policía.* Madrid: Centro de Investigaciones Sociológicas.

Martín Villa, Rodolfo. 1984. *Al servicio del Estado.* Barcelona: Planeta.

Marx, Gary T. 1970. "Civil Disorder and the Agents of Social Control." *Journal of Social Issues* 26 (1): 19–58.

———. 1972. "Civil Disorders and the Agents of Social Control." In *Muckraking Sociology,* edited by Gary T. Marx, 75–97. New Brunswick, N.J.: Transaction Books.

———. 1974. "Thoughts on a Neglected Category of Social Movement Participant: The Agent Provocateur and the Informant." *American Journal of Sociology* 80 (2):402–42.

———. 1979. "External Efforts to Damage or Facilitate Social Movements: Some Patterns, Explanations, Outcomes and Complications." In *The Dynamics of Social Movements,* edited by John McCarthy and Mayer N. Zald, 94–125. Cambridge, Mass.: Winthrop.

———. 1988. *Undercover: Police Surveillance in America.* Berkeley: University of California Press.

———. 1995a. "The Engineering of Social Control: The Search for the Silver Bullet." In *Crime and Inequality,* edited by J. Hagan and R. Peterson, 225–46. Stanford, Calif.: Stanford University Press.

————. 1995b. "Undercover in Comparative Perspective: Some Implications for Knowledge and Social Research." In *Undercover: Police Surveillance in Comparative Perspective*, edited by C. Fijnaut and Gary T. Marx, 323–36. The Hague: Kluwer Law International.

Mawby, R. J. 1992. *Comparative Policing Issues: The British and American Experience in International Perspective*. London: Routledge.

McAdam, Doug. 1982. *Political Process and the Development of Black Insurgency, 1930–1970*. Chicago: University of Chicago Press.

————. 1983. "Tactical Innovation and the Pace of Insurgency." *American Sociological Review* 48 (6): 735–54.

McCabe, Sarah, and Peter Wallington (with John Alderson, Larry Gostin, and Caroline Mason). 1988. *The Police, Public Order and Civil Liberties: Legacies of the Miners' Strike*. London: Routledge.

McCarthy, John, and Clark McPhail. 1997. "The Institutionalization of Protest." In *A Movement Society? Contentious Politics for a New Century*, edited by David Meyer and Sidney Tarrow. Boulder, Colo.: Rowland and Littlefield.

McCarthy, John, Clark McPhail, and Jackie Smith. 1994. "The Institutional Channeling of Protest: The Emergence and Development of U.S. Protest Management Systems." Paper presented at the World Congress of the International Sociological Association, Bielefeld, Germany.

————. 1996. "Images of Protest: Dimensions of Selection Bias in Media Coverage of Washington Demonstrations, 1982, 1991." *American Sociological Review* 61 (June): 478–99.

McCarthy, John, Clark McPhail, and John Crist. 1995. "The Emergence and Diffusion of Public Order Management Systems: Protest Cycles and Police Responses." Paper presented at the Conference on Cross-National Influences and Social Movement Research, Mont-Pélerin, Switzerland.

McClintock, Frederick, André Normandeau, Robert Philippe, and Jerome Skolnick. 1974. "Police et violence collective." In *Police, culture et société*, edited by Denis Szabo, 91–158. Montreal: Les Presses de l'Université de Montréal.

Medici, Sandro. 1979. *Vite di poliziotti*. Turin: Einaudi.

Melossi, Dario. 1990. *The State of Social Control*. New York: St. Martin's Press.

Michener, James. 1971. *Kent State (May 4, 1970): What Happened and Why*. New York: Random House.

Miliband, Ralph. 1982. *Capitalist Democracy in Britain*. Oxford: Oxford University Press.

Miller, Wilbur. 1977. *Cops and Bobbies: Police Authoriy in New York and London 1830–1870*. Chicago: University of Chicago Press.

Momboisse, Raymond M. 1967. *Riots, Revolts and Insurrections*. Springfield, Ill.: Charles C. Thomas.

Monet, Jean-Claude. 1990. "Maintien de l'ordre ou création du désordre? La conclusion de l'enquête administrative sur la manifestation du 23 mars 1979." In *La Manifestation*, edited by Pierre Favre, 229–44. Paris: Presse de la Fondation Nationale des Sciences Politiques.

Monjardet, Dominique. 1984. *La police au quotidien. Éléments de sociologie du travail policier*. Paris: GST-CNRS, Université de Paris-VII.

————. 1988. "Le maintien de l'ordre: technique et idéologies professionnelles des CRS." *Déviance et société* 12 (2): 101–26.

————. 1990. "La manifestation du côté du maintien de l'ordre." In *La Manifestation*, edited by Pierre Favre, 207–28. Paris: Presse de la Fondation Nationale des Sciences Politiques.

Monkkonen, Eric. 1981. *Police in Urban America 1860–1920*. Cambridge: Cambridge University Press.

Moore, Barrington, Jr. 1967. *The Social Origins of Dictatorship and Democracy*. London: Penguin.

Morgan, Jane. 1987. *Conflict and Order: The Police and Labour Disputes in England and Wales 1900–1939*. Oxford: Clarendon Press.

Morris, Aldon. 1993. "Birmingham Confrontation Reconsidered: An Analysis of the Dynamics and Tactics of Mobilization." *American Sociological Review* 58 (5): 621–36.

Morris, Terry. 1985. "The Case for a Riot Squad." *New Society* 29 (November): 373–74.

Muir, W. K., Jr. 1977. *Police: Street-Corner Politicians*. Chicago: University of Chicago Press.

Murdock, Graham. 1984. "Reporting the Riots: Images and Impact." In *Scarman and After*, edited by John Benyot, 73–95. Oxford: Pergamon Press.

Murphy, Patrick, John Williams, and Eric Dunning. 1990. *Football on Trial: Spectator Violence and Development in the Football World*. London: Routledge.

Narr, Wolf-Dieter. 1983. "Soziale Merkmale von Demonstrationen. Gutachten anläßlich der Anklage gegen Josef Leinen wegen 'Verdachts des Vergehens gegen das Versammlungsgesetz.'" In *Das Demonstrationsrecht*, edited by Sebastian Cobler, Reiner Geulen, and Wolf-Dieter Narr, 103–26. Reinbeck bei Hamburg: Rowohlt.

National Council for Civil Liberties. 1984. *Civil Liberties and the Miners' Dispute: First Report of the Independent Inquiry*. London: National Council for Civil Liberties.

Norris, Clive. 1989. "Avoiding Trouble: The Patrol Officer's Perception of Encounters with the Public." In *Police Research: Some Future Prospects*, edited by M. Weatheritt, 89–106. Aldershot: Avebury.

Northam, Gerry. 1988. *Shooting in the Dark*. London: Faber.

Ochs, Bob. 1985. "Managing an Anti-Apartheid Demonstration." *Campus Law Enforcement Journal* 15 (5): 11–12.

O'Donnell, Guillermo, and Philippe C. Schmitter. 1986. *Transitions from Authoritarian Rule: Tentative Conclusions about Uncertain Democracies*. Baltimore: Johns Hopkins University Press.

Oliva, Gianni. 1992. *Storia dei carabinieri. Immagine e autorappresentazione dell'Arma (1814–1992)*. Milan: Leonardo.

Palidda, Salvatore. 1993. "Sapere di polizia e sicurezza a livello locale." Florence: European University Institute (manuscript).

———. 1995. "Polizia e Sicurezza Urbana." Florence: European University Institute (manuscript).

Palmer, Stanley. 1988. *Police and Protest in England and Ireland 1780–1850*. Cambridge: Cambridge University Press.

Paul, Gerhard, and Klaus-Michael Mallmann, eds. 1995. *Die Gestapo—Mythos und Realität*. Darmstadt: Wissenschaftliche Buchgesellschaft.

Pearson, Geoffrey. 1983. *Hooligan*. London: Macmillan.

Pizzorno, Alessandro. 1993. "Le difficoltà del consociativismo." In *Le radici della politica assoluta e altri saggi*, 285–313. Milan: Feltrinelli.

Polanyi, Karl. 1944. *The Great Transformation*. Boston: Beacon Press.

Polizei-Führungsakademie. 1986a. *Schlußbericht über das Seminar 'Polizei im demokratischen Verfassungsstaat—Soziale Konflikte und Arbeitskampf' vom 24.–26. September 1986*. Münster.

———. 1986b. *Schlußbericht über die Arbeitstagung 'Polizeieinsätze an der WAA Wackersdorf sowie am 7.6.86 am KKW Brokdorf und am 8.6.1986 in Hamburg' vom 26.–27. Juni 1986*. Münster.

———. 1987. *Schlußbericht über das Seminar 'Polizei im demokratischen Verfassungsstaat— Bürgerrechte und Staatsgewalt' vom 3.–5. Juni 1987*. Münster.

Polizei-Institut Hiltrup. 1971. *Polizei und Demonstationen. Schlußbericht über das Seminar für leitende Polizeibeamte vom 29.3.–2.4.71*. Hiltrup.

Post, Robert C. 1987. "Between Governance and Management: The History and Theory of the Public Forum." *UCLA Law Review* 34 (5 and 6): 1718–1835.

President's National Advisory Commission on Civil Disorders. 1968. *Report of the National Advisory Commission on Civil Disorders*. Washington, D.C.: U.S. Government Printing Office.

Preston, Paul. 1986. *The Triumph of Democracy in Spain*. London: Methuen.

———. 1987. *La Guerra Civil Española, 1936–1939*. Esplugues de Llobregat: Plaza and Janés.

Punch, M. 1985. *Conduct Unbecoming: The Social Construction of Police Deviance and Control*. London: Tavistock.

Quaker Action Group v. Hickel. 1969. 421 F. 2d 1111 (D.C. Cir.).

Quaker Action Group v. Morton. 1975. 516 F. 2d 717, 725 (D.C. Cir.).

Reed, David, and Olivia Adamson. 1985. *Miners' Strike 1984–1985: People versus State*. London: Larkin Publications.

Reinares, Fernando. 1990. "Sociogénesis y evolución del terrorismo en España." In *España: sociedad y política*, edited by Salvador Giner, 353–96. Madrid: Espasa Calpe.

Reiner, Robert. 1980. "Forces of Disorder." *New Society* 10 (April): 51–54.

———. 1991. *Chief Constables: Bobbies, Bosses or Bureaucrats?* Oxford: Oxford University Press.

———. 1992a. "Policing a Postmodern Society." *Modern Law Review* 55 (6): 761–81.

———. 1992b. *The Politics of the Police*. 2d ed. Hemel Hempstead, Hertfordshire: Harvester Wheatsheaf.

———. 1994. "Policing and the Police." In *The Oxford Handbook of Criminology*, edited by Mike Maguire, Rod Morgan, and Robert Reiner, 707–72. Oxford: Oxford University Press.

Reinhard, Hans. 1993. *Allgemeines Polizeirecht*. Bern: Haupt.

Reiter, Herbert. 1997a. "I progetti degli alleati per una riforma della polizia in Italia, 1943–1947." *Passato e Presente*, no. 42: 37–64.

———. 1997b. *Police and Public Order in Italy, 1944–1948: The Case of Florence*. Working Paper of the Schuman Center of the European University Institute, Florence.

Reith, Charles. 1938. *The Police Idea*. Oxford: Oxford University Press.

———. 1943. *British Police and the Democratic Ideal*. Oxford: Oxford University Press.

———. 1956. *A New Study of Police History*. London: Oliver and Boyd.

Riehle, Eckart. 1983. "Sicherheit im Vorfeld des Rechts." In *Der Mensch als Risiko*, edited by Manfred Max Wambach, 274–84. Frankfurt/Main: Suhrkamp.

Robertson, Geoffrey. 1989. Freedom, the Individual and the Law. London: Penguin.

Robinson, Cyril, and Richard Scaglio. 1987. "The Origin and Evolution of the Police Function in Society: Notes toward a Theory." *Law and Society Review* 21: 109–53.

Roddi, Cesare. 1953. *La polizia di Sicurezza*. Milan: Giuffrè.

Rodríguez, José Luis. 1994. *Reaccionarios y Golpistas. La extrema derecha en España: del tardofranquismo a la consolidación de la democracia (1967–1982)*. Madrid: Consejo Superior de Investigaciones Científicas.

Rodríguez-Granero, L. F. 1988. "Las tramas anti-ETA. La más sucia de las guerras." *Derechos Humanos* (dossier), 21–22.

Rothmayr, Christine. 1994. "Die Kulturpolitik der Stadt Zürich: Eine vergleichende Analyse der Ausgestaltung kulturpolitischer Massnahmen in den 70er und 80er Jahren." Zurich: Master's thesis, University of Zurich.

Roversi, Antonio. 1992. *Calcio, tifo e violenza*. Bologna: Il Mulino.

———, ed. 1990. *Calcio e violenza in Europa*. Bologna: Il Mulino.

Rubinstein, Jonathan. 1973. *City Police*. New York: Ballantine.

Sack, Fritz. 1984. "Die Reaktion von Gesellschaft, Politik und Staat auf die Studentenbewegung." In *Protest und Reaktion. Analysen zum Terrorismus*, vol. 4/2, edited by Fritz Sack and Heinz Steinert, 107–227. Opladen: Westdeutscher Verlag.

Sahid, Joseph. 1969. *Rights in Concord: Task Force Report to the National (Eisenhower) Commission on the Causes and Prevention of Violence*. Washington, D.C.: U.S. Government Printing Office.

Salerno, Luigi. 1952. *Enciclopedia di polizia, ad uso dei funzionari e impiegati di P.S., ufficiali e sottufficiali dei carabinieri, degli agenti di polizia e della guardia di finanza, magistrati, avvocati, sindaci e segretari comunali*. Milan: Hoepli.

Salvini, Alessandro. 1988. *Il rito aggressivo. Dall'aggressività simbolica al comportamento violento. Il caso dei tifosi ultrà*. Florence: Giunti Barbera.

Sánchez Soler, Mariano. 1993. *Los hijos del 20-N. Historia violenta del fascismo español*. Madrid: Ediciones Temas de Hoy.

Sandora, J. A., and R. C. Petersen. 1980. "Crowd Control and the Small Police Department." *FBI Law Enforcement Bulletin* 49 (12): 2–5.

Sannino, Antonio. 1985. "Le forze di polizia nel secondo dopoguerra (1945–1950)." *Storia contemporanea* 16: 427–85.

Sardino, Thomas. 1985. "The Demonstration Experience at Syracuse University." *Campus Law Enforcement Journal* 15 (5): 33–34.

Saxer, Urs. 1988. *Die Grundrechte und die Benutzung öffentlicher Strassen*. Zurich: Schulthess Polygraphischer Verlag.

Scarman, Lord. 1981. *The Brixton Disorders*. London: Penguin.

Scheerer, Sebastian. 1988. "Deutschland: Die ausgebürgerte Linke." In *Angriff auf das Herz des Staates*, vol. 1, edited by Henner Hess, Martin Moerings, Dieter Paas, Sebastian Scheerer, and Heinz Steinert, 193–429. Frankfurt/Main: Suhrkamp.

Schneider, Heinz-Jürgen. 1986. "Staatliche Sicherheitspolitik als Systemschutz. 'Innere Sicherheit' in der Geschichte der Bundesrepublik." In *Totalerfassung. "Sicherheitsgesetze," Volkszählung, neuer Personalausweis, Möglichkeiten zur Gegenwehr*, edited by Martin Kutscha and Norman Paech, 81–101. Cologne: Pahl-Rugenstein.

Scranton, William. 1970. *Report of the National Commission on Campus Unrest*. Washington, D.C.: U.S. Government Printing Office.

Silver, Allan. 1967. "The Demand for Order in Civil Society: A Review of Some Themes in the History of Urban Crime, Police, and Riot." In *The Police*, edited by David J. Bordua, 1–24. New York: John Wiley and Sons.

———. 1971. "Social and Ideological Bases of British Elite Reactions to Domestic Crises 1829–32." *Politics and Society* 1: 179–201.

Skocpol, Theda. 1979. *States and Social Revolutions: A Comparative Analysis of France, Russia, and China*. New York: Cambridge University Press.

Skokie v. National Socialist Party. 1978. 69 Ill. 2d 605, 373 N.E. 2d 21, 24.

Skolnick, Jerome H. 1966. *Justice without Trial: Law Enforcement in Democratic Society*. New York: John Wiley and Sons.

———. 1969a. *The Politics of Protest: Report to the National Commission on the Causes and Prevention of Violence*. New York: Simon and Schuster.

———. 1969b. *Rights in Conflict: A Task Force Report to the National [Eisenhower] Commission on the Causes and Prevention of Violence*. New York: Ballantine.

Smolla, Rodney A. 1992. *Free Speech in an Open Society*. New York: Knopf.

Snow, David, and Robert Benford. 1988. "Ideology, Frame Resonance, and Participant Mobilization." *International Social Movement Research* 1: 197–217.

Snowden, Frank M. 1989. *The Fascist Revolution in Tuscany, 1919–1922*. Cambridge and New York: Cambridge University Press.

Snyder, John V. 1985. "Forum over Substance: Cornelius v. NAACP Legal Defense and Education Fund." *Catholic University Law Review* 35 (1): 307–33.

Spitzer, Steven, and Andrew Scull. 1977. "Privatisation and Social Control." *Social Problems* 25: 18–29.

Stark, Rodney. 1972. *Police Riots: Collective Violence and Law Enforcement.* Belmont, Calif.: Wadsworth Publishing Company.

Staunton, Marie. 1985. *Free to Walk Together?* London: National Council for Civil Liberties.

Steedman, Carolyn. 1984. *Policing the Victorian Community.* London: Routledge.

Stevenson, John. 1977. "Social Control and the Prevention of Riots in England 1789–1829." In *Social Control in 19th Century Britain,* edited by A. Donajgrodski, 23–48. London: Croom Helm.

Stevenson, John, and Chris Cook. 1977. *The Slump.* London: Cape.

Steytler, N.C. 1989. "Policing 'Unrest': The Restoring of Authority." In *Acta Juridica,* edited by W. Scharf, 234–61. Cape Town: Faculty of Law, University of Cape Town.

Storch, Robert. 1975. "The Plague of Blue Locusts: Police Reform and Popular Resistance in Northern England 1840–57." *International Review of Social History* 20: 61–90.

———. 1976. "The Policeman as Domestic Missionary." *Journal of Social History* 9 (4): 481–509.

———. 1980. "Crime and Justice in 19th Century England." *History Today* 30: 32–36.

Storchi, Massimo. 1995. *Uscire dalla guerra. Ordine pubblico e forze politiche Modena 1945–1946.* Milan: Franco Angeli.

Sumner, Colin. 1982. "'Political Hooliganism' and 'Rampaging Mobs': The National Press Coverage of the Toxteth 'Riots.'" In *Crime, Justice and the Mass Media,* edited by Colin Sumner, 25–35. Cambridge: Cropwood Conference Series.

Sunday Times Insight Team. 1985. *Strike.* London: Coronet.

Szabo, Mate. 1995. "Police Interventions at Protest Events in the Press in Hungary." Paper presented at the conference on the theme "The Policing of Mass Demonstrations in Contemporary Democracies," Florence, European University Institute.

Szikinger, Istvan. 1995. "The Institutional Framework of Handling Protest and Demonstrations in Hungary." Paper presented at the Conference on the theme "The Policing of Mass Demonstrations in Contemporary Democracies," Florence, European University Institute.

Taft, P., and P. Ross. 1979. "American Labor Violence: Its Causes, Character, and Outcome." In *Violence in America,* edited by H. D. Graham and T. R. Gurr, 187–241. Beverly Hills, Calif.: Sage.

Tamames, Ramón. 1973. *La República. La Era de Franco.* Madrid: Alianza/Alfaguara.

Tarrow, Sidney. 1983. *Struggling to Reform: Social Movement and Policy Change During Cycles of Protest.* Ithaca, N.Y.: Cornell University, Western Societies Program, Occasional Paper No. 15.

———. 1989a. *Democracy and Disorder: Protest Politics in Italy, 1965–1975.* Oxford: Oxford University Press.

———. 1989b. *Struggle, Politics, and Reform: Collective Action, Social Movements, and Cycles of Protest.* Western Society Papers, 21. Ithaca, N.Y.: Cornell University Press.

———. 1994. *Power in Movement: Social Movements, Collective Action and Mass Politics in the Modern State.* New York: Cambridge University Press.

Tezanos, José Felix. 1989. "La crisis del franquismo y la transición democrática en España." In *La transición democrática española,* edited by José Felix Tezanos, Ramón Cotarelo, and Andrés de Blas, 9–30. Madrid: Editorial Sistema.

Tezanos, José Felix, Ramón Cotarelo, and Andrés de Blas, eds. *La transición democrática española.* Madrid: Editorial Sistema.

Thompson, Edward P. 1968. *The Making of the English Working Class.* London: Penguin.

———. 1975. *Whigs and Hunters: The Origin of the Black Act.* London: Penguin.
———. 1992. *Customs in Common.* London: Merlin.
Thornton, Peter 1985. *We Protest.* London: National Council for Civil Liberties.
Thurmond Smith, Phillip. 1985. *Policing Victorian London.* Westport, Conn.: Greenwood.
Tilly, Charles. 1978. *From Mobilization to Revolution.* Reading, Mass.: Addison-Wesley.
———. 1990. *Coercion, Capital, and European States, AD 990–1990.* Oxford: Basil Blackwell.
———. 1995. *Popular Contention in Great Britain 1758–1834.* Cambridge: Harvard University Press.
Triani, Giorgio. 1994. "Curva sud e Lega nord: dai calci alla politica." In *Tifo e supertifo. La passione, la malattia, la violenza,* edited by Giorgio Triani, 59–61. Naples: Edizioni Scientifiche Italiane.
Tribe, Lawrence H. 1988. *American Constitutional Law.* New York: Foundation Press.
Trum, Hansjörg. 1981. "Polizeipsychologie im Rahmen eines institutionalisierten psychologischen Dienstes." In *Handbuch der angewandten Psychologie,* vol. 3, *Markt und Umwelt,* edited by Henning Haase and Walter Holt, 701–15. Landsberg am Lech: Moderne Industrie.
Uglow, Stephen. 1988. *Policing Liberal Society.* London: Oxford University Press.
United States Army Military Police School. 1972a. "Confrontation Management." MP 564V–LP, pp. 1–14 in *SEADOC: Civil Disturbance Orientation Course Textbook.* Fort Gordon, Ga.: United States Army Military Police School.
———. 1972b. "Operational Tasks and Techniques." MP 574V, pp. 1–30 in *SEADOC: Civil Disturbance Orientation Course Textbook.* Fort Gordon, Ga.: United States Army Military Police School.
———. 1972c. "Orientation." ATSMP-DCAST-DDM, p. 1 in *SEADOC: Civil Disturbance Orientation Course Textbook.* Fort Gordon, Ga.: United States Army Military Police School.
———. 1972d. "Special Orders for All Military Personnel Engaged in Civil Disturbance Operations." ATSMP-DRI-MPS&A, pp. 1–2 in *SEADOC: Civil Disturbance Orientation Course Textbook.* Fort Gordon, Ga.: United States Army Military Police School.
United States v. Eichman. 1990. 110 S. Ct. 2404.
Vogler, Richard. 1991. *Reading the Riot Act: The Magistracy, the Police and the Army in Civil Disorder.* Milton Keynes: Open University Press.
Volpi, Mauro. 1983. "Costituzione e polizia." *Politica del diritto* 14: 91–116.
Volta, Paolo. 1994. "Una proposta di metodo e di merito: l'esperienza di Genova." In *Tifo e supertifo. La passione, la malattia, la violenza,* edited by Giorgio Triani, 71–75. Naples: Edizioni Scientifiche Italiane.
Waddington, David. 1992. *Contemporary Issues in Public Disorders: A Comparative and Historical Approach.* London: Routledge.
———. 1993. *Policing Public Disorder.* London: Routledge.
Waddington, David, Karen Jones, and Chas Critcher. 1989. *Flashpoints: Studies in Public Disorder.* London: Routledge.
Waddington, P. A. J. 1987. "Towards Paramilitarism: Dilemmas in Policing Public Disorder." *British Journal of Criminology* 27: 37–46.
———. 1991. *The Strong Arm of the Law.* Oxford: Clarendon Press.
———. 1992. "An Inquiry into the Police Response to, and Investigation of, Events in Boipatong on 17 June 1992." Submitted to the Commission of Inquiry Regarding the Prevention of Public Violence and Intimidation, His Honour Mr. Justice Goldstone, Chairman. Pretoria (unpublished).
———. 1993a. "'The Case against Paramilitary Policing' Considered." *British Journal of Criminology* 33 (3): 353–73.

———. 1993b. "Dying in a Ditch: The Use of Police Powers in Public Order." *International Journal of Sociology* 21: 335–53.

———. 1994a. "Coercion and Accommodation: Policing Public Order after the Public Order Act." *British Journal of Sociology* 45: 367–85.

———. 1994b. *Liberty and Order: Public Order Policing in a Capital City.* London: U.C.L. Press.

———. 1995. "Public Order Policing: Citizenship and Moral Ambiguity." In *Core Issues in Policing,* edited by F. Leishman, B. Loveday, and S. P. Savage, 114–30. London: Longman.

Walker, Daniel. 1968. *Rights in Conflict: Chicago's 78 Brutal Days. Report of the Chicago Study Team of the National [Eisenhower] Commission on the Causes and Prevention of Violence.* New York: Grossett and Dunlap.

Walker, Jack L. 1969. "The Diffusion of Innovations among the American States." *American Political Science Review* 63: 880–99.

Wallington, Peter T., ed. 1984. *Civil Liberties 1984.* Oxford: Martin Robertson/Cobden Trust.

Watts v. United States. 1969. 394 U.S. 705, 708.

Watts-Miller, William. 1987. "Party Politics, Class Interest and the Reform of the British Police 1829–56." *Police Studies* 10 (1): 42–60.

Weber, Max. [1922] 1974. *Economia e società.* 2 vols. Milan: Edizioni di comunità.

Weinberger, Barbara. 1991. *Keeping the Peace? Policing Strikes in Britain, 1906–1926.* Oxford: Berg.

Weitzer, R., and C. Beattie. 1994. "Police Killings in South Africa: Criminal Trials 1986–1992." *Policing and Society* 4: 99–118.

Wells, Tom. 1994. *The War Within: America's Battle over Vietnam.* Berkeley: University of California Press.

Werkentin, Falco. 1984. *Die Restauration der deutschen Polizei. Innere Rüstung von 1945 bis zur deutschen Notstandsgesetzgebung.* Frankfurt/Main: Campus.

———. 1988. "Der Staat, der Staat ist in Gefahr . . . Kontinuität und Formwandel innerer Rüstung in der Bundesrepublik." *Prokla* 18: 97–117.

Westergaard, John, and Henrietta Resler. 1975. *Class in a Capitalist Society.* London: Heinemann.

Whitaker, Charles. 1964. "The Causes and Effect upon Public Order of Planned Mass Violations of Our Laws." *The Police Chief* 34 (4): 12–22.

———. 1966. "The Effects of Planned, Mass Disobedience of Our Laws." *FBI Law Enforcement Bulletin* 35 (9): 9–13, 25.

Willems, Helmut, Roland Eckert, Harald Goldbach, and Toni Loosen. 1988. *Demonstranten und Polizisten. Motive, Erfahrungen und Eskalationsbedingungen.* Weinheim and Munich: Juventa.

Williams, Juan. 1987. *Eyes on the Prize: America's Civil Rights Years, 1954–1965.* New York: Viking Penguin.

Winter, Martin. 1991. "Polizei—Politik—Protest. Untersuchung zum politischen Selbstverständnis der Polizei in der Bundesrepublik Deutschland zwischen 1960 und 1990." Erlangen-Nürnberg, Diplomarbeit (manuscript).

———. 1997. *Police Philosophy and Protest Policing in the Federal Republic of Germany, 1960–1990.* Working Paper of the Schuman Centre of the European University Institute, Florence.

Wisler, Dominique. 1995. "Protest Policing and Diffusion: Some Thoughts on the Swiss Case." Paper presented at the conference on cross-national influences and social movement research, Mont-Pélerin, June 15–18.

Wisler, Dominique, Hanspeter Kriesi, and José Barranco. 1995. "Protest Policing in
    Switzerland: Five Cities Compared." Paper prepared for the workshop on protest polic-
    ing, European Institute, Florence, April 4.
Wisler, Dominique, José Barranco, and Marco Tackenberg. 1996. "Police, Mass Demon-
    strations, and Politics." Paper presented at the Second European Conference on Social
    Movements, Vitoria, Spain. October.
Worden, R. E. 1989. "Situational and Attitudinal Explanations of Police Behavior. A
    Theoretical Reappraisal and Empirical Reassessment." *Law and Society Review* 23 (4):
    667–711.
Wright, P. 1985. *Policing the Coal Industry Dispute in South Yorkshire*. Sheffield: South
    Yorkshire Police.
Zwerman, Gilda. 1987. "Domestic Counter-Terrorism: U.S. Government Responses to
    Political Violence on the Left in the Reagan Era." *Social Justice* 14 (2): 31–63.

Contributors

Rocco De Biasi is author of *Gregory Bateson* (1996) and editor of the special edition of the journal *Aut Aut* (1995) focusing on Erving Goffman's "Frame Analysis." He is working on a book about fans, culture, and rituals, and is temporary lecturer in sociology in the Faculty of Sciences of Education of the University of Genoa.

Donatella della Porta is professor of political science at the University of Florence. She carried out research in Italy, France, Spain, the Federal Republic of Germany, and the United States. Her main fields of research include social movements, political violence, terrorism, political corruption, maladministration, public order, and the police. Her publications include *Social Movements, Political Violence, and the State* (1995), *Movimenti collecttivi e sistema politico in Italia* (1996), and *Social Movements: An Introduction* (co-author, 1998). In 1997, she was a visiting scholar at the Wissenschaftszentrum für Sozialforschung in Berlin.

Olivier Fillieule is a researcher at CNRS (CRESAL) and teaches political science at the Institute of Political Science in Paris (Science Po). His main fields of research include social movements, gay politics, public order, and the police. He has published three books, among them *Stratégie de la rue: Les manifestations en France* (1997). He is chief editor of *Les Cahiers de la sécurité intérieure*.

Oscar Jaime-Jiménez is currently official research fellow at the Political Science and Sociology Faculty of the Universidad Nacional de Educación a Distancia in Madrid. His articles have been published in Spanish academic journals. He is researching issues related to intelligence services and to the police response to terrorism in Spain.

Fabien Jobard is an assistant in law and political science at the University of Rouen, France. He is author of a forthcoming book on the police use of force in the United States and Great Britain. His research focuses on police activities in the field of drug enforcement.

Hanspeter Kriesi teaches political science at the University of Geneva. He is a specialist of comparative and Swiss politics. His research interests include social movements, electoral behavior, direct democracy, social stratification, and questions of attitude formation. Currently he is engaged in the Swiss national election study and in research on the role of information in the process of attitude formation in Swiss environmental and energy policy.

Gary T. Marx is professor emeritus at the Massachusetts Institute of Technology and professor of sociology at the University of Colorado, Boulder. His publications include *Protest and Prejudice* (1967), *Undercover: Police Surveillance in America* (1988), *Collective Behavior and Collective Behavior Process* (1988, coauthored with Doug McAdam), and *Undercover: Police Surveillance in Comparative Perspective* (1993, coedited with Cyrille Fijnaut).

John McCarthy is ordinary professor of sociology and a member of the Life Cycle Institute at the Catholic University of America in Washington, D.C. He continues his research on protest events, the policing of protest, and the role of social movement organizations in the mobilization of citizen action. He is coauthor (with Jim Castelli) of *Power Organizing* (forthcoming) and coeditor (with Doug McAdam and Mayer N. Zald) of *Comparative Perspectives on Social Movements* (1996).

Clark McPhail is professor of sociology at the University of Illinois at Urbana-Champaign. He first studied protest policing during the 1967 antiwar demonstrations at the University of South Carolina and civil rights protests following the 1968 Orangeburg massacre. His publications include *The Myth of the Madding Crowd* (1991) and numerous articles on collective action in temporary gatherings. He is collaborating with John McCarthy in the collection and analysis of police and mass media archival and direct observation records of collective action in Washington, D.C., demonstrations.

Fernando Reinares is titular professor of sociology, Jean Monnet Chair in European Political Studies, and NATO research fellow at the Universidad Nacional de Educación a Distancia in Madrid. Previously, he held teaching positions at Stanford University, the University of North Carolina (Chapel Hill), St. Anthony's College in Oxford, and Beijing Foreign Studies University. He is the author of several books and many articles on terrorism, counterterrorism, social conflict, collective action, political change, and European integration.

Robert Reiner is professor of criminology in the law department at the London School of Economics and director of its Mannheim Centre for Criminology and Criminal Justice. His books include *The Blue-Coated Worker* (1978), *The Politics of the Police* (1985), and *Chief Constables* (1991). He has published more than one hundred papers on policing and criminal justice topics.

Herbert Reiter is a researcher in history at the University of Halle in Germany. He carried out his research in the Federal Republic of Germany, the German Democratic Republic, Italy, France, Belgium, Switzerland, Great Britain, and the United States. His main fields of research are the history of political asylum, the democratic movements in Germany in the nineteenth century, and the reorganization of the police in Italy and Germany after 1945. He is the author of *Politisches Asyl im 19. Jahrhundert. Die deutschen politischen Flüchtlinge des Vormärz und der Revolution von 1848/49 in Europa und den USA* (1992). In 1994 and 1995 he received a research grant from the H. F. Guggenheim Foundation.

David Schweingruber is a Ph.D. candidate in sociology at the University of Illinois at Urbana-Champaign. As a research assistant on the Collective Action Project, he has been involved with the creation and implementation of a system for observing and recording collective action in demonstrations. He is preparing a dissertation on the training and organization of door-to-door salespersons.

P. A. J. Waddington is professor of sociology at the University of Reading, England. He has published extensively on the police and policing. His most recent books include *The Strong Arm of the Law* (1991), *Calling the Police* (1993), and *Liberty and Order* (1994). He is currently writing a general analysis of policing in liberal democracies.

Martin Winter is a social scientist at the University of Halle in Germany. He recently completed his Ph.D. thesis, titled "Politikum Polzei—Macht und Funktion der Polizei in der Bundesrepublik Deutschland."

Dominique Wisler teaches at the department of political science at the University of Geneva. He has published on social movements, political violence, and protest policing, and is currently directing a project of the Swiss National Foundation of Sciences on the media framing of riots in a cross-country perspective.

Index